QUANTITATIVE SOCIAL RESEARCH METHODS

QUANTITATIVE SOCIAL RESEARCH METHODS

Kultar Singh

lications

ew Delhi • Singapore

First published in 2007 by

Sage Publications India Pvt Ltd
B1/I1, Mohan Cooperative Industrial Area
Mathura Road
New Delhi 110 044
www.sagepub.in

Sage Publications Inc
2455 Teller Road
Thousand Oaks, California 91320

Sage Publications Ltd
1 Oliver's Yard, 55 City Road
London EC1Y 1SP

Sage Publications Asia-Pacific Pte Ltd
33 Pekin Street
#02-01 Far East Square
Singapore 048763

Published by Vivek Mehra for Sage Publications India Pvt Ltd, typeset in 10.5/12.5 Aldine 401 BT by Star Compugraphics Private Limited, Delhi and printed at Chaman Enterprises, New Delhi.

Library of Congress Cataloging-in-Publication Data

Singh, Kultar, 1976–
      Quantitative social research methods/Kultar Singh.
         p.   cm.
      Includes bibliographical references and index.
      1. Social sciences—Research—Methodology. I. Title.

H62.S47757   300.72—dc22   2007   2006037461

ISBN: 978–0–7619–3383–0 (PB)   978–81–7829–525–1 (India–PB)

Sage Production Team: Abantika Banerjee, Neha Kohli, Mathew P.J. and Santosh Rawat

In loving memory of my grandparents *(nani, dada* and *dadi)*

CONTENTS

LIST OF TABLES

LIST OF FIGURES

LIST OF BOXES

LIST OF ABBREVIATIONS

ADR	average discontinuation rate
ANCOVA	analysis of covariance
ANOVA	analysis of variance
AR	auto-regressive
ARCH	auto-regressive conditional heterescedastic
ARIMA	Auto Regressive Integrated Moving Average Model
ASFR	age-specific fertility rate
BMI	body mass index
CBA	cost-benefit analysis
CBR	cost-benefit ratio
CCA	command coverage area
CI	confidence interval
CPM/PERT	Critical Path Method/Programme Evaluation and Review Technique
CPR	contraceptive prevalence rate
DALY	disability adjusted life years
DP	discriminating power
DPEP	District Primary Education Programme
DV	dependent variable
EDP	eco-domestic product
EH	environment health
EIA	environment impact assessment
EKC	environmental Kuznet curve
EMS	environment management system

EPI	Extended Programme of Immunization
ERR	economic rate of return
EXPAR	exponential auto-regressive
GDP	gross domestic product
GFR	general fertility rate
GLS	generalized least square
GNP	gross national product
GRR	gross reproductive rate
ICDS	Integrated Child Development Scheme
ICMR	Indian Council of Medical Research
IDD	iodine deficiency disorder
IMR	infant mortality rate
IRR	internal rate of return
IRWR	internal renewable water resources
ISSA	integrated system for survey analysis
IV	independent variable
JFM	Joint Forest Management
LAM	lactational amenorrhea method
LFA	logical framework approach
MA	moving average
MANCOVA	multiple analysis of covariance
MANOVA	multiple analysis of variance
MAR	missing at random
MCA	multiple correspondence analysis
MCAR	missing completely at random
MDA	multiple discriminant analysis
MDS	multidimensional scaling
MFA	multiway frequency analysis
MIS	management information system
MLE	maximum likelihood estimation
MMR	maternal mortality rate
MNP	minimum needs programme
MUAC	mid-upper arm circumference
NAEMA	National Accounting Matrix including Environmental Accounts
NFHS	National Family Health Survey
NMAR	not missing at random

NMR	neonatal mortality rate
NNP	net national product
NPE	National Policy on Education
NPV	net present value
NRA	natural resource accounting
NRR	net reproduction rate
NSV	non scalpel vasectomy
NUDIST	Non Numeric Unstructured Data Indexing Searching and Theorizing
OLSE	ordinary least square
PCA	principal component analysis
PCR	principal component regression
PD	pair wise deletion
PEM	protein energy malnutrition
PMR	perinatal mortality rate
PNMR	post-neonatal mortality
POA	plan of action
PPR	parity progression ratio
PPS	probability proportionate to size
PRA	participatory rural appraisal
PSU	primary sampling units
RRA	rapid rural appraisal
SE	standard error
SEEA	System of Integrated Environmental and Economic Accounting
SEM	structural equation modelling
SFM	Sustainable Forest Management
SPM	suspended particulate matter
SPSS	Statistical Package for Social Sciences
STI	sexually-transmitted infections
TAR	threshold auto-regressive
TFR	total fertility rate
UEE	Universal Elementary Education
UIP	Universal Immunization Programme
WHO	World Health Organization
WLSE	weighted least square
WTP	willingness to pay

PREFACE

Social research is a beautiful amalgamation of science and art. It tries to unveil hidden emotions and perceptions with clinical efficiency by solving complex riddles of development and growth against the backdrop of a prevailing socio-economic situation. This field fascinated me to such an extent that I started writing down my experiences and learning as a means to explore this fascinating world of social research.

When I started exploring social research, I realized that though there are various books available on social research that inspire interest, they often leave the reader stranded midway and one has to look out for other books. In pursuit of filling this vacuum, I have made a modest effort to put down my experiences and learning in the form of a book, which covers the entire spectrum of social research methods and its application. It starts from the basics and progresses thematically to advanced stages of research methods, data analysis and its application in the development sector.

This book is thematically arranged in two sections. The first section, covering seven chapters, discusses all aspects of social research methods, starting with a brief on development research techniques and continuing with the importance of social research, process, scope, sampling methodology to quantitative univariate, bivariate and multivariate data analysis with the help of software packages such as SPSS and Stata.

Chapter 1 explores the various development research techniques frequently used in the social decision-making process. Chapter 2 traverses the genesis, scope and importance of social research and covers research tools like monitoring and evaluation techniques in assessing development changes. The third chapter takes the theme further and explores various concepts of the research process with its manifold dimensions mainly identification of a problem, usage of adequate research tools, collection of data and its subsequent analysis. Chapter 4 discusses sampling in detail. It examines the basic concepts, types of sampling and its relevance and usage in social research.

The next three chapters of the first section detail all aspects of data analysis in an extensive manner. Chapter 5 covers all facets of data analysis with the use of appropriate statistical techniques, namely, univariate and bivariate analysis, and covers both non-parametric and parametric methods for hypothesis testing. This theme is continued further in Chapter 6, which examines all multivariate techniques from multiple regression to factor and cluster analysis in detail. Chapter 7 embarks on a different theme and examines the issue of analysis of quantitative data using two of the most frequently used quantitative software, namely, Stata and SPSS.

The second section, comprising five chapters, focuses on the application of social and development research methods covering the entire gamut of the development sector. It explores the application of research method and issues relevant to population health, nutrition, poverty and rural development, education, water and sanitation, environment and natural resource management along with other development research techniques and theories frequently used in social research.

Chapter 8 examines basic concepts/issues in each of these areas like demographic transition, fertility, mortality, family planning and their computer analysis by using appropriate software, like the software for anthropometric analysis. Chapter 9 focuses on education primarily in terms of elementary, secondary and adult education, the concerned policies and their impact.

Chapter 10 examines the issues of the water and sanitation sector focusing primarily on water management practices. Chapter 11 is concerned with the examination of the agrarian economy and the need to develop the non-farm sector economy. Chapter 12 is divided into two sections. The first section examines basic concepts of environment, poverty and health, focusing on issues of natural resources, biodiversity, conservation, pollution and waste-management. The second section deals with the growth and sustenance of development emphasizing the importance of natural resources management.

I have tried to convey my passion for social research through this book, to motivate readers to look at it not just as an academic exercise, but as an exercise to interpret social maladies. I sincerely hope that readers find this book useful and it serves as a guide to equip students with conceptual and practical research tools. I also hope it serves as a definitive reference for researchers, to help them carry out social research studies and procedures.

I have tried to organize the book in a way that clearly presents the various themes and focii that researchers encounter while doing research in a simple, clear, coherent and consistent manner. It is quite possible that despite my earnest efforts certain shortcomings might have remained. I will be grateful to readers for suggestions and a feedback.

Kultar Singh

ACKNOWLEDGEMENTS

There are infinite sets of opportunities that lie between a bubble and an ocean and if you want to praise an ocean for its infinite opportunities, then the real praise is due to each drop of the ocean for losing its identity to make an ocean. This book is the result of dedication, help and support received from many quarters.

I owe a great part of whatever little I have learned to my alma mater the Indian Institute of Forest Management (IIFM), where I learned my first lessons in social research, practiced theories and tested all development-oriented hypotheses. I also take this opportunity to thank the IIFM faculty and the student fraternity, that is, my batchmates, seniors and juniors for providing such an excellent environment for learning.

I will always be indebted to the ORG Centre for Social Research (a division of ACNielsen ORG-MARG Pvt. Ltd.), which provided me the opportunity to work on various facets of social research, covering the entire gamut of development issues. Thanks are especially due to my colleague at Lucknow, Sameer Shukla, who helped me learn my first practical lessons in social research. Thanks are also due to the immensely talented field team of Vishnu Shanker Tiwari and Devendra Singh, who helped me learn and realize all practical paradigms of social research, which helped me immensely in striking a balance between academic research and commercial research. I would also like to thank Dr C.V.S. Prasad, advisor, ORG Centre of Social Research, who was a constant source of inspiration for exploring new frontiers in social research.

I am also thankful to Amit Chakraborty, M&E officer, BASICS-II, for not only helping me out as a friend but also in providing invaluable tips on data analysis and SPSS. I owe my sincere gratitude to Dr Sridhar Srikantiah, team leader, BASICS-II, for helping me learn Epi Info and passing on his infectious work spirit.

I take this opportunity to sincerely thank Nitin, Swapnil and Dharmendra, all part of a dream named Sambodhi, for being with me throughout the startup process. This book would not have been possible without their unconditional support and love.

I also express my heartfelt gratitude to my batchmates and friends, especially Nikhil, my roommate who has always been like an elder brother, Radhika, Angshuman, Navin, Sonia, Joy,

Ashish, Amit, James and Kaustab, who have played a pivotal role in motivating me to strive for the best.

I take this opportunity to acknowledge the sacrifice my parents have made in providing me an education and supporting me in every endeavour, without whose support I would not have been able to achieve anything. I owe a lot of whatever little I have achieved to early lessons in dedication, honesty and sincerity taught by my uncle, Captain Swaraj Singh, which forms the core of my values. I will always be grateful to all my cousins Dharmendra, Yashvinder, Sukhvinder and Sarbjeet for their unconditional love, support and motivation. I am also grateful to my sister, Surjeet (Dolly), who has always shouldered the responsibility of the family, which helped me immensely in focusing on this book.

I take this opportunity to acknowledge the earnest efforts put in by the entire Sage Publications team, without whom the publication of this book would not have been possible.

SECTION I

CHAPTER 1

DEVELOPMENT RESEARCH TECHNIQUES

Social research covers the entire spectrum of the socio-development sector and is an amalgamation of various research techniques from the fields of economics, project management and other allied subjects. This volume starts with a brief introduction to various development research techniques that are frequently used for making informed social decisions about development action and programmes such as: (i) cost-benefit analysis, (ii) logical framework-approach, (iii) stakeholders' analysis, (iv) social assessment, (v) beneficiary assessment, (vi) social audit, (vii) welfare economics and (viii) game theory.

COST-BENEFIT ANALYSIS

Cost-benefit analysis (CBA)[1] is based on Jules Dupuit's concept of consumer's surplus theory. It first came to the fore in a study entitled 'On the Measurement of the Utility of Public Works' (Jules Dupuit, 1844). Cost-benefit analysis is a summative measure of analysing net benefits accruing due to project initiation, by identifying the benefits and costs involved in a project. As a framework, CBA helps in analysing the feasibility of a project by enumerating the benefits and costs involved in the project in monetary terms through a well-laid down and established analytical framework. It thus helps planners, policy-makers and implementation agencies to take informed decisions about the financial as well as economic viability of a project by enumerating its social costs and benefits.

FINANCIAL VERSUS ECONOMIC ANALYSIS

It is imperative to make a distinction between financial analysis and economic analysis before deliberating further on the concept of CBA. Cost-benefit analysis helps to make a decision after taking in account all costs and benefits of a project and discounting them to present value by defining it in terms of net present value (NPV), that is, the present value of the benefits versus the present value of the costs. This method is used extensively in social and development projects as it enumerates all relevant costs and benefits. But, as we are all aware, there are some social costs and benefits involved in projects that are difficult to quantify. For example, in the case of forestry land being diverted for irrigation purposes, the social cost in the form of loss of habitat or benefit accruing from the forest in the form of carbon sequestration are difficult to quantify and would not be taken into account in the case of financial analysis. But, in the case of economic analysis, all those social benefits and costs are taken into account as the emphasis is on relating all direct and indirect costs and benefits to their economic or real social values, by using shadow pricing. Shadow prices are needed because in reality actual market prices do not reflect social costs and benefits, especially in a country like India where the market mechanism functions imperfectly due to a number of economic and social obstacles.

Several criteria can be used in a CBA framework. It depends on the problem at hand, the objectives and the specific circumstances surrounding the project being valued. The criteria that can be used to select or rank projects include among others the NPV, the economic rate of return (ERR), the cost-benefit ratio (CBR), the value added criterion and various efficiency tests as per the research objective.

In a nutshell, the main difference between financial and economic analysis lies in the interpretation of what are to be considered as the costs and benefits and the nature of prices used for estimation. In the case of financial analysis, direct costs and direct benefits are estimated at constant market price and items that are not direct market transactions, such as depreciation, subsidies and interest payments are disregarded. In the case of economic analysis,[2] all direct and indirect benefits and costs are ascertained in monetary terms, which may result from the consumption of project outputs. All indirect benefits are ascertained using contingent valuation, which measures the consumers' willingness to pay (WTP) and can be computed by the area under the social demand curve.

METHODS TO CALCULATE COSTS AND BENEFITS

Cost-benefit analysis is a method of evaluating the economic viability of a project. It compares the total benefits of a project with its total costs based on the NPV of the project. It recommends the implementation of the project if the benefits exceed the costs. To calculate the costs and benefits of a project it is imperative to ascertain the useful life of the project, that is, the number of years over which the benefits and costs of the project are to be evaluated. The researcher then needs to enlist all the benefits and costs of the project for each year, irrespective of their monetary or non-monetary nature (see Table 1.1).

TABLE 1.1
Cost and Benefit Distribution Over N Number of Years

Description	Year 0	Year 1	...	Year N
Benefits	B0	B1	...	Bn
Costs	C0	C1	...	Cn

After enlisting all relevant benefits and costs accruing to the project, it is important to bring all future costs and benefits to a common denominator, that is, the present value, by discounting all relevant costs and benefits. The premise for discounting is based on the fact that a rupee spent today is more valuable than a rupee spent one or two years from now, since today's rupee can be invested and hence can generate extra income during this period.

Further, while calculating the discount rate, either the nominal values not adjusted for inflation or the real values adjusted for inflation may be used, but the calculations must be consistent for the entire CBA process. It is important, however, to differentiate between the cost of capital, which is defined as the discount rate applied to the stream of net cash flows, that reflects the opportunity cost to the providers of capital, and social discount rate, which is used in economic analysis as an equivalent of the discounting factor to the cost of capital and is usually lower than the financial discounting rate. In a majority of cases, the real discount rate adjusted for inflation is used. It is calculated as:[3]

Real discount rate = (nominal discount rate – expected rate of inflation) / (1 + expected rate of inflation)

After calculating the discount rate, the discount factor is calculated as:

Discount factor = 1/(1 + discount rate)* time

The discount factor is then applied to all future values of costs and benefits to assess present values of all costs and benefits, which are then added to determine the present value of the total costs and benefits of the project. The data thus collected paves the way for the calculation of the projected NPV, CBR and ERR, etc., to decide on the viability of the project.

Net Present Value (NPV)

The NVP is calculated by subtracting the total cost from the total benefit. It can also be defined as the resultant sum of the discounted value of the benefits that exceed or lag behind the discounted value of the costs at a discount factor of say d per cent per annum.

Cost-Benefit Ratio (CBR)

Cost-benefit ratio can be defined as the ratio between the present value of benefits to the present value of costs at a specified social discount rate defined as:

PV of benefits/PV of costs = x/y

The decision rule for deciding on the viability of project based on NPV and CBR is:

(I) If NPV ≥ 0, implement the project. Else, do not implement it.

Or

(II) If $\dfrac{B}{C} \geq 1$, implement the project. Else, do not implement it.

Economic Rate of Return (ERR)

The ERR is defined as the discount factor at which present value of benefits becomes equal to the present value of costs. It signifies that even after taking the time value of money into consideration, the incurred costs at the starting of the project would yield a compound return of E per cent per annum for the next N years.

Internal Rate of Return (IRR)

The IRR of a project is defined as the discount rate at which the NPV of the project becomes zero. Usually, as the discount rate rises, NPV of the project declines. The IRR is a measure of risks associated with the project. It is a measure of how high the discount rate can go without making the project infeasible, that is, without making the NPV negative. That is why a project that has an IRR greater than the social discount rate is considered a good project.

Sensitivity Analysis

Sensitivity analysis is usually done to ascertain the sensitivity or uncertainty of outcome as a result of change in input variables. In the case of CBA, viability of a project can change totally if the results are sensitive to the choice of discount rates, that is, a small change in the discount rate can affect the viability of a project greatly and, as a result, the project may no longer be viable.

LOGICAL FRAMEWORK APPROACH

The logical framework approach (LFA) according to Jackson (1997), provides a set of tools that can be used for planning, designing, implementing and evaluating projects. It can also be defined as an aid to systematic thinking in formulating projects. It provides a structured, logical approach for setting priorities and determining the intended results and activities of a project.

The LFA encapsulates intermittent concepts, which facilitate all aspects of planning, implementation and evaluation of a project. The LFA centres on a matrix, which is completed by following a standardized terminology and a series of principles. An LFA matrix[4] encapsulates vertical logic wherein project implementation designs are formulated in a hierarchical manner. At the first stage, project inputs are combined into activities and at later stages, the inputs are compared vis-à-vis the outputs, which are later combined synergistically to achieve the objective and hence the goal (see Figure 1.1 and Box 1.1).

The logical framework approach (also known as logframe approach) and logical framework analysis (also known as logframe analysis), therefore, is an attempt to think in an integrated, systematic and precise manner about (i) project objectives, (ii) the linkages between different levels, (iii) the assumptions about other factors that are needed for the connections between the different levels to be valid and (iv) how to assess the degree of fulfillment of the various levels of targets and objectives.

FIGURE 1.1
LFA Matrix

Narrative Summary	Objectively Verifiable Indicators	Means of Verification	Important Assumptions
Development Objective			
Immediate Objectives			
Outputs			
Activities			
Inputs			

BOX 1.1
Definition of Terms Used in a Logframe Matrix

Development objectives are defined as long-term goals, which a project aims to achieve in consonance with other development interventions.

Immediate objectives are representative of short-term goals, which signify a specific change in condition, to be achieved at the end of the project.

Output is defined as the result of a project's activities, which signifies the project's achievement contributing to a process of change.

Activities are specific tasks that are performed by the project staff to achieve the desired goals.

Input refers to all project resources provided by the implementation organizations.

The LFA matrix logic can be deconstructed into 'vertical logic' and 'horizontal logic'. 'Vertical logic' of the LFA matrix is used as a tool by programme managers to design an implementation strategy, while researchers use 'horizontal logic' to evaluate the impact/outcome of projects.

Table 1.2 demonstrates the use of horizontal logic of logframe analysis. In the present example, the key project goal was to increase the contraceptive prevalence rate (CPR) from 42.6 to 47.1 per cent and one of the objectives to achieve that goal was to create a conducive environment. In order to achieve the goal, activities scheduled to be carried out under the component objectives were listed down as output activities and for each output activity, indicators and means of verification were also assessed. For example, the involvement of pradhans and religious leaders in reproductive child health (RCH) camps was assessed through a survey.

STAKEHOLDERS' ANALYSIS

The process of social change does not take place in isolation. It requires a multitude of strategic interventions involving different sets of stakeholders in a coherent manner to bring out a sustained

TABLE 1.2
Review of District Action Plan Implementation in Meerut District—A Logical Framework Analysis

Particulars	Project Description	Indicators	Means of Verification	Outcome/Comments
Key project goal	Increase CPR from 42.6 to 47.1%	Current use of modern family-planning (FP) methods	Primary survey	Current use of modern FP methods work out to 42%
Component objective 1		Creating a conducive environment		
Output activities	Meeting with religious leaders	Number of religious leaders trained	Secondary information	28 religious leaders participated in a one-day workshop
	RCH and FP training programmes for village pradhan	Number of pradhans trained	Secondary information	96% trained, 31% reoriented at Primary Health Centre (PHC)/Community Health Centre (CHC)
	Orientation programme for elected representatives in Merrut City	Perception of pradhans and religious leaders on reasons for their being invited to attend FP training	Interview/survey	3/5th of the sampled pradhans and religious leaders reported attending the training workshop because they felt obliged to attend after receiving the invitation
	RCH camp for religious leaders	Involvement of pradhans and religious leaders in RCH camps	Interview/survey	1 pradhan and 6 religious leaders out of the sampled 30 (each) confirmed contributing to the programme
	Dissemination of FP information among the masses	Counselling by pradhans and religious leaders for the use of FP methods	Interview/survey	0.6% of users reported pradhans/religious leaders as the motivator
		% of sampled EWs reporting a meeting with religious leaders/pradhans on FP information/services	Interview/survey	Less than 1%

Horizontal Logic: Determinant of Monitoring and Evaluation Plan.

desirable change. Thus, to assess the impact of a social change, it is necessary to do a stakeholders' analysis to have the views of all partners associated in the process.

The first step in conducting a stakeholders' analysis is to identify the primary and secondary stakeholders. Primary stakeholders are beneficiaries who are directly affected by a particular programme, while secondary stakeholders are persons who are indirectly impacted by the programme.

After identifying the stakeholders, researchers should try to identify their interest in various project objectives and outputs. However, it is not easy to identify their interests especially if they are hidden, multiple, or are in contradiction with the stated objectives of the organization or individual. After identifying the objectives, the researchers need to relate each stakeholder to the proposed objectives and activities of the specific project or policy.

The identification of the stakeholders' interests is followed by an assessment of the power and influence the stakeholders can have on a project or policy. Stakeholders' interrelationships are as critical to consider as their individual relationship to the project or policy. Stakeholders' analysis helps the researchers gather information about the social, economic, political and legal status of the stakeholders as also their relationships of authority and control and their relative negotiating positions.

OUTPUT OF STAKEHOLDERS ANALYSIS

Stakeholders' analysis serves as an analytical tool, which helps in determining the role and importance of various stakeholders, that is, primary and secondary stakeholders in project design and implementation. It can also suggest a strategy to foster partnerships among the stakeholders.

a) Stakeholders' analysis identifies the potential winners and losers resulting from a project's activities. It tries to list out the individuals or groups who will be positively or negatively affected by the project.
b) It ascertains the stakeholders' commitment to the goals of the project and their ownership of the project. Ownership determines the stakeholders' willingness to go with the project's goals. A low level of ownership means that the stakeholder cannot be counted on and that the stakeholders' weak commitment may affect other stakeholders.
c) The likelihood of the stakeholders' assistance in a project's development objectives is evaluated.

SOCIAL ASSESSMENT

Social assessment[5] ascertains the project's responsiveness to social development concerns. It provides a framework for beneficiaries to participate in the project planning, monitoring and implementation process. Thus, it facilitates the participation process of all relevant stakeholders in the project design and implementation.

Participation of stakeholders in the planning and designing process ensures that their concerns and issues form part of the project implementation processes. Further, participation during implementation increases the chances that people who are intended to benefit can ultimately avail equitable access to development opportunities. Thus, it allows the implementing agency to articulate the project's development outcome and impact, and establish meaningful indicators to monitor and evaluate them. It helps in lending a helping hand to the vulnerable and poor to voice their concerns during project formulation.

The quality of social assessment is another important criteria, which is emphasized by the World Bank in terms of five entry points: (i) social diversity and gender analysis, (ii) institutional rules and behaviour, (iii) stakeholders, (iv) participation and (v) social risk and vulnerability. Of these criteria, institutional rules and behaviour, and participation are discussed in detail.

INSTITUTIONAL RULES AND BEHAVIOUR

Social analysis as proposed by the World Bank looks at an institution's rules and behaviour. It analyses the role an institution plays in affecting change and ensuring community participation through techniques as listed next:

Analytic Work on Institutions

Social assessment as a process starts by analysing the institution's rules and behaviour. It helps in appraising the institutional capacity of the project-implementing agency. Social analysis focuses on institutional rules and behaviours, both formal and informal, which is likely to affect the project's development objectives. It analyses groups' characteristics, relationships (intra-group and inter-group) with institutions and the community.

It is important that while studying institutions, both written and unwritten codes/behaviours/norms of both formal and informal institutions are studied. The emphasis should be on analysing people's access to opportunity—their inclusiveness, their accountability, their accessibility and their ownership, rather than their efficiency as providers of goods or services. Social assessment considers all people who work in the implementing institutions as stakeholders in the project and also involves them in the assessment process.

PARTICIPATION

a) *Analysing the equity and effectiveness of participation:* Researchers, while using participation as a tool of social analysis, need to first examine the degree to which stakeholders affected by a project can participate in the opportunities created by the project. Researchers should also analyse the existing modes of participation to improve the effectiveness of stakeholders' participation.

b) *Equity of opportunity to participate in benefits:* Researchers, after analysing an institution's rules and effectiveness of participation of stakeholders, need to assess whether the assets and capabilities of the groups provides equity of opportunity in reaping the benefits of the project. The assets of these groups can be physical or financial.

   It is important to point out here that the groups' capabilities are as important as their assets. It also analyses the status of stakeholders' health, education, skills and experience. The assessment also analyses the organizational resources or the social capital stakeholders enjoy, that is, what is the level of relationship among peer groups and within communities. It treats social capital as an important asset, which can lower transaction costs and help establish networks to promote economic activity.

The capability and assets thus generated allows people to function, exercising their freedom to convert their entitlements, in the form of command over goods and services. The assessment, thus, can help in showing that development is not a matter of increasing supplies of commodities, but of enhancing the capabilities of people.

c) *Organizing effective participation:* Social analysis first analyses the traditional system/way in which people express interests. After this, the social process of inclusion and exclusion is studied to understand the local and traditional forms of participation. After taking into account all relevant factors, an effective participation framework is designed along with the community.

SOCIAL CAPITAL

It is very difficult to define social capital in exact terms as the mere mention of the term portrays vivid and abstract images. Unlike other forms of capital such as natural, physical, financial and human capital, social capital is at a very nascent stage in terms of its appeal. Further, it is very difficult to measure as the definition of social capital is very abstract and varies a great deal across cultures.

Social capital comprises varied norms, rules, association and networks that hold individuals and communities together. Research studies have further corroborated the fact that social capital/cohesion is critical for societies, especially for poor and disadvantaged communities to prosper economically. Poor people are the most disadvantaged people in every aspect; they suffer from poverty but cannot raise their voice as they do not have a voice of their own. They do not have a collective voice because they lack social capital or affiliations to formal and informal institutions.

It is imperative in such a situation that both formal and informal networks and institutions are strengthened and the participation of poor and disadvantaged people is ensured. Panchayati raj institutions (PRIs)[6] are an example of formal institutions that can make an immense contribution in lending a voice to the poor. Its decentralized decision-making process coupled with the reservation of seats for members of the disadvantaged community are steps which can ensure the participation of poor people in the decision-making process.

Social capital or networks can be classified on the basis of geographical domain into two types, namely, geographic social capital networks and non-geographic social capital networks. Geographic social capital networks are networks within a particular geographical region or subdivision whereas non-geographic social capital networks are networks of individuals who share the same values but may not belong to the same geographic region (Dasgupta, 2000).

Besides classifying social capital on the basis of geographical domain, researchers have also tried to classify social capital on the basis of the hierarchy and nature of association formed, that is, into horizontal and vertical associations.

Horizontal Association

Social capital is also defined in terms of horizontal associations between people characterized by networks, associations and norms, which strengthen community participation.[7] It can increase coordination and cooperation, especially among poor people, who face social exclusion and are subjected to severe social poverty.

Vertical and Horizontal Associations

Social capital in its broader sense involves both vertical as well as horizontal associations between people. This view emphasizes a concerted and coherent approach, combining both horizontal and vertical associations, to give communities a sense of identity and common purpose. But vertical association are paramount in bridging ties that transcend various social divides like religion and caste, otherwise horizontal ties can become a basis for the pursuit of narrow interests characterized by limited mobility and association.

Measuring Social Capital

Social capital in its broadest sense includes both the social and political environment, which defines social structures and also helps in enabling norms to develop. This definition in broad terms encompasses all aspects of social capital, but provides a serious challenge to devise strategies and policies to measure social capital. It is actually very difficult to list down the features or notions that can be associated with norms, associations and networks. Researchers can, to some extent, associate certain indicators in the case of formal networks and associations, but it is very difficult to even list down the norms and rules that govern informal institutions and networks.

Social capital has been measured in a number of innovative ways through quantitative,[8] qualitative and comparative methodology, though still a composite or agreed upon measure is far from sight. The reason is the comprehensive definition of social capital, which is multidimensional in nature and incorporates different levels of analysis. Further, any attempt to measure the properties of abstract concepts such as 'community' and 'network' is problematic, as definition and perception may vary from researcher to researcher. Though there have been surveys which have tried to measure social capital as a measure of trust in the government, voting trends, membership in civic organizations, no conclusive measurement process or strategy has been devised yet to measure social capital. Hopefully new surveys and methodologies will produce more direct and accurate indicators.

SOCIAL AUDIT[9]

Social audit is different from social assessment but some organizations use the terms interchangeably. The term is used to describe evaluations that focus on the likely impact on jobs, the community and the environment if a particular enterprise or industry were to close or relocate. Social audit is also used to signify the evaluation of outcome indicators or results vis-à-vis the objective or goal specified by an organization. Social auditing, thus, is also defined as a process that enables an organization to assess and demonstrate its social and economic benefits. It measures the extent to which an organization lives up to the shared values and objectives it has envisioned and committed to. It provides an assessment of the impact of an organization's non-financial objectives by regularly monitoring its performance by involving all stakeholders.

Social audit, as the name specifies, clearly points to the fact that these audits are concerned with the social consequence of a particular action. Initially these evaluations had no common structure or method other than the term social audit. But later on some sort of commonality was established across evaluations.

BACKGROUND

The first recorded methodology for social audit was developed in 1978 at Beechwood College and between 1978 and 1984, social audit training was given at Beechwood. The methodology was documented and published[10] (*Social Audit—A Management Tool for Co-operative Working*) in 1981 by Third System Organization (TSO) as an organizational tool for democratic organizations to measure their social performance and achievement. Social audit strategy is based on three key elements, namely, social targets, internal view and external view as a process of auditing.

The social audit process, detailed in subsequent sections, is in consonance with the process that is specified in the social audit toolkit designed and published by TSO, though the term social audit in its various forms and adaptations are used in developing countries.

THE SOCIAL AUDIT PROCESS

The social audit process is defined as the way in which social audit is planned and carried out. It encompasses various steps related to preparation for managing the social audit, that is, setting the criteria and target, monitoring progress and finally evaluating the flow of benefits. At the end of each of the elements, audit teams use internal verifiable indicators to monitor the project's activities and actions.

The social audit team, while conducting the audit, plans each exercise and element of the process in such a way that the process is useful for the organization during the final measurement analysis also. The social audit process is concerned with the practical application of the exercises and overall methodology.

Setting up an Audit Team

After deciding about the social audit process, the management board prepares the terms of reference for the audit team. The management board then appoints an audit team that is entrusted with the responsibility of carrying out the social audit. In the case of an external agency, the management board and audit team ethically should not consist of members from the organization whose audit needs to be done.

Statement of Purpose

After setting up an audit team, the next step is to establish the statement of purpose, defining the underlying culture of the organization. This helps to develop the value base of the organization. It draws on the major principles stated in the organization's charter, vision and goal, the statements about the purpose of the organization and organizational rules and norms made in the course of managing the organization. The value base is then used as the basis for setting the criteria to monitor consistency between the stated values of the organization and its general and specific performance.

Purpose of the Organization

Purpose of the organization signifies a clear and concise statement of the organization's stated purpose and objectives. The audit team develops the purpose of the organization in consonance with the organization's stated objective, in response to the key problems and issues highlighted by the organization. It defines the organization's central objectives in terms of the outputs expected by the beneficiaries and users. It defines the organization's success and relates directly to the problem of the beneficiaries that it seeks to address.

Organizational Rules

Organizational rules characterize the internal management rules and values that have been agreed on and are followed in the day-to-day functioning of the organization. Organizational rules are rules that not only shape the day-to-day functioning of the organization but also its future.

Value Base

The value base is drawn from the components of the statement of purpose by highlighting the key guiding principles stated and envisioned in the organization's philosophy. The vision, mission and legal charter provide the broad-based values governing the organization and represent the main strategies thus devised to address problems.

The purpose of the organization represents the values of the target groups' problems, which need to be addressed. It also takes into account the organizational rules, which represent the values of the staff, board members and employees. These values then serve as the benchmark for all measurement criteria and project appraisal decisions. These values are tested against stakeholders' interests in the exercise of the external and internal views of the social audit.

External View

The external view tries to take an unbiased view of the situation as researchers interact with a wide range of stakeholders associated with the organization. The purpose is to inform stakeholders about the organization's activities in order to obtain a response to the information. Besides, it aims to elicit stakeholders' attitudes and perceptions about the services provided.

Internal View

Internal view is an important constituent for assessing the attitudes and ideas of the staff, board members and other close associates and stakeholders about how the organization operates. It provides important information about the internal systems and structures of the organization. It also tests the ability of the organization to meet the needs of its users and clients.

Target Setting

While setting targets, researchers need to collate all draft targets and compile them into a single document. These targets then need to be prioritized before being put into a planning framework. Furthermore, specific issues and actions from each of the associated elements, such as the statement of purpose, the external view and the internal view, can be identified and integrated into the target setting process.

Social Targets

Social audit teams use social targets sheets as a series of planning tools to set targets, which ultimately helps in promoting good practice. These social targets together provide the planned and actual framework for measurement.

Social Audit Reporting

The audit team after completing the social audit exercise needs to prepare its report. It is important to point out that the method and style of presentation should be informative and understandable. Further, the report needs to be concise and clear. The report thus prepared should be disseminated to all stakeholders in a workshop/seminar/meeting. The report along with the main points should be put forward for discussion at a forum such as an annual general meeting.

Internal Verification Indicators

Internal verification indicators provide the audit team with an internal method of monitoring the process of social audit in consonance with the established principles of the organization. This provides verification of the results and thus enables the organization to set its own standards and criteria in relation to the values established in the methodology by the stakeholders.

BENEFICIARY ASSESSMENT

Beneficiary assessment is defined as a qualitative research tool that is used for improving the impact of development operations by analysing the views of the intended beneficiaries regarding an ongoing reform/process. This process starts as a consultation with project beneficiaries and other stakeholders to help them in designing development activities and to list down any potential constraints and also in obtaining feedback on reactions to intervention during the implementation process.

Beneficiary assessment, like social assessment, provides the target population with the opportunity to voice their opinions, needs and concerns regarding the development process. Thus, it is also a process of (i) listening to the issues and concerns of poor and disadvantaged beneficiaries and (ii) obtaining feedback on project interventions.

Beneficiary assessment is a qualitative method of investigation and evaluation that relies primarily on three data collection techniques:

a) In-depth interviews.
b) Structured and unstructured focus group discussions.
c) Direct observation.
d) Participant observation.

Beneficiary assessment, thus, is a low-cost option as interviewing and observation can be carried out with individual beneficiaries or with groups with a smaller sample size.

WELFARE ECONOMICS

Welfare economics is a branch of economics that attempts to maximize the level of social welfare by examining the economic activities of individuals who comprise a society. It assesses how different forms of economic activity and allocation of scarce resources affects an individual's well-being. Welfare economics takes a bottom-up approach. It assumes the individual as the basic unit of measurement and analyses the correlation between individual choices and collective choices or between individual welfare and social welfare. Social welfare signifies a collective welfare state of a society and is a resultant of individual welfare functions of a society. It can be ascertained in terms of utility or in terms of money.

WELFARE ECONOMICS: TWO APPROACHES

There are two approaches to welfare economics: the neoclassical approach and the new welfare economics approach. The neoclassical approach can be defined as an amalgamation of classical economic ideas and theories of the marginal utility school of thought. Classical economists used a materialistic concept of wealth but theory of utility defines satisfaction of consumer' wants as a utility function, hence the emphasis is on wealth to be conceived at the subjective level. It is based on premise that all individuals have a similar utility function, which can be summed up together to have a social welfare function.

The new welfare economics approach is based on the work of Pareto, Hicks and Kaldor. Welfare theory discusses the relationship between the values of many individuals and the possibility of social desirability of various alternatives. It addresses the issue of efficiency through criteria such as Pareto efficiency and the Kaldor-Hicks criterion (see Box 1.2).

Efficiency

Efficiency is a general term, but in welfare economics it corresponds to the concept of Pareto efficiency.[11] According to the definition of social welfare, social welfare function is optimal if no individuals can be made better off without making someone else worse off or in other words a system is not Pareto-optimal if some individual can be made better off without anyone being made worse off.

It is widely debated and concluded that Pareto-optimality is quite adequate as a concept of efficiency but not as a concept that defines optimality. Amartya Sen elaborated that an economy can be Pareto-optimal, yet it can still be perfectly disgusting by any ethical standard and concluded that there is nothing so special and inherent about Pareto-optimality, which implies maximization of social welfare.

BOX 1.2
Kaldor and Hicks Criterion

Nicholas Kaldor and John Hicks defined Kaldor-Hicks efficiency in relation to Pareto efficiency. In the case of Pareto efficiency, an outcome is termed to be more efficient if at least one person is made better off and nobody is made worse off, but under Kaldor and Hicks criterion, a more efficient outcome can make some people worse off. The key difference between Kaldor-Hicks efficiency and Pareto efficiency is the question of compensation. Kaldor-Hicks efficiency does not require compensation, and thus does not necessarily make each party better off. But, Pareto efficiency does require making every person better off. The Kaldor-Hicks method is used as test of Pareto efficiency to determine whether a system is moving towards Pareto efficiency.

Concept of Utility, Marginal Utility and the Indifference Curve

Utility as a concept is the core of welfare economics and is defined as the pleasure or satisfaction the consumer wants. Total utility increases as more of a good is consumed whereas marginal utility usually decreases with each additional increase in the consumption of a good. The phenomenon is also known as the law of diminishing marginal utility. Quite naturally, as human beings, we have a certain threshold of satisfaction and after that threshold of satisfaction is achieved, the consumer will no longer receive the same pleasure from consumption.

A model that tries to understand and describe individual human behaviour is based on the concept of utility maximization and is defined by the formula:

$$\max U = f(x,y)$$

On the basis of this formula, utility function can be defined as a function of the quantities of two goods consumed. The consumer is expected to experience satiation with the increased consumption of any good, that is, the utility function for an individual will exhibit diminishing marginal utility. A curve plotted to describe utility function is called the indifference curve.

A set of indifference curves is actually a map of a utility function, or, in other words, utility is constant along an indifference curve. An indifference curve shows all combinations of the two products that yield the same level of satisfaction for an individual. Further, as a characteristic, indifference curves do not intersect and bow inwards towards the origin.

Concept of Income Distribution and Production Possibility Frontier

Consumer utility can be combined in various ways to draw infinite consumer and production equilibrium, which yield Pareto-optimal results. Production equilibrium are determined from the production possibility frontier (PPF), which represents the point at which an economy produces its goods and services in the most efficient manner and thus allocates its resources in the best way possible. But, it also shows that there is limit to production and, hence, to achieve efficiency it is imperative to decide on the best combination of goods and services that need to be produced. There are as many optima as there are points on the aggregate production possibility frontier. Each Pareto optimum corresponds to a different income distribution in the economy.

The question that now arises is how to determine the best possible scenario and the answer lies in the social welfare function, which states the relative importance of the individuals who comprise society and hence there is a need for social welfare maximization.

Social Welfare Maximization

A social welfare function is defined as a function, which represents the measure of welfare of society. From the social welfare function, various utility functions can be derived on the PPF. Thus, this entire utility frontier can give a social utility frontier. Each point on such a social utility frontier signifies an efficient allocation of an economy's resources, which is the Pareto optimum. Though all points on the social utility frontier are Pareto efficient, only one point corresponds to a point where social welfare is maximized.

Arrows Impossibility Theorem

The theory of social choice is based on the connection between individual value and collective choice. The question really is in what way can individual choice be translated into collective choice. In the early 1950s, problems relating to rules for collective choice persuaded Kenneth Arrow, economics laureate in 1972, to examine the likely rules for aggregating individual preferences, where majority rule was only one of the many alternatives. His conclusion was that no aggregation rule exists that satisfies the five axioms he postulated. This popularly came to be known as Arrows Impossibility Theorem.

Amartya Sen in his book *Collective Choice and Social Welfare* dealt with problems like majority rule, individual rights and the availability of information about individual welfare. A well-known prerequisite for collective decision-making is that it should be non-dictatorial, that is, it should not reflect the values of any single individual. The minimum requirement for protecting individual rights is that the rule should respect the individual preferences of some people in some dimension.

Sen then pointed to the fundamental dilemma by showing that no collective decision rule can fulfill such minimal requirements of individual rights and the other axiom in Arrows Impossibility Theorem.

GAME THEORY

Game theory[12] is a branch of mathematical analysis (which has roots in welfare economics) that deals with the decision-making process in a conflict situation. Today, however, game theory has become a dominant tool for analysing economic and social issues.

In game theory we assume rational behaviour where each player tries to maximize his payoff irrespective of what other players are doing, or, in other words, each player has a set of moves that are in accordance with the rules of the game to maximize his rewards while his opponents adopt counter strategies to maximize their rewards.

DEFINITION OF GAME

The definition of a game is the central and key concept of game theory. A game has players or agents who receive certain payoffs,[13] which depend on the actions or strategies they choose to pursue. A strategy consists of a description of what the agent will do under each possible set of circumstances that may arise.

Game theory can be broadly classified into two branches, namely, non-cooperative game theory and cooperative game theory depending on the players' moves and cooperative behaviour. In the case of non-cooperative game theory, players work independently without assuming/knowing anything about what the other players are doing, whereas in the case of cooperative game theory, players may cooperate with one another.

In the case of non-cooperative game theory, each player tries to maximize his payoff and as he is not aware of the other players' moves, strategy and timing of the players' strategy are crucial in determining the outcome of the game. The term 'non-cooperative' means that this branch of game theory explicitly models the process of players making choices out of their own interest. Cooperation can, and often does, arise in non-cooperative models of games, when players find it in their own best interests.

STRATEGIC AND EXTENSIVE FORM OF GAMES

Strategic form/normal form is the basic type of game studied in non-cooperative game theory. A strategic form consists of a list of each player's strategies, that is, what a player can do in a game and the resulting payoffs. These are presented in a table with a cell for each strategy combination.

In the extensive form of the game, players make their moves in turns and there is more than one move in the game and everyone knows the previous moves of all opponents. It is also called a game tree as we can depict with a tree how a game is played, by depicting the order in which players make their moves and the information each player has at each decision point.

Dominating Strategy

It is possible in some games to choose a strategy that dominates all other strategies and gives a player a better payoff than his opponent, regardless of the opponent's strategies. As players are assumed to be rational, they decide on the strategy which results in the outcome they prefer most, given what their opponents do. If, in a game, each player has a dominant strategy, and each player plays the dominant strategy, then that combination of strategies and the corresponding payoffs constitute the dominant strategy equilibrium.

In the case of complete information game, each player knows about the payoffs of all the players under all possible actions, all the nodes in the game and all the structures of the game. A game has perfect information when at any point in time only one player makes a move and knows all the actions which have been made until then.

Nash Equilibrium

In 1950, John Nash[14] demonstrated that finite games always have an equilibrium point at which point all players choose actions that are best for them given their opponents' choices. Nash equilibrium, also called strategic equilibrium, is a list of strategies, one for each player, which has the property that no player can unilaterally change his strategy and get a better payoff. Nash equilibrium was taken a step further through the work of John von Neumann and Oskar Morgenstern. However, they only managed to solve non-cooperative games in the case of 'pure rivalries' (that is, zero-sum).

The Nash bargaining game is a two player non-cooperative game where the players attempt to divide a good between themselves. Each player requests an amount of the good. If his or her requests are compatible, each player receives the amount requested; if not, each player receives nothing. The simplest form of the Nash bargaining game assumes the utility function for each player to be a linear function of the amount of good they get.

Zero-sum Game

In a zero-sum game, the sum of the payoffs of all the players for each outcome of the game is zero, which signifies that if one player is able to improve his payoff by using some good strategy, the payoff of the other players is going to decrease or in other terms one player's gain is the other player's loss.

OPERATIONS RESEARCH

Operations research is defined as the study concerned with optimal resource allocation. Mathematically speaking, it tries to maximize the return or benefits against the specified constraints. Operations research thus tries to maximize benefits by using various algorithms and models that characterize the relation between objective function and constraint. For example, in case the relations between objective function and constraint are linear then a linear programming model is used and if it is non-linear then a non-linear programming model is used. It is important to point out that programming models must be representative of the original situation.

Some of the operations research models that are used frequently in the study of optimum resource allocation are discussed next.

LINEAR PROGRAMMING

Linear programming takes its name from the fact that here the objective function as well as the specified constraints are all related linearly to the decision variable. It involves an objective function, signified either by maximization of profit or minimization of cost, against a specified set of constraints.

NETWORK FLOW PROGRAMMING

Network flow programming is a special case of the linear programming model. In fact, formulating and solving network problems such as assignment problem, shortest route problem and transshipment problem, etc., via linear programming is called network flow programming. Thus, any network flow problem can also be designated as a minimum cost network flow programming.

INTEGER PROGRAMMING

Integer programming, as the name suggests, is concerned with an objective function, wherein variables can take discrete values and in most cases the values are integers. Integer programming does not allow variables to take all real values but limits them to take predetermined values within a given range.

NON-LINEAR PROGRAMMING

In non-linear programming, the objective function as well as the specified constraints are related non-linearly with the decision variable and hence models/appropriate algorithms are much more varied than linear programming.

Dynamic Programming

The dynamic programming model defines process in terms of states, decision and returns, not as an objective function. In a situation where a process moves through a dynamic phase and when a decision causes transition to a new state and with every state a return is realized, then dynamic programming models are used to ascertain the sequence that maximizes the total return taking into account all states and returns realized.

Stochastic Processes

Stochastic processes are used whenever processes in a model are governed by the probability theory. The stochastic model depicts activities, events and states in which a system can be found, for example, the number of persons in a queue, price of an asset, etc., in dynamic state and time.

In such a dynamic state, both the state and time could be either discrete or continuous. The discrete time system model is known as the Markov chain model and the continuous time system is known as the Markov process.

Simulation

Simulation is a very general technique, which is used in simulating a system on which results are desired. In case of simulation, a system is modelled in such a way that values for random variables are not known. Then values for the variables are drawn randomly from their known probability distributions, for example, Poisson distribution and normal distribution and the system response is recorded for each observation/value. Thus by simulating a system and by putting random values and recording the responses for each observation, the resulting statistics can be ascertained.

Notes

1. Cost-benefit analysis is a relatively simple and widely used technique for deciding whether to make a change. As its name suggests, to use the technique simply add up the value of the benefits of a course of action and subtract the costs associated with it.
2. Shadow pricing is an important methodology of economic analysis. Here the significant items of direct and indirect costs and benefits are adjusted to their economic, or real, social values. This is based on the premise that market prices of inputs and outputs tend to differ significantly from their social values, mainly due to the presence of externalities and price distortions in the economy.
3. In social projects, the social discount rate is used as an equivalent of the discounting factor to the cost of capital. This is the rate at which society values future benefits.
4. Logical framework analysis, besides being a project implementation tool, is also an excellent tool for understanding the practical indicators of project performance and for supporting monitoring and evaluation methods.

5. Social assessment is also defined as a process through which development planners learn from cultural values and actual behaviour. For more details on social assessment please refer to the World Bank website: http://www.worldbank.org/socialanalysissourcebook/home.htm.

6. The process of decentralization was given a boost by the 73rd and 74th Amendments to the Constitution in 1992.

7. For more details on the measurement aspect, please refer to the World Bank website: http://lnweb18.worldbank.org/ESSD/sdvext.nsf/09ByDocName/SocialCapital.

8. In the case of quantitative methodology, Knack and Keefer (1997) used indicators of trust and civic norms from the World Values Survey for a sample of 29 market economies. They use these measures as proxies for the strength of civic associations in order to test two different propositions on the effects of social capital on economic growth, the 'Olson effects' (associations stifle growth through rent-seeking) and 'Putnam effects' (associations facilitate growth by increasing trust).

9. For details on social audit, please refer to the *Social Audit Toolkit* (Freer, 2000); *Social Auditing for Small Organizations: The Workbook for Trainers and Practitioners* (Pearce et al., 1996) and http://www.locallivelihoods.com/socialov.htm.

10. It was not until the New Economic Foundation (NEF) in London, established in 1984, started to work on social audit in conjunction with the Strathclyde Community Business Ltd (SCB) in the early 1990s that any alternative method to the social audit toolkit was developed.

11. There are a number of conditions that, most economists agree, may lead to inefficiency. They include: imperfect market structures, factor allocation inefficiencies, market failures and externalities, price discrimination, long-run declining average costs, certain types of taxes and tariffs.

12. The earliest example of a formal game-theoretic analysis is the study of a duopoly by Antoine Cournot in 1838. The mathematician Emile Borel suggested a formal theory of games in 1921, which was taken further by the mathematician John von Neumann in 1928 in a 'Theory of Parlor Games' (von Neumann, 1928).

13. A payoff is a number, also called utility, which reflects the desirability of an outcome to a player, for whatever reason. When the outcome is random, payoffs are usually weighted with their probabilities. The expected payoff incorporates the player's attitude towards risks.

14. Nash was a mathematical genius whose 27-page dissertation, 'Non-Cooperative Games', written in 1950 when he was 21, was honoured with the Nobel Prize in Economics in 1994.

CHAPTER 2

SOCIAL RESEARCH: GENESIS AND SCOPE

Developing countries today face the great challenge of balancing growth with equity and justice. Growth, in all its fairness, should translate into equitable opportunity for all, but as is observed, the distributional effect of growth often does not trickle down to the majority of the socially and economically disadvantaged community. It is imperative in these situations to embark on a process of developmental change to improve the quality of life of the majority of the disadvantaged community. Developmental change, however, is not an act that can be carried out in isolation. It requires a multitude of strategic interventions supported by well-executed development planning, communication strategy and research and monitoring exercises.

Social research[1] plays an essential part in every development process of social change. It can lead implementing organizations to undertake constructive action programmes, to take the cue for mid-course correction or to ascertain the change that the programme has made vis-à-vis the expectation levels. The present chapter explores the very idea of social research/development research and the role social research can play in the process of developmental change. It also explains the importance of monitoring and evaluation as an important research tool.

SOCIAL RESEARCH/DEVELOPMENT RESEARCH: THE IDEA

All major social issues or problems in any developing country, especially in a country like India, arise from developmental backwardness coupled with the norms and practices of the prevailing social structure. Their struggle with the interrelated development issues of assuring quality of life to individuals, checking population growth and poverty and resource allocation makes them even more vulnerable to fall into the trap of a vicious downward spiral of developmental backwardness. India has staggering population-related problems, with a current population of more than one billion and a population growth rate of more than 2 per cent, which is compounded by the fact that one-fourth of the total population still lives below the poverty line. In addition, India's natural and environmental resources are deteriorating: more than half of India's total land area is degraded or is prone to soil erosion; dense and closed forests have been markedly declining; and widespread water scarcity and water pollution still exist.

Developing countries, in particular India, today face an uphill task of bringing about a turnaround on various social fronts, namely, improving health and nutritional indicators, increasing literacy rates, reducing poverty and conserving natural and environmental resources. This calls for intervention at all levels of the social and developmental process. It requires initiative from the government and a combined and fitting response from social institutions, that is, implementing organizations, in accelerating the process of social change, by intervening at various levels, for better socio-economic development in India.

Intervention targeted at various levels of the development process aims to affect changes in every facet of the socio-development process in a stipulated time frame by way of project-specific intervention. Research plays an instrumental role at all stages of planned intervention, starting with designing of programmatic intervention, by inquiring about the outcomes sought. It also helps in tracking the intervention's impact by conducting an inquiry into the outcomes sought vis-à-vis the resources used and the sustained change that the intervention has been able to make. It is clear, therefore, that social research can make an immense contribution to society at large, by linking research with programmes of sustained social action. Research can guide implementing organizations to undertake constructive action for mid-course correction by ascertaining the change the programme has made vis-à-vis the expectation levels.

Although some of the issues and linkages among nutritional indices, low educational indicators, population growth, sustainable development, natural resource conservation, poverty and the environment have received attention from researchers and policy-makers, working out a coherent and concerted strategy still seems to be a far-fetched idea.

THE PROCESS OF DEVELOPMENTAL CHANGE: PROGRAMME/PROJECT APPROACH

The socio-economic development scenario today asks for a concerted effort at all stages of development planning and intervention to bring about social change. Every development process is aimed at improving conditions in various realms of life. Interventions targeted at various levels of the development process aim to affect changes in the socio-development process in a stipulated time frame by way of project-specific interventions or in the form of a programmatic approach (wherein the stipulated time frame is not a precondition).

PROGRAMME

A programme is a coherent, organized and well-defined plan or intervention, composed of objectives, activities and means. A programme has a structured and well-defined goal, which can be broken down into objectives, activities and means. A project is a time-bound intervention that has a specific beginning and end, whereas a programme does not necessarily follow a time-bound approach.

Project

All targeted interventions, at any level of the socio-development process, usually subscribes to either a project or a programme approach. Project management can be defined as the planning, scheduling and controlling of a series of integrated tasks so that the goals of the project are achieved successfully in the best interests of the project's stakeholders. Effective project management requires good leadership, teamwork, planning and coordination, and better results to the satisfaction of the customers and project staff. Thus, a project is also defined as an endeavour to create a unique product, service or feature that results in customer (beneficiary) satisfaction and delight. This definition serves to highlight some essential features of a project, namely, (i) it is a time-bound process, that is, it has a definite beginning and an end and (ii) it is unique in some way either in its approach or in the features it has.

Though every project is unique in some way, based on broad features, projects can be broken down into:

a) *Separate activities:* These are tasks where each activity has an associated duration or completion time.
b) *Precedence relationships:* Precedence relationships govern the order in which planners/policy-makers may perform the activities. For example, a family-planning programme project may start with establishing the goal of increasing CPR and may have some broad objectives and activities such as the marketing and distribution of contraceptives. These activities could be backed by an efficient project management approach to bring all these activities together in a coherent way to complete the project.

Constituents of a Project

As mentioned earlier, all projects can be broken down into separate activities, that is, tasks. The project approach has several constituents, which make up the very core of the development process. These are:

a) Mission.
b) Vision.
c) Goal.
d) Objective.
e) Criteria.
f) Indicator.

Mission

The mission statement defines the very existence of a project/intervention. It signifies the very soul of the project. It can also be defined as the constant guiding force of the project/organization. It is to the project/organization what the preamble is to the constitution.

Vision

The vision portrays an idealistic view of what the project strives to achieve after completion. A vision statement provides focus and direction for the project. It is a statement that details the project outcomes to the impacted beneficiaries/stakeholders. It serves as a reference and guiding point during the life of the project and can be used for testing whether the project is on track. The vision statement is short and comprises a few statements and is usually developed by taking inputs from a cross-section of the stakeholders. It is written to be meaningful to both project team members and stakeholders and should state clearly how things would be better once the project is completed.

The vision statement for a large project, however, is much broader and this usually occurs because large projects address a more diverse set of clients, stakeholders and business processes.

Goal

The goal statement[2] provides the overall context of the project, that is, what the project is trying to accomplish. It takes its guidance from the project's vision statement and is always in consonance with it. The context of the project is established in a goal statement by stating the project's object of study, its purpose, its quality focus and its viewpoint.

The goal[3] for every project can be defined as the agreement between the project implementer/seeker and the project provider about what needs to be accomplished through the project. It points out to the direction to be taken and serves as the pivotal point for assessing whether the project outcomes are correct. In the project management life cycle, the goal is bound by a number of objective statements.

Objectives

Objectives are concrete statements describing what the project is trying to achieve. They are more specific statements about the expectations for the programme and describe the outcomes, behaviours, or a performance that the programme's target group should demonstrate at its conclusion to confirm that the target group has learned something. Objectives can also be defined as a statement of certain behaviours that, if exhibited by the target group, indicate that they have some skill, attitude, or knowledge (Fitz-Gibbon and Morris, 1978).

Objectives should be written at the initial stages of the project so that they can be evaluated at the conclusion of the project to determine if they were achieved. As mentioned earlier, goal statements can be broad in nature but objectives[4] should adhere to well-defined SMART criteria (specific, measurable, attainable/achievable, realistic and time-bound).

a) *Specific:* An objective should always be specific about the task or target it wants to accomplish.
b) *Measurable:* It should be measurable. Means and measures of verification should be established to assess whether objective has been met.
c) *Attainable:* It should always be within attainable limits, because formulation of an objective that cannot be achieved affects the morale of the project staff.
d) *Realistic:* The objectives should be set realistically after taking in account the available human and financial resources.
e) *Time-bound:* It should be attainable within a realistically stipulated time frame.

Goal statements, in actual terms, can be deconstructed into a set of necessary and sufficient objective statements, that is, every objective if combined must be accomplished to reach the goal. It is imperative, however, to define and agree on the project objectives before the project starts as deliverables of the project are created based on the objectives. Preferably a meeting between all major stakeholders should decide on the objectives to gain a consensus on what they are trying to accomplish. In keeping with the criteria just mentioned, it should be ensured that each objective broadly defines the (i) outcome, that is, what the project tries to accomplish, (ii) a time frame within which it would accomplish the tasks, (iii) means of measurement and verification and (iv) a plan to describe how it envisages to achieve the objectives.

Criteria

Criteria can be defined as a standard based on which things are judged. A criterion thus adds meaning and operationality to a principle without itself being a direct measure of performance. In other words, criteria sums up the information provided by indicators, which can be further integrated in a summative measure known as principle.

Indicator

An indicator can be defined as a variable that is used to infer attributes encompassed by criteria. If good health is decided as one of the criterion of a healthy body then people's exposure to sickness or disease can be used as one of indicators to sum up the criterion signifying a healthy body.

Besides being used extensively in quantitative research, principle, criteria and indicator are also used extensively in the qualitative research framework (see Box 2.1).

BOX 2.1
Qualitative Monitoring/Evaluation Framework: The Principle, Criteria and Indicator Approach

In qualitative research, researchers often use principle, criteria and indicator as components of a monitoring and evaluation framework. Principle comes at the top of the hierarchy followed by criteria and indicators.

Principle at the top of the hierarchy forms the basis of reasoning, based on which the criteria and indicators can be defined. A principle is usually centred around a core concept based on natural truths, societal values and traditional values as well as on scientific knowledge. Usually principles can be expressed concisely, for example, the principle of sustainable development.

Now if we take sustainable development as a principle, then we can take optimum utilization and intergeneration equity as the criteria that sum up sustainable development. Lower down the hierarchy, we can take yield per capita and benefit shared among beneficiaries as indicators to sum up optimum utilization and intergeneration equity respectively.

ASSESSING DEVELOPMENTAL CHANGE: MONITORING AND EVALUATION

Once an intervention has been developed and implemented through the project/programme approach, it must be monitored and evaluated to ensure that:

a) It has been successfully implemented.
b) It is properly targeted on the problem.
c) It is having the expected impact upon the problem.

However, monitoring and evaluation are more than just tools to show the success or failure of intervention. They enable researchers to investigate how particular changes are brought about. In other words, they can help an organization to design/extract, from past and ongoing activities, relevant information that can subsequently be used as the basis for building programmatic orientation, reorientation and planning. Without monitoring and evaluation it would be very difficult to track the course of work, that is, whether progress and success can be claimed, whether performance measures and outputs are in consonance with the input involved in the project and how future efforts might be improved (see Box 2.2).

BOX 2.2
Terms Frequently Used in Monitoring and Evaluation

Inputs: Inputs are defined as any human, physical and financial resource that are used to undertake a project or initiative.
Outcomes: Outcomes are consequences/results of an intervention and they can arise during and after an intervention.
Outputs: Outputs are the direct results of an implementation process and they arise only during the implementation period.
Performance indicators: Performance indicators are measures of verification that determine whether a target is achieved and how well it has been achieved.
Performance measures: Performance measures are means of verification, which try to capture the output and outcome by measuring performance indicators.

MONITORING

Monitoring, as the name suggests, involves tracking the progress of an act on a continuous basis. It can be defined as a function that monitors the ongoing process of intervention to provide the project staff, programme managers and key stakeholders indications about the progress of, or lack thereof, in achieving the targets. It does so by measuring inputs and outputs and any changes in output due to change in input.

Monitoring, though, has its limitations; it cannot comment on broader outcomes and the overall goal of the project and for this evaluation is required. Nevertheless, it plays an equally important role in tracking the process indicators of a project.

Tracking Specific Projects

Monitoring is generally used to assess the progress of projects and to provide important cues about the response of various initiatives, interventions and approaches. Thus, devising the monitoring process is not an act that can be carried out in isolation and it involves personnel from policy management, the finance department, field staff and officers implementing the project on the ground.

THE MONITORING PROCESS

The monitoring process must start with the designing of a monitoring framework or monitoring information system. This includes: (i) setting inputs, that is, the additional resources that need to be put in and a resource allocation plan, (ii) setting outputs and performance indicators, that is, project deliverables against the resource utilized, (iii) a time frame for each task and activity, including a start and end date and milestones for regular review of inputs and outputs, (iv) devising a financial accountability/auditing system and to do so planners will need to identify all possible forms of spending before the project begins and (v) devising a management information system, where all project staff provide necessary information in a user-friendly form and within the specified timetable.

EVALUATION

Evaluation is different from monitoring in many ways. Monitoring usually provides information regarding performance of process indicators, whereas evaluation assesses the performance of impact indicators. Monitoring is an internal process where all concerned project staff devise a monitoring system, while evaluation is usually done by an external agency to assess the project's achievements. Evaluation is a selective exercise that attempts to systematically and objectively assess progress towards the achievement of an outcome. It is defined as the process of aggregating and analysing various types and forms of data to evaluate the outcome of the project vis-à-vis the inputs used. More specifically, Walberg and Haertel (1990: 756) define evaluation as a careful, rigorous examination of an intervention, programme, institution, organizational variable, or policy. The focus is on understanding and improving the thing evaluated as we do in the case of formative evaluation, or in summarizing, describing, or judging planned and unplanned outcomes in the form of summative evaluation.

Evaluation is not a one-time event, but it is an exercise that can be carried out at different points of time, having different objectives and scope in response to evolving needs for evaluating the effectiveness of projects or even to comprehend the learning during the effort. Thus, all evaluations, including project evaluations that assess performance, effectiveness and other criteria, need to be linked to the outcomes as opposed to immediate outputs.

TIMING OF EVALUATION

Monitoring can only assess whether a project is being implemented and managed appropriately, but the scope of evaluation goes far beyond that as it evaluates outcomes and allows researchers to go a step further and assess the impact of the project. Concurrent monitoring might provide an indication to assess whether outcomes match the targets that were set, but to have an assessment of whether changes in output and ground conditions are due to programme efforts, it is imperative to do a comprehensive evaluation.

THE EVALUATION PROCESS

Evaluation as a process starts with the process of identifying the task, activities or initiatives that need to be evaluated. Effective evaluation can take place only if other processes, including monitoring, have been carefully followed and there is detailed information about project activities and tasks carried out to achieve the desired goal. The first step involves assigning an evaluation agency (external) the task of evaluating the project's outcome or performance against the laid out objectives. The process does not end with evaluation by the external agency. It is taken further by ensuring that the evaluation results are disseminated to all project stakeholders and cues are taken for further programme improvement.

EVALUATION AS PART OF THE PLANNING-EVALUATION CYCLE

Evaluation is often construed as part of a larger managerial cycle. It forms an integral part of any planning process and is also referred to as the planning-evaluation cycle. Both planners and evaluators describe the planning-evaluation cycle in different ways and, usually, the first stage of such a cycle is the planning phase, which is designed to elaborate a set of potential actions, programmes, or technologies to select the best for implementation. Depending on the organization and the problem being addressed, a planning process could involve any or all of these stages:

a) Identification of the research problem.
b) Conceptualization of the research problem and the probable options.
c) Listing all probable options and implications of selecting a probable option.
d) Evaluation of all probable options.
e) Selection and implementation of the best probable option.

Although these stages are usually considered as a part of the planning process, each stage requires a lot of evaluation work. Managers in charge of the planning process also need to have expertise in conceptualizing and detailing the research problem and options, to make a choice of the best available option. Evaluation aims to provide feedback to a variety of stakeholders including sponsors, donors, client groups, administrators, staff and other beneficiaries to help in decision-making. Evaluations aim to supplement programme efforts in utilizing available resources in an effective and efficient way to achieve the desired outcome (see Box 2.3).

BOX 2.3
Evaluating Effectiveness and Efficiency

Effectiveness: Effectiveness and efficiency are often confused and are even used as synonyms, but they are very different concepts. Management guru Peter Drucker defines effectiveness in terms of doing the right things and in the case of project intervention it is judged by comparing the objectives with the results directly attributable to the programme, with regard to both quantities, for example, number of persons, man days or quantifiable resources involved in the programme, and quality, for example, desired outcomes. Effectiveness is obtained by dividing expected results and actual results and thus is always expressed in terms of a percentage and has no units.
Efficiency: Efficiency is defined as doing things right, that is, getting the most from allocated resources. It is not expressed as a percentage because the value is obtained by relating two different elements to each other—outcomes in comparison with inputs or resources used. It is evaluated by assessing whether (i) the best possible results were attained with the activities/means available, (ii) results can be improved by organizing or managing the activities, means, or resources differently, (iii) it is possible to reduce the quantity or quality of the activities, means and resources without affecting the quality of the results.

EVALUATION STRATEGIES

Evaluation strategies signify a broad, overarching and encompassing perspective on evaluation. Evaluation strategies/studies[5] can be further classified on the basis of methods/models adopted for evaluation or on the basis of the purpose of evaluation.[6]

Classification Based on the Method/Model Adopted for Evaluation

Evaluation strategies can be further classified into three major groups described next:

Scientific Method
Scientific methods were probably the first methods adopted that provided an insight into evaluation strategy. Scientific methods are based on ethics and values laid out in the social sciences. They prioritize and evaluate the accuracy, objectivity, reliability and validity of the information generated. The scientific method includes experimental methods such as experimental and quasi-experimental designs; econometric-oriented designs, cost-effectiveness and cost-benefit analysis.

Project Management-Oriented Method
Project management-oriented methods are widely used nowadays in operations research, social research and even in development planning and management. The Programme Evaluation and Review Technique (PERT) and Critical Path Method (CPM),[7] as part of network analysis, are probably the best-known management-oriented models (see Box 2.4). Some researchers also consider 'logframe analysis' as a management-oriented evaluation method.

Qualitative Method
Qualitative research method focuses on the importance of observation, the need to reveal the hidden areas and the value of subjective human interpretation in the evaluation process as propounded in 'grounded theory' (Glaser and Strauss, 1967).

BOX 2.4
Network Analysis

Network analysis, a vital technique in project management, is used widely for the planning, management and control of projects. It enables project managers to evaluate different options/alternatives to suggest an approach that shall successfully manage a project through to successful completion. Network analysis is not as complex as the name suggests and can be easily used by non-technical personnel, by using project management software such as Microsoft Project. Network analysis broadly encompasses two different techniques that were developed independently in the late 1950s, namely, PERT and CPM.

These approaches were developed for purposes other than network analysis; PERT was developed by the United States Navy for planning and managing its missile programme. The emphasis was on completing the programme in the shortest possible time. The Dupont company developed CPM and the emphasis was on the trade-off between the cost of the project and its overall completion time. Modern commercial software packages do not differentiate between PERT and CPM and include options for completion times and project completion time/project cost trade-off analysis.

Classification Based on the Purpose of Evaluation

Evaluation strategies based on the purpose of evaluation can be categorized into formative[8] and summative evaluation.

Formative Evaluation

Formative evaluation, as the name suggests, provides the initial feedback needed to strengthen the intervention or policy formulation. It examines the programme's delivery process, quality of implementation and the impact of organizational inputs on the desired outcomes. Formative evaluations[9] are performed to assess whether a programme is working well or not and if the programme is not working well then what are the modifications required.

Formative evaluation usually requires the same data as summative evaluation, though the research design and methodology adopted for formative evaluation may differ. The main difference is in the case of data analysis procedures. In the case of formative evaluation, usually complex analysis procedures are used to explore the impact of interventions but causal relationship are not performed. This is because the purpose of formative evaluation is to ensure that the programme is moving in the right direction in a timely manner and that there are no gaps between strategies devised and outcome sought and if there are gaps, it helps programme managers in addressing the gap through formulation of strategies.

Formative evaluation can be subdivided into the following categories:

a) *Needs assessment:* This determines the programme's needs from the perspective of all stakeholders.
b) *Feasibility assessment:* It assess the feasibility of a programme, policy or a concept for implantation. It analyses both the technical and financial viability of an intervention.
c) *Process evaluation:* Process evaluation evaluates the impact of an intervention on process indicators. For example, whether an intervention targeted to increase family-planning awareness has any impact on group meetings between eligible couples is studied through process evaluation. It investigates the process of delivering the output.

Summative Evaluations

Summative evaluations are more specific than formative evaluations. They try to identify the impact of a programme's activities and tasks in achieving its objectives. It tries to examine the effects or outcomes of a programme/intervention by ascertaining whether the outcomes are in consonance with the desired objective. It determines the overall impact of the programme beyond the immediate target outcomes.

Summative evaluation can also be subdivided into:

a) *Outcome evaluations:* These try to analyse the impact of a programme's service delivery and organizational input on desired outcome.
b) *Impact evaluation:* Impact evaluation ascertains the project impact by analysing whether the project's activities and tasks have been successful in achieving the desired objective and goal. It, therefore, assesses the overall effects of the programme as a whole.
c) *Cost-effectiveness and cost-benefit analysis:* This assesses the benefit that is going to accrue from the project vis-à-vis the cost that is going to be involved in the project.
d) *Meta-analysis:*[10] Meta-analysis integrates the outcome estimates from multiple studies to arrive at an overall or summary judgement on an evaluation question.

SOCIAL RESEARCH/DEVELOPMENT RESEARCH: CLASSIFICATION BASED ON THE NATURE OF THE PROJECT/RESEARCH OBJECTIVE

The process of social change is not an act in isolation. It requires a multitude of strategic interventions involving different sets of stakeholders in a coherent manner to bring about a sustained desirable change. In a bid to respond to such a multitude of strategies, social research too takes different shapes. Social research can be classified into various categories based on the nature of the project/clientele and the research objective the study strives to achieve.

CLASSIFICATION BASED ON THE NATURE OF THE PROJECT/CLIENTELE

The research process, based on the nature of the project can be broadly classified into two categories: (i) customized research and (ii) syndicated research.

Customized Research

A customized research process is specific to the client's need/project objective. It takes into account the specific need of the client and the research methodology and design strictly adhere to the terms of reference provided by the client. Furthermore, it follows the timeline and deliverables as suggested by the client.

Syndicated Research

Syndicated research can be defined as a research product based on a concept, which is then marketed to various clients who subscribe to the product as per their need. Microfinance credit rating, rural index and Environment Management System (EMS) all fall under the category of syndicated research. As it is a syndicated product, the budget and timeline depends on the nature of the project.

SOCIAL RESEARCH BASED ON RESEARCH OBJECTIVE

As mentioned earlier, objectives are the pivotal points around which one needs to assess whether a project has achieved the expected outcomes or not and that is the reason it is advised that objectives be written down at the initials stages of the project so that they can be evaluated at the conclusion to determine if they were achieved. Social research based on the nature of the research objective can be classified into different types mentioned next:

a) *Action research:* Action research can be defined as programme evaluation of a highly practical nature. Professor John Elliott, dean of the School of Education at UEA, has defined action research as 'the study of a social situation with a view to improving the quality of action within it'(Elliott, 1991).

b) *Applied research:* Applied research can be defined as research linking basic research methods to practical situations. Assessing inequality using the Lorentz curve for a village/state or assessing the improvement in environmental conditions with the increase in income, etc., are examples.

c) *Concurrent monitoring:* Though the name suggests that concurrent monitoring is a type of monitoring method, it is more often used as an evaluation tool in determining accountability in activities related to inputs. It ascertains the on-going measures of progress and thus helps in determining the successful features of the programme, the shortcomings of the programme and whether the implementation process and the stakeholders are progressing in the expected manner. It provides important cues about the progress of the project and allows project staff to determine the direction of programme and to learn from the programme results.

d) *Cost-benefit analysis:* Cost-benefit analysis determines accountability in outputs related to inputs and thus suggests the technical feasibility of projects. Cost-benefit analysis is a summative measure of analysing net benefits accruing due to project initiation, by identifying the benefits and cost involved in the project. As a framework CBA helps in analysing the feasibility of a project by enumerating the benefits and costs involved in the project in monetary terms within a well-laid down analytical framework.

e) *Feasibility assessment:* Feasibility assessment determines the technical and financial capability of a programme. For example, edible salt is currently fortified with iodine and experimentation is on for the double fortification of salt with iodine and iron, the technical feasibility of which needs to be assessed before policy formulation and large-scale implementation.

f) *Impact evaluation:* Impact evaluation tries to assess the impact of strategic interventions on outcomes by finding statistically significant relationships. It examines the extent to which the project impacted on the problem and involves: (i) identifying the relationship between the results of the project, that is, the outputs and inputs, (ii) assessing what happened to the problem in the target area and what are the things that could have affected change and whether it can be statistically proved that the change is due to programme intervention and (iii) identifying aspects of intervention that affected the change.

g) *Process evaluation:* It seeks to find statistically significant relationships between activities and inputs. It examines the process involved in setting up and running the project. Process evaluations are focused in evaluating the performance of process indicators and provide insights about the process, that is, the managerial and administrative aspects of the project. It provides (i) an assessment of the way in which the tasks and activities were planned and carried out, (ii) identifies key elements or best practices by assessing the involvement of project managers and stakeholders, (iii) problems encountered during project implementation (iv) strategies devised to overcome problems and (v) the extent to which the project was successful in carrying the tasks as planned.

h) *Needs assessment:* Needs assessment tries to find service delivery gaps or unmet needs to re-establish priorities. It is based on continuous efforts to learn about the target respondents' needs and aspirations from the workers themselves and then develop responsive training and development programmes. It determines the current status of participants' and potential participants' expertise and knowledge. A needs assessment allows programme planners to determine the needs, desires and goals of the potential participants and/or their parents, teachers and other stakeholders.

The first step of the needs assessment process involves the identification of the management, project teams and other stakeholders with the needs assessment expectations and process. The next step involves research tool preparation, which entails adapting needs assessment questionnaires to the local context, training data collectors, establishing and orienting the project team and communicating to the target respondents about the purpose of the research.

i) *Operations research:* Operations research is another approach that is widely used to assess evaluation using a systems model and most operations research[11] studies involve the construction of a mathematical model. Operations research envisages maximizing benefits against a set of constraints by ensuring optimum utilization of resources. It does so by using logical and mathematical relationships/modelling that represent the situation under study. Mathematical models and algorithm describe important relationships between variables including an objective function with which alternative solutions are evaluated against constraints to suggest feasible options and values. Examples of these are linear programming, network flow programming, integer programming, non-linear programming, stochastic processes, discrete/continuous time Markov chains and simulation.

j) *Organizational development:* This is carried out to create change agents or process of change in the organization. Here it is important to note that change agents define a broader term as it could mean a change in organizational dynamics, values, structure or functioning. It is an important tool to assess whether organization dynamics, values, structure or functioning are in consonance with the vision or goal the organization seeks.

NOTES

1. The terms social research and development research are used interchangeably, though some authors have covered the topics differently depending on the problem or issue they have dealt with.
2. Goal statement is defined as 'an intended and prespecified outcome of a planned programme' (Eraut, 1994).
3. Rossi and Freeman (1982) have argued that, 'Goal-setting must lead to the operationalization of the desired outcome—a statement that specifies the condition to be dealt with and establishes a criterion of success...' (Rossi and Freeman, 1982: 56).

4. Tyler (1950) and Mager (1962) specify that objectives should also identify (i) the audience, (ii) the behaviour of the target population, (iii) the conditions under which the behaviour will be exhibited, and (iv) the degree/criterion of success.
5. There are three basic types of questions in evaluation research and studies classified on the basis of response to questions: descriptive, normative and impact. In the case of descriptive study, the researchers describe the goals, objectives, start-up procedures, implementation processes and anticipated outcomes of a programme. In case of normative studies, researchers evaluate the programme's goals and objectives by multiple values whereas in impact studies, researchers evaluate programme goals and objectives in terms of outcomes.
6. For further information, please refer to the research methods knowledge base of William Trochim, Cornell University (www.socialresearchmethods.net/kb/index.htm)
7. CPM/PERT models are available on Microsoft Project software and are an essential part of any project management application.
8. Scriven (1991) coined the terms used for two of the functions evaluation most frequently serves: formative and summative.
9. The origin of the term 'formative' evaluation clearly signifies that programme improvement is the purpose of most formative evaluations. This implies that the programme will be continued and can be bettered.
10. Meta-analysis is a set of statistical techniques for combining information from different studies to derive an overall estimate of an effect and is discussed in detail in Chapter 4.
11. The stream of operations research deals with optimizing resource utilization in a resource-constrained environment.

CHAPTER 3

RESEARCH PROCESS

The previous chapter emphasized the importance and need of a social research process to be in place to design, plan, implement and improve any developmental change process. The present chapter lists the various steps of the research process in detail starting with problem identification and conceptualization of the research plan to the preparation of the research report. Research as a process starts with the identification of the problem and moves ahead with the exploration of various probable solutions to that problem. It can be described as a researcher's quest to identify the problem and to solve it in the best possible way.

The first step in solving a research problem is the identification of the research problem and the various options/alternatives that are available to solve the problem in the best possible way (see Figure 3.1). The researcher should then identify/determine the information that is already available and the best possible research design needed to collect information, taking into account the time and cost factors. Finally, the information obtained must be assessed/analysed objectively to help in making an informed decision about the best possible way of solving the problem. This systematic

FIGURE 3.1
Social Research Process

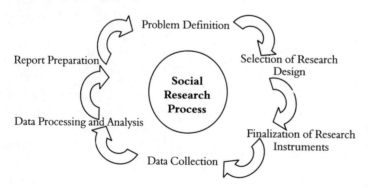

approach to decision-making is referred to as the research process. The process can be broadly defined as a combination of following steps:

a) Problem definition.
b) Selection of research design.
c) Finalization of research instruments.
d) Data collection.
e) Data processing and analysis.
f) Report preparation.

PROBLEM DEFINITION

As mentioned earlier, research as a process starts with problem identification. It may sound simple, but often it is the most difficult part. In the socio-development scenario, it is even more challenging to lay down the problem area and research needs exactly because of non-controllable extraneous factors and externalities involved in the process. More so, as every socio-development process has a social and human angle attached to it, which makes the task even more difficult. For example, it is very challenging to establish linkages between environment and poverty, environment and health, or for that matter between natural resource degradation and population, and it is even more difficult to lay down the research objective precisely, which can be assessed using an objective approach/tools.

The identification of the problem area then leads to the formulation of the research objective, which is the core of the research process. All subsequent steps in the research process, that is, selection of research design, research instruments and analysis take their cue from the objectives.

SELECTION OF RESEARCH DESIGN

In quantitative research, the primary aim is to determine the relationship between an independent variable and another set of dependent or outcome variables in a population. Research design,[1] according to Kerlinger is the plan, structure and strategy of investigation conceived to obtain answers to research questions and to control variance (see Figure 3.2).

Quantitative research designs[2] can be broadly divided into two types, namely, exploratory research and conclusive research.

EXPLORATORY RESEARCH

Exploratory research, as the name suggests, is often conducted to explore the research issue and is usually done when the alternative options have not been clearly defined or their scope is unclear. Exploratory research allows researchers to explore issues in detail in order to familiarize themselves

FIGURE 3.2
Quantitative Research Design Classification

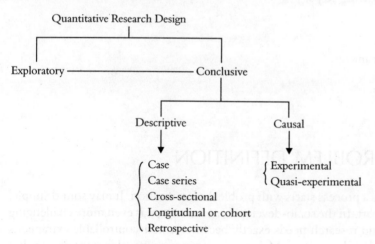

with the problem or concept to be studied. Familiarization with the concept helps researchers in formulating research hypothesis.

Exploratory research is the initial research, which forms the basis of more conclusive research. It can even help in determining the research design, sampling methodology and data collection method. In some cases, exploratory research serves as the formative research to test concepts before they are put into practice.

Exploratory research, as mentioned earlier, explores the issue further, hence it relies more on secondary research, that is, the review of available literature and/or data, or qualitative research approaches such as informal discussions with primary and secondary stakeholders, project staff, donor agencies and more formal approaches, like in-depth interviews, focus groups or case studies. Exploratory research thus cannot provide a conclusive answer to research problems and usually are not considered useful for decision-making, but they can provide significant insights to a given situation. However, the results thus obtained cannot be generalized and should be interpreted with caution as they may or may not be representative of the population being studied.

CONCLUSIVE RESEARCH

Conclusive research can further be classified into descriptive research and causal research.

Descriptive Research

Descriptive research, as the name suggests, enumerates descriptive data about the population being studied and does not try to establish a causal relationship between events. This is also one of its major limitations as it cannot help determine what causes a specific behaviour or occurrence. It is used to describe an event, a happening or to provide a factual and accurate description of the population being studied. It provides the number of times something occurs and helps in determining the descriptive statistics about a population, that is, the average number of occurrences or frequency of occurrences. In a descriptive study, things are measured as they are, whereas in an experimental study researchers take measurements, try some intervention and then take measurements again to see the impact of that intervention.

Descriptive research can be further classified into the following types:

a) Case study.
b) Case series study.
c) Cross-sectional study.
d) Longitudinal change.
e) Retrospective study.

Case is the simplest kind of descriptive study, which reports data on only one subject, individual or social process. For example, the study of an HIV patient or of a voluntary institution that is performing well. Case studies are now used worldwide as an accepted tool to document innovative approaches, success stories and failures. Case series is the descriptive study of a few cases. For example, studying success stories of resource-based self-help groups to identify their commonality would be a case series. Cross-sectional studies portray a snap shot of the prevalent situation as in these studies variables of interest in a sample are assessed only once to determine the relationships between them. The most commonly seen surveys use the cross-sectional design, which asks questions of people at one point in time. In the case of a longitudinal design, the same questions are asked at two or more points in time. Longitudinal design can be further classified into three subtypes: (i) trend study, (ii) cohort study and (iii) panel study.

a) *Trend study* can be defined as a repeated cross-sectional design where the same set of questions are asked to different sets of people/target population at different points in time. In trend studies, the variables of interest are assessed as a function of time.
b) *Cohort study* is a trend study that studies changes in cohorts, that is, the same set of people who experience the same kind of life or the same events over time. In prospective or cohort studies, some variables are assessed at the start of a study then after a period of time the outcomes are determined. For example, assessing the impact of a communication campaign on awareness levels of a target audience, would be a cohort study.
c) *Panel study* asks the same set of questions to the same people over time and is used to assess changes in the panel respondent's characteristics over times. In a nutshell, trend studies essentially look at how concepts/variables of interest change over time; cohort studies look at how the behaviour of the same set of people changes over time; and panel studies look at how people change over time.

Case-control studies compare cases with a particular characteristic of control subjects, that is, subjects without the attribute in order to determine a causal effect, for example, cases of tuberculosis and the number of cigarettes smoked per day. Case-control studies are also known as retrospective studies because they focus on conditions, which might have resulted in subjects becoming cases.

Causal Research

Causal research is defined as a research design where the main emphasis is on determining a cause and effect relationship. It is undertaken to determine which variable might be causing a certain behaviour, that is, whether there is a cause and effect relationship between variables and if a relationship exists then what is the nature of the causal relationship. In order to determine causality, it is important to hold one variable constant to assess change in the other variable and then measure the changes in the other variable. Causal research by nature is not very easy as it is very difficult to ascertain the causal relationship between the observed variable and the variable of interest. In fact, the causal relationship could be due to other factors, especially when dealing with people's attitudes and perceptions. There are often much deeper psychological factors, which even the respondent may not be aware of while responding to a question.

There are two research methods/designs for exploring the cause and effect relationship between variables: (i) experimental studies and (ii) quasi-experimental studies.

Experimental Studies

Experimental studies are characterized by a control group and an experimental group and subjects are assigned randomly to either group. Researchers try to maintain control over all factors that may affect the result of an experiment as experimentation[3] is still believed to be and is used as one of the most important research designs for establishing causality between variables. It allows the researcher to manipulate a specific independent variable in order to determine what effect this manipulation would have on other dependent variables. Another important criterion, while following the experimental research design, is to decide on the setting of the experiment, that is, whether it should take place in a natural setting or in an artificial one.

Experimental studies/designs[4] are also known as longitudinal or repeated-measure studies. They are also referred to as interventions, because of the use of control and experimental groups.

Time series is the simplest form of experiment, where one or more measurements are taken on all subjects before and after a treatment and it could either be a single subject design or a multiple subject design. In the case of a single subject design, measurements are taken repeatedly before and after an intervention on one or a few subjects.

The very nature of a time series design can also pose some problems as any change that is observed could be due to something other than the treatment. The subjects might do better on the second test because of their experience/learning during the first test or there could be some other extraneous factors that may result in a difference between the results of the first and second test such as change in weather, change in aptitude or change in diet. Crossover design, where the subjects are normally given two treatments, one being the real treatment, the other a control or reference treatment, can solve this problem. In the case of a crossover design, as the name suggests, half the subjects first receive control treatment, whereas the other half receive experimental treatment and after a sufficient period of time, which should allow the treatment to wash out, the treatments are crossed over. Further, any effect of retesting or of change that happened during successive tests can then be subtracted out by an appropriate analysis and we can also use multiple crossover designs involving several treatments to sort out this problem.

In certain situations, the treatment effect is unlikely to wash out between measurements. It then becomes imperative to use a control group. In these designs, though all subjects are measured, only an experimental group receives the treatment and when subjects are measured again, then any change in the experimental group is compared with the change in the control group to assess the effect of the treatment.

In another case of experimentation, that is, in the case of a randomized controlled trial, subjects are assigned randomly to experimental and control groups. It minimizes the chance that either group is not representative of the population they belong to. Further, if the subjects are masked to the identity of the treatment, the design is called single blind controlled trial.

The term blind experiment means that the subjects do not know which group they belong to, that is, they do not know whether they belong to the experimental group or the control group. In a double blind experiment, even the researchers and facilitators do not know who is in which group. These precautions/measures are taken by the research team to avoid the Hawthorne effect[5] and the placebo effect. The Hawthorne effect is defined as the tendency of human beings to temporarily improve their performance when they are aware it is being studied, especially in a scenario where they think they have been singled out for some experimental treatment. The placebo effect refers to the tendency of some subjects to respond positively to a new treatment just because they expect it to work, although the treatment may be entirely ineffective.

In such a case, researchers first need to randomly select a control group, statistically equal to the treatment group. Though the subjects are assigned randomly to each group, it is important to ensure that both groups are from the same population. To do so, researchers should match population characteristics to ensure that the groups match in their distributional characteristics.

There is nothing sacrosanct about having only one control and treatment group and researchers may have more than one control or treatment group. Researchers can have full and partial treatment groups based on the nature of the treatment. The experiment procedure starts with a pre-test and ends with a post-test. It is important to point out that researchers can conduct multiple post-tests at any time during the experiment. Researchers need to analyse the findings based primarily on differences in the post-test scores of the experimental and control groups.

Quasi-experimental Studies

Quasi-experimental studies, as the name suggests, have some attributes of experimental research design as they involve some controls over extraneous variables when full experimental control is lacking. Thus, in some cases, where the situation demands partial control, these designs may be the only way to evaluate the effect of the independent variable of interest. Further, as quasi-experimental studies lack control, this research design is often used in the area of medicine where, for ethical reasons, it is not possible to create a truly controlled group. Quasi-experiment[6] is a type of quantitative research design conducted to explain relationships and/or clarify why certain events happen.

The objective of adopting a quasi-experimental design is to assess causality. It analyses the difference in treatment and control group to look for causality in situations when complete control is not possible. These designs were developed to examine causality in situations where it is not practical or possible to have complete control over the subjects.

Quasi-experiments are relatively strong in terms of internal validity and use matching instead of randomization. Thus, quasi-experimental designs lack at least one of the other two properties that characterize true experiments, namely, randomization and a control group.

FINALIZATION OF RESEARCH INSTRUMENTS

DESK RESEARCH

The first step to the finalization of research instruments is to do desk research. Desk research, as the name implies, is analysis/documentation of available information for preparing survey instruments, finalizing sampling and operation plans and developing a list of indicators for the study. It usually involves review of secondary literature, that is, related studies, schedules, etc.

DEVELOPMENT OF RESEARCH INSTRUMENTS

Development of research tools/instruments forms the next step after the finalization of research design. Finalization of research instruments needs to be done in consultation with all research partners and the core study team members need to develop the research instruments in consonance with the research objectives and designated tasks.

DESIGNING RESEARCH TOOLS/INSTRUMENTS

Designing research instruments depends on various factors such as the research problem, type of survey design and nature of information that needs to be collected. In the case of a quantitative survey, structured questionnaires and schedules are preferred whereas in the case of qualitative research, semi-structured questionnaires or discussion guidelines are preferred. However, it is not as easy as it sounds. There are other factors that need to be considered.

Though survey is the most preferred option, it suffers from some problems too. Researchers can make inferences, but cannot be sure of the cause and effect relationship as they can be in the case of experimental or quasi-experimental research. Other weaknesses of the survey method include:

a) *Reactivity:* Respondents' bias arises because they may give morally desirable responses or feel good responses.
b) *Mismatched sampling frame:* In surveys it is difficult to ascertain the adequate number and type of people who are representative of the population.
c) *Non-response rate:* However hard researchers may try, there are always going to be people who will not participate in surveys. This leads to high a non-response rate.

d) *Measurement error:* Like respondent and interviewer bias, there is always going to be some bias because of the failure of the survey instrument or methodology in measuring the desired attribute.

The next section looks at the important procedure of designing a survey instrument, which can contribute a lot in minimizing measurement error and interviewer error to some extent.

Survey Instrument

Survey instruments[7] can be broadly classified into two categories: (i) questionnaires and (ii) interviews. A questionnaire is almost always self-administered, allowing respondents to fill them out themselves. All the researcher has to do is to arrange for the delivery and collection of the questionnaires.

An interview is typically defined as a face-to-face discussion or communication via some technology like the telephone or computer between an interviewer and a respondent. There are three subtypes of interviews: (i) unstructured, which allows a free flow of communication in the course of the interview or questionnaire administration, (ii) structured, where the information that needs to be culled out from the respondents is already decided and (iii) semi-structured, which restricts certain kinds of communications but allows manoeuvring freedom on the discussion of certain topics.

Type of Question

Usually research questionnaires contain question of three basic types: (i) open-ended questions, (ii) dichotomous questions and (iii) multiple-response questions.

a) *Open-ended questions:* Open-ended questions are questions that do not have pre-coded options. These are used extensively in formative research or qualitative research when researchers want to capture the respondent's responses verbatim.

b) *Dichotomous questions:* Dichotomous questions have two possible answers like yes/no, true/false or agree/disagree responses. Surveys often use dichotomous questions when they are looking for a lead question.

c) *Multiple-response questions:* There are several questions that may have many probable answers, for example, knowledge regarding ways in which HIV/AIDS can spread. It is highly probable that most of the respondents would be aware of more than one probable way, thus it becomes imperative to frame questions as multiple-response questions.

Besides the type of question, there are various other attributes/norms that need to be adhered to while designing research instruments. These are discussed next.

Mutual Exclusivity

In the case of a multiple-response question, it is imperative to have response items that are mutually exclusive otherwise a bias could be introduced.

Non-exhaustive Response Set

Bias can also be introduced when the response alternatives available to the respondent leaves out valid choices they would otherwise make. The most common example is leaving out such responses as 'not applicable' or 'don't know' when, in fact, respondents may well be neutral or may actually not know, rather than be hiding their 'true' responses which the researcher is trying to force out by omitting these categories.

Order of Questions

The order of questions plays an important role in designing the survey instrument. The first paragraph should be clearly related to the announced purpose of the survey. Location details (state/district/village) could follow later together with background information questions. The survey should then proceed to attitude questions, sequencing from general and less sensitive items towards more specific and more sensitive ones.

Filter Items/Skip Questions

Filter items/skip questions are ones that allow for the elimination/filtering of unqualified respondents. For example, sometimes the researcher may have to ask the respondent one question in order to determine if they are qualified or experienced enough to answer a subsequent one. This can be done using a filter or skip question. For instance, the researcher may want to ask one question if the respondent has used a family-planning method and a different question if the respondent has not used any family-planning method. In this case, the researcher constructs a filter question to determine whether the respondent has ever used a family-planning method:

1) Have you ever used a family-planning method?

   a) Yes
   b) No

2) Please specify the family-planning method you have used?

Filter questions can get very complex. Sometimes, the researcher has to have multiple filter questions in order to direct the respondents to the correct subsequent questions. However, the researcher must always try to avoid having more than three levels for any question as too many filter questions and jump questions can confuse the interviewer and may even discourage the respondent from continuing with the survey. Researchers generally use graphics like arrows to indicate the question to which the skip question leads, or, alternatively, researchers can use instructions.

Cross-check Items

Cross-check items are check items which help researchers in tracking data consistency in research questionnaire. The researcher can ask the respondent's age at one point and date of birth at another to cross-check both the survey items. Split-form interview is an extension of this, wherein the questionnaire is administered to different related respondents, for example, a husband and wife separately with a view towards cross-checking for consistency.

Caution Taken in Phrasing Questions

a) *Is the question really necessary?* First and foremost, researchers always need to ask whether the question is really necessary, that is, they must examine each question to see if the question needs to be asked at all and if it needs to be asked then what level of detail is required. For example, do you need the age of each child or just the number of children under 16?

b) *Double-barrelled questions/compounded items:* Researchers can often find a double-barrelled question by looking for the conjunction 'and' in the question. For example, the question 'What do you think of the proposed changes in the country's economic policy and foreign policy?' is a double-barrelled one.

   Items with compound clauses may not be multidimensional, but may involve undue complexity. For example, the question, 'Have you ever faced complications after using the oral pill and whether you have consulted any doctor for the same?' is better broken into two items: 'Have you ever faced complications after using the oral pill?' and the follow-up question, 'If you have answered yes to the previous question, whether you have consulted any doctor for the complications?'

c) *Is the question specific or it is leading to ambiguity?* Sometimes we ask our questions too generally and the information we obtain is more difficult to interpret. Questions should be specific, avoiding generalities for if it is possible for respondents to interpret questions in dissimilar terms, they will.

d) *Is the question sufficiently general?* Sufficiently general question such as what is your opinion about India's policy should be avoided as it leaves scope of ambiguity. It is not clear in the question whether the researcher is asking about the country's economic policy, foreign policy, or domestic policy.

e) *Is the wording personal?* Personal wording in any scenario should be avoided, more so in the case of sensitive/controversial issues.

f) *Is the wording too direct?* Questions need to be specific but not direct as they may not get any response and may rattle the respondent.

g) *Loaded questions:* Sometimes the researcher's own biases can also creep in and may affect the wording of the questions. For example, the questions 'Do you still smoke?' or 'Do you still beat your wife' are loaded ones as the researcher has already loaded his bias into the questions to get a desired response.

h) *Recall items:* People's ability to recall the past is very limited. They may not be able to recall something, which happened more than six month ago. Thus, if recall is necessary, the time frame should be as recent as possible. In rural areas, festival like Holi, Diwali and Id or even Hindu calendar months like Sawan could be mentioned as a reference point.

i) *Unfamiliar terms and jargon:* Unfamiliar terms and jargon could cause a lot of problems for the respondents not only in understanding the question, but it may also confuse them. Take, for example, a question like 'Do you think India is moving away from a socialistic model of development?' Terms such as 'socialistic model of development' are not likely to be well understood by typical survey populations. When a term not in popular usage has to necessarily be used in an item, the interviewer must precede the item with a brief explanation. Wherever possible, familiar terms should be substituted for unfamiliar terms.

j) *Questions requiring inaccessible information:* Sometime, a question may use familiar terms, but require information most respondents would not know or would not like to share. Take, for example, a question such as 'What is your family income?'. Now, if the investigator asks this question to a family member other than the head of household/chief wage earner in an agrarian economy setup, then he may not get an appropriate answer.

k) *Complexity and memory overload:* In complex research issues, sometimes the researcher tries to frame the questionnaire in a manner as complex as the research issue, without realizing that by doing so he is likely to overtax the respondent. The more complex the research objective or issue, the easier it is to overload memory. If there are over five alternatives, a show card should be used to allow the respondent to view the alternatives, not simply hear them orally in an interview situation.

l) *Problem of dangling alternatives:* For example, 'Would you say that you very strongly approve, strongly disapprove', presents 'dangling alternatives', which the respondent must memorize before even understanding the question. This can result in first-presented response, or in negativity. Besides grammar, it is important to ensure that the survey instrument takes into account the language and dialect people speak in the region where the survey is going to be conducted, either at the tool formulation stage or at the translation stage (see Box 3.1).

BOX 3.1
Translation of Survey Items into Vernacular Languages

One of the key issues in a large nationwide study is translation of survey items into the regional/vernacular languages. Thus, while translating survey tools, researchers should take care of semantic equivalence, conceptual equivalence and normative equivalence of survey items (Behling and Law, 2000).

This is done through the translation/back translation method where independent translators translate from one language to another, and then back again, to see if the original and re-translated items remain the same.

PRE-TESTING AND FINALIZATION OF RESEARCH INSTRUMENTS

All the research instruments developed for the study should be thoroughly tested in order to ascertain their suitability in actual field conditions. Professionals with the support of field executives need to carry out the pre-testing exercise.

Pre-testing is considered an essential step in survey research. It is not only critical for identifying questionnaire problems but it also helps in removing ambiguities and other sources of bias and error. It can also highlight any problem interviewers may have regarding the language of the questions and the skip patterns.

Regarding pre-testing, Converse and Presser (1986) argue that a minimum of two pre-tests are necessary. They suggest that the first pre-test should have twice the number of items as the final pre-test, as one of the purposes of the pre-test is to identify weaker items and drop them from the survey. Items may also be dropped if the first pre-test shows that they have little variance to be accounted.

Pre-testing incorporates different methods or combinations of methods. These techniques have different strengths and weaknesses. Some of these techniques are highlighted in the next section.

Types of Pre-testing

Pre-testing techniques[8] can be further classified into two major categories based on the methodology and approach used for pre-testing: (i) pre-field techniques and (ii) field techniques. Pre-field techniques are generally used at the initial stages of research instrument development through respondent focus groups and interviews.

In the field type of pre-testing, questionnaires are tested under field conditions and include techniques such as behaviour coding, interviewer and respondent debriefings and the analysis of non-response items and response distributions.

Pre-field Techniques

a) *Focus groups:* Focus group helps in identifying variations in questionnaire items, language, or interpretation of questions and pre-coded options. Self-administered questionnaires can be pre-tested in a focus group, to learn about the appearance and formatting of the questionnaires. Focus groups also produce information and insights that may be less accessible without the group.

b) *Cognitive laboratory interviews:* Cognitive laboratory interviews are also generally used early in the questionnaire.

Field Techniques

a) *Behaviour coding:* Behaviour coding, as the name suggests, depends on interactions between the respondent and the interviewer to decide about the relevancy of language, content and interpretation of questionnaire items.

 The focus of behaviour coding is on how the respondent answered the question and how the interviewer tried to ask the question. For example, if a respondent asks for clarification after hearing the question, it is likely that some aspect of the question may have caused confusion.

b) *Interviewer debriefing:* It tries to minimize interviewer bias by making questions simple and clear. It tries to assess whether the interviewer has understood the question correctly.

MEASUREMENT SCALES

There are four types of scales that are used in measurement: nominal, ordinal, interval, and ratio scales. In fact, they follow a hierarchy of measurement scales, nominal being at the lowest rung of the hierarchy and even application of statistical procedure are classified in relation to the scale used. They are categorized into two groups: categorical and continuous scale data, where nominal and ordinal scales are categorized together as categorical data while interval and ratio scales are grouped together as continuous data.

Nominal data having unordered scales are called nominal scales, for example, the gender categories male and female. Categorical data having ordered scales are called ordinal scale. In the case of continuous data, scales representing interval data are called interval scales and data having both equal intervals and an absolute zero point are called ratio scales.

a) *Nominal variables:* The values of the nominal variable data have no numeric meaning as no mathematical operation except counting can be done on the data. They are, in fact, used for classifying whether the individual items belong to some distinctively different categories. For example, we can say that individuals are different in terms of variables like gender, race, colour, caste, etc. However, apart from counting, no other mathematical operation can be carried out on these variables.

b) *Ordinal variables:* Ordinal variables, unlike nominal variables, allow us to rank the items we measure in terms of order and we can specify that higher order items definitely represent more of the quality extent represented by the variable, but we still cannot tell how much more than the other item. A typical example of an ordinal variable is the rating assigned to the impact of a programme, like excellent, average and poor. Now we can say that x per cent rated the programme as excellent, y per cent rated it as average and another z per cent rated it poor, but researchers cannot say for sure that the difference between excellent and average is same as that of average and poor. In the case of ordinal variables, only certain mathematical variables such as greater than or less than are feasible and only measures such as median and range can be calculated.

c) *Interval variables:* Interval variables provide more flexibility in terms of measurement as it not only allows us to rank the measured items but can also help in quantifying the size of the difference between them. For example, temperature, as measured in degrees Fahrenheit or Celsius, constitutes an interval scale. We can say that a temperature of 80 degrees is higher than a temperature of 40 degrees, but still we cannot say 80 degree is twice as hot as 40 degrees. Another example is the measure of time using the BC/AD system (here the initial point of reference is assumed to be zero). We have simply constructed a reference scale to measure time, which does not have a true or rational zero.

d) *Ratio variables:* Ratio variables measured by scale not only have equidistant points, but also have a rational zero. Thus, in addition to all the properties of interval variables, they feature an identifiable absolute zero point. A typical example of a ratio scale is the Kelvin temperature scale. In this case we can not only say that a temperature of 60 degrees is higher than one of 20 degrees, we can also specify that a temperature of 60 degrees is three times as hot as a temperature of 20 degrees. Most of the variables we use to measure in field situations conform to ratio scale properties, though most statistical data analysis procedures do not distinguish between the interval and ratio properties of the measurement scales.

Attitudinal Scales

Attitudinal scales are composite scales, which try to bring objectivity into subjective concepts of aptitude and attitude. They measure underlying traits and behaviours such as trust, joy, patience, happiness or verbal ability. Thus, attitudinal scales are also defined as measures that try to quantify abstract and subjective behaviour and attitudes.

A scale is always unidimensional, which means it has construct and content validity. It is important to point out that the terms scale, index or benchmark should be used with caution. Index is a specialized scale, wherein highly correlated individual items are taken together to form a scale (see Box 3.2). The next section lists some of the most widely used attitude scales in social research.

Thurstone Scales

Thurstone scales, developed in 1929 by Thurstone and Chave, is one of the best-used techniques in attitude measurement for measuring a core attitude when there are multiple dimensions or concerns around that attitude. In Thurstone scaling, researchers usually ask a panel of judges to comment on relevant and conceivable questions (say 100 questions) to develop a scale.

The usual procedure of Thurstone scaling involves judges, who rank opinion statements into a set of order. Judges then sort out the statements as favourable or unfavourable vis-à-vis the variable of interest. When the judges are finished, for each judge the statement slips will be ordered into numbered piles. Each statement is allotted the number of its pile. Next, the slips are sorted out by statement and the median pile value is determined for each statement. Statements are then sorted out into piles as per their median value. The researchers then select some statements from each pile to construct a scale, giving preference to those statements the judges agreed on while ranking. Further, researchers can administer the questionnaire to the panel to analyse inter-rater reliability. Researchers can also use the discrimination index to avoid non-homogenous items.[9]

BOX 3.2
Benchmark and Indexes

Benchmark: Benchmark, as the name suggests, is the standard or target value, accepted by professional associations or a group of organizations. It may be composed of one or more items. The observed values are compared against the benchmark value to ascertain the project's performance.

Indexes: Indexes are summative measures, constituting a set of items, which measure the latent underlying variable's characteristics. Further, all items in an index are highly correlated with each other.

Likert Scales or Summated Ratings Scale

The summated ratings scale/Likert scale was developed in 1932 by Rensis Likert as a five-point, bipolar response scale. It tries to assess people's agreement/disagreement, approval/disapproval on a five-point scale.

In constructing a Likert scale, a large number of statements are collected. In the next step, ambiguous, irrelevant statements are omitted. The remaining statements are then given to a few respondents who are asked to indicate their reaction to them using a five-point rating system: strongly approve, approve, undecided, disapprove and strongly disapprove. These categories are then assigned values of 5, 4, 3, 2 and 1 respectively. The correlation between statement scores and the total score is then ascertained. Those statements, which have a high correlation with the total score are then selected for the final scale. Researchers can also use index of discriminating power to select appropriate items for the scale (see Box 3.3).

BOX 3.3
Index of Discriminating Power

Index of discriminating power (DP): Index of discriminating power is used as a criterion for choosing more appropriate Likert items over other probable items. Scale items whose mean scores of the top 25 per cent of the respondent's score is different from the bottom 25 per cent of the respondent's scores have high DP coefficients.

Guttman Scaling

Guttman scaling, also known as scalogram analysis, was developed in the 1940s as a proposed method for scaling attitude items. It is based on the fact that attitudes can be arranged in an order that a respondent, who positively answers to a particular item, also responds positively to other items lower in rank.

It is based on the assumption that ordering of certain stimuli is possible. Thus, if an individual dominates a stimulus, he will also dominate other stimuli. These scales are also defined as ones in which the items constitute a one-dimensional series such that an answer to a given item predicts the answer to all previous items in the series. The scoring system is based on how closely they follow a pattern of an ever-increasing hardened attitude towards some topic in the important questions.

Coefficient of scalability (which can be abbreviated as Cs)[10] is the standard method for assessing whether a set of items forms a Guttman scale. It usually follows that Cs should be .60 or higher for the items to be considered a Guttman scale.

$$Cs = 1 - E/X$$

Where E is the number of Guttman error
X is the number of errors expected by chance

Stouffer's H technique is a variant which gives greater stability to Guttman scale by basing each Guttman scale position on three or more items, rather than just one.

Mokken Scales

Mokken scales are similar to Guttman scales but they are probabilistic whereas Guttman scales are deterministic, that is, in a Mokken scale, a respondent answering all items positively will have a significantly greater probability than answering a null answer to a less difficult item. Whereas, in a perfect Guttman scale, answering an item positively indicates that the respondents will answer all less difficult items positively also.

Loevinger's H coefficient measures the conformity of a set of items to the Mokken scale. Loevinger's H is based on the ratio of observed Guttman errors to total errors expected under the null hypothesis.

Semantic Differential

The semantic differential scaling procedure was developed by Osgood in the 1950s to deal with attitudes such as emotions and feelings. It measures people's reactions to words and concepts in terms of ratings on polar scales and is based on the idea that people think dichotomously or in terms of polar opposites while forming opinion such as good-bad, or right-wrong.

In order to formulate a suitable semantic differential scale, several factors need to be considered the most important being the need to consider whether the scale is balanced or not. In fact, the semantic differential scale can be used with any adjective by collecting response patterns to analyse for scaling purposes. In order to quantify a semantic differential, a Likert-type scale is used and the endpoints are assumed to be extremes such as 'very bad' or 'very good' and another important consideration is to ensure that the scale is balanced, that is, either side of the indifferent cues have an equal number of cues.

RELIABILITY AND VALIDITY

The terms reliability and validity are generally used as synonyms, though they have very different meanings when applied in statistics. Reliability and validity are two very important concepts that deal with the psychological characteristics of measurement and its precision. As we all know, measurements are seldom perfect, especially in the case of questionnaire responses or processes, which are difficult to measure precisely and thus often result in measurement errors. Besides, reliability and validity, precision and accuracy of instruments/tests are two other terms that are often confused by people while reporting measured outcomes (see Box 3.4).

BOX 3.4
Precision and Accuracy

People often confuse the concepts of precision and accuracy, especially those who do not have a mathematical background. Precision signifies perfection in an instrument and assesses how finely an estimate is specified, whereas accuracy refers to how close an estimate is to the true value. Precision relates to the quality of a process through which a result is obtained, while accuracy relates to the quality of the result. It is important to note that estimates can be precise without being accurate, as in case of a computer output containing results specified to the fourth or sixth decimal place.

Reliability[11]

Reliability signifies the issue of consistency of measures, that is, the ability of a measurement instrument to measure the same thing each time it is used. There are three important factors involved in assessing reliability, the first being stability, which entails asking whether a measure is stable over time so that researchers can be confident that results relating to the measure for a sample of respondents will not fluctuate. The second issue is that of internal reliability, which seeks to assess whether the indicators that make up the scale or index are consistent. Inter-observer consistency is another key factor, which may arise due to the involvement of more than one observer in activities such as recording of observation or translation of data into categories.

Validity[12]

Validity tries to assess whether a measure of a concept really measures that concept, that is, the extent to which the concept measures the thing it was designed to measure. Thus, when people raise questions about the relation between a person's IQ test and his general level of intelligence, it signifies that they doubt the measurement validity of IQ tests in relation to the concept of intelligence. Thus, while IQ tests will have high reliability they might have low validity with respect to job performance. Thus, for a research study to be accurate, it is imperative that the findings are both reliable and valid.

It is important to point here that although reliability and validity are two different concepts, they are related in some way because validity presumes reliability, which means that if a measure is not reliable it cannot be valid, though the opposite is not true and a study can be reliable even if it is not valid. There are various threats to validity as well as reliability and some of these can be avoided if internal validity is ensured. This can be done if the researchers use the most appropriate research design for their study.

Methods of Measuring Reliability

There are four good methods of measuring reliability:

Test-retest Technique   Test-retest technique is generally used to administer the same research instrument/test/survey or measure to the same group of people twice under the same conditions, but at different points in time. Reliability estimates are expressed in the form of a correlation co-efficient, which is a measure of the correlation between two scores in the same group.

Multiple Forms   Multiple forms are also known by other names such as parallel forms and disguised test-retest. It tests the reliability of the research instrument by mixing up the questions in the research instrument and giving it to the same respondents again to assess whether it results in any different responses.

Inter-rater   Inter-rater reliability is used to assess the reliability of research tool instruments/tests when more than one rater/interviewer is involved in interviewing or content analysis. It is calculated by reporting the percentage of agreement on the same subject between different raters or inter-viewers.

Split-half Reliability   In the case of the split-half reliability method, as the name suggests, half of the indicators, tests, instruments, or surveys, are analysed assuming it to be the whole thing. Then, the results of this analysis are compared with the overall analysis, to assess the reliability of the indicators, tests or instruments. Nowadays, researcher use Cronbach's alpha[13] to test internal reliability and it correlates performance on each item with an overall score. Kuder-Richardson coefficient[14] is another technique, which is used nowadays to measure internal reliability (see Box 3.5). These techniques can be easily calculated by using statistical packages such as Statistical Package for Social Sciences (SPSS), an example of which is discussed in Chapter 7.

BOX 3.5
Internal and Inter-rater Reliability

Cronbach's alpha is a commonly used test of internal reliability. It calculates the average of all possible split-half reliability coefficients and a computed alpha coefficient varies between 1, denoting perfect internal reliability, and 0, denoting no internal reliability. The figure of .75 or more usually is treated as a rule of thumb to denote an accepted level of reliability.

Tau-equivalent:[15] Different measures have identical true scores but need not have equal error variances. It is believed that for alpha to be a correct measure of reliability, the items constituting it need to be at least Tau-equivalent and if this assumption is not met, alpha is considered as a lower bound estimate of reliability.

Congeneric measures: Congeneric measures are based on the assumption that different measures have only perfect correlation among their true scores. Thus, it is not necessary that measures would have identical error variances or true score errors.

Inter-rater reliability tries to ascertain the reliability of the single rating. It is defined as the extent to which two or more individuals agree on a rating system. It addresses the consistency of the implementation of a rating system. There are various ways in which inter-rater reliability can be ascertained, one of which is to analyse the 'intra-class' correlation, which assumes that the raters have the same mean. For purposes such as planning power for a proposed

(Box 3.5 continued)

(*Box 3.5 continued*)

study, it does matter whether the raters to be used will be exactly the same individuals. Bland and Altman(1999: 135–60) proposed a very good methodology. They advise researchers to use two methods, whose difference in scores can be plotted against the mean for each subject.

Methods of Measuring Validity

Researchers should be concerned with both external and internal validity. External validity signifies the extent to which a research study can be generalized to other situations.

Internal validity refers to the true causes, which result in an outcome. In other words, it signifies the (i) the rigour with which the study was conducted and (ii) the extent to which the designers of a study have taken into account alternative explanations for any causal relationships they explore (Huitt, 1998). Internal validity is constituted of four broad sub-categories as discussed below:

Face Validity   Face validity refers to validity that establishes the fact that the measure apparently reflects the content of the concept in question. Face validity is an intuitive process and is established by asking other people whether the measure seems to capture the concept that is the focus of attention. It is essentially an assertion on the part of the researchers that they have reasonably measured the concept they intended to measure.

Content Validity[16]   Content validity, as the name suggests, tries to assess whether the content of the measurement technique is in consonance with the known literature on the topic. If the researcher has concentrated only on some dimensions of a construct or concept, then it is believed that other indicators were overlooked and thus the study lacks content validity. It can easily be estimated from a review of the literature on the concept/construct topic or through consultation with experts in the field of the concept. Thus, this process ensures that the researcher has covered all the conceptual space. Content validity is usually established by content experts. Thus, it is imperative to ensure that experts do not take their knowledge for granted and do not consider other people to have the same level of intelligence.

Criterion Validity   Criterion validity is also known as instrumental validity. It draws an inference from test scores about performance and demonstrates the accuracy of a measure or procedure by comparing it with another standard valid procedure.

There are different forms of criterion validity: in concurrent validity, researchers seek to employ a criterion on which cases/subjects are known to differ and assess how well the criterion captures the actual behaviour; in the case of predictive validity, researchers use a future criterion measure to assess how well it estimates future events that have not happened yet.

Construct Validity   In construct validity, researchers are encouraged to deduce the hypothesis from a theory that is relevant to the concept. Construct validity can be further segmented into two sub-categories: convergent validity and discriminate validity. In the case of convergent validity, validity is gauged by comparing it to measures of the same concept developed through other methods to assess how well the items are together (convergent validity) or distinguish different people on certain behaviours (discriminate validity).

DATA COLLECTION

ORIENTATION OF PROFESSIONALS

Internal meetings-cum-workshops should be organized where all the professionals associated with the project are briefed on the objectives, methodology, research techniques, study instruments and guidelines for the training of field staff. This helps in creating a common understanding among all the professionals.

RECRUITMENT OF FIELD STAFF

The project coordinator/principal research investigator in association with the core team members needs to look after the recruitment of the field staff. The recruitment needs to be done from the existing panel of field personnel and also from among fresh candidates applying for jobs at the local field office in response to advertisements in the local newspapers. Candidates having the desired qualifications and experience in conducting surveys should be recruited for the study. Recruitment should be 20 per cent more than the actual requirement to make up for attrition after training and the dismissal of candidates whose work is not found to be up to the mark.

BRIEFING TO FIELD STAFF

The professionals involved in the study should be involved in briefing the field staff. All the field persons engaged for the survey should be given extensive training. The training sessions should consist of instructions in interviewing technique, field procedures for the survey, time schedules, detailed instructions on schedules and manuals and each item in the questionnaire followed by mock exercises between the participants.

FIELD WORK

Selection of Study Units and Respondents

Appropriate and required sample of respondent categories should be selected from survey areas using the sampling technique as commonly agreed. The core team members and the project associates need to be responsible for this exercise.

Operational Aspects of Fieldwork

The fieldwork for the study needs to be initiated immediately after the briefing/training of the field staff is complete. The entire team needs to work under the overall guidance of the project coordinator for the study.

Collection of Secondary Data

Some studies also involve the collection of secondary data along with the main survey data. This exercise can be a simultaneous activity along with the main survey. Prior appointment needs to be taken from the designated officials.

The team should collect all necessary secondary information from the records, registers and documents available at the respective offices and individuals. The secondary information needs to be collected using a standard information sheet prepared in line with the objectives of the study and finalized in consultation with the client. The core team members should also visit the field to oversee the progress of secondary data collection and the quality and completeness of the information collected.

Quality Control of Field Data and Monitoring

For proper monitoring of fieldwork and ensuring the quality of data collected it is imperative that emphasis be given to the following aspects of field-work.

a) Observation of some of the interviews/discussions carried out by the field staff.
b) Spot checks to verify the accuracy of the information collected.
c) Back checks.
d) Maintenance of log sheets by field executives indicating team performance.
e) Visits by the concerned research professionals for monitoring fieldwork and providing technical guidance to the field staff.

DATA PROCESSING AND ANALYSIS

The system analyst needs to look after data processing and analysis. The project coordinator and the core team members should provide inputs at various stages of data processing and analysis.

Once the research data has been collected, the process of preparing it for analysis begins. Quantitative data will need to be sorted and coded and even qualitative data will need to be indexed or categorized, in preparation for analysis.

Coding

Coding is defined as the process of conceptualizing research data and classifying them into meaningful and relevant categories for the purpose of data analysis and interpretation. A number is assigned to each category, in the form of a code, for example, in the case of the gender variable, code 1 is assigned to males and code 2 is assigned to females. Coding formats may be included on the questionnaire, or can also be developed after the data have been collected in cases where respondents' replies do not fall into pre-coded response categories, that is, in the case of open-ended questions and for pre-coded questions which have an 'other' code.

The basic rules for the development of the coding scheme known as the coding frame for quantitative data are that the codes must be mutually exclusive, coding formats for each item must be comprehensive and the codes must be applied consistently whereas coding rules for qualitative data permit the allocation of responses to more than one category in order to facilitate conceptual development.

Interview data can be hand coded by the interviewer during or after the interview, that is, field coding can be done directly on to the paper questionnaire. However, it often requires coding in the office by a coder, or a team of coders.

a) *Coding boxes:* While designing questionnaires, coding boxes should be allocated for each question. It is important to point out that each coding box must contain only one number and for answers that have been allocated a two-digit code, two coding boxes need to be provided—one for each number.

b) *Coding transfer sheets:* In a majority of the cases, pre-coded questionnaires are used for data entry though in some cases coding transfer sheets for each questionnaire, containing the transferred codes from each question, are also used. Coding transfer sheets are used in cases where the investigator does not wish to clutter the questionnaire with numerical codes and coding boxes, but it doubles the administrative effort and entry costs.

    Irrespective of the method used, they should specify exactly where in the individual's computer records each item of data is to be placed. This is usually done by allocating variable names to each question, which are stored in the computer's data entry programme in a predefined sequence as well as on the coding frame.

c) *Numerical values for codes:* In the case of quantitative analysis, it is essential that the collected information is coded either quantitatively in the form of a measurement such as weight in kilograms or 'qualitatively' in the form of a category so that the numbers in each group can be counted. Thus, for gender the groups are male and female; for marital status the groups are married, single, widowed, divorced and separated. Further, each of the categorized groups to be analysed require a numeric value before they can be entered on to the computer, counted and analysed. For example, dichotomous responses such as male and female choices could be scored 1 and 2 respectively.

d) *Coding open questions:* Open-ended questions form an integral part of questionnaire as it allows respondents to use their own words and form their own response categories. Open-ended questions responses are then listed by the investigator after the data has been collected, which can be grouped by theme for the development of an appropriate coding framework. Even in the case of a structured questionnaire, pre-coded response options have the provision for the 'others' category thus making it imperative that a list is prepared to develop a coding frame for the various 'other' response choices that were offered to respondents and whose replies did not fit the codes given.

e) *Coding closed questions:* Closed-ended questions require that any groupings should be defined before the data are collected. The response is then allocated to the pre-defined category, with a number assigned. The response is then itself an item of data ready for transfer to coding boxes, data entry and analysis.

DATA ENTRY ON TO THE COMPUTER

As with the coding, the process of verification of office data entry involves two data entry persons independently entering the data. This is also known as double data entry. Double data entry should be supported by the use of a computer programme, which can check for any differences in the two data sets, which then have to be resolved and corrected by a member of the research team.

Human coding and entry or direct electronic data entry are usually preferred. With the latter, the computer displays each question on the screen and prompts the interviewer to input the response directly, whereupon it is programmed to store it under the correct code. Coded data is stored in the form of a data table in a computer file. Statistical software packages contain facilities for entering the data, which can be read directly by that package, although many packages can translate data typed into other programmes. The semi-structured schedules and the in-depth interviews would be entered with the help of latest data entry software packages.[17] Integrated System for Survey Analysis (ISSA 6.0) is a very good software having inbuilt checks.

To ensure data quality, researchers usually key in all the data twice from raw schedule and the second data entry is done by a different key entry operator whose job also includes verifying mismatches between the original and second entries. It is observed that this kind of 'double entry' provides a high 99.8 per cent accuracy rate for all data entered.

CREATION OF THE SYSTEM FILE

The computer package chosen for analysis will have the facility for the creation of a system file before the data can be entered. For example, the Statistical Package for the Social Sciences (SPSS) system file will require the labelling of all the variables and their response choices, the number of columns to be assigned to each and determination of which codes are to be assigned as missing in the analyses. This should be done before the coding has been completed so that it is ready before the data entry is due to start.

CLEANING THE DATA

Once the data has been stored in computer readable form, the next task is to eliminate the more obvious errors that will have occurred during the data collection, coding and input stages. An edit programme will need to be specified. This should look at missing values, skips, range checks and checks for inconsistency.

An edit programme will require a set of instructions for the computer package used that will automatically examine, and draw attention to, any record that appears to have an error in it.

a) *Range checks:* For data fields containing information about continuous variables like height and weight, observations should fall within a specified range. Thus, if the height of an adult male falls outside the normal range it should be checked.

b) *Consistency checks:* Often certain combinations of within-range values of different variables are either logically impossible or very unlikely. Data entry programme shall have some checks to ensure data consistency, for example, a person who has undergone sterilization should not be using the spacing method of birth control. These checks will not eliminate all the errors introduced during the data collection, coding and data input phases, but will certainly minimize the errors. There is no substitute for careful recording of data, coding, data entry and verification.

c) *Missing values and data checks:* There are two types of missing values: first, where a question is deliberately blank because it did not apply to the individual respondent or where a reply was expected but was not given, which is known as an inadequate response. Such missing cases can occur because the respondent refused or did not answer the question, or because the interviewer forgot to ask it.

It is also customary to use 9 or 99 (as close ended codes for options) for questions, which do not apply to the respondent (NAs); for example, skips in the questionnaire will be employed so that men will not be asked about specific questions. The inadequate and do not apply response codes are then set as missing on the computer, so they are not routinely included in the analyses.

CHECKING FOR BIAS IN THE ANALYSES

Response Bias

Response bias is one of the most common phenomenons, which is observed during data collection. As much information as possible should be collected about non-responders to research in order that the differences between responders and non-responders to a research study can be analysed, and the extent of any resulting bias assessed.

In order to check for age bias, for example, the investigator should compare the age structure of the respondents with that of the non-responders, or that of the study population as a whole.

Interviewer Bias

In practical situations, interviewer bias is more commonly observed than response bias. Where more than one enumerator, interviewer or observer has been used, comparisons should be made between the data collected by each one. As there is bound to be some variation in the way an interviewer asks a particular question and the only way to remove interviewer bias is to provide rigorous training followed by field exercise.

ANALYSIS OF DATA

The core team members and the system analyst under the guidance of the project coordinator shall prepare the analysis/tabulation plan. The tabulation plan will be finalized in consultation with the client. The required tables can then be generated using the latest version of analysis software[18] like Stata, SAS, or SPSS. Though in the case of qualitative analysis, researchers shall first focus on transcription of qualitative data, which can later be used during content analysis (see Box 3.6).

BOX 3.6
Transcription and Content Analysis

In qualitative research it is believed that data analysis is as good as transcription of raw data. Transcription is an important stage in qualitative data analysis and almost all qualitative research studies involve some degree of transcription. Transcription is not about jotting up or summing up what a researcher, interviewer or transcriber feels. It is all about what the respondent feels.

The recorded cassettes of the focus group discussion/in-depth interviews are transcripted in the desired language by the transcriptors/project associates with the guidance of the core team members. The content analysis of the focus group discussions and the final analysis of the qualitative schedule needs to be done by the core team members with the help of the in-house qualitative researchers.

PREPARATION OF REPORT

The next step after analysis of data is to prepare the report. Though it is not necessary that in a research project the report shall be submitted only after data analysis. As per the terms agreed upon or requirements of the study, the following reports could be prepared at different stages of the study:

a) Pre-testing report.
b) An inception report prior to initiation of fieldwork.
c) A mid-term evaluation report.
d) Draft report.
e) Final report.

A report generally consists of the following sections:

a) Executive summary.
b) Introduction/background.
c) Findings.
d) Summary, conclusion and recommendation.

The executive summary is the portion of the report that most people read. Though not as a rule but ideally this section should be around three to five pages long, with bullets providing as much information as possible. It should contain all relevant information starting from project background, research methodology to findings and recommendations so that the reader has an overall understanding of the basics of the project.

The introduction should include all relevant information necessary to understand the context and implementation of the programme from its inception through the current reporting period. It clearly describes the goal and objectives that the project expects to achieve. Next, it should detail the research objectives of the study and research design and methodology adopted to assess the research objectives. It should also clearly specify the study area and sample size of the study, besides detailing out the timeline of the project.

The findings are the soul of the evaluation report. It presents the results of the various instruments described in the methodology section. Findings present in chapters shall align itself to research objectives of the study. Further findings may or may not be summed up in one chapter; it may be presented in two or three chapters depending on the objectives and complexities of the project.

The last section of the report shall comprise of conclusions, discussions and recommendations. It provides a final interpretation of success or failure of the project and how the programme can be improved. In presenting this information, some of the key points discussed are (i) whether the project achieved the desired result, (ii) certainty that the programme caused the results and (iii) recommendation to improve the programme.

Notes

1. A design is a plan that dictates when and from whom measurements will be gathered during the course of an evaluation. The first and obvious reason for using a design is to ensure a well-organized evaluation study: all the right people will take part in the evaluation at the right times (Fitz-Gibbon and Morris, 1978: 10).
2. Evaluation designs generally fall into one of four types: (i) experimental, (ii) quasi-experimental, (iii) survey, or (iv) naturalistic.
3. Experimentation represents the process of data collection and so refers to the information necessary to describe the interrelationships within a set of data. It involves considerations such as the number of cases, sampling methods, identification of variables and their scale types, identification of repeated measures and replications.
4. Cook and Campbell (1979) mention 10 types of experimental design, all using randomization of subjects into treatment and control groups.
5. The Hawthorne effect is so named because the effect was first observed while Elton Mayo was carrying out pioneering research in industrial psychology at the Hawthorne plant of Northern Electric.
6. Some authors, on the contrary, argue that case studies are a prototype of quasi-experimental design if pursued systematically.
7. Survey research is the method of gathering data from respondents thought to be representative of some population, using an instrument composed of closed structure or open-ended items and survey instrument is the schedule of questions or response items to be posed to respondents.
8. Pre-testing is used to assess reliability of the research instrument and if there is any remaining doubt about the reliability of one or more items, the researcher should consider split sample comparisons, where two versions of the same item appear on two different survey forms administered randomly.
9. Q-dispersion is usually used to have a measure of item ranking measurement, which is quite similar in nature to standard deviation.

10. The coefficient of reproducibility (Cr) is an alternative measure for assessing whether a set of items form a Guttman scale and is defined as:

$$Cr = 1 - E/N$$

Where E refers to number of choices and N denotes the number of subjects.

11. For a brief but in-depth discussion of reliability, including statistical formulae for calculating reliability, see Thorndike et al. (1991).

12. The Joint Committee of the American Educational Research Association, American Psychological Association, adds that 'validity ... refers to the appropriateness, meaningfulness, and usefulness of the specific inferences made from data'.

13. Cronbach's alpha was popularized in 1951 by an article by Cronbach on the work in the 1940s by Guttman. The widely accepted cutoff is that alpha should be .70 or higher for a set of items to be considered a scale.

14. Kuder-Richardson is a special case of Cronbach's alpha for ordinal categories.

15. Psychometric literature classifies indicator sets for variables into three categories, that is, congeneric sets, which are presumed to have passed some test of convergent validity such as Cronbach's alpha. Tau equivalents also have equal variance for the indicators. Parallel indicators are Tau-equivalent having equal reliability coefficients.

16. Content validity is based on the extent to which a measurement reflects the specific intended domain of content (Carmines and Zeller, 1991: 20).

17. SPSS and SAS also have software for data entry such as SPSS Data Entry II and SAS FSPFSEDIT respectively.

18. Statistical packages are available to assist in the quantitative analysis of data. Most data base packages will be able to provide descriptive statistics like simple frequencies, average scores and so on, but specific package such as SPSS, Stata for quantitative analysis are frequently used (details are provided in Chapter 7).

CHAPTER 4

SAMPLING AND SAMPLE SIZE ESTIMATION

The Roman Empire was the first form of government to gather extensive data about population, area and wealth of the territories that it controlled. Since then governments have used data collection as an important precursor to making policies. It is this human quest for collection and analysis of data that has given rise to sampling and various sampling methods. This chapter discusses the basic concepts and relevance of sampling, types of sampling distribution and sample size estimation.

SAMPLE

A sample can be defined as a finite part of a statistical population whose properties are used to make estimates about the population as a whole (Webster, 1985). When dealing with people, it can be defined as a set of target respondents selected from a larger population for the purpose of a survey.

POPULATION

A population is a group of individuals, objects, or items from among which samples are taken for measurement. For example, a group of HIV affected patients or students studying in a class would be considered a sample.

SAMPLING FRAME

The sampling frame is defined as the frame of entities from which sampling units are selected for a survey. For example, a list of registered voters in a constituency may be the sampling frame for an opinion poll survey of that area. The sampling frame can also be defined as that subset of the population, which provides a broad and detailed framework for selection of sampling units.

SAMPLING

Sampling is defined as the process of selection of sampling units from the population to estimate population parameters in such a way that the sample truly represents the population. Researchers aim to draw conclusions about populations from samples by using inferential statistics to determine a population's characteristics by directly observing only a sample of the population.

Survey or data collection exercise can be broadly classified into two types, namely, census survey, where data is collected from each member of the population of interest, and sample survey, where data is to be collected from some selected members of the population. The choice of conducting a census survey or a sample survey is that of the researcher.

Researchers often go for sample surveys for several obvious reasons, the primary one being that sample surveys have fewer costs involved than census surveys. Second, time is another constraint that prompts researchers to opt for census surveys. Looking sensibly at things, if a researcher can predict a population parameter with a confidence level of say 95 per cent by selecting a few hundred units from the population, then it does not make sense to survey the whole population.

In the social sciences it is not feasible to collect data from the entire population on the variables of interest. So, researchers first identify a population parameter they want to estimate and at the next stage they select a representative sample of the population from the whole population to estimate the population parameters for sample statistics. Researchers make inferences about the population on the assumption that the sampling units are randomly sampled from an infinitely large population and thus represent the population. Inference is based on an assumption that the sample size is large enough to represent the normal distribution, a special distribution that is described in detail in subsequent sections.

PARAMETERS AND STATISTICS

The terms parameter and statistics are often used interchangeably by people although they are two very different concepts. The statistical characteristics of populations are called parameters and the statistical characteristics of a sample are known as statistics. The mean, variance and correlation of variable in a population are examples of parameters. Conventionally, parameters are represented with Greek letters like μ and π for mean and proportion.

Samples are selected from populations in such a way that they can provide an idea about the parameters. The basic idea of sampling is to extrapolate the statistics computed from sampled data to make inferences about the population from which the sample was derived. For example, the mean of the data in a sample is termed as the unbiased estimator of population mean from which that sample was drawn. Statistics are often assigned Roman letters, like X and s.

In a nutshell, we can differentiate a parameter as an entity that is inferred and the estimate as an entity that is used to infer it, and thus they are not the same. Parameters are summaries of the population, whereas estimates are summaries of the sample.

PROBABILITY

Probability, derived from the verb probe, essentially is a study of uncertainty. It owes its origin to the study of games of chance and gambling during the sixteenth century and is now used widely in almost all areas ranging from statistics, econometrics to financial modelling and engineering. It was popularized by Blaise Pascal and Pierre de Fermat in the seventeenth century, when they introduced probability theory as a branch of mathematics.

Probability[1] is defined as the likelihood of the occurrence of an event, whose likelihood value can range from zero to one. A probability of zero means that the occurrence of that event is impossible and a probability of one denotes that the likelihood of the occurrence of that event is sure. However, in reality, probabilities range from zero to one but never attain the value of zero or one. For example, if a coin were tossed, the probability of the coin landing on its head face or its tail face would be 50–50 in both cases.

The classical approach to probability refers to the relative frequency of an event, given that the experiment is repeated an infinite number of times. In the case of an independent event, the probability of one event does not affect the probability of other events; the probabilities may be multiplied together to find the probability of the joint event. The probability of a thunderstorm and the probability of a coin landing on its head face when flipped is the product of two individual probabilities.

As mentioned earlier, the emphasis on the sampling process is on the way a sample is selected to represent the population to reflect the population's characteristics. But often researchers do not know about the population characteristic and in the end it becomes very difficult to accurately ascertain whether a sample was representative of the entire population. This is where the theory of probability comes to the rescue. If a sample is drawn, according to the laws of probability, then the degree to which the sample mirrors the population can be calculated in probabilistic terms. Hence, researchers will be in a position to state that the probability of the sample being representative of the population to a certain degree.

Without doubt, the development of the probability theory has increased the scope of statistical applications. So data collected using probabilistic measures can be approximated accurately by certain probability distributions, and the results of probability distributions can be further used in analysing statistical data. It can be used to test the reliability of statistical inferences and to indicate the kind and amount of data required for a particular problem. However, to do so you have to select a sample in such a way that the distribution of the sample mirrors the population distributions. For example, how is the variable of interest distributed in the population? To understand it better it is imperative to understand models of distribution and sampling distribution.

MODELS OF DISTRIBUTION

Models of distribution are nothing but models of the frequency distribution representing population units. These are also called probability models or probability distributions,[2] and are characterized by an algebraic expression, which is used to describe the relative frequency for every possible score. Though probability is a general term, which is used quite frequently as a synonym of likelihood, statisticians define it much more precisely. They define probability of an event as the theoretical relative frequency of the event in a model of the population.

The models of distribution[3] can be different assuming continuous measurement or discrete measurement. For discrete outcome experiments, the probability of a simple outcome can be calculated using its probability function.

DISCRETE PROBABILITY DISTRIBUTION

If x is a simple outcome (for example, $x = 0$) and P(x) is probability of occurance of that outcome, then the function can be calculated by summing up all probabilities.

$$F(x) = \Sigma\, P(x)$$

In the case of a discrete probability function, the following distribution models are found:

a) Binomial distribution (also known as Bernoulli distribution).[4]
b) Negative binomial.
c) Poisson distribution.
d) Geometric distribution.
e) Multinomial distribution.

The two most frequently used distributions are binomial and Poisson, which are discussed in brief for reference.

Binomial Probability Distribution

Binomial distribution, also known as 'Bernoulli distribution' is a probability distribution, which expresses the probability of one set of dichotomous alternative/options, that is, 'yes' or 'no or 'success' or 'failure' or a classification such as male or female.

In a binomial distribution, the probability of a success is denoted by p and probability of failure is denoted by q, wherein $p = 1 - q$. Further, the shape and location of a binomial distribution changes as p changes for a given n or as n changes for a given p.

Poisson Probability Distribution

Poisson distribution is a discrete probability distribution and is used widely in statistical work. It was developed by the Frenchman, Simeon Poisson (1781–1840). This happens in cases where the chance of any individual event being a success is small. The distribution is used to describe the behaviour of rare events, for example, the number of accidents on the road. All Poisson distributions are skewed to the right and that is the reason Poisson probability distribution is also known as probability distribution of rare events.

CONTINUOUS PROBABILITY DISTRIBUTION

Continuous variable/measurement means every score on the continuum of scores is possible, or there are an infinite number of scores. In this case, no single score can have a relative frequency because if it did, the total area would necessarily be greater than 1. For this reason, probability is defined over a range of scores rather than a single score.

For continuous outcome experiments, the probability of an event is defined as the area under a probability density curve. The probability density curve is determined by the appropriate integral of the function represented as:

$$F(x) = \int f(x)\, dx$$

The various types of continuous probability distribution are:

a) Normal distribution.
b) Log-normal distribution.
c) Gamma distribution.
d) Rayleigh distribution.
e) Beta distribution.
f) Chi-square distribution.
g) F distribution.
h) T distribution.
i) Weibull distribution.
j) Extreme value distribution.
k) Exponential/negative exponential distribution.

Some of the continuous probability distributions that are not used very frequently are explained next in brief for reference. Distributions such as normal distribution, T distribution, chi-square distribution and F distribution, which have extensive application in sampling theory, are dealt with separately in the next section.

Gamma Distribution

Gamma distribution depicts the distribution of a variable, bounded at one side. It depicts distribution of time taken by exactly *k* independent events to occur. Gamma distribution is based on two parameter α and θ and is frequently used in queuing theory and reliability analysis.

Beta Distribution

Beta distribution is the distribution of variables that are bounded at both sides and ranges between 0 and 1. It also depends on two parameters *a* and *b* and is equivalent to uniform distribution in the domain of 0 and 1.

Log-normal Distribution

Log-normal distribution, as the name suggests, is a distribution wherein the parameter of population does not follow the normal distribution but logarithm of parameter does follow normal distribution. Log-normal distribution assumes only positive values and is widely used to describe characteristics of rainfall distribution.

Weibull Distribution

Weibull distribution is widely used in survival function analysis. Its distribution depends on the parameter β and based on the value of β, it can take the shape of other distributions.

Rayleigh Distribution

The Rayleigh distribution is a special case of the Weibull distribution. Rayleigh distribution is widely used in radiation physics, because of its properties of providing distribution of radial error when the errors in two mutually perpendicular axes are independent.

Negative Exponential Distribution

Negative exponential distribution is often used to model relatively rare events such as the spread of an epidemic. The negative exponential distribution is presented in Figure 4.1.

FIGURE 4.1
Negative Exponential Distribution

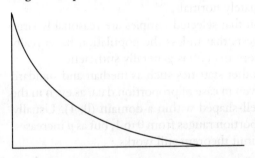

Gaussian Distribution/Normal Distribution

A. de Moivre first expressed the normal curve in a paper in 1733 (de Moivre, 1733). Though it is also known today as Gaussian distribution, after Gauss who stated that when many independent random factors act in an additive manner, the data follows a bell-shaped distribution. The distribution does occur frequently and is probably the most widely used statistical distribution, because it has some special mathematical properties, which form the basis of many statistical tests.

Normal distribution is an approximation of binomial distribution, which tends to the form of a continuous curve when n becomes large.

SAMPLING DISTRIBUTION

Sampling distribution describes the distribution of probabilities associated with a statistic of a random sample selected from the population. It is different from population distribution as it portrays the frequency distribution of the sample mean and not the population mean.

Let us assume that instead of taking just one sample, a researcher goes on taking an infinite number of samples from the same population. He then calculates the average of each sample to plot them on a histogram, in terms of frequency distribution of sample means (calculated from an infinite number of samples), also known as sampling distribution. Interestingly, in most of the cases, the sample mean would converge on the same central value, adhering to the famous bell-shaped distribution. This unique but interesting property of sampling distribution is emphasized greatly in the central limit theorem as a key to all statistical theory and applications.

Central Limit Theorem

According to the central limit theorem, the distribution of the mean of a random sample taken from a population assumes normal distribution with increase in sample size. Thus if samples of large sizes are drawn from a population that is not normally distributed, the successive sample mean will form a distribution that would be approximately normal.

The central limit theorem works on the assumption that selected samples are reasonably large and they are representative of the population. It suggests that unless the population has a really different and unusual distribution, a sample size of more than 30 is generally sufficient.

The central theorem applies to the distribution of other statistics such as median and standard deviation, but not in the case of range. It is applicable even in case of proportion data, as even in the case of the proportion curve, distribution becomes bell-shaped within a domain (0, 1). Usually, the normal distribution ranges from $-\infty$ to $+\infty$ and proportion ranges from 0 to 1, but as n increases, the width of the bell becomes very small and central limit theorem still works.

Normal Distribution

The normal distribution[5] is important, not only because it symbolizes the most observed phenomenon, but also because in most cases, it approximates the other prevalent functions. That is why it can be used as an approximation of other well-known distributions such as binomial and Poisson distributions. Further, even the distribution of important test statistics either follow normal distribution or they can be derived from the normal distribution.

Normal distribution is a class of distribution, whose exact shape depends on two key parameters: mean and standard deviation (see Figure 4.2).

FIGURE 4.2
Normal Distribution

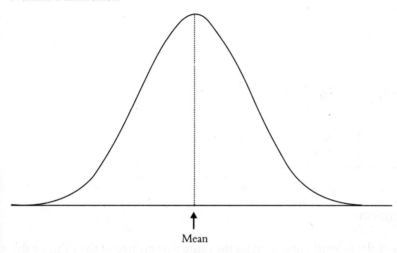

Mean

$$f(x \mid \mu, \sigma) = \frac{1}{\sqrt{2\pi}\sigma} e^{\frac{1}{2}\left(\frac{x-\mu}{\sigma}\right)^2}$$

Normal distribution[6] is a symmetric distribution, often described as bell-shaped, because of its peak at the centre of the distribution and well spread out tails at both ends. Its symmetrical property ensures that the curve behaves the same to the left and right of some central point. In the case of an asymmetrical normal distribution, all measures of central tendency, that is, mean, median and mode, fall in the same place.

In the case of normal distribution, the total area under the curve is equal to 1. Another characteristic property of the normal distribution is that 95 per cent of the total values or observations fall within the range of standard deviation of ±2 and around 68 per cent of all of its observations fall within a range of ±1 standard deviation from the mean (see Figure 4.3). In most statistical theories and applications, normal distribution gives way to standard normal distribution, which is defined as the probability distribution, having zero mean and unit variance.

BASIS OF SAMPLING THEORY

The basis of sampling theory, which is key to estimation and significance testing depends on (i) standard normal distribution, (ii) the T distribution, (iii) the chi-square and (iv) the F distribution. The next section lists the role of these distributions in estimation and significance testing.

FIGURE 4.3
Characteristics of Normal Distribution

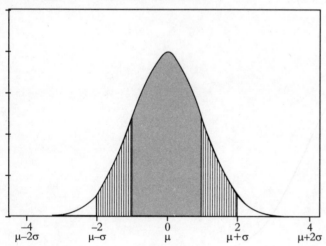

Standard Normal Distribution

The important characteristics of the normal curve remain the same irrespective of the value of the parameter and normal distributions can be referred to a single table of the normal curve by standardizing a variable to a common mean and standard deviation. Thus, it is useful to consider a standard normal distribution curve whose mean is 0 and area under curve is 1. Normal distributions can be transformed to standard normal distributions by the formula:

$$z = \frac{X - \mu}{\sigma}$$

Where X signifies observation values from the original normal distribution, μ is the mean and σ is the standard deviation of original normal distribution. The standard normal distribution is also referred as the z distribution, wherein z score reflects the number of standard deviations a score is above or below the mean (see Figure 4.4). Though it is important to point out here that the z distribution will only be a normal distribution if the original distribution follows the condition of normal distribution. The area enclosed by one standard deviation on either side of the mean constitutes 68 per cent of the area of the curve.

Standard Scores

It is important to point out that though unit normal z scores are useful, but to apply them to various application they needs to be transformed. In these scenario, one transforms them to scales that are used more frequently or have more convenient means and standard deviations. For example, if one were to multiply each z score by 10 and then add 200 to the product, the resulting new standard scores would have a mean of 200 and a standard deviation of 10.

FIGURE 4.4
Characteristics of Standard Normal Distribution

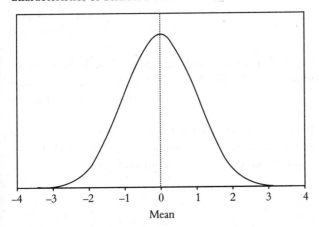

Mean

There are various other standard score scales in common use on which z scores can be transformed. In general, if a z score is transformed via the following formula:

$$Z = Bz + A$$

then the z score has a mean of A and a standard deviation of B. Transformation of raw data or observed function is a usual phenomenon and in a majority of the cases, researchers go beyond the z score to do logarithmic and inverse transformation of the function (see Box 4.1)

BOX 4.1
Data Transformation to Attain Uniform Variance

Transformation or conversion of a function into another function is usually done to suit the demand of the estimation procedure, test statistics or a mathematical algorithm the researcher wishes to employ for analysis or estimation.

Transformation is carried out in cases where statistical techniques, such as t tests and analysis of variance, require that the data follow a distribution of a particular kind. Researchers do a transformation to suit the demand that data must come from a population, which follows a normal distribution. Researcher often carry out the transformation by taking the logarithm, square root or some other function of the data to analyse the transformed data. Log-linear, logit and probit models are the best examples, where researchers use transformed functions to predict categorical dependent variables.

Student T-Density Function

The T distribution was developed by W.S. Gosset and published under the pseudonym 'Student'. Thus, it is also referred to as student's T distribution. T distributions are a class of distributions varying according to degree of freedom.

T distribution in many ways is like a normal distribution, that is, it is symmetric about the mean and it never touches the horizontal axis. Further, the total area under curve in T distribution is equal to 1, as in the case of normal distribution. However, the T distribution curve is flatter than the standard normal distribution, but as sample size increases, it approaches the standard normal distribution curve (see Figure 4.5).

The T distribution has only one parameter, that is, the degree of freedom. The larger the degree of freedom, the closer T density is to the normal density. Further, the mean of T distribution is 0 and standard deviation is referred as √df/df-2.

T distribution can be correlated with normal distribution and chi-square distribution. Let us assume that we have two independent random variable distributed as the standard normal distribution and chi-square distribution with $(n-1)$ d.f.; then the random variable will be defined by the formula $(n-1)Z/\alpha^2$ would have T distribution with $(n-1)$ d.f.

In the case of a large sample size, say n more than 30, the new random variable would have an expected value equal to 0 having variance close to 1. T distribution statistic is also related to f statistic as f statistics is the square of T distribution having two degrees of freedom d.f.$_1$ and d.f.$_2$.

FIGURE 4.5
Characteristics of T Distribution

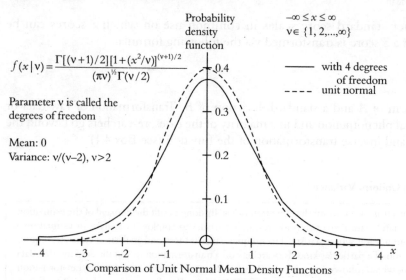

$$f(x\,|\,v)=\frac{\Gamma[(v+1)/2][1+(x^2/v)]^{(v+1)/2}}{(\pi v)^{\frac{1}{2}}\Gamma(v/2)}$$

Parameter v is called the degrees of freedom

Mean: 0
Variance: v/(v–2), v>2

Probability density function

$-\infty \le x \le \infty$
$v \in \{1, 2,...,\infty\}$

—— with 4 degrees of freedom
---- unit normal

Comparison of Unit Normal Mean Density Functions

Source: Johnson and Kotz (1970); K.M. Portier (2001).

Chi-square Density Function

For a large sample size, the sampling distribution of x^2 can be closely approximated by a continuous curve known as chi-square distribution. The x^2 distribution has only one parameter the number of degree of freedom. As in case of T distribution, there is a distribution for each degree of freedom and for a very small number of degrees of freedom the distribution is skewed to the right and as the number of the degree of freedom increases, the curve become more symmetrical (see Figure 4.6).

Like T distribution, chi-square distribution also depends on the degree of freedom. The shape of a specific chi-square distribution varies with the degree of freedom. The chi-square distribution curve is skewed for a very small degree of freedom but for a very large degree of freedom, the

FIGURE 4.6
Characteristics of Chi-square Distribution

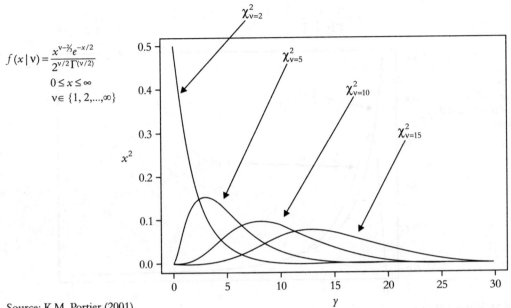

$$f(x \mid v) = \frac{x^{v-\frac{2}{2}}e^{-x/2}}{2^{v/2}\Gamma(v/2)}$$

$$0 \le x \le \infty$$

$$v \in \{1, 2,...,\infty\}$$

Source: K.M. Portier (2001).

chi-square looks like a normal curve. The peak of a chi-square distribution curve with 1 or 2 degrees of freedom occurs at 0 and for a curve with 3 or more degrees of freedom the peak occurs at d.f.-2.

The entire chi-square distribution lies to the right of the vertical axis. It is an asymmetric curve, which stretches over the positive side of the line and has a long right tail.

Chi-square distribution has variance, which is twice of its d.f., and its mode is equal to (d.f.- 2).

Relation of Chi-square Distribution to Normal Distribution
The chi-square distribution is also related to the sampling distribution of the variance. The sample variance is described as a sum of the squares of standard normal variables N (0, 1).

Relation of Chi-square Distribution to F Distribution
Chi-square is related to F distribution. F distribution statistics in relation to chi-square distribution is expressed as F = chi-square/d.f.$_1$, wherein d.f.1 = d.f. of the chi-square table.

F Distribution

F distribution is defined as the distribution of the ratio of two independent sampling estimates of variance from standard normal distributions. Like the shape of T and chi-square distributions, the shape of a particular F distribution curve depends on the degree of freedom. F distribution though has two degrees of freedom, one degree of freedom for the numerator and another degree of freedom for the denominator and each set gives a different curve (see Figure 4.7).

FIGURE 4.7
Characteristics of F Distribution

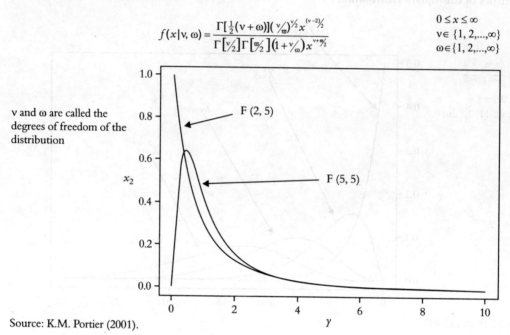

$$f(x|v, \omega) = \frac{\Gamma[\frac{1}{2}(v+\omega)](\frac{v}{\omega})^{v/2} x^{(v-2)/2}}{\Gamma[\frac{v}{2}]\Gamma[\frac{\omega}{2}](1+\frac{v}{\omega})x^{v+\omega/2}}$$

$0 \leq x \leq \infty$

$v \in \{1, 2,...,\infty\}$

$\omega \in \{1, 2,...,\infty\}$

v and ω are called the degrees of freedom of the distribution

Source: K.M. Portier (2001).

The units of F distributions are denoted by F, which assumes only non-negative values. F distribution is continuous in nature and assumes only non-negative values. As the degree of freedom increases, the peak of the curve shifts to the right and its skewness decreases.

F distribution's main application is in testing the quality of two independent population variances based on independent random samples.

TEST FOR NORMALITY

One of the key assumption in applying major statistical techniques is normality of the variable under study. Thus before using any of these statistical techniques, it is imperative to ensure that the concerned variable follows normal distribution. There are various statistical tests such as Kolmogorov-Smirnov test, Levene or the Shapiro-Wilks' W test to ensure that the assumption of normality holds true.

Shapiro-Wilks' W Test

D'Agostino and Stevens (1986) describe Shapiro-Wilk W test, developed by Shapiro and Wilk (1965) as one of the best tests of normality. The test statistics W can be described as the correlation between a data and their normal score. Further, it can be used in samples as large as 1,000–2,000 or as small as 3–5. In the Shapiro-Wilk test, W is given by

$$W = (\Sigma a_i x_{(i)})^2 / (\Sigma (x_i - \overline{x})^2)$$

where $x(i)$ is the i-th largest order statistic and x is the sample mean. The function uses the approximations given by Royston (1982) to compute the coefficients a_i, $i = 1, ..., n$, and obtains the significance level of the W statistic.

Kolmogorov-Smirnov Test

The Kolmogorov-Smirnov test assess deviations of a particular distribution from normal distribution. It does so by quantifying the difference in the spread of a particular distribution with an ideal normal distribution.

The Kolmogorov-Smirnov test computes the test statistics D. If the statistic is significant, then researchers can reject the hypothesis that the sample comes from a normally distributed population. In the case of computer software generated result, P value can be used to ascertain the normality. In case the P value is less than the specified value say .05, then researchers can conclude that the population is normally distributed.

Lilliefors' Test for Normality

Lilliefors' test for normality is a special case of the Kolmogorov-Smirnov test. Lilliefors test looks at the maximum difference between the sample distribution and population distribution to test the normality of the population's distribution. It does so by making a comparison between a sample cumulative distribution function and the ideal standard normal cumulative distribution function.

In case researchers find that the sample cumulative distribution closely resembles the standard normal cumulative distribution function, then they can conclude that the sample is drawn from a population having a normal distribution function. In case there is no close resemblance between the two functions, researchers can reject the hypothesis that the sample is drawn from a population having a normal distribution function.

Anderson-Darling Test

The Anderson-Darling test, defined as a modification of the Kolmogorov-Smirnov test is used to test whether a set of data came from a specific distribution population. The Anderson-Darling test is more sensitive to deviations in tails, that is, it assigns more weight to the tails than does the Kolmogorov-Smirnov test. The Anderson-Darling test, unlike the Kolmogorov-Smirnov test, uses specific distribution functions in calculating critical values. Thus, it is more sensitive to a specific distribution.

In the case of the Anderson-Darling test, the null hypothesis assumes that the data follows a specified distribution whereas the alternate hypothesis specifies that the data does not follow the specified distribution.

In the Anderson-Darling test, the value of test statistics depends on the specified distribution that is being tested. The computed value of Anderson-Darling test statistics 'A' is compared with the tabulated value of a specified distribution and null hypothesis is rejected if test statistic A is found to be greater than the critical value.

Bartlett's Test

Bartlett's test, also known as Bartlett's test of sphericity, is a very useful test to determine the equality of variances. It is used to test whether homogeneity of variance exists across n samples. Bartlett uses chi-square statistics with $(n - 1)$ degree of freedom as test statistics to verify equality of variances, whereas the Levene test uses F test as test statistics.

There are various statistical tests that are based on the assumption that t variances are equal across groups or samples. The Bartlett test along with Levene test is best suited to verify that assumption. Nowadays, however, researchers prefer Levene's test to Bartlett's test for testing equality of variances.

Levene's Test

Levene's test provides another way to test differences in variances. The test is used to assess if n samples have equal variances. In Levene's test, instead of analysing variances across groups, researchers analyse deviation around the median in each group. If the deviation is more in one group compared to others, then there is a strong probability that the samples belong to different populations. The significance of this hypothesis can be tested using F test to conclude whether homogeneity of variance exist across samples. Levene's test is also regarded as an alternative to Bartlett's test and is less sensitive than the Bartlett test to capture departures from normality.

SAMPLING

Sampling can be defined as the process or technique of selecting a suitable sample, representative of the population from which it is taken, for the purpose of determining parameters or characteristics of the whole population. There are two types of sampling: (i) probability sampling and (ii) non-probability sampling.

PROBABILITY SAMPLING

In the case of probability sampling, the probability or chance of every unit in the population being included in the sample is known due to randomization involved in the process. Thus, the probability sampling[7] method is also defined as a method of sampling that utilizes some form of random selection.[8] In order to adhere to a random selection method, researchers must choose sampled units in such a way that the different units in the population have equal probabilities of being chosen and random numbers could be easily generated from a random number table or calculator.

Simple Random Sampling

In the case of simple random sampling, every unit of the population has a known, non-zero probability of being selected, which implies equal probability of every unit being selected. Researchers begin with a list of N observations that comprises the entire population from which one wishes to extract a simple random sample. One can then generate k random case numbers (without replacement) in the range from 1 to N to select the respective cases into the final sample. This is done by first selecting an arbitrary start in consonance with a random number followed by the selection of a subsequent unit as per the subsequent random number generated.

For example, let us assume a voting area have, 1,000 votes and assume that the researchers want to select 100 of them for an opinion poll. The researchers might put all their names in a box and then pull 100 names out. Now this way each voter will have an equal chance of being selected. We can also easily calculate the probability of a given person being chosen, since we know the sample size (n) and the population (N) and it becomes a simple matter of division:

$n/N \times 100$ or $100/1000 \times 100 = 10\%$

Simple random sampling can be further classified into two categories mentioned next:

a) *Simple random sampling with replacement:* In this case, selected units are replaced back into the sampling frame before the next selection is made so that even the previous selected unit has a chance of selection.
b) *Simple random sampling without replacement:* In this case, the units once selected cannot be replaced back into the sampling frame hence it does not allow the same selected unit to be picked again.

Systematic Random Sampling

In the case of systematic random sampling, the unit is selected on a random basis and then additional sampling units are selected at an evenly spaced interval until all desired units are selected. The various steps to achieve a systematic random sample are:

a) Number the units in the population from 1 to N.
b) Decide on the n (sample size) that you want or need where

  $i = N/n = $ the interval size.

c) Randomly select an integer between 1 to i.
d) Select every i-th unit.

In systematic sampling, one unit in a sample is first selected then the selection of subsequent samples is dependent on the preceding unit selected. Hence, there is the possibility of an order bias. In case the sampling frame lists are arranged in a pattern, and if the selection process matches with that pattern, then the whole idea of randomization would be defeated and we would either have overestimation or underestimation. If, however, we assume that the sampling frame list is randomly ordered, then in that case systematic sampling is mathematically equivalent to simple random sampling. If the list is stratified based on some criteria, then in that case systematic sampling is equivalent to stratified sampling.

Repeated systematic sampling is a variant of systematic sampling which tries to avoid the possibility of order biases due to periodicity or presence of some pattern in the sampling frame. This is usually done by culling out several smaller systematic samples, each having a different random start, thus minimizing the possibility of falling prey to periodicity in the sampling frame. Further, we can have an idea of the variance of estimate in the entire sample by looking at the variability in the sub-sample.

For example, if we have a population that only has $N = 500$ people in it and we want to take a sample of $n = 100$ to use systematic sampling, the population must be listed in a random order. The sampling fraction would be $f = 500/100 = 20\%$. In this case, the interval size k is equal to $N/n = 500/100 = 5$. Now, select a random integer from 1 to 5. In our example, imagine that you chose 2. Now, to select the sample, start with the second unit in the list and take every k-th unit (every fifth unit because $k = 5$). You would be sampling units 2, 7, 12, 17 and so on to 500 and you should wind up with 100 units in your sample.

Stratified Random Sampling

Stratified random sampling, sometimes also called proportional or quota random sampling, involves dividing the population into mutually exclusive and mutually exhaustive subgroups/strata and then taking a simple random sample in each subgroup/strata.

Subgroups can be based on different indicators like sex, age group, religion or geographical regions. However, it is to be noted that stratification does not mean the absence of randomness. Further, it is also believed that stratified random sampling generally has more precision than simple random sampling, but this is true only in case we have more homogeneous strata, because variability within groups of a homogeneous stratum is lower than the variability for the population as a whole. That is, confidence intervals will be narrower for stratified sampling than for simple random sampling of the same population. Stratified random sampling has some advantages over random sampling, for in the case of stratified random sampling, researchers can have the facility to generate separate results for each stratum, which can not only provide important information about that stratum but can also provide comparative results between strata. For example, if we assume that the researchers want to ensure a sample of 10 voters from a group of 100 voters contains both male and female voters in the same proportions as in the population, they have to first divide that population into males and females. In this case, let us say there are 60 male voters and 40 female voters. The number of males and females in the sample is going to be:

Number of males in the sample = $(10/100) \times 60 = 6$
Number of females in the sample = $(10/100) \times 40 = 4$

Researchers can further select six males and four females in the sample using either the simple random method or the systematic random sampling method.

Stratified random sampling can be further segregated into (i) proportionate stratified random sampling, where each stratum has same sampling fraction and (ii) disproportionate stratified random sampling where each stratum has different sampling fractions, that is, disproportionate numbers of subjects are drawn from some stratum compared to others. Disproportionate stratified sampling is also used in over sampling of certain subpopulations to allow separate statistical analysis with precision. Another reason for using a disproportionate stratified sampling is the higher cost per sampling unit in some stratum compared to others.

It is important to point out here that while calculating significance levels and confidence levels for the entire sample under disproportionate stratified sampling, cases must be weighted to ensure that proportionality is restored. Since weighting reduces precision estimates of stratified sampling, as a result disproportionate stratified samples tend to be less precise than proportionate stratified samples. Thus, in the case of proportionate stratified sampling precision is not reduced as compared to simple random sampling, whereas in the case of disproportionate stratified samples, standard error estimates may be either more or less precise than those based on simple random samples.

Cluster Sampling

Cluster sampling signifies that instead of selecting individual units from the population, entire group or clusters are selected at random. In cluster sampling, first we divide the population into clusters (usually along geographic boundaries). Then we randomly select some clusters from all clusters formed to measure all units within sampled clusters in the end.

Though often in practical situations, a two-stage cluster sample design[9] is used where a random sample of clusters is selected and within each cluster a random sample of subjects are selected. Further, the two-stage design can be expanded into a multi-stage one, in which samples of clusters are selected within previously selected clusters. There are also special variants of cluster sampling, such as World Health Organization (WHO) recommended 30 by 7 cluster sample technique for evaluating immunization programmes (see Box 4.2).

BOX 4.2
WHO Recommended 30 by 7 Cluster Sample Technique for Extended Programme of Immunization

The 30 by 7 cluster sample is widely used by WHO to estimate immunization coverage. Though it is a type of two-stage cluster sampling, it is different from the two-stage cluster sampling as in the case of a 30 by 7 cluster sample only the first household in each cluster is randomly selected.

The sample size for the 30 by 7 cluster sample is set at 210, which provides estimates within 10 percentage points of the true population percentage. In most situations this is adequate, though in case of high immunization coverage, estimating within 10 percentage points is not very informative and in these situations the sample size needs to be increased. This could be done either by increasing the number of clusters or the sample size per cluster.

Further, as in the case 30 by 7 cluster sample, every eligible individual in the household is interviewed, not all the 210 sampled respondents are independent. This may introduce bias into the estimate because subjects in the same household tend to be homogeneous with respect to immunization, though this bias could be easily avoided by randomly selecting one child per household, but in that case, the number of households that need to be visited to interview seven respondents per cluster would probably be more than earlier.

Cluster sampling has limitations in the form of a high degree of intra-cluster homogeneity, though a benefit of this type of cluster sample is that researchers do not have to collect information about all clusters as a list of the units in the population are only needed for selected clusters. Cluster sampling is generally used with some important modifications, that is, while selecting clusters variables are selected according to probability proportionate to the size criteria, such as the population size, the number of health facilities in the region, or the number of immunizations given in a week. This type of cluster sample is said to be self-weighting[10] because every unit in the population has the same chance of being selected. But in case researchers do not have information about the measure of the size of the clusters prior to sample selection, then all clusters will have the same chance or probability of selection, rather than the probability being related to their size. Thus, in this case, first a list of clusters is prepared and then a sampling interval (SI)[11] is calculated by dividing the total number of clusters in the domain by the number of clusters to be selected. In the next stage, a random number is selected between one and the sampling interval and subsequent units are chosen by adding the sampling interval to the selected random number. However, in such a situation the sample is not self-weighting as in this case, the probability of selecting a cluster is not based on the number of households in the cluster, and the procedure leads to sample elements having differing probabilities of selection.

Procedures for Selecting Sample Households

In the next stage, selection of sample households can be done by segmentation and a random walk method described next:

a) *Segmentation method:* Segmentation method is widely used in the case of a large cluster size. In the segmentation method, sample clusters are divided into smaller segments of approximately equal size. One cluster is selected randomly from each cluster and all households in the chosen segment are then interviewed. It is important to point out, though, that the size of the segment should be the same as the target number of sample households selected per cluster.

b) *Random walk method:* The random walk method used in the expanded programme of immunization cluster surveys is relatively widely known. The method entails (i) randomly choosing a starting point and a direction of travel within a sample cluster, (ii) conducting an interview in the nearest household and (iii) continuously choosing the next nearest household for an interview until the target number of interviews has been obtained.

Theoretically, clusters should be chosen so that they are as heterogeneous as possible, that is, though each cluster is representative of the population, the subjects within each cluster are diverse in nature. In that case, only a sample of the clusters would be required to be taken to capture all the variability in the population. In practice, however, clusters are often defined based on geographic regions or political boundaries, because of time and cost factors. In such a condition, though clusters may be very different from one another, sampled units within each cluster have a very high probability of being similar to other units. Because of this, for a fixed sample size, the variance from a cluster sample is usually larger than that from a simple random sample and, therefore, the estimates are less precise.

Multi-stage Sampling

All the methods of sampling discussed so far are examples of simple random sampling strategies. In most real life social research, however, researchers need to use sampling methods that are considerably more complex than simple random sampling. Multi-stage sampling is one such sampling strategy, which is generally used in more complex survey designs. Multi-stage sampling, as the name suggests, involves the selection of units at more than one stage. The number of stages in a multi-stage sampling strategy varies depending on convenience and availability of suitable sampling frames at different stages. For example, in the case of a five-stage sampling exercise, states may be sampled at the first level; then the sampling may move on to select cities, schools, classes and finally students. The probability proportionate to size sampling (PPS)[12] is used at each of the hierarchical levels, that is, successive units are selected according to the number of units/stages it contains.

Area sampling is a type of multi-stage sampling, where geographic units form the primary sampling units. In area sampling, the overall area to be covered in a survey is divided into smaller units from which further units are selected.

Non-probability Sampling

Unlike probability sampling, non-probability sampling does not involve the process of random selection, that is, in the case on non-probability sampling, the probability of selection of each sampling unit is not known. It implies that non-probability samples cannot depend upon the rationale of the probability theory and hence we cannot estimate population parameters from sample statistics. Further, in the case of non-probability samples, we do not have a rational way to prove/know whether the selected sample is representative of the population.

In general, researchers prefer probabilistic sampling methods over non-probabilistic ones, but in applied social research due to constraints such as time and cost and objectives of the research study there are circumstances when it is not feasible to adopt a random process of selection and in those circumstances usually non-probabilistic sampling is adopted. Further, there are instances, such as in the case of anthropological studies, or in the study of natural resource usage patterns where there is no need of probabilistic sampling, as estimation of the results is never an objective.

Non-probability sampling methods[13] can be classified into two broad types: accidental or purposive. Most sampling methods are purposive in nature because researchers usually approach the sampling problem with a specific plan in mind.

Accidental or Convenience Sampling

In the case of convenience sampling, as the name suggests, sampling units are selected out of convenience, for example, in clinical practice, researchers are forced to use clients who are available as samples, as they do not have many options.

Purposive Sampling

Purposive sampling, as the name suggests, is done with a purpose, which means that selection of sampling units is purposive in nature. Purposive sampling can be very useful for situations where you need to reach a targeted sample quickly and where a random process of selection or proportionality is not the primary concern.

Quota Sampling

In quota sampling, as the name indicates, sampling is done as per the fixed quota. Quota sampling is further classified into two broad types: proportional and non-proportional quota sampling. In proportional quota sampling, researchers proportionally allocate sampling units corresponding to the population size of the strata, whereas in the case of non-proportional quota sampling, a minimum number of sampled units are selected in each category, irrespective of the population size of the strata.

Expert Sampling

Expert sampling[14] involves selecting a sample of persons, who are known to have demonstrable experience and expertise in a particular area of study interest. Researchers resort to expert sampling because it serves as the best way to elicit the views of persons who have specific expertise in the study area. Expert sampling, in some cases, may also be used to provide evidence for the validity of another sampling approach chosen for the study.

Snowball/Chain Sampling

Snowball sampling[15] is generally used in the case of explorative research study/design, where researchers do not have much lead information. It starts by identifying respondents who meet the criteria for selection/inclusion in the study and can give lead for another set of respondents/information to move further in the study. Snowball sampling is especially useful when you are trying to reach populations that are inaccessible or difficult to find, for example, in the case of identifying injecting drug users.

Heterogeneity Sampling

In the case of heterogeneity sampling, samples are selected to include all opinions or views. Researchers use some form of heterogeneity sampling when their primary interest is in getting a broad spectrum of ideas and not in identifying the average ones.

Maximum Variation Sampling

Maximum variation sampling involves purposefully picking respondents depicting a wide range of extremes on dimension of interest studied.

SAMPLING ERROR

Sampling error is that part of total error in research, which occurs due to the sampling process, and this is one of the most frequent causes that makes a sample unrepresentative of its population. It is defined as the differences between the sample and the population, which occurs solely due to the nature or process in which particular units have been selected.

There are two basic causes for sampling error, the first is chance, that is, due to chance some unusual/variant units, which exist in every population, get selected as there is always a possibility of such selection. Researchers can avoid this error by increasing sample size, which would minimize the probability of selection of unusual/variant units. The second cause of sampling error is sampling bias, that is, the tendency to favour the selection of units that have particular characteristics. Sampling bias is usually the result of a poor sampling plan and most notable is the bias of selection when for some reason some units have no chance of appearing in the sample.

NON-SAMPLING ERROR

The other part of error in research process, which is not due to the sampling process, is known as non-sampling error and this type of error can occur whether a census or a sample is being used. Non-sampling error may be due to human error, that is, error made by the interviewer, if he is not able to communicate the objective of the study or he is not able to cull out the response from respondents or it could be due to fault in the research tool/instrument. Thus, a non-sampling error is also defined as an error that results solely from the manner in which the observations are made and the reason could be researchers' fault in designing questionnaires, interviewers' negligence in asking questions, or even analysts' negligence in analysing data.

The simplest example of non-sampling error is inaccurate measurements due to poor procedures and poor measurement tools. For example, consider the observation of human weights; if people are asked to state their own weights themselves, no two answers will be of equal reliability. Further, even if weighing is done by the interviewer, error could still be there because of fault in the weighing instrument used or the weighing norms used. Responses, therefore, will not be of comparable validity unless all persons are weighed under the same circumstances.

BIAS REDUCTION TECHNIQUES

Re-sampling and bias reduction techniques such as bootstrap and jackknifing are the most effective tools for bias reduction. They are non-biased estimators. In re-sampling, researchers can create a population by repeatedly sampling values from the sample. Let us take an example, where the researcher has a sample of 15 observations and wants to assess the proximity of the sample mean to the true population mean. The researcher then jots down each observation's value on a chit and put all the chits in a box. He can then select a number of chits, with replacements from the box to create many pseudo samples. The distribution of the means of all selected samples would accurately give the mean of the entire population.

Re-sampling methods are closely linked to bootstrapping methods. According to a well-known legend, Baron Munchausen saved himself from drowning in a quicksand by pulling himself up using only his bootstraps. Bootstrapping provides an estimation of parameter values, which also provides an estimation of parameter values and standard errors associated with them. The basic bootstrapping technique relies on the Monte Carlo algorithm. It is a mechanism for generating a set of numbers at random.

Bootstrap, as a scheme, envisages generating subsets of the data on the basis of random sampling with replacements, which ensures that each set of data is equally represented in the randomization scheme. It is important to point out here that the key feature of the bootstrap method are concerned with over-sampling as there is no constraint upon the number of times that a set of data can be sampled. In the case of the bootstrap method, the original sample is compared with the reference set of values to get the exact p-value.

Jackknifing is a bias reduction technique that provides an estimate of the parameters in the function and measures their stability with respect to changes in the sample. It is carried out by omitting one or more cases from the analysis in turn and running the analysis to construct the relevant function. From each one of the analysis different values for each of the parameters are obtained and based on these an estimate of parameter values and standard estimates are assessed. It re-computes the data by leaving one observation out each time and does a bit of logical folding to provide estimators of coefficients and error that will reduce bias.

Comparing the bootstrap and jackknife methods, both re-use data to provide an estimate of how the observed value of a statistics changes with the changing sample. Both examine the variation in the sample as the sample changes; however, the jackknife method generates a new coefficient, which has a standard error associated with it. The bootstrap method directly calculates a standard error associated with full sample estimate.

SAMPLING PROBLEMS

In practical situations, due to various constraints, there are several problems such as mismatched sampling frames and non-response, which need to be sorted out before analysing data. The next section describes various types of sampling problems.

MISMATCHED SAMPLING FRAMES

There are several instances when the sampling frame does not match with the primary sampling unit that needs to be selected. This problem occurs especially in the case of demographic studies wherein the purpose is to obtain a complete list of all eligible individuals living in the household to generate a sampling frame for selection of eligible individuals. If in a household there is more than one eligible individual for selection, and only one individual per household needs to be selected then it is imperative that interviewers are provided with some information in the form of a selection grid such as the Kish table to select an individual.

ANALYSING NON-RESPONSE

One of the most serious problems in a sample survey is non-response, that is, failure to obtain information for selected households or failure to interview eligible individuals and there are several strategies that are adopted to deal with non-response.

a) *Population comparison:* In order to account for non-response, survey averages are compared with population averages, especially in the case of demographic variables such as gender, marriage age and income. Though, in several cases, population values may not be available, however, on occasion, certain sources may provide population values for comparison. At the next stage, deviation of the sample average and the population average is assessed to study the impact of such a bias on the variables of interest.

b) *Comparison to external estimate:* Another strategy to analyse the impact of non-response rate is to compare the survey estimate with some external estimate, but the problem with this approach is that the difference could be due to lots of other factors such as time of survey or the way in which the questions were asked.

c) *Intensive post-sampling:* The second approach of intensive post-sampling envisages boosting the sample by making efforts to interview a sample of non-respondents. Though it is not feasible in the majority of the cases due to the costs involved and the problem of time overrun.

d) *Wave extrapolation:* Extrapolation methods are based on the principle that individuals who respond less readily are similar to non-respondents. Wave extrapolation is the commonest type of extrapolation, which is used to analyse the non-response rate. It does so by analysing the average of fall-back response rates assuming that person responded late are similar to non-respondents. This method involves little marginal expense and therefore is highly recommended.

WEIGHTING

The researcher can achieve a self-weighting sample by applying methods such as probability proportion to size (PPS) but in certain circumstances such as non-response and stratification, it becomes imperative to assign weight before analysing data.

a) *Weighting for non-response:* Let us assume that in a behaviour surveillance survey among HIV patients, the rate of non-response is quite high among female respondents because they are not very forthcoming in discussing such an issue. If the researcher wants to analyse the different behavioural traits among HIV patients by gender, then in such cases it becomes necessary to assign more weight to female responses than male responses. Because observed distributions do not conform to the true population, researchers need to weight responses to adjust accordingly.

For example, if the true proportion of HIV patients in the population by gender is 50–50, and in survey we were able to interview only 20 females and 80 males, then researchers can weight each female response by 4.0, which would give 80 females and 80 males. But, in that case the total sample size would increase from 100 to 160. Thus, to calculate all percentage on a sample size of 100, researchers need to further weight the scale back to 100. This could be achieved by further weighting both females and males by 5/8.

b) *Weighting in case of under-representation of strata:* In certain socio-economic surveys, researchers may often find themselves in a situation where the data shows under-representation of a given strata. This could happen either due to non-response or due to disproportionate stratified sampling. In such cases, weights need to be assigned to under-represented strata before going on with the analysis.

c) *Weighting to account for the probability of selection:* In true probabilistic sampling, that is, in a random sampling procedure, each individual has an equal chance of being selected. Though in reality, individuals may not have an equal chance of selection. In the majority of demographic surveys, where all eligible members in a household are listed, each household, not individual, has an equal chance of selection. Thus, eligible members within households with more eligible people have a lower chance of being selected and, as a result, they are often under-represented. It becomes imperative in those situations that a weighting adjustment is made before going forward with the analysis.

Dealing with Missing Data

Missing data can be due to various factors such as interviewer's fault in administering questions leaving certain questions blank or the respondent declining to respond to certain questions, due to some human error in data coding and data entry. This poses serious problems for researchers. While analysing, they need to decide what to do with the missing values—whether they should leave cases with missing data out of analysis or impute values before analysis.

Little and Rubin (1987) worked a lot on the process of data imputation and stressed that imputation depends on the pattern/mechanism that causes values to be missing.

Missing values are classified into three types: (i) values that are not missing completely at random (NMAR), (ii) values missing at random (MAR) and (iii) values missing completely at random (MCAR). In the case of NMAR and MAR, researchers can ignore the missing values but in the case of NMAR, it becomes imperative to use missing value data techniques.

Little and Rubin (1987) suggested three techniques to handle data with missing values: (i) complete case analysis (list-wise deletion), (ii) available case methods (pair-wise deletion) and (iii) filling in the missing values with estimated scores (imputation).

List-wise Deletion

In list-wise deletion, all cases pertaining to the variable of interest are deleted and the remaining data is analysed using conventional data analysis methods. The advantages of this method are: (i) simplicity, since standard analysis can be applied without modification and (ii) comparability of univariate statistics, since these are all calculated with a common sample base of cases. However, there are disadvantages particularly due to the potential loss of information in discarding incomplete cases.

Pair-wise Deletion

In pair-wise deletion (PD), unlike list-wise deletion, cases pertaining to each moment is estimated separately using cases with values for the pertinent variables. Pair-wise deletion uses all cases where the variable of interest is present and thus it has the advantage of being simple and also increases the sample size. But, its disadvantage is that the sample base changes from variable to variable according to the pattern of missing data.

Imputation

Imputation envisages replacing missing value with estimated value through some mathematic and statistical model. It is important to point out, however, that an imputation model should be chosen in consonance with the pattern of missing values and the data analysis method. In particular, the model should be flexible enough to preserve the associations or relationships among variables that will be the focus of later investigation. Therefore, a flexible imputation model that preserves a large number of associations is desired because it may be used for a variety of post-implementation analyses. Some of the most frequently used imputation methods are described next.

a) *Mean substitution:* Mean substitution was once the most common method of imputation of missing values but nowadays it is no longer preferred. In the case of mean substitution, substituted mean

FIGURE 4.8
Missing Value Analysis Using SPSS

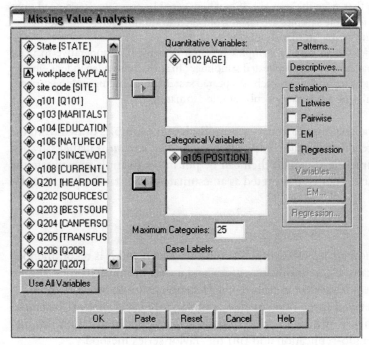

values reduce the variance of the variable and its correlation with other variables. However, it is advised that the value of group mean should be substituted for a categorical variable having high correlation with the variable, which has missing values.

The Statistical Package for Social Sciences (SPSS) provides options for replacing missing values and it can be accessed via the menu item Analyse, Missing Value Analysis. It provides facilities for both quantitative variables and categorical variables. It supports estimation such as list wise, pair wise, regression and expectation maximization (see Figure 4.8).

b) *Regression analysis:* Regression analysis, as the name suggests, envisage fitting a regression model for each variable having missing values. It does by doing a regression analysis in cases without missing data to predict values for the cases with missing data. But, this method suffers from the same problem as mean substitution: all cases with the same values on the independent variables will be imputed with the same value on the missing variable. That is the reason some researchers prefer stochastic substitution, which uses the regression technique but also adds a random value to the predicted result.

c) *Maximum likelihood estimation (MLE):* SPSS provides the facility of using MLE through Expectation Maximization (EM) algorithm in the SPSS missing values option. Maximum likelihood estimation is considered a better option than multiple regression as it does not work on the basis of statistical assumption as regression does. That is why it is one the most commonly used methods for imputation.

d) *Multiple imputation (MI):* Multiple imputation is a very effective method of imputing data. As the name suggests, MI imputes each missing value with a set of possible values. These multiple imputed data sets are then analysed in turn and the results are combined to make inferential statements that reflect missing data uncertainty in terms of p-values.

e) *Hotdeck method:* Stata and some other statistical packages implement the hotdeck method for imputation. In the hotdeck method, at the first stage the user specifies which variables from the strata need to be focused on. At the next stage, multiple samples are taken from each stratum to derive the estimate of the missing value for the given variable in that stratum.

f) *Adjustment to complex research designs:* In case of complex research designs, it is imperative to make adjustments for estimating variance including replicated sampling.[16] In such cases, independent samples are drawn from the population by using designs such as repeated systematic sampling and the variance of samples is estimated by analysing variability of sub-sample estimates.

Let U be a parameter such as the response to a survey item. Each of the samples drawn from the population can be used to estimate a mean for the population such as $u_1, u_2,..., u_t$. Further, all such samples can be pooled to get sample mean, which then can be put into a formula to estimate the sampling variance of $\ddot{u}$, whose square root is interpreted as an estimate of the standard error and is represented by the formula:

$$v(\ddot{u}) = \text{SUM } (u_i - \ddot{u})^2/t(t-1)$$

It is imperative to ask, however, how many sub-samples should be drawn and it is recommended that in the case of a descriptive statistics, a minimum of four and a maximum of 10 sub-samples should be drawn. For multivariate analysis, the number of sub-samples should be 20 or more.

Lee, Forthofer and Lorimar detailed three other methods of variance estimation: (i) balanced repeated replication, used primarily in paired selection designs, (ii) repeated replication through jackknifing, which is based on pseudo-replication and (iii) the Taylor series method.

SAMPLE SIZE ESTIMATION

SAMPLE SIZE

Sampling is done basically to achieve two broad objectives: (i) to estimate a population parameter or (ii) to test a hypothesis.

Sample size plays an important role in determining how closely the sampling distribution represents the normal distribution. Despite the assurance given by the central limit theorem, it is true that as the sample size increases, sample distribution approaches normal even if the distribution of the variable in the population is normal. But, in case the researcher opts for a smaller sample size, then those tests can be used only in case the variable of interest is normally distributed.

Researchers, in general, have to deliberate on various considerations before deciding on the adequate sample size, which shall represent the population. The main consideration are (i) precision in estimates one wishes to achieve, (ii) statistical level of confidence one wishes to use and (iii) variability or variance one expects to find in the population.

Standard Error

Researchers, while deciding on adequate sample size need to first decide on the precision they want or the extent of error they are willing to allow for parameter estimation. The extent of error, signifying a difference between a sample statistics and the population parameter, is also defined as the standard error. It is important to point out that the standard error is different from standard deviation (see Box 4.3).

Estimation of the unknown value of a population parameter will always have some error due to sampling no matter how hard we try. Thus, in order to present the true picture of the estimates of population characteristics, researchers also need to mention the standard errors of the estimates. Standard error is a measure of accuracy that determines the probable errors that arise due to the fact that estimates are based on random samples from the entire population and not on a complete population census.

Standard error is thus also defined as a statistic, which signifies the accuracy of an estimate. It helps us in assessing how different estimates such as sample mean would be from population parameters such as population mean. The widely used statistics for standard error are listed next.

BOX 4.3
How Standard Deviation is Different from Standard Error

Standard deviation signifies the spread of distribution. The term standard deviation is generally used for the variability of sample distribution, though it is also used to mean population variability. In the majority of the cases, researchers are not aware of population deviation and compute deviation around the sample mean to estimate the population mean.

Standard error, on the other hand, means the precision of the sample mean in estimating the population mean. Thus, while standard deviation is usually related to sample statistics, standard error is always attached to a parameter. Standard error is inversely related to sample size, that is, the standard error decreases with an increase in sample size and increases with decrease in sample size.

Standard Error for the Mean

Standard error of mean decreases as the sample size increases though it decreases by a factor of $n^{1/2}$ not n. Standard error for the mean is described as:

$$S/n^{1/2}$$

Thus, in case the researcher wants to reduce the error by 50 per cent, the sample size needs to be increased four times, which is not very cost effective. In the case of a finite population of size N, the standard error of the sample mean of size n, is described as:

$$S \times [(N - n)/(nN)]^{1/2}$$

Standard error for the multiplication of two independent means $\bar{x}_1 \times \bar{x}_2$ is defined as:

$$\{\bar{x}_1 S_2^2/n_2 + \bar{x}_2 S_1^2/n_1\}^{1/2}$$

Standard error for two dependent means $\bar{x}_1 + \bar{x}_2$ is:

$$\{S_1^2/n_1 + S_2^2/n_2 + 2r \times [(S_1^2/n_1)(S_2^2/n_2)]^{1/2}\}^{1/2}$$

Standard Error for the Proportion

Standard error for proportion is defined in terms of p and q $(1 - p)$, that is, the probability of the success or failure of an occurrence of an event respectively. It is also defined mathematically as:

$$[P(1 - P)/n]^{1/2}$$

In the case of a finite population of size N, the standard error of the sample proportion is described as:

$$[P(1 - P)(N - n)/(nN)]^{1/2}$$

Level of Confidence

The confidence intervals for the mean gives us a range of values around the mean where we expect that the true population mean is located. For example, if the mean in a sample is 14 and the lower and upper limits of the confidence interval are 10 and 20 respectively at 95 per cent level of confidence, then the researcher can conclude that there is a 95 per cent probability that the population mean is greater than 10 and lower than 20. The researcher has the flexibility of deciding on a tighter confidence level by setting the p-level to a smaller value.

It is important to point out that the width of the confidence interval depends on the sample size and on the variation of data values. The larger the sample size, the more reliable is its mean and the larger the variation, the less reliable is its mean.

Variability or Variance in Population

Variance or variability in a population is defined in terms of deviation from the population mean. Population variance plays a very important role in determining adequate sample size. In the case of large variability in population, the sample size needs to be adequately boosted to capture the spread or variability of population.

Sample size computation depends upon two key parameters, namely, the extent of precision required and the standard deviation or variance of the population. But, in the majority of the cases, researchers do not have any information about population variance and they have to depend on estimation of population variance by computing deviations around the sample mean.

SAMPLE SIZE DECISION WHEN ESTIMATING THE MEAN

The first critical task, after deciding on the research design and sampling methodology is to decide on the adequate sample. In the majority of the cases, researchers would be interested in estimating the population mean. The required sample size for estimating the population mean depends upon the precision the researchers require and the standard deviation of the population.

Further, as mentioned earlier, the confidence level too depends upon the sample size and the larger the sample, the higher is the associated confidence. But, a large sample means a burden on the resources and thus every researchers' quest remains to find the smallest sample size that will provide the desirable confidence.

$$E = Z \; \sigma/n^{1/2}$$

Where E is the extent of precision the researchers desire and σ is standard deviation of the population. In case the researchers do not have an idea about the standard deviation of population, then the method followed would remain the same, except that an estimate of the population standard deviation may be used. Sometimes, researchers may undertake a pilot survey to ascertain standard deviation and if that is not feasible then standard deviation of the sample may be used.

SAMPLE SIZE DECISION WHEN ESTIMATING PROPORTION

Sample size decision for estimating proportion is based on similar considerations as in the case of estimating the mean. It depends on the proportion the researchers want to estimate and the standard error they are willing to allow.

Standard error depends on the sample size and precision increases with increase in sample size. However, one cannot just opt for a large sample size to improve precision, in fact, the task is to decide upon the sample size that will be adequate to provide the desirable precision.

For a variable scored 0 or 1, for no or yes, the standard error (SE) of the estimated proportion p, based on the random sample observations, is given by:

$$SE = [p(1 - p)/n]^{1/2}$$

Where p is the proportion obtaining a score of 1 and n is the sample size. In probabilistic terms, researchers also categorize p as the success of an event and $1 - p$ as the failure of the event. Standard error is the standard deviation of the range of possible estimate values.

The formulae suggest that sample size is inversely proportional to the level of standard error and research. Based on researchers' objectives and population characteristics researchers can decide upon the error that they need to allow for. In case researchers are not sure about the error, they can opt for the worst case scenario, that is, maximum standard error at $p = 0.5$, when 50 per cent of the respondents say yes and 50 per cent say no. Under this extreme condition, the sample size, n, can then be expressed as the largest integer less than or equal to:

$$n = 0.25/SE^2$$

Based on the SE the researcher can decide upon the sample size. That is, in case SE is 0.01 (that is, 1 per cent), a sample size of 2500 will be needed. Similarly, for 5 per cent a sample size of 100 would be enough.

SAMPLE SIZE DECISION IN COMPLEX SAMPLING DESIGN

In practical situations, simple random sampling is rarely used and often researchers have to resort to complex sampling procedures. Selection of a complex sampling procedure instead of a simple random sampling procedure thus affects the probability of selection of elementary sampling units and hence the precision as compared to a simple random sampling procedure. As a result, a complex sampling design has sampling errors much larger than a simple random sample of the same size. To have an idea about sample size requirements in a complex sampling design, it is necessary to have an idea about the design effect and the effective sample size.

Design Effect

Design effect (DEFF), as the name suggests, signifies increased sampling error due to complex survey design. It is defined as a factor that reflects the effect on the precision of a survey estimate due to the difference between the use of complex survey designs such as cluster or stratified random sampling as compared to simple random sampling.

In simpler terms, the design effect for a variable is the ratio of variance estimated using a complex survey design to variance estimated using simple random sampling design for a particular sample statistic. Design effect is a coefficient, which reflects how the sampling design affects the variance estimation of population characteristics due to complex survey designs as compared to simple random sampling. A DEFF coefficient of 1 means that the sampling design is equivalent to simple random sampling and a DEFF of greater than 1 means that the sampling design has reduced precision of estimate compared to simple random sampling, as usually happens in the case of cluster sampling. Similarly, a DEFF of less than 1 means that the sampling design has increased precision compared to simple random sampling and this is usually observed in the case of stratified sampling.

Researchers in a majority of health and demographic studies opt for multi-stage cluster sampling and in all those studies variances of estimates are usually larger than in a simple survey. Researchers usually assume that cluster sampling does not affect estimates themselves, but only affect their variances.

Thus as mentioned earlier, DEFF is essentially the ratio of the actual variance, under the sampling method actually used, to the variance computed under the assumption of simple random sampling. For example, interpretation of a value of DEFF of, say, 3, means that the sample variance is three times bigger than it would be if the survey were based on the simple random process of selection. In other words, we can also suggest that in case of simple random sampling, only one-third of the sample cases would have been sufficient if a simple random sample were used instead of the cluster sample with its DEFF of 3.

In the case of complex cluster sampling design, two key component of DEFF are intra-class correlation and the cluster sample sizes. Thus, DEFF is calculated as follows:

$$\text{DEFF} = 1 + \acute{\alpha}(n - 1)$$

where design effect is also represented as DEFF, $\acute{\alpha}$ is the intra-class correlation for the variable of interest and n is the average size of the cluster.

Studies have shown that design effect increases as intra-class correlation increases and the cluster sizes increase. The intra-class correlation is defined as the likelihood that two elements in the same cluster have the same value, for a given variable of interest, as compared to two elements chosen completely at random in the population. A value of 0.30 signifies that the elements in the cluster are about 30 per cent more likely to have the same value as compared to two elements chosen at random in the survey. Let us take an example where clustering is done based on social stratification. In such a case, the socio-economic profile of two individuals in the same stratum would be more likely to have the same value than if selected completely at random.

Design effect is not a constant entity and it varies from survey to survey, and even within the same survey, it may vary from one variable to another variable. Respondents of the same clusters are likely to have similar socio-economic characteristics like access to health and education facilities, but are not likely to have similar disability characteristics.

Besides using DEFF as a measure of assessing effectiveness due to a complex survey design, researchers also use DEFT, which is the square root of DEFF. Since DEFT is the square root of DEFF, it is less variable than DEFF and may be used to reduce variability and to estimate confidence intervals. DEFT also provides evidence of how sample standard error and confidence intervals, increase as a result of using a complex design. Thus, a DEFT value of 3 signifies that the confidence interval is three times as large as it would have been in the case of a simple random sample.

Effective Sample Size

In practical situations, researchers often have to resort to a complex sampling methodology instead of a simple random sampling methodology. In such situations, there is strong probability of losing effectiveness, if researchers go with the sample size, as they would have taken in the case of a simple random sampling. Effective sample size is defined as the sample size, which researchers would have selected in the case of a simple random sampling.

To explain it further, let us take an example of one-stage cluster sampling, where the selection of a unit from the same cluster adds less new information (because of strong intra-cluster correlation) than a completely independent selection would have added. In such cases, the sample is not as varied or representative as it would have been in a random sample and to make it representative researchers increase the sample size. In actual practice, however, by doing so researchers reduce the effective sample size.

SAMPLE SIZE DECISION WHILE TESTING A HYPOTHESIS

In a majority of the cases in social research, a hypothesis is propounded and a decision has to be made about the correctness of the hypothesis. Sample size decision in the case of hypothesis testing becomes a relevant and important point. The next section lists sample designs used in the case of testing a hypothesis when a change has to be assessed.

Sample Size Decision Assessing Change

After planning and implementing a specific intervention, the researchers' primary task remains to measure and compare changes in behavioural indicators over time. The sample size decision in this case also depends on the power, that is, the efficiency to detect and measure change, besides depending on the level of statistical significance.

The sample size required to assess change for a given variable of interest depends upon several factors such as (i) the initial value of the variable of interest, (ii) the expected change the programme was designed to make, which needs to be detected, (iii) the appropriate significance level, that is, assigning probability to conclude that an observed change is a reflection of programme intervention and did not occur by chance and (iv) the appropriate power, that is, the probability to conclude that the study has been able to detect a specified change.

Based on this consideration the required sample size (n) for a variable of interest as a proportion for a given group is given by:

$$n = \frac{D[Z_{1-\alpha}\sqrt{2P(1-P)} + Z_{1-\beta}\sqrt{P_1(1-P_1) + P_2(1-P_2)}]^2}{(P_2 - P_1)^2}$$

where:

D = design effect
P_1 = the estimated proportion at the time of the first survey
P_2 = the proportion expected at the time of survey
$Z_{1-\alpha}$ = the z-score corresponding to a significance level
$Z_{1-\beta}$ = the z-score corresponding to power

The most important parameter in this formula is design affect, which as described earlier is the factor by which the sample size has to increase in order to have the same precision as a simple random sample.

Further, as design effect is the ratio of the actual variance, under the sampling method actually used, to the variance computed under the assumption of simple random sampling, it is very difficult to compute beforehand, unless researchers do a pilot study or use data from a similar study done earlier. Researchers often use the standard value of $D = 2.0$ in two-stage cluster sampling based on the assumption number of cluster sample sizes are moderately small.

NOTES

1. Probability is an instrument to measure the likelihood of the occurrence of an event. There are five major approaches of assigning probability: classical approach, relative frequency approach, subjective approach, anchoring and the Delphi technique.

2. It is important to mention that whilst probability distribution stands for population distribution, frequency distribution stands for sample distribution.

3. A distribution function of a continuous random variable X is a mathematical relation that gives for each number x, the probability that the value of X is less than or equal to x. Whereas in the case of discrete random variables, the distribution function is often given as the probability associated with each possible discrete value of the random variable.

4. This is the simplest probability model—a single trial between two possible outcomes such as the toss of a coin. The distribution depends upon a single parameter 'p' representing the probability attributed to one defined outcome out of the two possible outcomes.

5. One reason the normal distribution is important is that a wide variety of naturally occurring random variables such as the height and weight of all creatures are distributed evenly around a central value, average, or norm.

6. There is not one normal distribution but many, called a family of distributions. Each member of the family is defined by its mean and SD, the parameters, which specify the particular theoretical normal distribution.

7. Probability sampling also tends in practice to be characterized by (i) the use of lists or sampling frames to select the sample, (ii) clearly defined sample selection procedures and (iii) the possibility of estimating sampling error.

8. A sample is a random sample if the probability density describing the probability for the observation of X_1, X_2,... is given by a product

$$f(x_1, x_2,..., x_n) = g(x_1)g(x_2)...g(x_n)$$

This implies in particular that the X_i are independent, that is, the result of any observation does not influence any other observations.

9. The two-stage cluster design involves a sampling frame involving two steps: (i) selection of first-stage or primary units and (ii) selection of elementary sampling units within the primary units. In many applications, for example, villages and/or city blocks are chosen at the first stage and a sample of households from each at the second.

10. Weights compensate for unequal probabilities of selection. The standard method for correcting for these unequal probabilities is to apply sampling weights to the survey data during analysis by multiplying the indicator value by the weight. The appropriate sampling weight for each sample subject is simply the reciprocal of the probability of selection of that subject, or the inverse of the probability.

11. It is important to note that in selecting sample clusters, decimal points in the sampling interval be retained. The rule to be followed is that when the decimal part of the sample selection number is less than 0.5, the lower numbered cluster is chosen, and when the decimal part of the sample selection number is 0.5 or greater, the higher numbered cluster is chosen.

12. The term probability proportionate to size means that larger clusters are given a greater chance of selection than smaller clusters. The use of the PPS selection procedure requires that a sampling frame of clusters with measures of size be available or developed before sample selection is done.

13. There are about 16 different types of purposive sampling. They are briefly discussed in the following section. See Patton (1990: 169-86) for a detailed study.

14. Critical case sampling is a variant of expert sampling, in which the sample is a set of cases or individuals identified by experts as being particularly significant.

15. Snowball sampling is also referred to as network sampling by some authors (see Little and Rubin, 1987).

16. Lee et al. (1989) studied the issue in great detail. These authors set forth a number of different strategies for variance estimation for complex samples.

CHAPTER 5

DATA ANALYSIS

In a bid to move from data to information, we need to analyse data using appropriate statistical techniques. The present chapter explains univariate and bivariate data analysis for both metric and non-metric data in detail. It also describes the parametric and non-parametric methods for paired and unpaired samples. First, though, it is imperative to have an idea of a variable, its nature and data type.

VARIABLE

A variable[1] is defined as the attribute of a case, which varies for different cases. Its variability is usually captured in a measurement scale, varying between two scale values to potentially an infinite number of scale values for binary scale or continuous metric scale.

Research as a process is nothing but an attempt to collect information about the variable of interest and assessing change in that variable as a function of the internal and external environment. The process of grouping observations about the variable of interest in a systematic and coherent way provides us data, which could be qualitative or quantitative in nature, depending on the nature and type of observation. For the sake of simplicity, as of now we can segregate qualitative data by words, picture or images and quantitative data by numbers on which we can perform basic mathematical operations.

Returning to the definition of a variable, instead of defining variable as an attribute of a case, some researchers prefer to say that the variable takes on a number of values. For example, the variable gender can have two values, male and female. Variables can be further classified into three categories:

a) *Dependent variable:* Dependent variable is also referred to by some researchers as response variable / outcome variable. It is defined as a variable, which might be modified, by some treatment or exposure, or a variable, which we are trying to predict through research.

b) *Independent variable:* Independent variable also referred to as explanatory variable is a variable which explains any influences/change in response in the variable of interest.

c) *Extraneous variable:* Extraneous variable is a variable that is not part of the study as per conceptualized design, but may affect the outcome of a study.

TYPES OF DATA

Data can be broadly classified as: (i) qualitative data and (ii) quantitative data based on the objects they measure.

Qualitative data measures behaviour which is not computable by arithmetic relations and is represented by pictures, words, or images. Qualitative data is also called categorical data, as they can be classified into categories such as class, individual, object, or the process they fall in.

Quantitative data is a numerical record that results from a process of measurement and on which basic mathematical operations can be done, for example, though we may represent gender variable values, male and female as 1 and 2, but as no mathematical operation can be done on these values (adding 1 and 2 does not make any sense), the data remains qualitative in nature.

Quantitative data can be further classified into metric and non-metric data based on the metric properties defining distances between scale values (see Figure 5.1). Scales are of different types and vary in terms of the ways in which they define the relationships between scale values. The simplest of these scales are binary scales where there are just two categories, one for the cases that possess those characteristics and one for the cases that do not. Nominal scales and ordinal scales can have several categories depending on the variables of interest, for example, in the case of gender we have only two categories, male and female, but in the case of occupational qualification, we can have several categories, depending on the way we decide to define categories.

a) *Non-metric data:* Data collected from binary scales, nominal scales and ordinal scales are jointly termed as non-metric data, that is, they do not possess a meter with which distance between scale values can be measured.

b) *Metric data:* Though for some scales there is metric data with which we can define distances between scale values.

FIGURE 5.1
Classification of Data Types

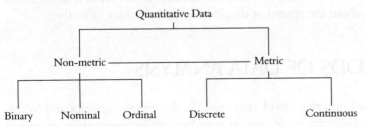

Metric data can be further classified into two groups: (i) discrete data and (ii) continuous data. Discrete data is countable data, for example, the number of students in a class. When the variables are measurable, they are expressed on a continuous scale also termed as continuous data. An example would be measuring the height of a person.

CHOICE OF DATA ANALYSIS

The choice of data analysis depends on several factors such as type of variable, nature of variable, shape of the distribution of a variable and the study design adopted to collect information about variables. While talking about the level of measurement, quantitative variables take several values, frequently called levels of measurement, which affect the type of data analysis that is appropriate. As discussed in Chapter 2, numbers can be assigned to the attributes of a nominal variable but numbers are just labels. These numbers do not indicate any order. Further, in the case of an ordinal variable, the attributes are ordered. Although the ordinal level of measurement yields a ranking of attributes, no assumptions can be made about the distance between the classifications. For example, we cannot assume that the distance between any person perceiving the impact of a programme to be excellent and good is the same as that between good and average.

Interval and ratio variables have additional measurement properties as compared to nominal and ordinal variables. In interval variables, attributes are assumed to be equally spaced. For instance, the difference between a temperature of 20 degrees and 25 degrees on the Fahrenheit temperature scale is the same as the difference between 40 degrees and 45 degrees. Likewise, the time difference between AD 1980 and AD 1982 is same as that between AD 1992 and AD 1994. But even in the case of an interval variable, we cannot assume that a temperature of 40 degrees is twice as hot as a temperature of 20 degrees. This is due to the fact that the ratio of the two observations are uninterpretable because of the absence of a rational zero for the variable. Thus, in order to do ratio analysis, ratio variables having equal intervals and a rational zero point should be used. For instance, weight is a ratio variable and in the case of weight, researchers can compute ratios of observations and can safely conclude that a person of 80 kg is twice as heavy as a person weighing 40 kg.

Variables distribution also plays a key role in determining the nature of data analysis. After data collection, it is advisable to look at the variable distribution to assess the type of analysis that could be done with the data or whether variable distribution is appropriate for a statistical test or estimation purpose or whether it needs to be transformed. Further, an examination of variable data analysis would also provide an indication about the spread of distribution and presence of outliers.

METHODS OF DATA ANALYSIS

Statistical methods can be classified into two broad categories: (i) descriptive statistics and (ii) inferential statistics (see Figure 5.2). Descriptive statistics are used to describe, summarize, or explain a given set of data, whereas inferential statistics use statistics computed from a sample to infer about the population concerned by making inferences from the samples about the populations from which they have been drawn.

FIGURE 5.2
Method of Data Analysis

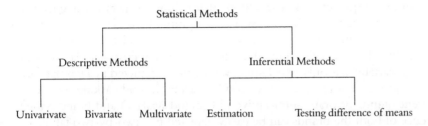

Descriptive statistics can be further segmented into statistics describing (i) non-metric data and (ii) metric data (see Figure 5.3).

FIGURE 5.3
Descriptive Analysis Type

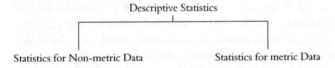

DESCRIPTIVE METHODS FOR NON-METRIC DATA

Univariate Analysis

Univariate analysis, as the name suggests, provides analytical information about one variable, which could be metric or non-metric in nature. Non-metric data (binary, nominal and ordinal) is best displayed in the form of tables or charts for further analysis. Frequency or one-way tables, depicting information in a row or column is the simplest method for analysing non-metric data. They are often used as one of the exploratory procedures to review how different categories of values are distributed in the sample.

In the case of binary variables, we have to display information about only two categories, for example, the number of respondents saying yes or no to a question. Though, in the case of nominal data, there may be three or more categories and data display does not matter as far as relative standing is concerned. Charts and graphs can also be used interchangeably to refer to graphical display. Charts for non-metric data are limited largely to bar charts and pie charts.[2]

Bivariate Analysis

The first step in data analysis of non-metric data is construction of a bivariate cross-tabulation, which is sometimes also referred to as contingency or a two-way table.[3] In a contingency table, nominal frequencies are displayed in cells of cross-tabulation in such a way that each cell in the table represents a unique combination of specific values of cross-tabulated variables. Thus, cross-tabulation allows us to examine frequencies of observations that belong to specific categories on more than one variable. Cross-tabulation is the easiest way of summarizing data and can be of any size in terms of rows and columns. It generally allows us to identify relationships between the cross-tabulated variables based on the cell values. The simplest form of cross-tabulation is the two-by-two table where each variable has only two distinct values and is depicted in a tabular form having two rows and two columns. For example, if we conduct a simple study asking females to choose one of two different brands of oral contraceptive pill (brand Mala-D and brand Saheli) then comparative preference of both the brands can be easily depicted in a two-by-two table.

Bivariate analysis and coefficient of association depend on the nature of variables.

Coefficient for Nominal Variable

Pearson Chi-square   The Pearson chi-square[4] coefficient n is the most common coefficient of association, which is calculated to assess the significance of the relationship between categorical variables. It is used to test the null hypothesis that observations are independent of each other. It is computed as the difference between observed frequencies shown in the cells of cross-tabulation and expected frequencies that would be obtained if variables were truly independent. For example, in case we ask 20 teachers and 20 village influencers to choose between two brands of iodized salt, Tata and Annapurna, and if there is no relationship between preference and respondents' profile, we would expect about an equal number of choices of Tata and Annapurna brand for each set of respondents. The chi-square test becomes more significant as the numbers deviate more from the expected pattern, that is, as the preference of teachers and village influencers differs.

The formula for computation of chi-square is:

$$= \frac{\Sigma(\text{observed frequency} - \text{expected frequency})^2}{(\text{expected frequency})}$$

Where χ^2 value and its significance level depend on the total number of observations and the number of cells in the table.

In accordance with the principles mentioned, relatively small deviations of the relative frequencies across cells from the expected pattern will prove significant if the number of observations is large.

In order to complete the χ^2 test, the degree of freedom also needs to be considered. Further, this is on the assumption that the expected frequencies are not very small. Chi-square[5] tests the underlying probabilities in each cell; and in case the expected cell frequencies are less than 5, it becomes very difficult to estimate the underlying probabilities in each cell with precision.

Maximum-likelihood Chi-square Maximum-likelihood chi-square distribution, as the name suggests, is based on the maximum-likelihood theory. Though maximum-likelihood chi-square takes a natural log of observed and expected frequencies, the resultant value is very close in magnitude to the Pearson chi-square statistic and is calculated as:

$$2 \sum_{\text{all cells}} O \ln (O/E)$$

ln = natural logarithm
O = observed frequency for a cell
E = expected frequency for a cell

Tshuprow's T[6] Tshuprow's T is a chi-square-based measure of association, which in mathematical terms is equal to the square root of chi-square divided by the sample size (n) and multiplied by the number of times the square root of the number of degrees of freedom. Mathematically it can also be expressed as:

$$T = \text{SQRT } [X^2/(n*\text{SQRT } ((r-1)\ (c-1)))]$$

Where r is the number of rows and c is the number of columns

As per the formula, T is inversely proportional to the number of rows and columns; hence T is less than 1.0 for non-square tables (tables having unequal number of rows and columns). Thus, the smaller the square of the table, the more T will be less than 1.0.

Yates Correction Chi-square distribution is a continuous distribution whereas the frequencies being analysed are not continuous. Thus, in order to improve the approximation of chi-square, Yates correction is applied. It does so by reducing the absolute value of differences between expected and observed frequencies in small two-by-two tables. It is usually applied in case of cross-tabulations, when a table contains only small-observed frequencies, so that some expected frequencies become less than 10.

Fisher Exact Test Fisher exact test is an alternative to chi-square test for two-by-two tables, when the sample is very small. Its null hypothesis is based on the rationale that there is no difference between the observed value and the expected value. It, therefore, computes the likelihood of obtaining cell frequencies as uneven as or worse than the ones that were observed assuming that the two variables are not related. Though in the case of a small sample size, probability can be computed by counting all probable tables that can be constructed based on the marginal frequencies.

Contingency Coefficient Contingency coefficient is used to test the strength between the variables in case of tables larger than two-by-two tables. It is interpreted in the same way as Cramer's coefficient. It varies between 0 and 1, where 0 signifies complete independence. Coefficient of contingency[7] is a chi-square distribution based measure of the relation between two categorical variables.

Contingency coefficient has one disadvantage as compared to chi-square statistics because of the limit of the size of the table (it can reach the limit of 1 only if the number of categories is unlimited) (Siegel, 1956: 201). The formula for calculating the chi-square is:

$$C = \frac{\chi^2}{\chi^2 + N}$$

The steps is to calculate chi-square characteristics are:

a) Calculate the statistics chi-square using the formula:

$$\chi^2 = \frac{\Sigma(f_0 - f_e)^2}{f_e}$$

b) Enter chi-square in contingency coefficient formula.

Coefficient Phi   The phi correlation coefficient is an agreement index for special case of two-by-two tables in which both variables are dichotomous. The phi coefficient can vary from –1 to 1, however the upper limit of phi depends on the relationship among the marginal. Phi coefficient assumes the value of 0 if the two variables are statistically independent. It is important to point out that phi, unlike chi-square, is not affected by total sample size.

Cramer's V   Cramer's V is a measure of agreement which is used in case of large tables. It is preferred over phi-square coefficient in case of two-by-two tables as in case of large tables phi-square can have value substantially larger than unity. In those cases it is better to use Crammer's V computed as:

$$V = \frac{\chi^2}{N \, \text{Min} \, (r-1)(c-1)}$$

Cramer's V varies between 0 and 1 for all sizes of tables.

The various measures of association for nominal variables have been discussed here. The researcher needs to carefully select the appropriate coefficient keeping in mind the nature of the data and the research objective (see Box 5.1).

BOX 5.1
Selection of Appropriate Coefficient for Nominal Variable

In case researchers want to analyse contingency tables with two rows and two columns, either Fisher's exact test or the chi-square test can be used. In case researchers want to use a measure based on the maximum likelihood theory, the maximum-likelihood chi-square can be used. Fisher's test is preferred in case the calculation is done using a computer. Chi-square test should not be used in cases when the cell frequencies in the contingency table are less than six. In case researchers want to opt for better approximation than chi-square for two-by-two tables, Yates correction should be used, though in the case of larger sample sizes, the Yates' correction makes little difference.

In case both the variables are dichotomous, phi correlation coefficient should be used. Cramer's V is preferred over the phi-square coefficient in the case of larger tables. Researchers can also use contingency coefficients for larger table, that is, tables having more than four cells.

Measures Based on Proportional Reduction of Error Principle

Another important measure to ascertain measure of association is based on proportional reduction of error principle. Coefficient of measure of association varies between 0 and 1, where a value of 0 signifies absence of any association between the two variables and coefficient value of 1 characterizes a perfect relationship between the two variables.

Lambda   Lambda measures the strength of association between two nominal variables. In Lambda the idea of an association between nominal variables is similar to that between ordinal variables but the computation approach is slightly different as in the case of a nominal variable, categories are just labels and doesn't possess inherent order. Lambda is based on the following calculation:

Numbers of errors eliminated
Numbers of original errors

Lambda varies from 0, indicating no association, to 1, indicating perfect association. Lambda's computation approach is based on proportional reduction in error method and involves mode as a basis for computing prediction errors. A lambda value of 0.30 signifies that by using an independent variable to predict a dependent variable, the researcher has reduced error by 30 per cent. It is important to point out that lambda is an asymmetrical measure of association and the result will be different based on the dependent and independent variables selected.

Uncertainty Coefficients   Uncertainty coefficients signifies the proportion of uncertainty in the dependent variable, which is explained by the independent variable. It uses a logarithmic function to ascertain the uncertainty in the dependent variable and then calculates the proportion of uncertainty, which could be eliminated by looking at the categories in the independent variable. It ranges from 0 to 1, wherein 0 indicates no reduction in uncertainty of the dependent variable and a value of 1 indicates the complete elimination of uncertainty. It can easily be computed using SPSS, using its cross-tab module (see Box 5.2).

BOX 5.2
Nominal Coefficient Using SPSS

Researchers can easily compute nominal coefficient in SPSS via the Analyse menu item and Descriptive sub-item. Further, in the Cross-tabs dialogue box, the researcher can enter variables in the dependent variable and independent variable dialogue boxes. Later he can click on the statistics window to open the cross-tab statistics window (see Figure 5.4). The researcher can then click on the measures he want for nominal coefficients, that is, the contingency coefficient, lambda, phi, Cramer's V and uncertainty coefficient. However, it is important to point out that Tshuprow's T is not supported in SPSS (or SAS).

FIGURE 5.4
Cross-tab Statistics Window

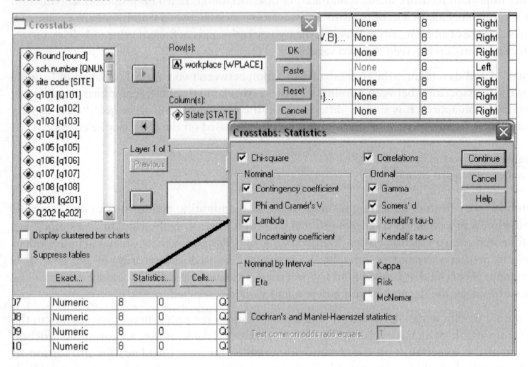

Statistics for Categories

a) *Per cent difference:* Per cent difference,[8] as the name suggests, simply analyses the per cent difference between the first and second columns in either row. It is defined as the simplest of all measures of association. Lets us take an example mentioned in Table 5.1.

TABLE 5.1
Educational Characteristics by Gender: Cell Proportion

Characteristics	Male	Female
Literate	20 (25%)	0 (0%)
Illiterate	60 (75%)	80 (100%)

In this example, the percentage difference is 25 per cent and it will be the same whichever row is selected. We can interpret from this table that gender makes a 25 per cent difference in the literacy levels of the sampled people. It is important to note that the per cent difference is asymmetric. The independent variable forms the columns, while the dependent variable is the row variable and reversing the independent and the dependent variables will lead to a different result.

b) *Yule's Q:* Yule's Q,[9] named after the statistician, Quetelet, is one of the most popular measures of association for categorical data. It is based on the odds ratio principle. It compares each observation with each other observation, termed as pairs. Yule's Q is based on the difference between concordant pairs (those pairs of cases which are higher or lower on both variables) and discordant pair (those pair of cases which are higher on one variable and lower on the other variable). Let us take the example in Table 5.2, where numbers are measured and in this case Q equals $(ad - bc)/(ad + bc)$, which, for the data given in Table 5.2 means Q = (20*60 – 10*40)/(20*60 + 10*40) = 800/1600 = .50.

TABLE 5.2
Educational Characteristics by Gender: Cell Numbers

Characteristics	Male	Female
Literate	$a = 20$	$b = 10$
Illiterate	$c = 40$	$d = 60$

Yule's Q can vary from –1 to +1 symbolising perfect negative to perfect positive associations respectively. Yule's Q is a symmetrical measure and the results do not vary based on which variable is in the row or column.

c) *Yule's Y:* Yule's Y is also based on odds ratio, though it uses the geometric mean of diagonal and off-diagonal pairs to calculate measures of association. It can be expressed mathematically as:

$$Y = \{SQRT(P) - SQRT(Q)\}/\{SQRT(P) + SQRT(Q)\}$$

Like Yule's Q, Yule's Y[10] is also symmetrical in nature and the result does not vary based on which variable is in the row or column. It is important to point out here that like nominal measures of association, which can be easily computed using the SPSS, it does not offer Yule's Q or Yule's Y but it offer gamma, which is identical to Yule's Q for two-by-two tables.

Statistics for Ordinal/Ranked Variable

Ordinal measures are signified by their emphasis on ranking and pairs, for example, assume that researchers asked respondents to indicate their interest in watching movies on a 4-point scale: (1) always, (2) usually, (3) sometimes and (4) never interested. Here the researchers desire relative coefficient from ranking pairs, based on the assumption that rank order of one pair predicts the rank order of the other pair.

a) *Spearman's R:* In certain cases, researchers are required to assess the extent of association between two ordinally-scaled variables. In such cases, Spearman's R is calculated as the measure of association between the ranked variables. It is important to point out that it assumes that the variables under consideration were measured on at least an ordinal scale.

b) *Kendall's tau:* Kendall's tau like Spearman's R is calculated from ordinally-ranked data. Though it is comparable to Spearman's R in terms of its statistical power, its result is quite different in magnitude because of its underlying logic. Siegel and Castellan (1988) express the relationship of the two measures in terms of the inequality:

$$-1 < = 3 * \text{Kendall's tau} - 2 * \text{Spearman's R} < = 1$$

Kendall's tau values vary between –1 and +1, where a negative correlation signifies that as the order of one variable increases, the order of the other variable decreases. A positive correlation signifies an increase in the order of a variable in consonance with increase in the order of the other variable. It is important to point out that while Spearman's R is a regular correlation coefficient as computed from ranks, Kendall's tau can be described as a measure representing probability.

Two different variants of Kendall's tau are computed. These are known as tau-b and tau-c. These measures differ only with regard to how tied ranks are handled as Kendall's tau-b is calculated in case of censored data.

c) *Tau-b:* This is also similar to Somers' d but includes both verson of *T*, *Tx* and *Ty* expressed in the formula:

$$T = \frac{C - D}{(C + D + Tx\, C + Ty + D)}$$

It varies between –1 and +1 only when the table is square in nature, that is, the number of rows is equal to the number of columns.

d) *Tau-c:* Tau-b is generally used when the number of rows and columns in a table are the same; in other cases the use of Tau-c is preferred:

$$Tau\text{-}c = \frac{2m(C - D)}{N^2(M - 1)}$$

m is the smaller of rows or columns

e) *Gamma:* Gamma is another measure of association, which is based on the principle of proportional reduction of error. It is a measure similar to tau, but is stronger and more frequently used. Gamma calculates the number of pairs in a cross-tabulation having the same rank order of inequality on both variables and compares this with the number of pairs having the reverse rank order of inequality on both variables. It takes the difference between concordance and discordance and divides this by the total number of both concordant and discordant pairs and is expressed as:

$$G = \frac{C - D}{C + D}$$

This indicator can range in value from –1 to +1, indicating perfect negative association and perfect positive association, respectively. When the value of gamma is near 0, there is little or no evident association between the two variables. Gamma is a symmetrical measure of association and thus its value is the same regardless of which variable is the dependent variable.

In case two or more subjects are given the same ranks, then gamma[11]statistic is preferred to Spearman's R or Kendall's tau. Gamma is based on similar assumption as used by Spearman's R or Kendall's tau; though in terms of interpretation, it is more similar to Kendall's tau than Spearman's R.

f) *Somers' d:* Somers' d[12] is a measure which is used to predict a one directional relationship. It is an asymmetric measure. In many ways it is similar to gamma except that it considers all those pairs which are tied on one variable but not on the other. The numerator of the equation is the same as that of a gamma measurement, but the denominator adds a value, T, which measures the number of ties on variable x, but not on variable y. The general formula is:

$$G = \frac{C - D}{C + D + T}$$

Though this section has listed various measures of association for ordinal variables, researchers need to carefully select the appropriate coefficient keeping in mind the nature of the data and the research objective (see Box 5.3).

BOX 5.3
Coefficient to Use in Case of Ordinal/Ranked Variables

Though there are various measures of association for ordinal variables, Spearman's R is the most common measure. Of the other measures, Gamma coefficient and Somer's d are fast becoming very popular.

In a nutshell, Gamma, based on proportional reduction of error, provides a somewhat loose interpretation of association, but it is always larger than tau-b, tau-c or Somer's d. Further, tau-b is best for tables having the same number of rows and columns, tau-c for rectangular tables, whereas Somers' d is preferred for asymmetric measures.

Statistics for Mixed Variables

a) *Eta:* Eta squared statistics can be used to measure associations when the independent variable is nominal and the dependent variable is on interval scale. Eta squared is also known as a correlation ratio. It is computed as a proportion of the total variability in the dependent variable that can be accounted for by knowing the categories of the independent variable.

Statistics take the variance of the dependent variable as an index of error by using the mean of the variable to make a prediction of each case. This is compared with the variance in each sub-group of the independent variable and is computed as:

$$n^2 = \frac{\text{original variance} - \text{within group variance}}{\text{original variance}}$$

Eta square is always positive and ranges from 0 to 1.

To assess the association among one nominal and one ordinal variable, the coefficient of determination is used and for describing the association between one ordinal and one interval variable, Jaspen coefficient and multiserial correlation are used.

In SPSS, while going for cross-tab the researcher will notice some statistics options such as Cohen's kappa risk and Cochran-Mantel-Haenszel test. The next section discusses statistics in brief.

b) *Cohen's kappa:* Cohen's kappa is used in cases when tables have the same categories in the columns as in the rows, for example, measuring agreement between two raters. It measures the agreement internal consistency based on a contingency table. Cohen's kappa measures the extent to which two raters give the same ratings to the same set of objects. The set of possible values for one rater forms the columns whereas the set of possible values for the second rater forms the rows. It can be defined as:

Kappa K = [observed concordance – concordance by chance]/[1 – concordance by chance]

c) *Risk:* In the case of tables having two rows and two columns, risk statistics are used for relative risk estimates and the odds ratio.

   (i) Relative risk: The relative risk is the ratio of the yes probability i.e., the probability of an event happening for the two-row groups. It can be defined as:

   Relative risk (RR) = $p1/p2$

   (ii) Odds ratio: Odds ratio, as the name suggests, is a ratio of two odds. Researchers can calculate odds ratio in two ways. In the first case, the researcher can use ratio of two odds and in the other case cross-product ratio can be used. The first way is to use the ratio of two separate odds. The first odds of success in the first row are odds 1 and the second odds of success in the second row are odds 2. Each odd can be defined as:

   odds 1 = $p1/(1 - p1)$
   odds 2 = $p2/(1 - p2)$

d) *Cochran-Mantel-Haenszel and Mantel-Haenszel tests:* In cases where there are more than two explanatory variables, that is, usually one is the explanatory variable and the other is the control variable, it is advised to conduct three tests. That is, (i) Cochran-Mantel-Haenszel test to test the conditional independence of two variables X and Y, (ii) the Mantel-Haenszel test to estimate the strength of its association and (iii) the Breslow-Day test to test the homogeneity of the odds ratio.

DESCRIPTIVE STATISTICS FOR METRIC DATA

Descriptive statistics, as the name suggests, describes the properties of a group or data score. Researchers use descriptive statistics to have a first hand feel of data, that is, in the case of categorical data counts, proportions, rates and ratios are calculated, whereas in the case of quantitative data, measures of distributional shape, location and spread are described.

FREQUENCY DISTRIBUTIONS

Frequency distribution (an arrangement in which the frequencies or percentages of the occurrence of event are shown) is the most important way of describing quantitative data. Further, in case a variable has a wide range of values, researchers may prefer to use a grouped frequency distribution where data values are grouped into intervals, 0–4, 5–9, 10–14, etc., and the frequencies of the intervals are shown. Frequency distribution of data can be expressed in the form of a histogram (see Figure 5.5), frequency polygon and ogive, depending on the frequency or cumulative frequency, which is plotted on the y-axis.

FIGURE 5.5
Frequency Distribution: Histogram

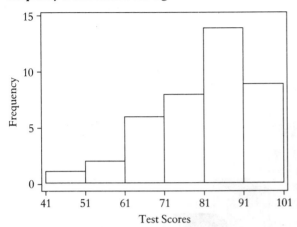

GRAPHIC REPRESENTATION OF DATA

Graphic representation of data is another very effective way of summarizing data in two-dimensional space. Graphical representation of data is a better visual medium of representing data, not only because of its visual appeal but also for interpretation by users. There are various ways in which data can be represented, like bar graphs, line graphs and pie graphs.

A bar graph uses vertical bars to represent the observation of each group, where the height of the bars represents the frequencies on the vertical axis for the group depicted on the horizontal axis (see Figure 5.6a). A line graph uses lines to depict information about one or more variables. Usually it is used to compare information about two variables, but in the case of a single line graph, information is depicted to represent a trend over time, for example, with years on the *x*-axis and the related variable on the *y*-axis (see Figure 5.6b). A pie chart is a circle graph divided into various pieces wherein each piece displays the related information proportional to size. Pie charts are used to display the sizes of parts that make up a whole (see Figure 5.6c). A scatter plot is used to depict the relationship between two quantitative variables, where the independent variable is represented on the horizontal axis and the dependent variable is represented on the vertical axis.

The type of description appropriate to an analysis depends on the nature of data and variable and hence further classification into univariate, bivariate and multivariate analysis. In the case of one variable, it is imperative to describe the shape of distribution through graphs such as histograms, stem-and-leaf plots, or box plots to deconstruct the data's symmetry, dispersion, and modality.

One of the key measures of summarizing univariate data is to ascertain the location of data characterized by its centre. The most common statistical measures of the location of the centre of the data are mean, median and mode. After ascertaining the location of the data, it is imperative to assess the spread of data around its centre. The most common summary measures of spread are

FIGURE 5.6a
Graphical Representation: Bar Chart

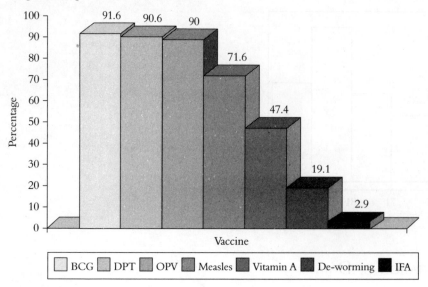

FIGURE 5.6b
Graphical Representation: Line Chart

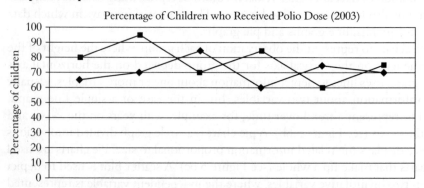

standard deviation, interquartile range and range. There are other measures of distribution such as skewness or kurtosis, which are also commonly used to make useful inferences about data.

UNIVARIATE ANALYSIS

Measures of Central Tendency

Univariate analysis is all about studying the attributes or distribution of a single variable of interest and measures of central tendency are the most important technique in univariate analysis, which

FIGURE 5.6c
Graphical Representation: Pie Chart

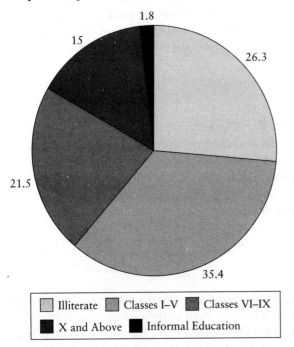

▨ Illiterate	▨ Classes I–V	▨ Classes VI–IX
■ X and Above	■ Informal Education	

provides information about the central location of a distribution. The three most frequently used measures of central tendency, which will be discussed in subsequent sections, are mode, median and mean.

Mode

Mode can be defined as the most frequently occurring value in a group of observations. It is that value in a distribution, which occurs with greatest frequency and is, thus, necessarily not unique.

If the scores for a given sample distributions are:

32   32   35   36   37   38   38   39   39   39   40   40   42   45

Then the mode would be 39 because a score of 39 occurs three times, more than any other score. The mode is determined by finding the attribute, which is most often observed and it can be applied to both quantitative and qualitative data and is very easy to calculate. It can be easily calculated by counting the number of times each attribute or observation occurs in the data.

However, the mode is most commonly employed with nominal variables and is generally less used for other levels. A distribution can have more than one mode, for example, in cases when two or more observations are tied for the highest frequency. Thus, a data set with two observations tied for most occurrences are known as bimodal, and sets of observations with more than two modes are referred to as multimodal.

Mode is very good measure for ascertaining the location of distribution in the case of nominal data, because in that case other measures of location cannot be used. But if the nature of data presents the flexibility to use other measures, mode is not such a good measure of location, because there can be more than one mode or even no mode. When the mean and the median are known, it is possible to estimate the mode for the unimodal distribution using the other two averages as follows:

Mode $\approx$ 3(median) – 2(mean)

Median

Median is defined as the middle value in an ordered arrangement of observations. It is a measure of central tendency if all items are arranged either in ascending or descending order of magnitude. In the case of an ungrouped frequency distribution, if the n values are arranged in ascending or descending order of magnitude, the median is the middle value if n is odd. When n is even, the median is the mean of two middle values. That is, if $X_1, X_2, \ldots, X_N$ is a random sample sorted from smallest value to largest value, then the median is defined as:

$Y = Y_{(N+1)/2}$, if N is odd.

$Y = (Y_{N/2} + Y_{(N/2)+1})/2$, if N is even.

The median is often used to summarize the location of a distribution. In the case of qualitative data, median is the most appropriate measure of central tendency. Even in the case of quantitative data, median provides a better measure of location than the mean when there are some extremely large or small observations. Even in the case of a skewed distribution, the median and the range may be better than other measures to indicate where the observed data are concentrated. Further, the median can be used with ordinal, interval, or ratio measurements and no assumptions need be made about the shape of the distribution. The median is not affected by extreme values and it is not much affected by changes in a few cases.

Mean

The arithmetic mean is the most commonly used and accepted measure of central tendency. It is obtained by adding all observations and dividing the sum by the number of observations. This should be used in the case of interval or ratio data. Its computation can be expressed mathematically by the formula:

Mean $= \bar{x} = \Sigma X_i / n$

The mean uses all of the observations, and each observation affects the mean. In the case of the arithmetic mean, the sum of the deviations of the individual items from the arithmetic mean is 0. In the case of a highly-skewed distribution, the arithmetic mean may get distorted on account of a few items with extreme values, but it is still the most widely used measure of location. Mean, as a measure of central tendency, is a preferred indicator both as a description of the data and as an estimate of the parameter. It is important to point out that for the calculation of the mean, data needs to be on an interval or ratio scale.

Mean has various important mathematical properties, which make it a universally used statistical indicator. According to the central limit theorem, as sample size increases the distribution of mean of a random sample taken from any population approaches normal distribution. It is this property of mean which makes it quite useful in inferential statistics and estimation. Further, just by looking at the position of the mean vis-à-vis other measures of central tendency, an inference can be made about the nature of distribution (see Box 5.4).

BOX 5.4
Skewed Distribution and Position of Mean, Median and Mode

In case a variable is normally distributed, then the mean, median and mode all fall at the same place. Though, when the variable is skewed to the left, the mean is pulled to the left the most, the median is pulled to the left the second most, and the mode is least affected. Therefore, mean < median < mode.

In case the variable is skewed to the right, then the mean is pulled to the right the most, the median is pulled to the right the second most and the mode is least affected. Therefore, mean > median > mode.

Based on the observation on position of mean, median and mode as explained here, researchers can conclude that if the mean is less than the median in observed distribution, then the distribution is definitely skewed to the left and in case the mean is greater than the median, then the distribution is skewed to the right.

Besides arithmetic mean, some other averages used frequently in data analysis are described next.

Geometric Mean

Geometric mean is another measure of central tendency, like the arithmetic mean, but is quite different from it because of its computation. The geometric mean of n positive values is computed by multiplying all n positive values and taking n-th root of the resulting value. It is preferred over the arithmetic mean in case some values are quite large in magnitude than other values.

Harmonic Mean

Harmonic mean is usually computed for variables expressed as rate per unit of time. In such cases, harmonic mean provides the correct mean. The harmonic mean (H) is computed as:

$$H = n/[\Sigma(1/x(i))]$$

The harmonic mean is never larger than the arithmetic mean and the geometric mean and the arithmetic mean is never less than the geometric mean and harmonic mean.

A few of the more common alternative location measures are:

Mid-mean

Mid-mean, as the name suggests, computes the mean using the data between the 25th and 75th percentiles.

Trimmed Mean

Trimmed mean is a special measure of the central tendency, which is very useful in case of outlier values as it is computed by trimming 5 per cent of the points in both the lower and upper tails. It can also be defined as the mean for data between the 5th and 95th percentiles.

Winsorized Mean

Winsorized mean is very similar to trimmed mean. In winsorized mean, instead of trimming 5 per cent of the points in both the lower and upper tails, all data values below the 5th percentile are made equal to the 5th percentile and all data greater than the 95th percentile are set equal to the 95th percentile before calculating the mean.

Mid-range

Mid-range is defined as the average of the smallest and the largest value taken from the distribution and is represented as:

Mid-range = (smallest + largest)/2

It is important to point out that the mid-mean, trimmed mean and winsorized mean are not affected greatly by the presence of outliers and in the case of normal symmetric distribution, their estimate is also closer to the mean. The mid-range, based on the average of two extreme values, is not very useful as a robust indicator for calculating the average.

Shape of Distribution

Skewed Distribution

Skewed distribution summarizes the shape of distribution. It measures the extent to which the sample distribution deviates from normal distribution. It refers to the asymmetry of the distribution around its mean. As a result, unlike symmetrical distribution, in the case of skewed distribution all measures of central tendency fall at different point. Skewness can be computed by the following formula:

Skewness = $\Sigma(x_i - \bar{x})^3/[(n - 1)S^3]$, where n is at least 2

Based on the formula it is clear that skewness will take on a value of 0 when the distribution is symmetrical in nature. A positively-skewed distribution is asymmetrical in nature and is characterized by long tails extending to the right, that is, in the positive direction. For example, in the case of a difficult examination, very few students would score high marks and the majority would fail mis-erably. The resulting distribution would most likely be positively skewed.

In the case of a positively-skewed distribution, the variable is skewed to the right (see Figure 5.7). Thus, the mean is pulled to the right the most, the median is pulled to the right the second most, and the mode is least affected. Therefore, the mean is greater than the median and the median is greater than the mode. It is very easy to remember this because in a positively-skewed distribution, the extreme scores are larger, thus the mean is larger than the median.

A negatively-skewed distribution is asymmetric in nature and is characterized by long tails extending to the left, that is, in the negative direction (see Figure 5.8). In the case of a negative distribution, the variable is skewed to the left. Thus, the mean is pulled to the left the most, the median is pulled to the left the second most, and the mode is least affected.

FIGURE 5.7
Positively-skewed Distribution

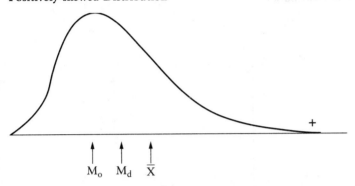

FIGURE 5.8
Negatively-skewed Distribution

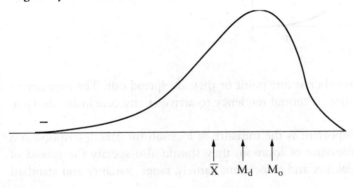

Kurtosis

Skewness refers to the symmetrical nature of distribution, whereas kurtosis refers to peakedness of the curve (see Figure 5.9). It is computed by the formula:

Kurtosis $= \Sigma(x_i - \bar{x})^4/[(n-1)S^4]$, where n is at least 2

Standard normal distribution has kurtosis[13] of +3 irrespective of the mean or standard deviation of distribution. A distribution having a kurtosis value of more than 3 is more peaked than a normal distribution and is termed as being leptokurtic in nature. A distribution having a value of less than 3 is said to be flatter than a normal distribution and is also known as platykurtic.

Thus, before starting an analysis it is quite useful to have a look at the data. It would provide information about the measure of central tendency and the shape of distribution.

Spread of the Distribution/Measures of Variability

The measure of central tendency does not capture the variability in distribution; hence measure of spread or dispersion is also very essential. Spread refers to the extent of variation among cases,

FIGURE 5.9
Figure Showing Kurtosis (Peaked Nature of Distribution)

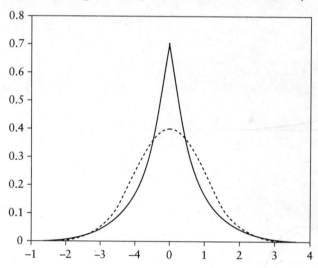

that is, whether cases are clustered together at one point or they are spread out. The measure of dispersion is as essential as the measure of central tendency to arrive at any conclusive decision about the nature of the data.

The measure of dispersion is as important as the measure of location for data description and whenever researchers describe the measure of location, they should also specify the spread of distribution. Statistics measuring variability and dispersion, namely, range, variance and standard deviation are discussed next.

Range

Range is the simplest measure of dispersion and is used widely whenever a variable is measured at least at the ordinal level but cannot be used with nominal variables because the measure makes sense only when cases are ordered.

It is computed as the difference between the highest and lowest value. Range is based solely on the extreme values, thus it cannot truly reveal the body of measurement. A range of 0 means there is no variation in the cases, but unlike the index of dispersion, the range has no upper limit. Whenever range is mentioned, its upper and lower limits are mentioned to make a reader aware about the spread.

Quartiles

Median divides a data set into two equal halves; similarly, quartile divides an arranged data set equally into four groups. The method used to find the position of quartiles is same as that used for the median. The lower quartile, represented by Q1, defines a position where 25 per cent of the values are smaller and 75 per cent are larger. The second quartile is equivalent to the median and divides data into two equal halves. The upper quartile represented by Q3 defines a position, where 75 per cent of the values are smaller and 25 per cent are larger.

Percentiles

Percentiles use a similar concept as that of quartiles and is widely used when data are ranked from the lowest to the highest value. The n-th percentile like the quartile represents a point, which separates the lower n per cent of measurement from the upper $(100 - n)$ per cent and 25th percentile corresponds to the first quartile Q1, etc.

The advantage of percentiles is that they may be subdivided into 100 parts. Quartiles and percentiles are also referred to as quintiles. Besides assessing the spread of distribution, percentile also provides important information about the relative standing of a score in the distribution (see Box 5.6).

Inter-quartile Range

The inter-quartile range (IQR) contains half of the measurements taken and is centred upon the median and thus is described as a good measure of dispersion. It does not have special properties of standard deviation but is unaffected by the presence of outliers in the data.

The lower quartile defines a position where 25 per cent of the values are smaller and 75 per cent are larger and the upper quartile define a position where 75 per cent of the values are smaller. These two quartiles, represented as Q1 and Q3, cut the upper and lower 25 per cent of the cases from the range. The IQR is defined as difference between the upper and lower quartile.

$$IQR = Q3 - Q1$$

Inter-quartile range, like range, requires at least an ordinal level of measurement, but unlike the range it is appropriately sensitive to outliers.

BOX 5.5
Measures of Relative Standing

Measures of relative standing provide very important information about the position of a score in relation to the other scores in a distribution of data. Percentile rank is one such very commonly used measure of relative standing. It tells researchers about the percentage of scores that would fall below a specified score. A percentile rank of 70 indicates that 70 per cent of the scores would fall below that score.

In case researchers do not want to use percentile ranks, they can use the z score as a measure of relative standing. A z score tells researchers about the standard deviations (SD) a raw score falls from the mean. A SD of 3 indicates that a score falls below three standard deviations above the mean. A SD of –2.0 indicates that the score falls two standard deviations below the mean.

Mean Absolute Deviation (MAD)

Mean squared deviation is obtained by dividing the sum of the squared deviation by sample size, i.e., n. Researchers also argue that dividing the sum by $n - 1$ provides a better and unbiased estimate. Mathematically it can be expressed as:

$$MAD = \Sigma |(x_i - \bar{x})|/n$$

Mean absolute deviation is widely used as a measure of variability. But unlike range and quartile deviation, its computation takes into account every observation and, as a result, is effected by outliers. It is, therefore, often used in small samples that include extreme values.

Variance and Standard Deviation

The standard deviation provides the best measure of dispersion for interval/ratio measurements and is the most widely used statistical measure after mean. It provides the average measurement of data from mean.

The variance, symbolized by s^2, is another measure of variability. The standard deviation, represented by s, is defined as the positive square root of the variance. Variance is expressed by the formula:

$$s^2 = \frac{\sum_{i=1}^{N}(X_i - \overline{X})^2}{N-1}$$

Variance makes deviation much larger than it actually is, hence to remove the effect they are un-squared by taking the square root of the squared deviations in the process of computing standard deviation.

Coefficient of Variation

Coefficient of variation (CV) is defined as the absolute relative deviation with respect to the sample mean and s calculated by dividing standard deviation by sample mean, expressed in percentage:

$$CV = 100 \ |S/\bar{x}|\%$$

Coefficient of variation is a ratio of two similar terms; hence it is independent of the unit of measurement. It reflects the variation in a distribution relative to the mean. But unlike deviation, confidence intervals for the coefficient of variation are not used as they are very tedious to calculate.

Coefficient of variation is used to represent the relationship of the standard deviation to the mean and it also tells about the 'representativeness' of the mean observed in a sample to that of the population. It is believed that, when CV is less than 10 per cent, the estimate is accepted as a true measure of the population.

All measures of variability such as range, quartile, standard deviation, etc., are not only very useful indicators for measuring the spread of distribution, but they also provide useful information about shape of the distribution (see Box 5.7).

BIVARIATE ANALYSIS

Often in practical situations, researchers are interested in describing associations between variables. They try to ascertain how two variables are related with each other, that is, whether a change in one affects the other. The measures of association depend on the nature of the data and could be positive, negative or neutral. The next section further explains the concept and measurement of relationship in detail.

BOX 5.6
Interpreting Spread of Distribution

There are various ways in which the spread of distribution can be interpreted. In one such way, researchers can interpret the spread of a distribution by just looking at the proportion of cases, which are covered by a measure of dispersion, for example, in the case of an interquartile range, researchers can safely conclude that the measure always cover 50 per cent of the cases.

Measures characterizing spread of distribution also provide important information about the shape of distribution. Based on measures such as range, quartiles and standard deviation, researchers can infer about the shape of distribution, that is, whether the distribution is close to a normal distribution, whether it is symmetrical or whether it follows an unknown or 'irregular' shape.

In case the distribution of the raw score is close to a normal distribution, then researchers can conclude that approximately 95 per cent of the cases would fall within four SD bands from the mean. In case the distribution is normal and symmetric, researchers can conclude that at least 89 per cent of the cases would fall within four SD bands from the mean. Further, in case distribution is multimodal or asymmetric, the researcher can still conclude that a minimum, 75 per cent of the cases would be covered within the four-SD from mean.

THE CONCEPT OF RELATIONSHIP

The concept of associating relationship is key to all measures of bivariate analysis. Thus, while defining relationship, researchers can define one variable as a function of another variable. Researchers can then assess whether a change in one variable results in change in the other variable to ascertain the relationship. It is important to point out that the relationship between two variables could be a simple association or it could be a causal relationship.

Whatever may be the nature of the relationship, the first step in examining the relationship starts with the construction of a bivariate table. Usually, bivariate tables are set up with the independent variable as the variable in the columns and the dependent variable in the rows.

MEASUREMENT OF RELATIONSHIP

Measures of relationship, in case of association is indicated by correlation coefficients, which signify the strength and the direction of association between the variables. Further, in case of regression analysis, researchers can determine the strength and measure of relationship by ascertaining the value of the regression coefficient.

MEASURES OF ASSOCIATION BETWEEN TWO VARIABLES

There are many ways of evaluating the type, direction and strength of such relationships. Measures may include two or more variables. Selection of appropriate measures of association depend on several factors such as type of distribution, that is, whether the variable follows a discrete distribution or a continuous distribution, data characteristics and measurement level of data. For example, in case both variables are nominal then Yule's Q, lambda test or contingency coefficient can be used.

ANALYSING AND REPORTING ASSOCIATION BETWEEN VARIABLES

Researchers while analysing association need to concentrate on ascertaining several points, that is, whether an association exists and if an association exists, what is the extent of the association? What really is the direction of the association? And what is the nature of the association?

To answer these questions it is imperative at the first stage to analyse a batch of data by depicting them in tabular or graphic form. In the case of nominal and ordinal data, researchers do not have to go for complex analysis; they can ascertain the existence of an association by inspecting the tables.

Besides ascertaining the existence of an association, it is imperative to assess whether the association is statistically significant or large enough to be important. The direction of an association also provides very important information about the measure of association in case of ordinal or higher variables, though in the case of nominal variables, it is meaningless. Thus, in the majority of cases, both positive and negative association can be defined where a positive value indicates that with the increase or decrease of one variable, the other variable also increases/decreases together and a negative value indicates that as one variable increases, the other decreases.

Researcher can also ascertain the nature of the association by simply inspecting the tabular or graphic display of a bivariate distribution. For example, researchers can easily conclude from a scatter plot about the linear nature of relationship, that is, a constant amount of change in one variable being associated with a constant amount of change in the other variable. Further, when the dependent variable is on an interval-ratio scale, regression analysis can also provide the measure, extent and strength of association between the dependent and the independent variable. It measures the extent of variance in the dependent variable, which is explained by the independent variable.

CORRELATION

Correlation is one of the most widely used measures of association between two or more variables. In its simplest form it signifies the relationship between two variables, that is, whether an increase in one variable results in the increase of the other variable. In a way, measures of correlation are employed to explore the presence or absence of a correlation, that is, whether or not there is correlation between the variables in an equation. The correlation coefficient also describes the direction of the correlation, that is, whether it is positive or negative, and the strength of the correlation, that is, whether an existing correlation is strong or weak.

Though there are various measures of correlation between nominal or ordinal data, Pearson product-moment correlation coefficient is a measure of linear association between two interval-ratio variables. The measure, represented by the letter r, varies from -1 to $+1$. A zero correlation indicates that there is no correlation between the variables.

A correlation coefficient indicates both the type of correlation as well as the strength of the relationship. The coefficient value determines the strength whereas the sign indicates whether variables change in the same direction or in opposite directions. A positive correlation indicates that as one variable increases, the other variable also increases in a similar way. A negative correlation, signified by a negative sign, indicates that there is an inverse relationship between the two variables, that is, an increase in one variable is associated with the decrease in the other variable. A zero correlation suggests that there is no systematic relationship between the two variables and any change in one variable is not associated with change in the other variable.

As a rule, correlation is considered to be very low if the coefficient has a value under 0.20 and is considered as low if the value ranges between 0.21 and 0.40. A coefficient value of above 0.70 is considered high.

Linear Correlation

Correlation, as defined earlier, measures both the nature and extent of the relationship between two or more variables. There are various measures of correlation, which are usually employed for nominal and ordinal data, but in most instances researcher use the Pearson product-moment correlation for interval-scaled data. Though it is important here to specify that correlation is a specific measure of association and not all measures of association can be defined in terms of correlation (see Box 5.8).

Pearson's correlation summarizes the relationship between variables by a straight line. The straight line is called the least squares line, because it is constructed in such a way that the sum of the squared distances of all the data points from the line is the lowest possible.

Significance of Correlations

It is imperative to assess whether the identified relationship between variables is statistically significant, that is, whether a correlation actually exists in the population. In other words, significance tries to assess whether variables in the population are related in the same way as shown in the study.

Significance test of correlation is based on the assumption that the distribution of the residual values follows the normal distribution, and that the variability of the residual values is the same for all values. Significance results are also a function of sample size. But, it is suggested, based on the Monte Carlo studies, that in case the sample size is 50 or more then it is very unlikely that serious bias would occur due to sampling, and in case of sample size of more than 100, researchers should not worry about the normality assumptions.

Significance test can be easily done by comparing computer-generated p value with the predetermined significance level, which in most cases is 0.05. In case the p value is less than 0.05, we can assume that the correlation is significant and it is a reflection of true population characteristic.

Based on the line of linear correlation between two variables, researchers can use 'multiple correlations', which is the correlation of multiple independent variables with a single dependent variable. But in case researchers want to control the other variable in multiple correlation variables, he can use 'partial correlation' by controlling other variables.

Coefficient of Determination

It is important to point out that the coefficient of correlation measures the type and strength of relationship but it does not provide information about causation. It can, however, offer very useful information and if squared, the coefficient of correlation gives the coefficient of determination. It describes the common degree of variability shared by two variables.

The coefficient of determination states the proportion of variance in one variable that is explained by the other variable. In case the coefficient of determination is 0.71, then it means that 71 per cent of the variance is accounted for by the other variable.

Correlation for Ordinal Variables

Ordinal measures are characterized by the presence of ranking and pairs. There are several measures such as Spearman's rho, gamma or Somers' d, Kendall's tau, which can be computed to determine the correlation between ordinal pairs. Gamma, Somers' d and Kendall's tau have already been explained in detail. Let us take a look at Spearman's rho to assess how it is different from other measures.

Spearman's Rho

Spearman's rho is very useful measure of association between two ordinal variables. It computes correlation between two ordered sets of variables by predicating one set from the other. Further, rho for ranked data equals Pearson's r for ranked data.

The formula for Spearman's rho is:

$$rho = \frac{1 - 6\Sigma D^2}{N(N^2 - 1)}$$

The only factor, which needs to be computed, is D, defined as the difference in ranks.

Correlation for Dichotomies

Dichotomies represent a special case of categorical data having only two categories, that is, 'yes' or 'no'. Researchers can, in fact, use various measures for assessing correlation for dichotomies such as bi-serial correlation and phi.

Bi-serial Correlation

Bi-serial correlation is a special case of correlation, which is used in the case of correlation between an interval variable and a dichotomous variable.

Phi

Phi is a special measure of association for dichotomous variables. Its value ranges from −1 to +1 and is the same as Pearson correlation, if computed from SPSS and both use the same algorithms.

BOX 5.7
Correlation as a Measure of Linear Association

Besides the layman, sometimes even researchers use the word 'correlation' as a synonym for 'association' forgetting the fact that the Pearson product-moment correlation coefficient or any other correlation coefficient for that matter is a measure of association for a specific set of variables computed in a specific way. Thus, while computing the measure of association such as gamma, we cannot use the word correlation and association interchangeably.

Further, in the majority of the cases, when researchers talk of association, they mean linear association because if the association is non-linear, the two variables might have a strong association but the correlation coefficient could be very small or even zero. In case the relationship is not linear then researchers should use another measure of association, called 'eta' instead of the Pearson coefficient (Loether and McTavish, 1988).

GENERAL LINEAR MODEL

The general linear model refers to a set of analysis techniques, which are based on linear models of single variables. Analysis of variance and simple regression are special cases of the general linear model. Overall, this class of analyses includes:

a) Simple and multiple linear regression.
b) Analysis of variance.
c) Analysis of covariance.
d) Mixed model analysis of variance.

The general linear model in modelling terminology, can be expressed as: $y = Xb + e$ where:

y is response variable,
X is explanatory variable,
b is a vector of unknown populations parameters, and
e is error component.

The general linear model expresses the response variable as function of the explanatory variable. In the case of analysis of variance, b would signify the unknown treatment effects and X the known criterion variable. For analysis of covariance, b signifies both treatment effects and regression coefficients, and X characterizes both explanatory and response variables.

As mentioned earlier, the general linear model assumes relationships to be linear. Hence, it uses the linear estimation technique to estimate the variance of unknown population parameters and may be estimated by:

a) Ordinary least squares (OLSE).
b) Weighted least squares (WLSE).
c) Generalized least squares (GLS).

In fact, several important statistical software packages include options for general linear model analysis. SPSS provides the facility of analysing the general linear model and researchers can access the option by clicking 'general linear model' under the 'analyse' menu option. SPSS further provides the facility of univariate, multivariate, repeated measures and variance components (see Figure 5.10).

FIGURE 5.10
General Linear Model Using SPSS

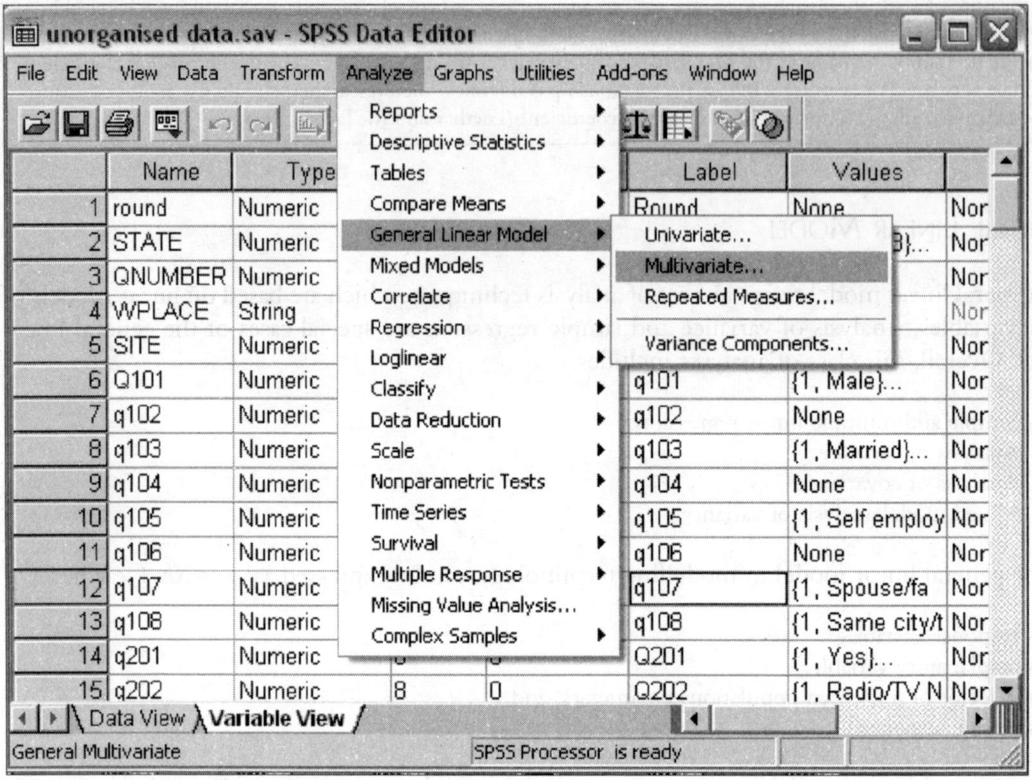

REGRESSION

Regression is one of the most frequently used techniques in social research. It is used in estimating the value of one variable based on the value of another variable. It does so by finding a line of best fit using ordinary least square method.[14] The relation between variables could be linear or non-linear and thus the regression equation could also be linear or non-linear. The most common form of regression, however, is linear regression, where the dependent variable is related to the independent variable in a linear way. The linear regression equation takes the following form:

$$Y = a + bx$$

Where Y is the dependent variable and x is the independent variable.

In a regression equation, *a* is defined as the intercept and *b* is known as the regression coefficient. The value of *b* indicates the change in the dependent variable for every unit change in the independent variable.

The regression line is a straight line, which is constructed by means of the method of least squares. The regression line is placed in such a position that the square of the vertical distance of observations from the line are the smallest possible. The line is also described as the line of best fit as it reduces the variance of all distances from the line. Further, researchers need to assess the distribution of data around the line of best fit to ascertain homoscedasticity and heteroscedasticity (see Box 5.8).

The regression coefficient is another widely used measure of association between two interval-ratio variables. The regression coefficient is an asymmetric measure of association and that is why the regression coefficient of the dependent variable on the independent variable is different from the regression coefficient of the independent variable on the dependent variable. Further, whether researchers should use an asymmetric measure of association or a symmetric measure depends on the application of the regression method. In case researchers are trying to predict one variable by another variable, then an asymmetric measure is preferred.

In regression analysis, the variable we are trying to predict is defined as the dependent variable and the variable that is used to predict the dependent variable, is known as the independent variable. Even the name clearly signifies that the dependent variable in some way depends upon the independent variable for prediction. Further, while plotting the variables to draw the regression line, by convention the dependent variable is plotted along the vertical axis and the independent variable along the horizontal axis.

By using the regression formula, researchers can compute R-squared, which measures the strength of an association in a bivariate regression and is also called as the coefficient of determination. It varies between 0 and 1 and represents the proportion of total variation in the dependent variable, which is accounted for by variation in the dependent variable. The regression coefficient is closely related to the Pearson product-moment correlation. The regression coefficient of the transformed variables (variables are transformed to *z* scores) is equal to the correlation coefficient.

BOX 5.8
Homoscedasticity and Heteroscedasticity

Homoscedasticity (homo = same, scedasis = scattering) as the name suggests, is used to describe the distribution of data points around the line of best fit and signifies that the data points are equally distributed around the line of best fit. *Heteroscedasticity* is the opposite of homoscedasticity and signifies that the data points are not equally distributed around the line of best fit or that the data is clustered around the line of best fit.

STATISTICAL INFERENCE

Statistical inferences, as the name suggests, are a set of methods, which use sample characteristics as inference to predict the nature of populations from which they were drawn. It is a way of generalizing from a sample to a population with an amount of confidence and certainty, usually represented in the form of a confidence level.

The two traditional forms of statistical inferences are estimation and hypothesis testing, which are most widely used by researchers. Estimation predicts the parameter of a population whereas hypothesis testing provides answer to hypothesis formulated by researchers by providing evidence to accept or reject the hypothesis.

INFERENTIAL STATISTICS

Inferential statistics represents a set of statistics, which is used to make inferences about a population from samples selected from the population. Besides estimating population parameters, it tests the statistical significance, to assess how accurately a sample predicts the population parameters. Inferential statistics are also used to test sample differences between two samples, to assess whether differences actually exist or are there just due to chance.

Inferential statistics are generally used for two purposes: (i) tests for difference of means and (ii) test for statistical significance, which is further subdivided into parametric and non-parametric, depending upon the distribution of parameters of population distribution characteristics.

ESTIMATION

Estimation assigns a value to a population parameter based on the value of sample statistics. The value assigned to a population based on the value of a sample statistics is defined as an estimate of the population parameter. The sample statistics used to estimate a population parameter is called an estimate of the population.

The process of estimation involves steps such as selection of a sample; collecting the required information, computing the value of sample statistics and assigning value to the corresponding parameter. It is important to point out that for the purpose of estimation, it is imperative that samples are selected from the population in a probabilistic manner, that is, samples are selected using a random process and each member of the population has a known, non-zero probability of being drawn.

Estimation, as a procedure is widely used to estimate population parameters by providing two-part answers: a point estimate of a parameter, which estimates a point value of population and an interval estimate of the parameter.

There are two forms of estimation: (i) point estimation and (ii) interval estimation.

Point estimation

Point estimate provides a single point estimate of a population parameter, which is most likely to represent the parameter. Researchers can select a sample to compute the value of sample statistics for a particular sample to give a point estimate of the corresponding population parameter, for example, a sample proportion may be viewed as the maximum likelihood point estimator of the population proportion.

Sample mean calculated from a selected sample is defined as the unbiased estimate of the population parameter, because the population mean would in anyway be the arithmetic average of all members of the population and the sample mean is the arithmetic average of all members of the sample. Besides, mean and standard deviation, other population parameters such as proportion can also be estimated from sample statistics. For example, to answer the question about the proportion of households that have access to television in rural areas, we can use the proportion having access to television from a simple random sample of households to make a point estimate of the proportion having access to television.

Inferential statistics and the process of estimation is based on the assumption that the sample is selected using a random selection process. But it is not practical in most instances to strictly adhere to a simple random sampling method and researchers often have to resort to complex stratified designs. In complex stratified designs, every member of the population has an unequal but known probability associated with it. Thus, researchers can still estimate the population parameter from the sample. The procedure becomes slightly more complicated, but the statistical principles remain the same.

Each sample taken from the population is expected to provide a different value of sample statistics and thus the population parameter estimated from the sample would also depend on the sample selected for estimation. It is believed that only one sample in a million would truly reflect the population.

A point estimate provides a single number to represent the population parameter, which, as discussed earlier, does not necessarily reflect the true value of the parameter. Thus, whenever we use point estimation we should always calculate the margin of error associated with the point of estimation. Interval estimates, the subject of the next section, enable us to describe the level of sampling variability in our procedures.

Interval Estimation

Interval estimation, as the name suggests, provides an interval that has a calculated likelihood of capturing the parameter, that is, instead of assigning a single value to a population parameter, an interval is constructed around the point estimate, and a probabilistic estimate that this interval contains the corresponding population parameter is made.

Each interval is constructed with regard to a given confidence level and is called the confidence interval. The confidence level associated with a confidence interval states with how much confidence we can say that that interval contains the true population parameter. A confidence interval constructed to estimate population is bound by lower and upper confidence limits. When we express it as a probability it is called confidence coefficient and is denoted by $1-\alpha$. It signifies that a 95 per cent confidence interval for the population will capture the parameter under study 95 per cent of the time, that is, even if the study is repeated an infinite number of times, 95 per cent of the times the value will fall in the calculated interval and only in 5 per cent of the times it might fail to capture the parameter.

But, in reality, we do not actually draw multiple samples and do not have the flexibility to repeat the study an infinite number of times. Thus, for a single sample, researchers can claim that they are 95 per cent confident that the interval reflects the true population mean.

In a bid to construct an interval estimate, researchers first need to choose a confidence level and then need to use the value of that confidence level to calculate the confidence limits. Researchers can select any value of confidence level based on tighter estimate they want to predict, but usually by convention it is 95 per cent in the social studies. In other words, to increase the likelihood that an interval will reflect the population parameter, the interval needs to be broadened.

Confidence Intervals for Proportions, Correlations and Means Correlations

Besides reporting the confidence interval for means, researchers can also compute confidence intervals for proportions, correlations and means correlations in a similar way. Researchers can draw a random sample of n cases from a population to ascertain the correlation between two variables, X and Y, in that population. From the sample, researchers can easily calculate the estimate of the correlation coefficient r, around which a 95 per cent confidence intervals can be constituted to estimate the population correlation ρ.

Proportions

In a similar way, researchers can draw a random sample of n cases from a population to estimate the unknown population proportion, say π. In the sample, the proportion of elements with the characteristic is p. Researcher can similarly construct a confidence interval of say around 95 per cent on π around p. The confidence interval would signify that around 95 per cent of the times, the estimates of proportion would fall in the mentioned interval.

Hypothesis Testing

A hypothesis is an assumption that we make about a population parameter. The hypothesis, which we wish to test, is called the null hypothesis because it implies that there is no difference between the true parameter and the hypothesis value so the difference between the true value and hypothesis value is nil. Hypothesis testing, as described by Neyman and Pearson, provides for certain decision rules about the null hypothesis. Hypothesis tests are procedures for making rational decisions about the reality of effects. Hypothesis testing starts with an assumption of 'no differences'.

Steps in Hypothesis Testing

Researchers while testing hypothesis usually employ the following steps, in a sequential manner to accept or reject null hypothesis.

a) Formulating a null and alternate hypothesis.
b) Selecting of appropriate level of significance.
c) Deciding on the location of critical region, based on the significance level.
d) Selecting an appropriate test statistics to find the relevant critical value of the chosen statistics from test statistics table, to define the boundary of the critical region.

e) Computing the observed value of the choosen statistics from the sample observations using test statistics.

f) Comparing the sample value of the chosen statistics with the tabulated value and if the computed statistics fall in the critical region, researchers can reject the null hypothesis, otherwise they can suggest that they do not have enough evidence to reject the null hypothesis and hence can accept an alternate hypothesis.

Null and Alternate Hypothesis

As mentioned earlier, null hypothesis assumes no difference between treatments or groups whereas an alternative hypothesis assumes some kind of difference between treatments or groups. Researchers usually aim to support the alternative hypothesis by showing that the data do not support the null hypothesis.

$$H_0: \mu_1 = \mu_2$$
$$H_1: \mu_1 \neq \mu_2$$

In this example, the null hypothesis assumes that the group means are equal while the alternative hypothesis assumes that the group means are not equal. Researchers can also define null hypothesis and alternative hypothesis in different sets of ways such as:

$$H_0: \mu_1 = \mu_2$$
$$H_1: \mu_1 > \mu_2$$

Where the null hypothesis is the same as in the previous example but the alternate hypothesis assumes that the second group mean is larger than the first.

Choosing a Level of Significance and Location of the Critical Region

The next step after the formulation of the null hypothesis is to choose a level of significance. The level of significance is defined as the probability a researcher is willing to accept or reject the null hypothesis when that hypothesis is true. In common practice a significance level of 0.05 is taken as the standard for a two-tailed test. The level of significance can vary depending on the nature and demand of the study.

The location of the critical region and the rejection region depends on the level of significance and type of test, that is one-tailed or two-tailed test. It is part of the sample space (critical region) where the null hypothesis H_0 is rejected. The size of this region is determined by the probability (α) of the sample point falling in the critical region when H_0 is true. α is also known as the level of significance, the probability of the value of the random variable falling in the critical region. Further, it is important to point out that the term statistical significance refers only to the rejection of a null hypothesis at some level of α and signifies that the observed difference between the sample statistic and the mean of the sampling distribution did not occur by chance alone. Lets take an example wherein $\alpha = 0.05$. We can draw the appropriate picture and find the z score for -0.025 and 0.025 (see Figure 5.11). The outside regions are called the rejection regions.

FIGURE 5.11
Figure Showing the Rejection Region for Z Score of –0.025 and 0.025

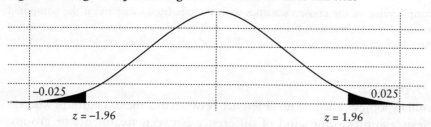

We call the shaded region the rejection region since if the value of z falls in this region we can say that the null hypothesis is very unlikely and we can reject the null hypothesis. It is important to note that the example given here shows the location of the critical region in the case of a two-tailed test. It is also important to point out at this point that if the alternative hypothesis has the form 'not equal to', then the test is said to be a two-tailed test and if the alternative hypothesis is an inequality (< or >), the test is one-tailed one (see Box 5.9).

BOX 5.9
Decision to Choose One-tailed Test or Two-tailed Test

> The researcher's decision to select a one-tailed test or a two-tailed test depends on the research objective and alternative hypothesis formulated. For example, in case of two sample t tests, the null hypothesis states that the mean of one sample is equal to the mean from another sample and in case of the two-tailed test, the alternative hypothesis would test that the mean of the two samples are not equal. The alternate hypothesis for a one-tailed test could have tested that the mean of one sample is greater than the mean calculated from another sample. Though in terms of statistics, the difference lies in the probability of area selected, that is, 5 per cent, 1 per cent or 0.1 per cent.

Let us take an example of a one-tailed test at a significance level of 0.05 with Z as the test statistics (see Figure 5.12). In this case the z score that corresponds to 0.05 is –1.96.

The critical region is the area that lies to the left of –1.96. If the z value is less than –1.96, then we will reject the null hypothesis and accept the alternative hypothesis. If it is greater than –1.96, we will fail to reject the null hypothesis and say that the test was not statistically significant.

Choosing Appropriate Test Statistics

The next step after deciding on the level of significance is to choose the appropriate test statistics. It is believed that:

a) If researchers know the detail of the parent population, they may apply the Z transformation statistics irrespective of the normality of the population and irrespective of the sample size.
b) If the variance of the parent population is unknown but the size of the sample is large, researchers may still apply the Z statistics since the estimate of the population variance from a large sample is a satisfactory estimate of true variance of population.

If the variance of the parent population is unknown and our sample is small we may apply the t statistics provided the true population is normal as for t statistics normality is crucial.

FIGURE 5.12
Figure Showing the Rejection Region for a One-tailed Test

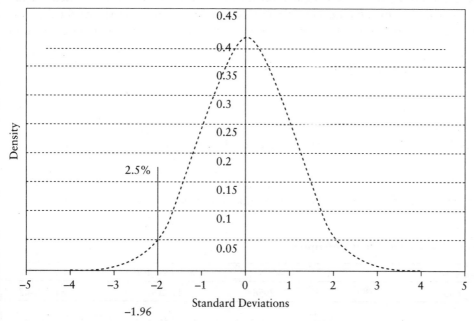

Deciding on the Acceptance and Rejection of a Hypothesis

Theoretically, at the next stage, researchers compute the observed value of the chosen statistics from the sample observations, using relevant formulae. Then to decide on the fate of the hypothesis, sample value of the chosen statistics is compared with the theoretical value that defines the critical region. If the observed value of the statistics falls in the critical region we reject the null hypothesis, otherwise we accept the null hypothesis.

In practice, though, researchers use computer programmes to decide on the acceptance and rejection of hypothesis. Most computer programmes compute p value and based on the value of p a decision is taken on the acceptance or rejection of the null hypothesis. P value is defined as the probability of getting a value of the test statistics as different or more different from the null hypothesis as specified by the significance level of the test. Thus, it is the probability of wrongly rejecting the null hypothesis if it is in fact true. It does so by comparing p value with the significance level and, if the p value is smaller than the significance level, the result is significant. In terms of null hypothesis and alternate hypothesis, it is true that smaller the p value, the more convincing is the rejection of the null hypothesis.

As mentioned earlier, nowadays all statistical software compute p value based on which we can comment about the hypothesis result. Researchers can compute almost all values such as sample mean, standard deviation and even p value corresponding to each test statistics using SPSS. The output generated has a standard error of the sample mean, t statistic, degrees of freedom and the all important p value.

Let us take the example of one-sample t test to compare the mean score of a sample to a known value and usually, the known value is a population mean. In SPSS it can be computed via the Analyse menu, Compare Means and One-sample t Test. Researchers then need to move the dependent variable into the Test Variables box and type in the value they wish to compare the sample to in the box called Test Value. In the present example, we are comparing mother's age at marriage in the sample to a known population value of say 21 years. The two proposed hypothesis in this case would be:

Hypotheses
Null: There is no significant difference between the sample mean and the population mean.
Alternate: There is a significant difference between the sample mean and the population mean.

SPSS Output   Table 5.3 is a sample output of a one-sample t test. We compared the mean level of female age at marriage for our sample to a known population value of 21 years (see Table 5.3).

TABLE 5.3
Testing Hypothesis: One-sample T Test Descriptives

	N	Mean	Std. Deviation	Std. Error Mean
Mother's age at marriage	19300	22.2958	11.2187	8.075E-02

First, we see the descriptive statistics. The mean of our sample is 22.2, which is slightly higher than our population mean of 21.

Our t value is 16 and our significance value is 0.00. So it can be interpreted that there is a significant difference between the two groups (the significance is less than 0.05) (see Table 5.4). Therefore, we can say that our sample mean of 22.2 is significantly greater than the population mean of 21.

TABLE 5.4
Testing Hypothesis: One-sample T Test

	Test Value=21				95% Confidence Interval of the Difference	
	t	df	Sig. (two-tailed)	Mean Difference	Lower	Upper
Mother's age at marriage	16.046	19299	.000	1.2958	1.1375	1.4540

Errors in Making a Decision

When researchers make a decision about competing hypotheses, there are two ways of being correct and two ways of making a mistake. The null hypothesis can be either true or false. Further, researchers will take a decision either to reject or not to reject the null hypothesis. If the null hypothesis is true and we reject it, we are making a type I error. A type II error occurs in the scenario where the null hypothesis is not true but we accept the hypothesis (see Table 5.5).

TABLE 5.5
Decision-making Matrix

Conclusions		Do not reject null hypothesis	Reject null hypothesis
True 'state of nature'	Null hypothesis	Correct conclusion	Type I error
	Alternative hypothesis	Type II error	Correct conclusion

Type I Error   There are usually two types of errors a researcher can make, type I error or a type II error. A type I error is characterized by false rejection of the null hypothesis and is referred by alpha (α) level. Alpha level or the significance level of the test, is the probability researchers are willing to take in the making of a type I error. In social research, alpha is usually set to a level of 0.05 though in case of clinical research it is usually set to 0.01, though there is nothing sacred about 0.05 or 0.01.

In case the test statistic is unlikely to have come from a population described by the null hypothesis, the null hypothesis will be rejected. This is usually done with the help of a p value as when the p value is smaller than the significance level α, the null hypothesis is rejected. Type I error would signify the probability of rejecting the null hypothesis when the null hypothesis is true, that is, we fail to capture the actual situation or change existent on the field. It can be minimized by increasing the sample size, though the extent to which the sample size can be increased depends on the cost and time available for the project.

Type II Error   Type II error corresponds to the acceptance of the false null hypothesis instead of its rejection. The probability of making a type II error is called beta (β), and the probability of avoiding a type II error is called power ($1 - \beta$). It is important to point out that both type I and type II errors are always going to be there in the decision-making process. The situation is further complicated by the fact that a reduction in probability of committing a type I error increases the risk of committing a type II error and vice versa. Thus, researchers have to find a balance between type I and type II errors they are willing to allow for.

Power of a Test

Power of a test is the probability of correctly rejecting a false null hypothesis. Its probability is one minus the probability of making a type II error (β). Further, as discussed earlier, type I and type II errors are correlated, that is, if we decrease the probability of making a type I error, we increase the probability of making a type II error.

Power refers to the probability of avoiding a type II error, or, more specifically, the ability of a statistical test to detect true differences of a particular size. Thus, power of a test is a very important criterion, which needs to be considered while deciding on the sample size in case the research objective is to detect a change say between baseline and end line. The power of the test depends on four things: sample size, the effect the researchers want to detect, the type I error specified and the spread of the sample. Based on these parameters, researchers can calculate the desired power for a study taking into account the desired significance level. In a majority of social surveys, researchers specify the power to be 0.80, the alpha level and the minimum effect size which researchers would like to detect and use the power equation to determine the appropriate sample size.

Thus, if researchers opt for less power, they may not be able to detect the effect they are trying to find. This is especially important in cases where the objective is to find a small difference or virtually no difference. That is why researchers have to emphasize greatly on developing methods for assessing and increasing power (see Cohen, 1998). The easiest way is to increase the sample size and if the sample is large, no matter how small or meaningless the difference, we would be able to detect the difference and the result will be 'statistically significant'.

Power as a Function of Sample Size and Variance   Power as a function of sample size and variance can be easily computed by referring to the two distributions of the parameters α and β. It depends on the overlap between the two distributions and the two distributions overlap a great deal when the means are close together compared to the condition when the means are farther apart. Thus, anything that affects the extent of overlapping will increase β, that is, the likelihood of making a type II error.

It is important to point out that sample size has an indirect effect on power. By increasing the sample size, researchers decrease the measure of variance, which in turn increases power. In other words, an increase in sample size modifies estimates of the standard deviation. Thus, when n is large, the study would have a lower standard error than when n is small. Though power increases with sample size, a balance should be there between the levels of power desired and the cost and time factor involved.

Power and the Size Effect   Effect size measures the magnitude of the treatment effect and in a majority of the cases we are interested in assessing whether a sample differs from a population, or whether two samples come from two different populations. The standardized difference between two population means, known as effect size will affect the power of the test.

It is well known that for a given effect size and type I error, an increased sample size would result in increase in power. It is also observed that while analysing two groups, power is generally maximized when the subjects are divided evenly between the two groups.

Effect Size

Effect size is a set of indices, which measure the magnitude of the treatment effect and is used widely in meta-analysis and power analysis. Effect size can be measured in different ways but the simplest measure is represented by Cohen's d as a ratio of a mean difference to a standard deviation in the form of a z score. Let us assume that an experimental group has a mean score of $s1$ and a control group has a mean score of $s2$ and a standard deviation is Sd. Then the effect size would be equal to $(s2 - s1)/Sd$. It is important to point out that in case of equality of variance, standard deviation of either group could be used.

As mentioned earlier, there are different ways of computing effect size. One such way is Glass's delta which is defined as the ratio of the mean difference between experimental and control group to standard deviation of control group. Effect size can also be computed as the correlation coefficient between the dichotomous explanatory variable and the continuous response variable.

META-ANALYSIS

Meta analysis is a combination of statistical techniques, which combine information from different studies to predict estimate of an effect. Meta-analysis tries to find patterns in findings of multiple studies to solve the research problem on hand.

Meta-analysis usually explores the relationship between one dependent variable and one independent variable. The extent of relationship varies among studies. There are some studies, which show a great extent of relationship and some studies do not show any relationship. It is pre-emptive in such situations to arrive at overall estimate by combining results from various studies.

While doing meta-analysis, at the first stage, researchers needs to formulate the relationship they are trying to establish. After formulating a hypothesis, they need to collate all studies that can provide information about the formulated hypothesis. Then they need to code all collated studies to compute the effect size. After computing the effect size, researchers should analyse the distribution of effect size to ascertain the relationship.

It is important to point out that while doing meta-analysis, care should be taken to exclude poorly-designed studies. But if poorly-designed studies are also included then weight assigned to poorly-designed studies should be different from those assigned to well-designed studies to avoid misleading results. Meta-analysis, as mentioned earlier, combines various set of results to give an overall result or an estimate. Researchers can compare the effect size obtained by two separate studies, by using the formula:

$$Z = (z_1 - z_2)/[(1/n_1 - 3) + (1/n_2 - 3)]^{1/2}$$

Where z_1 and z_2 are defined as the Fisher transformations of r, and $n1$ and $n2$ are the sample size for each study.

Researchers can even use statistical software for doing meta-analysis. It first creates a database of studies and then runs a meta-analysis to arrive at an overall estimate.

COMPARISON BETWEEN GROUPS

Besides assessing the relationship and association between variables, researchers often want to compare two groups on some variable to see if the groups are different. The two groups could be two samples selected from the same population or samples selected from different populations.

Researchers while comparing a sample with the population use significance tests to ascertain whether trends shown in the sample reflect the population trends, that is, whether statistics reflects the parameter. Similarly, while testing difference between groups, researchers use significance tests to know how significant differences are to predict that differences are real and truly represent the field situation.

There are many ways in which a group's characteristics can be compared with another group's characteristics. Researchers usually employ mean as a measure to compare groups but researchers can also make comparison by using (i) medians, (ii) proportions and (iii) distributions. In case two groups are compared on an ordinal variable, then the median should be used as a measure of comparison. Further, if researchers are interested in comparing the spread of a distribution, then they should use a measure of spread for comparison between two groups.

Researchers can use a variety of statistical significance methods, based on the research objective and data characteristics. Researchers can select appropriate statistical significance tests based on (i) the number of groups to be compared, (ii) process of selection of samples, (iii) the measurement level of the variables, (iv) the shape of the distributions and (v) the measure of comparison.

PARAMETRIC AND NON-PARAMETRIC METHODS

There are two basic families of statistical techniques and methods—parametric methods, which are based on data measured on an interval or ratio scale, and non-parametric methods, where the variables are measured on a nominal or ordinal scale. Thus, depending on the nature of data measurement, a whole range of parametric and non-parametric methods can be used to compare differences across groups on some variable (see Table 5.6).

TABLE 5.6
Parametric Test and Non-parametric Test

| | | Non-parametric Test | |
| | Parametric Test | Rank, Score or | Binomial (Two |
Goal	Gaussian Population	Measurement	Possible Outcomes)
Compare one group to a hypothetical value	One-sample t test	Wilcoxon test	Chi-square or binomial test
Compare two unpaired groups	Unpaired t test	Mann-Whitney test	Fisher's test
Compare two paired groups	Paired t test	Wilcoxon test	McNemar's test
Compare three or more unmatched groups	One-way ANOVA	Kruskal-Wallis test	Chi-square test
Compare three or more matched groups	Repeated-measures ANOVA	Friedman test	Cochran Q

Parametric tests assume that the variable of interest is normally distributed, thus allowing slightly more statistical power to detect differences across group. In the case of non-parametric methods, power associated with tests is typically very weak, even if the association is strong. Thus, in some cases, when the original variable is not distributed normally, the variable of interest is transformed to make it look more normal in their distribution and then parametric statistics are used on the transformed variables.

Non-parametric methods, as the name suggests, were developed to be used in cases where the researchers know nothing about the parameters of the variable of interest in the population and hence these methods are also called parameter-free methods or distribution-free methods. Thus, non-parametric methods do not rely on the estimation of parameters, such as the measure of central tendency and dispersion in describing the distribution of the variable of interest in the population. There are situations where parametric methods cannot be used because the data do not meet the assumption on which the test is based, hence non-parametric tests are used.

In many cases, parametric and non-parametric tests give the same answer. Further, for every parametric method there is a non-parametric method and vice-versa and they treat the variable in same way.

BRIEF OVERVIEW OF NON-PARAMETRIC METHODS

Basically, there is at least one non-parametric equivalent for each parametric type of test. In general, these tests fall into the following categories:

a) Tests of differences between groups (independent samples).
b) Tests of differences between variables (dependent samples).
c) Tests of relationships between variables.

Differences Between Independent Groups

There are several types of tests of significance which researchers can use based on whether the samples are related or independent. In case researchers want to compare groups using the mean value for the variable of interest, researchers can use the t test for independent samples in case the samples are drawn using a random process. Researchers can also use non-parametric alternatives for this test such as Wald-Wolfowitz runs test, the Mann-Whitney U test and the Kolmogorov-Smirnov two-sample test, when the samples are selected using non-probabilistic measures.

In case there are more than two groups, researchers can use analysis of variance as the parametric test and Kruskal-Wallis analysis of ranks and the median test as the non-parametric equivalents.

Differences Between Dependent Groups

There are several types of tests of significance which researchers can use in case of dependent or related samples. Researchers can use the t test for dependent samples, in case they want to compare the two variables measured in the same sample, and if the variables follow parametric distribution. An example could be comparing students' math skills at the beginning of the course with their skills at the end of the course. If the variables measured in the sample do not follow a parametric distribution, researchers can use non-parametric alternatives of the t test like the Sign test and Wilcoxon's matched pairs test. If the variables of interest are dichotomous in nature then McNemar's test can be used for ascertaining association.

In the case of more than two variables, researchers can use repeated measures ANOVA as the parametric test. In case variables measured in the sample do not follow parametric distribution, researchers can use a non-parametric equivalent of ANOVA like Friedman's two-way analysis of variance. In case the variables are measured in categories, the Cochran Q test can be used for analysing the association.

Non-parametric tests are many and diverse and thus require special attention. Thus, while employing any non-parametric test, it is advisable to keep in mind three key points: (i) when and under what conditions specific tests are employed, (ii) how test are computed and (iii) how their values are interpreted. For example, the Kolmogorov-Smirnov two-sample test is very sensitive to both differences in the location of distributions and differences in their shapes and Wilcoxon's matched pairs test is based on the assumption that the magnitude of difference can be easily ordered in a meaningful manner.

Non-parametric tests are less powerful statistically than parametric tests, hence researchers should be very careful in selecting appropriate non-parametric tests to detect even small effects. Generally, if the result of a study is critical then researchers need to run different related non-parametric tests before deciding on which test is to be used.

Large Data Sets and Non-parametric Methods

Parametric test are the first choice of researchers when the sample size is large, that is, when n is greater than 100. Because as sample size becomes very large, then as per the central limit theorem, sample means will follow the normal distribution, even if the population from which the sample is drawn is not normally distributed. Parametric methods have more statistical power than non-parametric tests.

Non-parametric methods are most appropriate when the sample sizes are small. But it is important to point out that meaningful tests can often not be performed if the sample sizes become too small.

PARAMETRIC TEST

Parametric test, as mentioned earlier, assumes that the sample comes from a normal distribution and is hence also known as a distribution test. The next section describes parametric tests based on the nature of groups, that is, (i) one-sample test, (ii) two-sample test and (iii) three or more sample test.

One-sample T Test

The one-sample test procedure determines whether the mean of a single variable differs from a specified constant. It is very similar to the z test, except for the fact that t test does not require knowledge of standard deviation of the population and is generally used in relatively small samples. One sample t test can be accessed in SPSS by moving to options under the menu item analyse, compare means and one-sample t test. The purpose is to compare the sample mean with the given population mean.

The objective is to decide whether to accept a null hypothesis:

$$H_0 = \mu = \mu_0$$

or to reject the null hypothesis in favour of the alternative hypothesis:

H_a: μ is significantly different from μ_0

The testing framework consists of computing the t statistics:

$$t = [(\bar{x} - \mu_0)n^{1/2}]/S$$

Where $\bar{x}$ is the estimated mean and S is the estimated variance based on n random observations.

Two-sample Test

Unpaired T Test

The independent samples t test procedure compares means for two groups of cases. In fact, there are two variants of unpaired t test based on the assumption of equal and unequal variances between two groups of cases.

In case of unpaired t test, subjects should be randomly assigned to two groups, so that researchers, after employing significance tests, can conclude that the difference in response is due to the treatment and not due to other factors. For example, in case researchers compare educational qualification for males and females. A person cannot be randomly assigned as male or female. In such situations, researchers should ensure that the differences in other factors are not contributing a significant difference in means. Differences in educational qualification may be influenced by factors such as socio-economic profile and not by sex alone.

Paired T Test

Paired t test is very similar to unpaired t test, except with the difference that paired t test is related to matched samples. It tests the difference between raw scores and is based on the assumption that data are measured on an interval/ratio scale. The test assumes that the observed data are from matched samples and are drawn from a population with a normal distribution.

Further, in case of paired t test, subjects are often tested in a before and after situation across time. It is important to point out that why repeated measure ANOVA is considered an extension of the paired t test.

Test: The paired t test is actually a test that the differences between the two observations are 0. So, if D represents the difference between observations, the hypotheses are:

H_o: D = 0 (the difference between the two observations is 0)
H_a: D = 0 (the difference is not 0)

The test statistic is t with $n - 1$ degrees of freedom. If the p value associated with t is low (< 0.05), there is evidence to reject the null hypothesis. Thus, you would have evidence that there is a difference in means across the paired observations.

Three-sample Test

Unpaired Test: ANOVA

The method of analysis of variance is used to test hypotheses that examine the difference between two or more means. ANOVA does this by examining the ratio of variability between two conditions and variability within each condition, that is, it breaks down the total variance of a variable into the additive component which then may be associated with various components.

It is also known as the F test and is used as (i) one way, when one criterion is used, (ii) two-way, when two criteria are used and (iii) N ways when more than two criteria are used. Though this is similar to the chi-square test and the z-test, it is employed when more than two variables are studied and it produces results that otherwise would have required several tests. The F statistics test the difference in group means to conclude whether groups formed by the values of independent variable are different enough not to have occurred by chance and if groups' means do not differ significantly then researchers can conclude that the independent variable did not have an impact on the dependent variable.

A t test would compare the likelihood of observing the difference in the mean number of words recalled for each group. An ANOVA test, on the other hand, would compare the variability that we observe between the two conditions to the variability observed within each condition.

In performing the ANOVA test, researchers simply try to determine if a certain number of population means are equal. In order to do that, researchers measure the difference of the sample means and compare that to the variability within the sample observations. The total variation can be split in components, i.e., within sample variation and between sample variations. That is why the test statistic is the ratio of the between-sample variation (MSB, 'between row mean square') and the within-sample variation (MSW, 'within row mean square'). If this ratio is close to 1, there is evidence that the population means are equal.

One-way ANOVA   It deals with one independent variable and one dependent variable. It examines whether groups formed by categories of independent variables are similar, for if the groups seem different then it is concluded that independent variable has an effect on the dependent variable.

Paired Test: Repeated Measure ANOVA

When a dependent variable is measured repeatedly at different points of time, that is, before and after treatment for all sample members, then the design is termed as repeated measures ANOVA.[15] In this design, there is one group of subjects and it is exposed to categories of independent variables. For example, five random groups are asked to take a performance test four times—once under each of the four levels of noise distraction.

The objective of repeated measure design is to test the same group of subjects at each category of independent variable. The levels are introduced to the subject in a counterbalanced manner to rule out the effects of practice and fatigue.

NON-PARAMETRIC TEST

Non-parametric tests, as mentioned earlier, do not assume anything about distribution and hence are also known as distribution-free tests. The next section describes parametric tests based on the nature of group, that is, (i) one-sample test, (ii) two-sample test and (iii) three or more sample test.

One-sample Test

Wilcoxon Rank Sum[16] Test

A Wilcoxon rank sum test[17] is different from Wilcoxon sign test as it compares the group's values with a hypothetical median. It does so by calculating the difference of each value from the hypothetical median. At the next stage, researchers rank the computed difference irrespective of their sign.

Researchers can then multiply the rank, which is lower than the hypothetical value by negative 1. After multiplication, they can sum up both positive ranks and negative ranks together to compute the sum of signed ranks. Based on the sum of signed rank, if Wilcoxon test statistics is near 0 then researcher can conclude that the data were really sampled from a population with the hypothetical median.

Chi-square Test

The chi-square test is only used with measures, which places cases into categories. The test indicates whether the results from the two measures are about what one would expect if the two were not related. A contingency table needs to be made and the chi-square test has to applied whenever the researchers want to decide whether membership in one category has a bearing on membership in another. A chi-square test compares the observed distributions with the distributions which would be expected if there was no relationship between the two set of categories. Researchers use the chi-square test[18] to determine whether the number of responses falling into different categories differ from chance. It is used in those cases where data are nominally scaled.

X^2 is calculated as follows:

$$X^2 = \sum \frac{(O - E)^2}{E}$$

Where O = observed frequency
E = expected frequency

Kolmogorov-Smirnov One-sample Test

The Kolmogorov-Smirnov one-sample test is an ordinal level, one-sample test, which is employed in those cases where the researchers are interested to know about the relationship between data and the expected values. The Kolmogorov-Smirnov one-sample test is used to test the hypothesis that a sample comes from a particular distribution, that is, it comes from a uniform, normal, binomial or Poisson distribution. It generally tests whether the observed value reflects the values of a specific distribution.

This test is concerned with the degree of agreement between a set of observed values and values specified by the null hypothesis. It is similar to the chi-square goodness of fit; though it is a more powerful alternative when its assumptions are met. The test statistics are computed from observed and expected values. But from these values, the test computes cumulative values of both observed and expected values. At the next stage, expected values are subtracted from observed values to compute the largest difference between expected and observed values. The Kolmogorov-Smirnov one-sample test use D as statistics, which is defined as the largest absolute difference between the cumulative observed values and the cumulative expected values on the basis of the hypothesized distribution. This computed difference is compared with the critical value (computed from the table) and if the difference is equal to or larger than critical value, difference is termed as significant and null hypothesis is rejected.

Researchers can compute the two-tailed significance level by using SPSS. It provides the probability that the observed distribution is not significantly different from the expected distribution. Researchers can access the Kolmogorov-Smirnov one-sample test in SPSS via the Statistics menu and the Non-parametric Tests sub-option. Researchers can select the desired test distribution and the desired criterion variables from the list of variables.

Two-sample Test

Independent Test/Unpaired

Mann-Whitney U Test   The Mann-Whitney test is a non-parametric test used to see whether two independent samples come from the population having the same distribution. This test is used instead of the independent group t test when sample populations make no assumptions about the normal distribution of the data or when the assumption of normality or equality of variance is not met. It tests the hypothesis to see whether two samples come from different or identical populations.

The hypotheses for the comparison of two independent groups are:

H_o: The two samples come from identical populations
H_a: The two samples come from different populations

The Mann-Whitney U test, like many non-parametric tests, uses the ranks of the data rather than their observed values to calculate the statistic based on the formula mentioned here:

$$U = \frac{n_1 n_2 + n_1(n_1 + 1) - R_1}{2}$$

Where U = Mann-Whitney statistic

n_1 = number of items in sample 1
n_2 = number of items in sample 2
R_1 = sum of ranks in sample 1

The test statistic for the Mann-Whitney test is U. This value is compared to the tabulated value of U statistics calculated from table. If U exceeds the critical value for U at some significance level (usually 0.05) it means that there is evidence to reject the null hypothesis in favour of the alternative hypothesis. Nowadays, computer-generated p values can be used to test significance levels to decide on the hypothesis (see Box 5.10).

BOX 5.10
Non-parametric Test for Two Independent Samples Using SPSS

A non-parametric test for two independent samples can be easily calculated using SPSS via the menu item Analyse, Non-parametric Tests, and Two Independent Samples. After clicking on the Two Independent Sample option, a new window, titled 'Two Independent Samples Tests', would pop up, in which the researcher can select the test type by clicking on the dialogue box (refer to Figure 5.13). At the next stage, the researcher can select the test variable and also the grouping variable by clicking on Define Groups to define the values for the two groups.

Kolmogorov-Smirnov Z Test   The Kolmogorov-Smirnov test for a single sample of data is used to test whether or not the sample of data is consistent with a specified distribution function. But in the case of more than two samples of data, it is used to test whether these two samples come from the same distribution or from different distributions. The test is based on the largest difference between the two cumulative distributions and relies on the fact that the value of the sample cumulative density function is normally distributed. It is based on the maximum absolute difference between the observed cumulative distribution functions for both samples and when this difference is significantly large, the two distributions are considered different.

Wald-Wolfowitz Runs Test   The Wald-Wolfowitz runs test analyses whether the number of runs in an ordering is random. It does so by ranking the observations from both groups, after combining the data value.

A run is defined as the succession of an identical letter (value), which is, followed and preceded by a different letter (value) or no letter at all. The test is based on the idea that too few or too many runs show that the items were not chosen randomly. If the two groups are from different distributions, the number of runs are expected to be less than a certain expected number, that is, the two groups should not be randomly scattered throughout the ranking. Based on the runs, researchers can conclude whether the apparently seen grouping is statistically significant or is it due to chance.

It is important to point out here that the Wald-Wolfowitz statistic is not affected by ties between subjects within the same sample, as in the case of tied observations, the order may be assigned by use of a random number table.

Two Dependent/Paired Groups

Sign Test   The sign test is one of the simplest non-parametric tests, which is used to test whether or not it seems likely that two data sets differ with respect to a measure of central tendency. This test is used in cases where two data sets or samples are not drawn independent of each other and do not require the assumption that the population is normally distributed, hence, this test is used most often in place of the one sample t test when the normality assumption is doubtful. This test can also be applied when the observations in a sample of data are ranks, that is, data is ranked as ordinal data rather than being direct measurements.

FIGURE 5.13
Non-parametric Test for Two Independent Samples Using SPSS

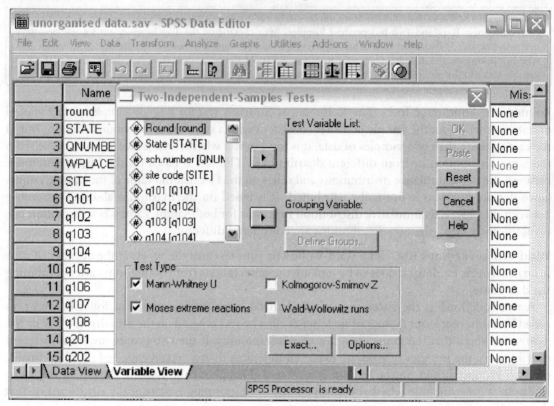

Its calculation is also very simple and can be calculated by subtracting the second score from the first score and the resulting sign of difference classified as either positive, negative, or tied is then used to calculate the test statistic. If the two variables are similarly distributed, the numbers of positive and negative differences will not be significantly different.

The sign test[19] is designed to test a hypothesis[20] about the location of a population distribution, that is, whether two variables have the same distribution. It is most often used to test hypothesis about a population median, and often involves the use of matched pairs or dependent samples, for example, before and after data, in which case it tests for a median difference of zero.

Wilcoxon Signed Ranks Test   Wilcoxon's test uses matched data and is equivalent to the paired t test, for example, before and after data, in which case it tests for a median difference of zero. It is used to test the hypothesis that the two variables have the same distribution and it makes no assumptions about the shapes of the distributions of the two variables. Hence, in many applications, this test is used in place of the one-sample t test when the normality assumption is doubtful. Further, this test can also be applied when the observations in a sample of data are ranks, that is, the data is ranked as ordinal data rather than being direct measurements.

Wilcoxon signed rank test is a modification of the sign test, which discards lot of information about the data. Wilcoxon signed rank test also takes into account the direction of the difference, besides taking into account the magnitude of the difference between each pair of scores. This test takes into account information about the magnitude of differences within pairs and gives more weight to pairs that show large differences than to pairs that show small differences. The test statistic is based on the ranks of the absolute values of the differences between the two variables[21] and should be used if the standard deviations of the two groups are not comparable.

Calculation of Wilcoxon test statistics is very easy and at the first stage, differences between each set of pairs is computed and then the absolute values of the differences is ranked from low to high. In the next step, the sum of the ranks of the differences is reported. In a nutshell, the Wilcoxon test analyses only the differences between the paired measurements for each subject.

Besides calculating Wilcoxon test statistics, researchers can test the significance by computer-generated p value. Null hypothesis states that there is no difference between the scores obtained before and after the exposure to stimulus. In case researchers have fixed the significance level at 0.05 and if computer-generated p value is less than 0.05 then researchers can conclude that the result is statistically significant and there is a difference between the scores before and after the stimulus.

McNemar Test The chi-square test of association and Fisher's exact test are both used when observations are independent, but McNemar Test is applicable when the research design involves a before and after situation and data are measured nominally.

McNemar's test[22] assesses the significance of changes in data due to stimuli and is used generally for dichotomous data of two independent samples. The null hypothesis states that there is no change despite the numerical difference in observed data. It tests the null hypothesis by analysing whether the counts in the cells above the diagonal differ from the counts below the diagonal and if the two counts differ significantly, researchers can conclude that the observed change is due to treatment between the before and after samples.

The McNemar test uses the chi-square distribution, based on this formula:

A	B	r_1
C	D	r_2
c_1	c_2	n

Chi-square = $(|a - d| - 1)^2)/(a + d)$
degrees-of-freedom = (rows – 1)(columns – 1) = 1

Three or More Samples

Independent Samples

Kruskal-Wallis Test[23]   The Kruskal-Wallis test (Kruskal and Wallis, 1952) is a non-parametric test used to compare three or more samples. It is used instead of the analysis of variance test when either the sampled populations are not normally distributed or sampled populations do not have equal variances. It is a logical extension of the Wilcoxon-Mann-Whitney test and is an alternative to the independent group ANOVA, when the assumption of normality or equality of variance is not met. This test uses rank rather than the original observations and is appropriate only when samples are independent.

This test is used to test the null hypothesis that sample come from identical populations against the alternate hypothesis that the sample come from different populations.

Test: The hypotheses for the comparison of two independent groups are:

H$_o$: The samples come from identical populations
H$_a$: They samples come from different populations

The test statistic for the Kruskal-Wallis test is H and is computed as:

$$H = \left[\frac{12}{N(N+1)} \sum_{i=1}^{k} \frac{R_i^2}{n_i} \right] - 3(N+1)$$

A large value of H tends to cast doubts on the assumption that the K samples used in the test are drawn from identically-distributed populations. This value is compared to a Kruskal-Wallis test table and if H exceeds the critical value for H at a specified significance level (usually 0.05) it means that there is evidence to reject the null hypothesis in favour of the alternative hypothesis. Nowadays, however, computer-generated p values, which can be easily calculated using SPSS, can be used to test the significance level to decide on the result (see Box 5.11).

Median Test   Median test,[24] as the name suggests, is based on the median as a measure of central tendency and is a more general alternative to the Kruskal-Wallis H test if several independent samples come from the same population. The test first combines the samples to calculate the combined median value and the result is displayed in a table in which the columns are the samples and the two rows reflect the sample counts above or below the pooled median value. Based on the tabulated result, it tests whether two or more independent samples differ in their median values for a variable of interest.

Jonckheere-Terpstra Test   The Jonckheere-Terpstra test is a non-parametric test, which is used to test for differences among several independent samples and is preferred to Kruskal-Wallis H test in the case of ranked data. It is used to test for ordered differences among classes, hence it requires that the independent samples be ordinally arranged on the variable of interest. Jonckheere-Terpstra tests the hypothesis that the within-sample magnitude of the studied variable increases as we move from samples low on the criterion to samples high on the criterion.

BOX 5.11
Non-parametric Test of K-independent Samples Using SPSS

Non-parametric test of k-independent samples can be easily calculated from SPSS by clicking the menu items: 'Analyse', 'Non-parametric Tests' and then 'K-Independent Samples'. In the 'Tests for Several Independent Samples' dialogue box under K-independent sample, select the 'Test Type' that needs to be done, that is, Kruskall-Wallis H, median, or Jonckheere-Terpstra test. At the next stage, enter the criterion variable in the 'Test Variable List' box from the list of variables. In the case of continuous criterion variables, enter a grouping variable in the 'Grouping Variable' box and click on 'Define Range' to enter the minimum and maximum values (see Figure 5.14). It is important to point out here that the Jonckheere-Terpstra test is available only when the 'SPSS Exact Tests module' is installed and is not available in the basic model.

FIGURE 5.14
Non-parametric Test of K-independent Sample Using SPSS

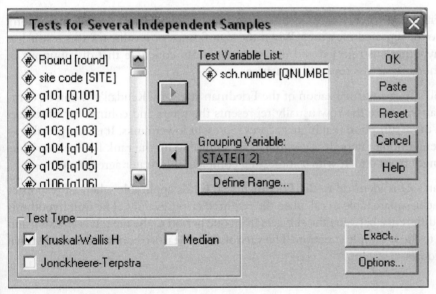

Dependent Samples

Friedman's Test   The Friedman test, also known as Friedman two-way analysis of variance is an analogue to parametric two-way analysis of variance. It tests the null hypothesis that measures from k-dependent samples come from the same population.

Friedman's test, like many non-parametric tests, uses the ranks of the data rather than their raw values to calculate the statistic. The test starts by ranking data in each column, where any tied observation is given the average of the rank to which they are tied. The test statistics are then calculated by measuring the extent to which ranks in each column vary from randomness, focusing on the sum of the ranks in each column. The test is based on the rationale that if the groups do not differ on the variable of interest, then the rankings of each subject will be random and there will be no difference in mean ranks between groups on the variable of interest.

Friedman's test, as mentioned, is an equivalent of parametric two-way analysis of variance, though unlike the parametric repeated measures ANOVA or paired t test, it does not make any assumption about the distribution of data. Further, since this test does not make a distribution assumption, it is not as powerful as the ANOVA. The Friedman test is typically used to test inter-rater reliability where the cases are judges and the variables are the items being judged, and it tries to test the hypothesis that there is no systematic difference in the ratings.

Test: The hypotheses for the comparison across repeated measures are

H_o: The distributions of mean ranks are the same across repeated measures.
H_a: The distributions of mean ranks are different across repeated measures.

The test statistic for Friedman's test[25] follows a chi-square distribution with $k-1$ degrees of freedom, where k is the number of repeated measures. When the significance or p value for this test is less than 0.05, the null hypothesis is rejected and the researchers can conclude that distributions of mean ranks are not the same across repeated measures.

Kendall's W   Kendall's W is a normalization of the Friedman statistics. Kendall's W can be computed from a data matrix, where the row usually represents the raters and column refers to data objects. It is based on the assumption that higher scores represent lower ranks. It is interpretable as a measure of agreement among raters. It is computed by summing up the rank for each variable. The coefficient W ranges from 0 to 1, with 1 indicating complete inter-rater agreement.

Cochran Q   Cochran's Q is identical to the Friedman test, but is applicable when all responses are binary. It uses the chi-square table to calculate the required critical values. The null hypothesis states that there is no difference between the subjects from one period to the next. It is an extension of the McNemar test to the k-sample situation. The variables are measured on the same individual or on matched individuals.

Notes

1. The opposite of a variable is a constant, that is, something that cannot vary, such as a single value or category of a variable.
2. In a pie chart, relative frequencies are represented in proportion to the size of each category by a slice of a circle.

3. If individual values are cross-classified by levels in two different attributes, such as gender and literate or not literate, then a contingency table is the tabulated counts for each combination of the levels of the two attributes, with the levels of one factor labelling the rows of the table, and the levels of the other factor labelling the table columns.

4. Chi-square, χ^2, is not the square of anything, it is just a name used to denote test.

5. Pearson's chi-square test for independence for a contingency table involves using a normal approximation to the actual distribution of the frequencies in the contingency table. This shall be avoided for contingency tables with expected cell frequencies less than 1, or when more than 20 per cent of the contingency table cells have expected cell frequencies less than 5. In such cases, an alternate test like Fisher's exact test for a two-by-two contingency table should be considered for a more accurate evaluation of the data.

6. T is a symmetrical measure. It does not matter which is the independent variable and may be used with nominal data or ordinal data.

7. The coefficient of contingency was proposed by Pearson, the originator of the chi-square test.

8. Per cent difference handles any level of data, including nominal variables such as gender. It is identical to Somers' d for the 2*2 case.

9. Q requires dichotomous data, which may be nominal or higher in level. Yule's Q is gamma for the case of two-by-two tables.

10. Yule's Y penalizes for near-weak monotonic relationships, similar to Somers' d, which is used far more commonly due to its more readily intuited meaning. Yule's Y is less sensitive than Yule's Q to differences in the marginal distributions of the two variables.

11. The gamma statistic was developed by Goodman and Kruskal. For details see Goodman and Kruskal (1954, 1959), Siegel (1956) and Siegel and Castellan (1988).

12. Sommer's d is an asymmetric measure of association related to tau-b (see Siegel and Castellan, 1988: 303–10).

13. Kurtosis is a measure of the heaviness of the tails in a distribution, relative to the normal distribution. A distribution with negative kurtosis such as uniform distribution is light-tailed relative to normal distribution, while a distribution with positive kurtosis such as the Cauchy distribution is heavy-tailed relative to normal distribution.

14. The method of least squares is a general method of finding estimated fitted values of parameters. Estimates are found such that the sum of the squared differences between the fitted values and the corresponding observed values is as small as possible. In the case of simple linear regression, this means placing the fitted line such that the sum of the squares of the vertical distances between the observed points and the fitted line is minimized.

15. In a repeated measure ANOVA, at least one factor is measured at each level for every subject. Thus, it is a within factor, for example, in an experiment in which each subject performs the same task twice, the trial number is a within factor. There may also be one or more factors that are measured at only one level for each subject, such as gender. This type of factor is a between or grouping factor.

16. This test is named after the statistician F. Wilcoxon and is used for ordinal data.

17. The Wilcoxon rank sum test compares one group with a hypothetical median and is very different from Wilcoxon matched pairs test which compare medians of two paired groups.

18. If the test is undertaken to examine whether the sample data adhere to a particular set of distribution, then it is called the test of goodness of fit.

19. The sign test is for two dependent samples, where the variable of interest is ordinal or higher.

20. The usual null hypothesis for this test is that there is no difference between the two treatments. If this is so, then the number of + signs (or – signs, for that matter) should have a binomial distribution 1 with $p = 0.5$, and $N =$ the number of subjects.

21. If there are tied ranks in data you are analysing with the Wilcoxon signed-ranks test, the statistic needs to be adjusted to compensate for the decreased variability of the sampling distribution. For details refer to Siegel and Castellan (1988: 94).

22. If a research design involves a before and after design and data are measured nominally, then the McNemar test is applicable.

23. The Kruskal-Wallis H-test goes by various names, including Kruskal-Wallis one-way analysis of variance by ranks (see Siegel and Castellan, 1988).
24. The median test is also called the Westenberg-Mood median test.
25. The Friedman test statistic is distributed approximately as chi-square, with $(k - 1)$ degrees of freedom, where k is the number of groups in the criterion variable, from $i = 1$ to k. Friedman chi-square is then computed by this formula:

$$\text{Chi-square}_{\text{Friedman}} = ([12/nk(k + 1)]*[\text{SUM}(T_i^2] - 3n(k + 1))$$

CHAPTER 6

MULTIVARIATE ANALYSIS

The previous chapter discussed data analysis techniques for one and two variables. The present chapter takes data analysis to an advanced stage wherein multivariate analysis methods are discussed quite elaborately. The realization that in many real life situations, it becomes necessary to analyse relationship among three or more variables led to the popularity of multivariate statistics. Besides, the term 'multivariate statistics' says it all—these techniques look at the pattern of relationships between several variables simultaneously.

The popularity of multivariate analysis can be attributed to other factors such as the advent of statistical software packages, which made complex computation very easy, and an increased emphasis on collection of large amounts of data involving several variables together. It thus become imperative that statistical methods were developed and applied to derive as much information as possible from the diversity of data, rather than restricting attention to subsets of it.

Multivariate data analysis methods are not an end in themselves and should be used with caution, taking into account the limitations of each method. Multivariate analysis should be seen as a complementary method to be used to run a rough preliminary investigation, to sort out ideas, or as a data reduction technique, to help summarize data and reduce the number of variables necessary to describe it. Multivariate analysis methods can also explore the causality and there are a range of methods which centre around the association between two set of variables, where one set of variable is the dependent variable.

Multivariate techniques can be further classified into two broad categories/situations: (i) when researchers know specifically about the dependent variable and the independent variable and try to assess the relationship between the dependent variable and the independent variable such as in the case of multiple regression, discriminate analysis, logistic regression and MANOVA, etc., and (ii) when researchers do not have any idea about the interdependency of the variables and have large set of data; they try to reduce the data by assessing a commonality among variables and try to group variables/cases according to commonality such as factor analysis, cluster analysis and multi-dimensional scaling.

Further, in situations where researchers have an idea about the interdependency of the variables, multivariate research statistics can be further classified based on the nature of the dependent variable, that is, whether it is metric or non-metric in nature (see Figure 6.1). In the case of data reduction techniques also, categorization depends on the nature of data type, that is, in the case of metric data, factor analysis, cluster analysis and metric multidimensional scaling can be performed, whereas in the case of non-metric data, non-metric multidimensional scaling and conjoint analysis are preferred.

FIGURE 6.1
Overview of Multivariate Research Techniques

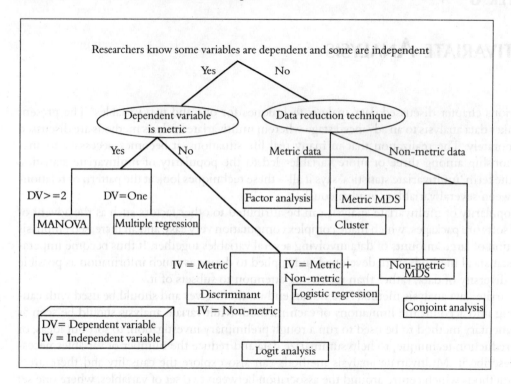

MULTIPLE LINEAR REGRESSION

Multiple regression, a straightforward generalization of simple regression, is the most commonly utilized multivariate technique. In simple regression, there is one dependent variable and one independent variable, whereas in multiple regression, there is one dependent variable and many independent variables. It examines the relationship between a single metric dependent variable and two or more metric independent variables. The technique relies upon determining the linear relationship with the lowest sum of squared variances and, therefore, assumptions of normality, linearity and equal variance should be checked before using multiple regression.

Multiple linear regressions take the following form:

$$Y = a + b_1x_1 + b_2x_2 + \dots + b_kx_k$$

Where y is a dependent variable and $x_1, x_2, \dots x_k$ are independent variables and $a, b_1, b_2 \dots b_k$ are the parameters/regression coefficient. The coefficient of each independent variable signifies the relation that the variable has with y, the dependent variable, when all the other independent variables are constant.

The regression surface, which is determined by a line in simple regression, is characterized by a plane or a higher-dimensional surface in multiple regression. It depicts the best prediction values of the dependent variable (Y) for a given independent variable (X). As we have seen in the case of linear regression, there are substantial variations from the line of best fit. In the case of multiple regression, similar variations occur from the fitted regression surface and likewise, deviation of a particular point from the nearest point on the predicted regression surface is called the residual value. The goal of multiple regression is similar to that of linear regression, which is to have a plane of best fit, where the values of the independent variables and the dependent variable that share a linear relationship, are as close to the observed dependent variable as possible. Thus, in a bid to construct a best-fit regression surface, the surface is computed in a way that the sums of the squared deviations of the observed points from that surface are minimized, hence, the process is also referred to as the least square estimation[1] (see Box 6.1).

BOX 6.1
Least Square Estimation and Correlation Among Variables

In the case of multivariate regression, the dependent variable should preferably be measured on an interval, continuous scale, though an ordinal scale can also be used. Independent variables should preferably be measured on interval scales, though ordinal scale measurements are also acceptable. Another condition for multiple regression is to ensure normality, that is, distribution of all studied variables should be normal and if they are not roughly normal, they need to be transformed before any analysis is done.

Another crucial condition for least squares estimation is that although the independent variables can be correlated, there must be no perfect correlation among them, or multicollinearity (a term used to denote the presence of a linear relationship among independent variables) should be avoided. If the correlation coefficient for these variables is equal to unity then it is not possible to obtain numerical values for each parameter separately and the method of least square doesn't work. Further, if the variables are not correlated at all (variables are orthogonal) there is no need to perform a multiple regression as each parameter can be estimated by a single regression equation.

Multiple regression analysis can easily be done using statistical software packages. In Stata, it can be computed using the 'mvreg' command followed by listing the dependent variable and the independent variables. In SPSS, it can be computed by clicking on the menu items Analyse, Regression and Linear Option. In linear regression, SPSS provides the option of selecting the method depending on how independent variables are entered into the analysis (see Figure 6.2). If all variables are entered in the block in a single step, then the process is termed as 'enter', while if the variables are removed from the block in a single step, the process is termed as 'remove'. SPSS also provides options such as forward variable selection, wherein variables are entered in the block one at a time based on the entry criteria and in the case of backward variable elimination, all the variables are entered in the block in a single step and then variables are removed one at a time based on the removal criteria. Stepwise variable entry and removal examines the variables in the block at each step for entry or removal based on the selected criterion. It is important to point out here that all variables must pass the tolerance criterion to be entered in the equation, regardless of the entry method specified. The default tolerance level is 0.0001. Further, a variable is not entered if it would cause the tolerance of another variable already in the model to drop below the tolerance criterion.

FIGURE 6.2
Multiple Linear Regression Using SPSS

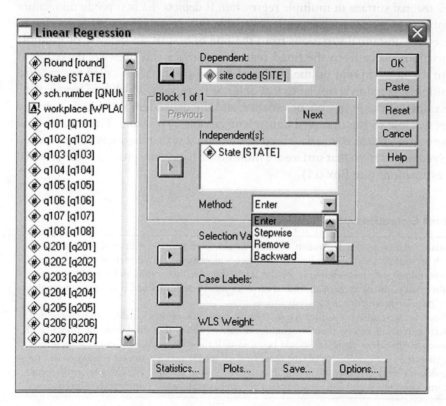

To explain multiple regression further, let us take an example from a salt traders' survey conducted in Uttar Pradesh (UP) among salt traders to assess stocking patterns and trade details. One of the key questions of the study was to assess dependence of stocking patterns of refined salt on the purchase price and the average monthly sale of refined salt. In this example, we have taken the purchase volume of refined salt as the dependent variable and the average monthly sale and purchase price as the independent variables and the variables have been entered using the 'enter' variable selection method (see Table 6.1).

TABLE 6.1
Variable Entered in an Equation Using the Enter Method[b]

Model	Variables Entered	Variables Removed	Method
1	Average monthly sale—Refined Purchase price—Refined[a]		Enter

a. All requested variables entered.
b. Dependent variable: Purchase volume at a time—refined.

The model summary presented in Table 6.2 helps in assessing the goodness of fit of a regression equation. It does so by computing a slightly different statistic called R^2-adjusted or R^2_{adj}.[2] The R-squared value for model is 0.663, which means that approximately 66 per cent of the variance of purchase volume is accounted for by the model. Further, it is widely accepted in the social and psychological applications that an R^2_{adj} of above 75 per cent is very good; between 50–75 per cent is good; between 25–50 per cent is fair and below 25 per cent is poor and in the given case, we can term the model to be good.

TABLE 6.2
Regression Model Summary Using Enter Method

Model	R	R Square	Adjusted R Square	Std. Error of the Estimate
1	0.663[a]	0.439	0.434	23027.784

a. Predictors: (Constant) average monthly sale—refined.
   Purchase price—refined.

Table 6.3 helps in assessing whether regressors/independent variables, taken together, are significantly associated with the dependent variable and this is assessed by the statistic F in the ANOVA part of the regression output. In this case, $F = 88.2$, $p < .001$. (SPSS output: Sig. $= .000$. It can be reported as $p < .001$), which means that the independent variables are significantly associated with the dependent variable.

TABLE 6.3
Regression Model: Analysis of Variance

Model	ANOVA[b]				
	Sum of Squares	df	Mean Square	F	Sig.
1 Regression	9.35E+10	2	4.676E+10	88.188	.000[a]
Residual	1.19E+11	225	530278841.6		
Total	2.13E+11	227			

a. Predictors: (Constant) average monthly sale—refined, purchase price—refined.
b. Dependent variable: Purchase volume at a time—refined.

TABLE 6.4
Standardized Coefficient of Variables Entered in an Equation

| | Coefficients[a] | | | | |
| | Unstandardized Coefficients | | Standardized Coefficients | | |
Model	B	Std. Error	Beta	t	Sig.
1 (Constant)	−36906.6	9943.172		−3.712	.000
Purchase price—Refined	7773.805	2153.472	.183	3.610	.000
Average monthly sale—Refined	1.814	.137	.670	13.217	.000

a. Dependent variable: Purchase volume at a time—refined.

After assessing the goodness of fit of the equation and the significant association of the independent variables and dependent variable, researchers should look at the impact of the independent variables in predicting the dependent variable by interpreting regression coefficients.

The regression coefficients or B coefficients represent the independent contributions of each independent variable to the prediction of the dependent variable (see Table 6.4). Now if we look at B coefficient of the independent variables, it can be interpreted from the table that the significance of all variables is statistically significant (significance level is less than 0.05 level).

The regression equation can be expressed as:

$$Y = -36906 + 7773pr + 1.814ms$$
pr-purchase price, refined
ms-average monthly sale

Let us consider the variable average monthly sale. We would expect an increase of 1.81 units in the purchase volume score for every one-unit increase in the variable, assuming that all other variables in the model are constant. The interpretation of much of the output of multiple regression is the same as it was for simple regression, though it is imperative in the case of multivariate regression to determine the variable accounting for most variance in the dependent variable (see Box 6.2), if we want to assess the impact of one variable on the other as in simple regression.

BOX 6.2
Determining the Variable Accounting for Most Variance in the Dependent Variable

Besides assessing regression coefficients, it is imperative to determine which are the variables that account for the most variance in Y. It is usually done by indicators mentioned below:

a) *Zero-order correlations:* Zero-order correlations assess the relationship between two variables, while ignoring the affect of another independent variable.
b) Variables having the largest absolute values of standardized beta weights are those that strongly predict Y.
c) *Darlington's usefulness criteria:* Darlington's useful criteria calculates change in R-squared after dropping a variable and it is based on the premise that if R-square drops considerably, then the independent variable is a useful predictor of the dependent variable.

It is important to understand what a 1.81 change in purchase volume really means, and how the strength of that coefficient might be compared to the coefficient of another variable, say purchase price refined (7773.8). To address this problem, we can refer to the column of beta coefficients, also known as standardized regression coefficients.[3] The beta coefficients are used by some researchers to compare the relative strength of the various predictors within the model. Because the beta coefficients are all measured in standard deviations, instead of the units of the variables, they can be compared to one another. In other words, the beta coefficients are the coefficients that you would obtain if the outcome and predictor variables were all transformed to standard scores, or z scores, before running the regression and the equation can be summed as:

$$ZY = .183pr + .670ms$$

Though usually, in the case of multivariate regression, we have one dependent variable and several independent variables, there are ways in which regression can be done even in the case of several dependent variables (see Box 6.3).

BOX 6.3
Regression with Many Predictors and/or Several Dependent Variables

Partial least square regression (PLSR): PLSR addresses the multicollinearity problem by computing latent vectors, which explains both independent variables and the dependent variables. It is frequently used in cases where the objective is to predict more than one dependent variable. It combines features from principal component analysis (PCA) and multiple linear regression as the score of the both units as well as the loadings of the variables can be plotted as in PCA, and the dependent variable can be estimated as in multiple linear regression.

Principal component regression (PCR): In the case of principal component regression, variance of the independent variables are computed through PCA and the scores of the units are used as independent variables in a standard multiple linear regression.

Ridge regression (RR): Ridge regression accommodates the multicollinearity problem by adding a small constant (the ridge) to the diagonal of the correlation matrix. This makes the computation of the estimates for MLR possible.

Reduced rank regression (RRR): In RRR, the dependent variables are submitted to a PCA and the scores of the units are then used as dependent variables in a series of standard MLR's where the original independent variables are used as predictors (a procedure akin to an inverse PCR).

NON-LINEAR REGRESSION

Multiple regression is based on the assumption that each bivariate relationship between the dependent and independent variables is linear and in case this assumption breaks, then researchers have to resort to non-linear regression for assessing the relationship.

An important type of curvilinear regression model is the polynomial regression model, which may contain one, two or more than two independent variables. In the case of the polynomial regression model, the independent variable could be of three or higher degrees. Polynomial regression, like multiple regression, can be interpreted by looking at R-squared and changes in R-squared.

MULTIVARIATE ANALYSIS OF VARIANCE (MANOVA)

Analysis of variance is a special case of regression model, which is generally used to analyse data collected using experimentation. Multivariate analysis of variance examines the relationship between several categorical independent variables and two or more metric dependent variables. Whereas ANOVA assesses the differences between groups, MANOVA examines the dependence relationship between a set of variables across a set of groups.

MANOVA is slightly different in that the independent variables are categorical and the dependent variable is metric. MANOVA, like ANOVA, can be classified into three broad categories based on the criterion used (see Box 6.4).

BOX 6.4
Classification of MANOVA

> *One-way MANOVA:* One-way MANOVA is similar to the one-way ANOVA (one criterion is used). It analyses the variance between one independent variable having multiple levels and multiple dependent variables.
>
> *Two-way MANOVA:* Two-way MANOVA is similar to the two-way ANOVA (two criterion are used). It analyses the variance between one dichotomous independent variable and multiple dependent variables.
>
> *Factorial MANOVA:* Factorial MANOVA is similar to the factorial ANOVA design (when more than two criterion are used). It analyses the variance between multiple nominal independent variables and multiple dependent variables. Factorial MANOVA can be further classified into three categories based on the subject design:
> a) *Factorial between subject design:* Factorial between subject designs is used when researchers want to compare a single variable for multiple groups.
> b) *Factorial within subject design:* In case of the within subject design, each respondent is measured on several variables. This is widely used in time-series studies.
> c) *Mixed between subject and within subject design:* In some situations, both between subject and within subject designs are important and thus both designs are used.

MANOVA: Testing Significance and Model-fit

F Test

Researchers while analysing MANOVA use the F test as the first step to test the null hypothesis that there is no difference in the means of the dependent variables for the different groups. Besides, taking into account the sum of squares between and within groups as in case of ANOVA, multivariate formula for computation of F also takes into account the covariance as well as group means. Besides F test there are also other significance tests for multiple dependent variables such as Hotelling T square, Wilks' lambda, or Pillai-Bartlett trace, which also follow the F distribution.

Post-Hoc Test

Researchers after using the F test for significance can use the post-hoc F test to make conclusions about the difference among the group means. MANOVA examines the model fit by determining the mean vector equivalents across groups. Post-hoc F test analyses whether the centroid of means of the dependent variables is the same for all the groups of the independent variables. Thus, based on the result of the post-hoc F test, researchers can determine the groups whose means differ significantly from other groups.

MANOVA as a model assumes normality of dependent variables, thus sample size is an important consideration. It requires at least 15–20 observations per cell though the presence of too many observations per cell can result in loss of the method's significance. MANOVA also works on the assumption that there are linear relationships among all pairs of dependent variables and all dependent variables shows equal levels of variance.

MANOVA Using SPSS

In SPSS there are several ways to run an ANOVA. The ANOVA and MANOVA procedures both have the same basic structure. In SPSS, ANOVA can be accessed via the Analyse and Compare Means option. For multiple analysis of variance, researchers need to select the GLM option. To use the GLM[4] option, researchers can click on Analyse, General Linear Model and Multivariate option. After selecting the option, researchers should move the dependents into the dependent variables box and the grouping variable into the fixed factor box (see Figure 6.3). Further, under 'options', researchers can select Descriptive Statistics and Homogeneity Tests.

FIGURE 6.3
MANOVA Using SPSS

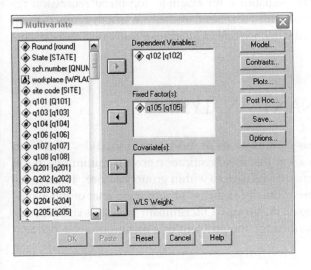

MULTIPLE ANALYSIS OF COVARIANCE (MANCOVA)

Multiple analysis of covariance (MANCOVA) is similar to MANOVA and the only difference is the addition of interval independents as 'covariates'. These covariates act as control variables, which try to reduce the error in the model and ensure the best fit.

MANCOVA analyses the mean differences among groups for a linear combination of dependent variables after adjusting for the covariate, for example, testing the difference in output by age group after adjusting for educational qualification.

Researchers can use MANCOVA in the same way as MANOVA. Researchers can click on Analyse, General Linear Model and Multivariate option for doing MANCOVA. In the multivariate option window, researchers can select the dependent variable to move it in the dependent variable box and factor variable into the fixed factor box. In addition, researchers need to specify the covariate, which has been used for adjustment. For example, in the case of testing the difference in output (productivity) by age group (after adjusting for educational qualification), educational qualification can be selected as the covariate.

REGRESSION: IN CASE OF CATEGORICAL DEPENDENT VARIABLES

In the case of multiple regression, dependent variables should preferably be measured on an interval continuous scale, though an ordinal scale can also be used as many interesting variables are categorical—patients may live or die, people may pass or fail. In these cases, it is imperative that the techniques evolved specially to deal with categorical dependent variables, such as discriminant analysis, probit analysis, log-linear regression and logistic regression, are used.

These techniques are applicable in different situations, for example, log-linear regression requires all independent variables to be categorical, whilst discriminant analysis strictly requires them all to be continuous. Logistic regression is used when we have a mixture of numerical and categorical independent variables.

DISCRIMINANT ANALYSIS

Discriminant analysis involves deriving linear combinations of independent variables which can discriminate between defined groups in such a way that misclassification error is minimized. It can be done by maximizing the between group variance relative to within group variance. Thus, it envisages predicting membership in two or more mutually exclusive groups from a set of independent variables, when there is no natural ordering on the groups. Discriminant analysis is an advantage over logistic regression, which is always described for the problem of a dichotomous dependent variable.

Discriminant analysis[5] can be thought of as just the inverse of one-way MANOVA, where the levels of the independent variable for MANOVA[6] become the categories of the dependent variable for discriminant analysis, and the dependent variables of the MANOVA become the independent variables for discriminant analysis.

Some researchers also define discriminant analysis as a scoring system that assigns score to each individual or object in the sample, which is the weighted average of the object's value on the set of dependent variables. Its application requires assignment of objects into mutually exclusive and exhaustive groups and the ability to classify observations correctly into constituents group is an important performance measure deciding success or failure of discriminant analysis.

The most common use of discriminant analysis is in cases where there are just two categories in the dependent variable; but it can also be used for multi-way categories. In a two-way discriminant function, the objective is to find a single linear combination of the independent variables that could discriminate between groups. It does so by building a linear discriminant function, which can then be used to classify the observations.

It is based on the assumption that independent variables must be metric and should have a high degree of normality. The overall fit is assessed by looking at the degree to which the group means differ and how well the model classifies it. It does so by looking at partial F values to determine which variables have the most impact on the discriminant function and higher the partial F, the more impact that variable has on the discriminant function.

Discriminant analysis uses a set of independent variables to separate cases based on defined categorical dependent variable. It does so by creating new variables based on linear combinations of the independent set provided by researchers. These new variables are defined so that they separate the groups as far apart as possible and effectiveness of the model in discriminating between groups is usually reported in terms of the classification efficiency, that is, how many cases would be correctly assigned to their groups using the new variables from discriminant function analysis. For example, a researcher may want to investigate which variables discriminate between eligible couples who decide (i) to adopt a spacing method, (ii) to adopt a permanent family-planning method, or (iii) not to adopt any family-planning method. For that purpose, the researcher would collect data on numerous variables in relation to the eligible couple's socio-economic profile as well their family and educational background. Discriminant analysis could then be used to determine which variable(s) are the best predictors of the eligible couple's subsequent family-planning method choice.

COMPUTATIONAL APPROACH

Discriminant analysis use three broad computational approaches to classify observations in groups based on the way in which independent variables are entered in equations.

a) *Forward stepwise analysis:* Forward stepwise analysis, as the name suggests, builds the discriminant model step-by-step. In this case, variables are entered one by one and at each step all variables are reviewed and evaluated to determine the variable, which contributes most in discriminating between groups and is included in the model.

b) *Backward stepwise analysis:* In the case of backward stepwise analysis, all variables are included in the model and then at each successive step the variable that contributes least to the prediction of group membership is eliminated. In the end only those variables are included in the model, which contribute the most to the discrimination between groups.

c) *F to enter, F to remove:* Forward stepwise analysis as well as backward stepwise analysis is guided by F to enter and F to remove values, as F value for a variable determines the statistical significance of a variable in discriminating between groups. It signifies the extent to which a variable makes an important contribution in classifying observation into groups.

INTERPRETING A TWO-GROUP DISCRIMINANT FUNCTION

A two-group discriminant function is like multiple regression and only difference is that the grouping variable is dichotomous in nature. Two-group discriminant analysis is also called the Fisher linear discriminant. In general, in the two-group case we fit a linear equation of the type:

$$Group = a + b_1 {*} x_1 + b_2 {*} x_2 + \dots + b_m {*} x_m$$

Where a is a constant and b_1 through b_m are regression coefficients.

Interpretation of the results of a two-group problem is similar to that of multiple regression. Like multiple regression, variables that have the largest regression coefficients are the ones that contribute most in classifying observations in groups.

MULTIPLE DISCRIMINANT ANALYSIS

Multiple discriminant analysis is an extension of the two-group discriminant function. It is used to classify a categorical dependent having more than two categories and is also termed as discriminant factor analysis. Multiple discriminant analysis, like PCA, depicts row of data matrix and mean vectors in a multidimensional space. The data axis and data space is determined in a way to attain optimal separation of the predefined groups.

DISCRIMINANT ANALYSIS USING SPSS

Discriminant analysis can be easily computed by using SPSS via the menu item Analyse, Classify and Discriminant option. Further, the discriminant analysis window can be accessed by clicking on the Discriminant option (see Figure 6.4). In the discriminant analysis window, the categorical dependent variable is placed in the Grouping Variable box wherein the range of the grouping variable is defined and independent variables are placed in the Independents box. After defining the grouping variable and independent variable, at the next stage the Statistics option needs to be clicked to select for means, univariate ANOVAs, Box's M, Fisher's coefficients and unstandardized coefficients. Researchers can also click on Classify to select for Priors Computed from Group Sizes and for a Summary Table.

FIGURE 6.4
Discriminant Analysis Using SPSS

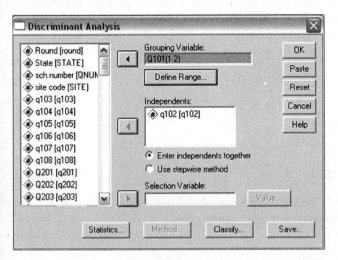

The goal of discriminant analysis is to describe how groups differ in terms of the values of the independent variable and testing whether or not difference between two groups are significant and using the discriminant function to predict group membership of an observation. To explain the methodology in detail, let us take the example of a salt trader's survey conducted in UP among salt traders to assess stocking pattern and trade details. In the present example, the volume purchased at a time and the average monthly sale of Baragara salt (big crystal salt) is taken as the dependent variable. Based on these variables, Baragara salt (big crystal salt type) is classified into two categories: iodized and non-iodized.

Tables 6.5 and 6.6 give the percentage of the variance accounted for by the one discriminant function generated and the significance of the function. Eigen values in Table 6.5 depicts how much per cent of variance each discrimination function contributes to the analysis. In the present case because there are two groups only one discriminant function was generated.

TABLE 6.5
Summary of Canonical Discriminant Functions—Eigen Value

Function	Eigen Value	% of Variance	Cumulative %	Canonical Correlation
1	.007[a]	100.0	100.0	.086

a. First 1 canonical discriminant functions were used in the analysis.

If Wilks' Lamda is low, the discriminant function is good.

TABLE 6.6
Summary of Canonical Discriminant Functions—Wilk's Lambda

Test of Function(s)	Wilks' Lambda	Chi-square	df	Sig.
1	.993	7.628	2	.022

The standardized canonical discriminant function coefficients in Table 6.7 give the standardized discriminant function coefficients for each discriminant function. The unstandardized canonical discriminant function coefficients are the regression weights for the prediction of a dichotomous dependent variable.

TABLE 6.7
Standardized Discriminant Function

	Function 1
Purchase volume at a time—Baragara	–.195
Average monthly sale—Baragara	1.116

The prior probabilities for groups table shows the prior probabilities set for each group. Table 6.8 is useful if you asked for priors to be computed from group sizes.

TABLE 6.8
Classification Statistics: Prior Probability for Groups

Whether Iodized Baragara	Prior	Cases Used in Analysis	
		Unweighted	Weighted
Yes	.974	1010	1010.000
No	.026	27	27.000
Total	1.000	1037	1037.000

Classification results (Table 6.9) describes the correctness of the categorization procedure. It can be seen that the procedure is accurate as 97.4 per cent of grouped cases are correctly classified.

TABLE 6.9
Classifications Results

		Whether Iodized Baragara	Predicted Group Membership		Total
			Yes	No	
Original	Count	Yes	1010	0	1010
		No	27	0	27
		Ungrouped cases	170	0	170
	%	Yes	100.0	.0	100.0
		No	100.0	.0	100.0
		Ungrouped cases	100.0	.0	100.0

Note: 97.4% of original grouped cases correctly classified.

LOGISTIC REGRESSION

Logistic regression sometimes referred to as 'choice model' is a variation of multiple regression that allows for the prediction of an event. Logistic regression is a statistical modelling method that is used for categorical dependent variables. It describes the relationship between the categorical dependent variables and one or more continuous and/or categorical independent variables.

Statistically speaking, logistical regression and linear least square regression are very different as the underlying algorithm and computational details are different, though from the practical standpoint they are almost identical. The difference lies in the nature of the dependent variable: with linear least squares regression, the dependant variable is a quantitative variable, while in the case of logistic regression, the dependent variable is a categorical variable.

In logistic regression contingency table is produced, which shows the classification of observations so as to study whether the observed and predicted events match. The sum of the events that were predicted to occur, which actually did occur, and the events that were predicted not to occur, which actually did not occur, divided by the total number of events, is a measure of the effectiveness of the model. This tool helps predict the choices consumers might make when presented with alternatives.

For example, researchers might be interested in predicting the relationship between chewing tobacco and throat cancer. The independent variable is the decision to chew tobacco (to chew tobacco or not to chew tobacco), and the dependent variable is whether to have throat cancer. In this case-control design, researchers have two levels in independent variables (to chew tobacco/not to chew tobacco) and two levels in dependent variables (throat cancer/no throat cancer).

Further, if researchers want to further explore the effect of age, they can add 'age' as continuous or categorical data as another dimension. Researchers, after formulating the hypothesis, then need to start with listing the data form of the data matrix in either case. Researchers can further categorize age into three age group, that is, under 40, 41–60, over 61 to have three age groups for the categorical age variable. In this case, it is possible to count the number of people in each cell of the contingency table. Table 6.10 summarizes the results of all three categorical variables in the form of a data matrix.

TABLE 6.10
A Person Smoking and Getting Cancer

Age Group	Lung Cancer	
Chewing tobacco	Yes	No
Under 25	20	5
25–45	30	10
Above 45	24	14
Not chewing tobacco		
Under 25	25	15
25–45	35	20
Above 45	45	25

Researchers can call it the 2(chewing tobacco)* 2(throat cancer)* 3(age group) contingency table, because researchers have two levels of habitually chewing tobacco, two levels of throat cancer and three levels of age groups.

The logistic regression model can be employed to test whether the practice of habitually chewing tobacco has an effect on throat cancer and whether the effect of age on throat cancer exists and whether there is an interaction between the habit of chewing tobacco and age group. Thus, logistic regression, by analysing associations tries to find the best-fit model that can predict the chance of throat cancer associated with the habit of chewing tobacco and age variables.

LOGISTIC REGRESSION USING SPSS

Logistic regression can be accessed via the menu item Analyse, Regression and Binary Logistic option. It is used to determine factors that affect the presence or absence of a characteristic when the dependent variable has two levels. Researchers can click on the binary logistic option to open the logistic regression window, where they can specify the dependent variables and covariates (see Figure 6.5). Also, the method of entering covariates in the equation, that is, enter, forward and backward should also be specified.

FIGURE 6.5
Logistic Regression Window Options

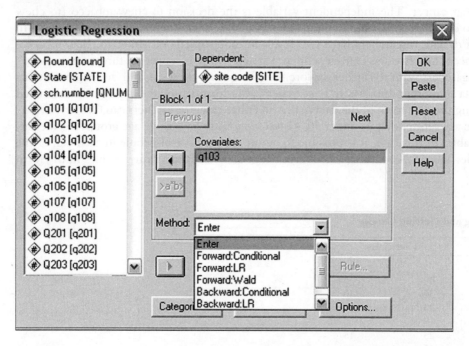

In a bid to explore the issue further, let us take an example wherein the dependent variable is traders currently stocking refined salt packets having the original value as 1 and 2 for stocking and not stocking respectively (see Table 6.11) and the independent variables are awareness regarding iodization (whose categorical coding is depicted in Table 6.12) and purchase price.

TABLE 6.11
Dependent Variable Encoding

Original Value	Internal Value
1	0
2	1

TABLE 6.12
Variable Frequency (Categorical Coding)

	Original Value and Internal Value		
Parameter	Value	Frequency	Coding
Whether Iodized (1)			
Q7G2			
Yes	1	1157	1.000
DK/CS	3	4	.000

Logistic regression applies maximum likelihood estimation after transforming the dependent variable into a logit variable. Thus it calculates changes in log odds of the dependent and not changes in the dependent itself as ordinary least square (OLS) does and estimates log likelihood function (see Table 6.13).

TABLE 6.13
Variable Model*

Dependent Variable	Currently Stocking Refined Salt Packets
Beginning block number 0	
Initial log likelihood function	
-2 log likelihood	64.454427

Note: *Constant is included in the model.

The independent variables entered in the equation are salt iodization and average purchase price of refined salt (see Table 6.14).

TABLE 6.14
Independent Variables Entered in the Equation

Beginning Block Number 1	Method: Enter
Variable(s) entered on step number 1	
Q7G2	Whether iodized
Q7G7	Purchase price (Rs/kg)

Estimation was terminated at iteration number 8 because log likelihood decreased by less than 0.01 per cent. Output tables for variable model provides the summary statistics, that is, the log likelihood function after iteration number 8 (Table 6.15), significance table (Table 6.16) and classification table for the dependent variable (Table 6.17), besides generating a summary of the variables statistics in the equation (Table 6.18).

TABLE 6.15
Summary Statistics

-2 log likelihood	52.576
Goodness of fit	699.764
Cox & Snell – R^2 **	.010
Nagelkerke – R^2 **	.188

Note: ** These are pseudo R-squares. Logistic regression does not have an equivalent to the R-squared that is found in OLS regression, but these are not R-square, so please be cautious.

TABLE 6.16
Testing Significance***

	Chi-square	df	Significance
Model	11.878	2	.0026
Block	11.878	2	.0026
Step	11.878	2	.0026

Note: ***In this example, the statistics for the step, model and block are the same because we have not used stepwise logistic regression or blocking. The value given in the significance column is the probability of obtaining the chi-square statistic (11.878) given that the null hypothesis is true, which of course, is the p value.

TABLE 6.17
Classification Table for Dependent Variable

Table row: Predicted Value Frequencies
Table column: Observed Value Frequencies
The Cut Value is 0.50

```
                     Predicted
                 Yes      No      Per cent Correct
                  Y    I   N
Observed          +———+———+
Yes       Y I 1156 I   0 I 100.00%
          +———+———+
No        N I  5 I   0 I  .00%
          +———+———+
          Overall  99.57%
```

TABLE 6.18
Summary of the Variables' Statistics in the Equation

Variables	B	SE	Wald	df	Sig.	R	Exp (B)
Iodization (1)	3.50	46.5298	.0057	1	.9400	.0000	33.1221
Monthly purchase	−1.3882	.4124	11.3286	1	.0008	−.3804	.2495
Constant	−3.4757	46.5516	.0056	1	.9405		

It thus follows that $\log(p/1-p) = b0 + b1*x1 + b2*x2 + b3*x3 + b3*x3 + b4*x4$

where p is the probability of stocking refined salt packets. Expressed in terms of the variables used in this example, the logistic regression equation is:

$$\log(p/1-p) = -3.475 + 3.5*\text{iodization} - 1.3882$$

Logistic regression has many analogies to ordinary least square regression, though the estimation approach is quite different. In logistic regression, logit coefficient corresponds to b coefficients in the least square regression and further the standard logit coefficient is equivalent to beta weights. In logistic regression, even a pseudo R-square statistics is available to summarize the strength of relationship, just like R-square does in OLS regression.

In logistic regression, by employing either the log likelihood test or the Wald statistics, researchers can easily test significance or best fit of a model. Though very large effects may result in large standard errors, small Wald chi-square values and small or zero partial R's, make assessing significance tests very difficult. In such situations, the log likelihood test of significance should be used.

INTERPRETING AND REPORTING LOGISTIC REGRESSION RESULTS

Logistic regression involves fitting the data in an equation in the form:

$$\text{logit }(p) = a + b_1x_1 + b_2x_2 + b_3x_3 + ...$$

The results are interpreted in the form of a log likelihood.

Log Likelihoods

Log likelihoods, a concept derived from maximum likelihood estimation (see Box 6.5), is a key concept in logistic regression. Likelihood just means probability, under a specified hypothesis.

BOX 6.5
Application of Maximum Likelihood Estimation

In classical statistical inference, we assume that a single population may generate a large number of random samples. Sample statistics are used to estimate the population parameters.

When applying the maximum likelihood example, we assume that the sample is fixed, but this sample can be generated by various different parent populations each having its own parameters. In the maximum likelihood approach, the sample is fixed but the parameters are assumed variable since they belong to different alternative parent populations. Among all possible set of parameters we choose the one that gives the maximum probability that its population would generate the sample actually observed.

In thinking about logistic regression, the null hypothesis is that all the coefficients in the regression equation take the value 0, and the hypothesis to be proved is that the model currently under consideration is accurate. We then work out the likelihood of observing the exact data we actually did observe under each of these hypotheses. The result is nearly always a very small number, and to make it easier to handle, we take its natural logarithm (that is, its log base e), giving us a log likelihood. Probabilities are always less than 1, so log likelihood's are always negative. Often, we work with negative log likelihoods for convenience.

Just like linear regression, logistic regression gives each regressor a coefficient b_1 which measures the regressor's independent contribution to variations in the dependent variable.

In case researchers try linear multiple regression for categorical variable, then they could run into problems as our predicted values can correspond to values greater than 1 or less than 0 but there are technical problems with dependent variables that can only take values of 0 and 1. What researchers want to predict from the knowledge of relevant independent variables is not a precise numerical value of the dependent variable, but rather the probability (p) that it is 1 rather than 0.

In order to predict values within these units, researchers use logit transformation. Logit (p) is the log (to base e) of the odds and odds are a function of p, the probability of a 1. Logit (p) is expressed as:

logit $(p) = \log (p/(1-p))$

While p can range from 0 to 1, logit can range from $-\infty$ to $+\infty$, which is appropriate for regression.

Thus, after transformation, researchers can state that the logit is a linearly related independent variable and data can be easily fitted into an equation of the form:

logit $(p) = a + b_1 x_1 + b_2 x_2 + b_3 x_3 + \ldots$

Logistic regression too, like linear regression, employs a best-fit regression equation, but the computation principle, or rather the estimation method, used is quite different. Logistic regression uses a maximum likelihood method, which maximizes the probability of getting the observed results given the fitted regression coefficient, instead of using the ordinary least square regression method, which are used in the case of linear regression for determining the line of best fit. Thus, goodness of fit and overall significance statistics used in logistic regression are different from those used in linear regression.

LOG-LINEAR, LOGIT AND PROBIT MODELS

Log-linear, logit and probit models are specialized cases of generalized linear models, which are frequently used for predicting categorical variables. Log-linear analysis is a type of multi-way frequency analysis and that is why sometimes log-linear analysis is also labelled as multi-way frequency analysis. Logit and probit models, in a similar way, try to predict the categorical variable by transforming the original variable.

The important difference between standard regression and these methods is the computation approach adopted. These methods differ from standard regression in substituting maximum likelihood estimation instead of using least squares estimation for estimating the dependent variable. Further, all these methods use transformed functions for predicting the dependent variable. The function used in log-linear analysis is the log of the dependent variable y, whereas in the case of the logit model, the transformed function is the natural log of the odds ratio. The probit model uses the inverse of the standard normal cumulative distribution as the transformed function to predict the categorical dependent variable.

In a bid to explore further log-linear analysis is used to determine if variables are related, to predict the expected frequencies of a dependent variable and to understand the relative importance of different independent variables in predicting a dependent and to confirm models using a goodness of fit test. Log-linear analysis is different from logistic regression in many ways. First, log-linear analysis, unlike binomial logistic regression, tries to predict the categorical nominal or ordinal variable. Second, in log-linear analysis, the categorical dependent variable follows Poisson distribution and even the transformed function is log not logit as in the case of logistic regression. Further, the prediction is based on the estimates of cell counts in a contingency table, not the logit of the dependent variable as in the case of logistic regression.

Probit and logit models deal with the problem of predicting a dependent variable, which is nominally or ordinally spaced. They differ as the probit response is assumed to be normally distributed, whereas in the case of logit, logistic distribution is assumed.

Logit models are a special class of log-linear models, which can be used to examine the relationship between a dichotomous dependent variable and one or more independent categorical variables. In discriminant analysis, the dependent variable is coded having a value of 0 and 1 and calculations are based on these values. In a logit model, the value of a dependent variable is based on the log odds. An odd ratio is the ratio between the frequencies of being in a particular category to being in another category.

The probit model, like the logit model, tries to predict the categorical dependent variable by assuming that the probit response is normally distributed. It is widely used to analyse dose-response data in medical studies. The probit model, like logit or logistic regression, focuses on transforming the dependent variables having values equal to 1. Unlike the logit model, which uses natural log of the odds ratio for transformation, the probit model uses the inverse of the standard normal cumulative distribution function for predicting the categorical variable.

The probit model can also be classified into ordinal probit represented as orprobit and multinomial probit represented as mprobit based on the type of predicted categorical variable.

Though both logit and probit use different transformation methods, usually they lead to the same conclusions for the same sort of data. Further, even the significance of a logit or probit model is tested in the same manner as for logistic regression. They also use −2 log likelihood for testing the model significance. Logit regression provides similar results to logistic regression as both use the maximum likelihood estimation method. However, some software programmes offers both logit regression and logistic regression with different output options (see Box 6.6).

BOX 6.6
Usage of Probit and Logit Models

SPSS provides the option of computing both logit and probit. Logit is available under menu item Analyse and sub-option Log-linear, whereas probit can be accessed via the menu item Analyse and the sub-option Regression.

The probit model, as mentioned earlier, is widely used for analysis of grouped dose-response data but it can also be used for other general purposes. In this procedure's dialogue boxes, researchers have to input covariate(s) and there must be at least one covariate. In probit, optionally, there can be one (and only one) categorical independent. If researchers specify a factor, probit includes it in the equation with a dummy variable for each level of the predictor and eliminates the intercept, so that the coefficient estimates are the predicted values for each level of the factor with the covariates set to 0.

In principle, one should use logit if one assumes that the categorical dependent reflects an underlying qualitative variable, as logit uses the binomial distribution, and use probit if one assumes that the dependent reflects an underlying quantitative variable as probit uses the cumulative normal distribution.

FIGURE 6.6a
Logit Model Using SPSS

FIGURE 6.6b
Probit Model Using SPSS

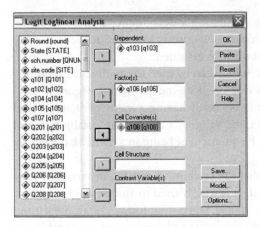

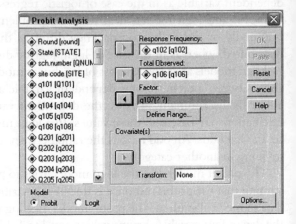

CANONICAL ANALYSIS

There are various ways in which the relationship between two or more variables can be assessed. Besides standard Pearson product moment correlation coefficients (r), there are various non-parametric measures of relationships that are based on the similarity of ranks in two variables. Canonical correlation[7] is an additional procedure for assessing the relationship between two sets of variables: one representing a set of independent variables and the other a set of dependent variables. In canonical correlation analysis, we seek two linear combinations: one for the dependent variable set and another for the independent variable set, or, in other words, it is used to seek correlation among several independent variables and several dependent variables simultaneously.

Canonical correlation[8] is different from multiple regressions in a way that while the former is used for many-to-many relationships, the latter is used for many-to-one relationships. Canonical correlation as in linear correlation tries to explain the percentage of variance in the dependent set explained by the independent set of variables along a given dimension.

In a bid to use canonical correlation analysis to test the significance of a relationship between canonical variates, data should meet the requirements of multivariate normality and homogeneity of variance.

It is particularly important when dependent variables are themselves correlated. In such cases, it can uncover complex relationships that reflect the structure between the dependent and independent variables. When only one dependent variable is available, canonical correlation reduces to multiple regression analysis.

The objective of the canonical relationship is to explain the relation of one set of variables by another such that linear correlation between the two set of variables is maximized. In canonical correlation, much like factor analysis, researchers can extract various sets of canonical correlation, each representing an independent pattern of relationship between the two latent variables. The first canonical correlation, like the first principal component analysis is the one, which explains most of the variance in relationship. In other words, the first canonical correlation explains the majority of the percentage variations in one set of variables explained by the other set.

INTERPRETING CANONICAL CORRELATION

Eigen value/Wilk's lambda is used as the criterion to explain variance in case of canonical correlation. Eigen values signify the amount of variance explained by each canonical correlation relating two sets of variables and is approximately equal to the square of canonical correlation. It is important to point out that Wilk's lambda is used in combination with the Bartlett's V to test significance of canonical correlation and if p value is less than 0.05, two sets of variables are significantly associated with canonical correlation.

Canonical weights are similar to beta weights in multiple regression analysis because they indicate the contribution of each variable to the variance of the respective within-set variance. Canonical weights tell about the relative contributions of the original x and y variables to the relationship between the x set and the y set. Further, like beta weights in multiple regression, canonical weights may also be affected due to multicollinearity. Thus, a structure correlation defining the correlation between the original variable and the composite provides a more stable source of information about the relative contribution of a variable.

CANONICAL CORRELATION IN SPSS

Canonical correlation in SPSS can be computed by selecting the menu item Analyse and then going to the General Linear Model option. Further, under General Linear Model the Multivariate option can be chosen. It is part of MANOVA in SPSS in which one set of variables is referred to as dependent and other as covariates.

In the MANOVA dialogue box, researchers can first enter a set of variables as dependent variables and a second set as covariates (see Figure 6.7). At the next stage, they need to click on Model and select Discriminant Analysis and click Continue.

FIGURE 6.7
Canonical Correlation (Multivariate Window)

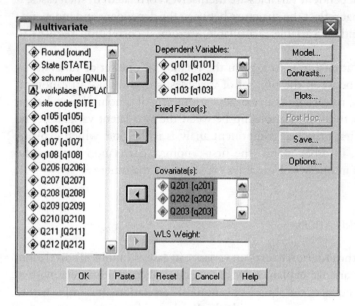

CONJOINT ANALYSIS

Conjoint analysis is concerned with the measurement of psychological judgements such as consumer preference. In most cases, consumers do not make choices based on a single attribute of a product, but on combing various attributes. They make judgements or trade-offs between various attributes to determine their final decision. To deconstruct the factors affecting their judgement-making process, it is imperative to analyse the trade-off between various alternatives.

In conjoint analysis, researchers try to deconstruct the overall responses so that the utility of each attribute can be inferred. It is thus defined as a compositional technique and a dependence technique, in that a level of preference for a combination of attributes and levels is developed. In this process, a part worth, or utility, is calculated for each level of attribute and combinations of attributes at specific levels are summed up to develop the overall preference for the attribute at each level.

Conjoint analysis thus predicts what products or services people will choose and assesses the weight people give to various factors which may have triggered their decision-making process. Depending on the utility of each attribute, ideal levels and combinations of attributes for products and services can be decided, which shall be most satisfying to the consumer. In other words, by using conjoint analysis, a service-providing organization can determine the features for their product or service, which can ensure maximum customer satisfaction. Conjoint analysis can be further segmented into (i) metric conjoint analysis, where the dependent variable has a metric value and (ii) non-metric conjoint analysis, where the dependent variable is non-metric in nature.

Conjoint analysis, though used primarily in market research study, is also used widely in development research by analysing stated preferences of consumers. It is the recommended approach to determine the willingness to pay for changes in the service level. A study was done in Kaliningrad[9] by Krüger where conjoint analysis was done to assess the willingness to pay for a package for services. The willingness to pay for water service was examined using stated preference techniques, that is, a stated preference bidding option consisting of a number of factors was devised. One of these factors was tariff and the rest were service factors like (i) water quality, (ii) smell, (iii) colour/clear water, (iv) pressure and (v) hours of water supply per day.

The choice of the service factors depends on the current standard of the supply, the feasible improvements and consumer requirements. Each of the factors has two, three or four levels, each of which describes a certain service level (see Table 6.19).

TABLE 6.19
Factors and Level for the Study

Factors	Levels
Water quality	As now
	Always safe to drink from tap
Smell	As now
	No smell at all
Supply and pressure	As now
	24-hour supply and pressure
	24-supply and good pressure
Cost	As now
	Plus10%
	Plus 25%
	Plus 50%

The respondents were given a choice to decide whether they prefer (i) to pay 50 per cent more to have water that is always safe to drink, with no smell at all and supplied 24-hours a day with good pressure, or (ii) to have water as of now and only pay 10 per cent more. If the water quality and supply are important issues to the respondent, and there is an ability to pay, the first option may be preferred. If saving money is important to the respondents and/or there is little ability to pay, the second option may be preferred.

Option one:
Water quality: Always safe to drink directly from the tap.
Smell: No smell at all.
Supply and pressure: Water supplied 24-hours a day and there is always good pressure.
Cost: An additional 50 per cent

Option two:
Water quality: As now.
Smell: As now.
Supply and pressure: As now.
Cost: An additional 10 per cent

The alternatives are described by a number of attributes, $x1$, $x2$, ..., xk, and these attributes are different for each respondent and each choice. The choice of the consumer reveals the consumer's preferences among the alternatives. A utility function was devised for the study and analysis showed the importance of the price difference between consumers with high income and consumers with low income.

CONJOINT ANALYSIS USING SPSS

Conjoint analysis can be easily done by using the SPSS advance model and researchers can use SPSS Conjoint's three procedures to develop product attributes. The first design generator—Orthoplan—is used to produce an orthogonal array of alternative potential products that combine different product features. It generates orthogonal main effects, fractional factorial designs and is not limited to two-level factors. Though in the majority of cases, researchers decide on the array of alternative option through pilot testing or based on some expert opinion. At the next stage, with the help of Plancards, researcher can quickly generate cards that respondents can sort to rank alternative products. Plancards is a utility procedure used to produce printed cards for a conjoint experiment, which needs to be sorted, ranked or rated by the subjects.

Then, at the end, analysis of the rated data is done by way of an ordinary least squares analysis of preference. It is important to note that the analysis is carried out on a plan file generated by Plancards, or a plan file input by the user using data list.

FACTOR ANALYSIS

In multivariate analysis, often volumes of data having many variables are analysed amidst the problem of multidimensionality. Multidimensionality is signified by a condition wherein groups of variables often move together and one reason for this is that more than one variable may be measuring the same driving principle governing the behaviour of the system. Researchers can simplify the problem by replacing a group of variables with a single new variable or to a smaller set of factors.

Factor analysis is concerned with identifying the underlying source of variation common to two or more variables. Factor analysis[10] first used by Charles Spearman (the term factor analysis was first introduced by Thurstone, 1931) is widely used nowadays as a data reduction or structure detection method. There are two objects of factor analysis: (i) to reduce the number of variables and (ii) to detect structure in the relationships between variables.

An assumption explicit in this common factor model is that the observed variation in each variable is attributable to the underlying common factors and to a specific factor. By contrast, there is no underlying measurement model with principal component; each principal component is an exact linear combination of the original variables.

Factor analysis can be either explanatory or confirmatory in nature. The objective of explanatory factor analysis is to identify these common factors and explain their relationship to observed data. Observed patterns of association in data determine the factor solution and the goal should be to infer factors structure from the patterns of correlation in the data.

In confirmatory factor analysis, we begin with strong prior notion that is sufficient to identify the model, that is, there is a single unique factor solution with no rotational indeterminacy. Rather than exploration, the goal is confirmation. We test our prior notion to see if it is consistent with the patterns in our data. The confirmatory approach has the advantage of providing goodness of fit tests for the models and standard errors for the parameters.

There are two main factor analysis methods:

a) *Common factor analysis*, which extracts factors based on the variance shared by the factors.
b) *Principal components analysis*[11], which extracts factors based on the total variance of the factors.

COMMON FACTOR ANALYSIS

Factor analysis differs from principal component analysis in a fundamental way. In factor analysis we study the inter-relationship among the variables in an effort to find a new set of variables fewer in number than the original variables and express what is common among the original variables.

PRINCIPAL COMPONENTS ANALYSIS

Principal components analysis is a data reduction technique, which re-expresses data in terms of components, which accounts for as much of available information as possible. The method generates a new set of variables, called principal components and each component is a linear combination of the original variables. All of the principal components are orthogonal to each other so there is no redundant information. The principal components as a whole form an orthogonal basis for the space of the data.

The principal components are extracted in such a fashion that the first principal component accounts for the largest amount of total variation in the data. The second principal component is defined as that weighted linear combination of observed variables, which is uncorrelated with the first linear combination and accounts for maximum amount of remaining total variation not already accounted by the first principal component. The first principal component is a single axis in space and when each observation is projected on that axis, the resulting values form a new variable having maximum variance. The second principal component is orthogonal to the first component and when observations are again projected on this axis, the resultant value forms a new variable having maximum variance among all possible choices of this second axis.

Thus, a full set of principal components is as large as the original set of variables, but in the majority of the cases, the sum of the variances of the first few principal components exceed 80 per cent of the total variance of the original data.

FACTOR ANALYSIS: STEPWISE APPROACH

The first step in factor analysis is to generate a correlation matrix among variables. Let us take a hypothetical example wherein out of six variables, three variables, namely, env1, env2 and env3 are related to the environment and three other variables, namely, pov1, pov2 and pov3 are related to poverty. The first step in the case of factor analysis is to calculate the correlation matrix, which details out the correlation among the mentioned variables as shown in Table 6.20.

TABLE 6.20
Correlation Matrix Showing Correlations Among Variables

Variable	env1	env2	env3	pov1	pov2	pov3
env1	1.00	.65	.65	.14	.15	.14
env2	.65	1.00	.73	.14	.18	.24
env3	.65	.73	1.00	.16	.24	.25
pov1	.14	.14	.16	1.00	.66	.59
pov2	.15	.18	.24	.66	1.00	.73
pov3	.14	.24	.25	.59	.73	1.00

The result shows that the variables symbolising environment and poverty attributes are highly correlated among themselves. The correlation across these two types of items is comparatively small.

Number of Factors to Extract

As discussed earlier, factor analysis and principal component analysis are data reduction methods, that is, they are methods for reducing the number of variables. But the key question that needs to be answered is, how many factors researchers want to extract considering that every successive factor account for less and less variability. Thus, the decision of the number of factors to extract depends on the situation when the researchers are certain there is very little random variability left.

Researchers start the process of deciding on the number of factors to extract through a correlation matrix, where the variances of all variables are equal to 1.0. Therefore, the total variance in that matrix is equal to the number of variables. For example, if we have 10 variables each with a variance of 1 then the total variability that can potentially be extracted is equal to 10 times 1. Researchers usually decide on the numbers of factors to be extracted based on certain criteria such as Eigen values, Kaiser criteria and scree test (see Box 6.7).

a) *Eigen value:* Eigen value[12] signifies the amount of variance explained by a factor. Thus, the sum of the Eigen values is equal to the number of variables. It helps in answering the question about the number of factors to be extracted.

b) *The Kaiser criterion*[13]: The Kaiser criterion proposed by Kaiser (1960) suggests that since an Eigen value is the amount of variance explained by one factor, there is no point in retaining factors that explain less variance than is contained in one variable. Thus, researchers should retain only those factors that have Eigen values greater than 1. This is probably the one most widely used criterion. In the mentioned example, using this criterion, we can retain two factors (principal components).

c) *The scree*[14] *test:* Scree test is a graphical method, which was first proposed by Cattell (1966)[15]. In a scree test, researchers plot successive Eigen values in a simple line plot and researchers look for a place where smooth decrease of Eigen values appears to level out abruptly.

BOX 6.7
Deciding on the Number of Factors to Extract

There are various indicators, which are used by researchers to decide on the number of factors that need to be extracted. Thus, it is imperative to decide on the indicator and level of indicator, which should be considered as the cut off to decide on the number of factors to be extracted. Kaiser's measure of statistical adequacy is one such measure, which signifies the extent to which every variable can be predicted by all other variables and it is widely believed that an overall measure of .80 or higher is very good, though a measure of under 0.50 is considered as poor.

The first factor extracted explains the most variance and the factors are extracted as long as the Eigen values are greater than 1.0 or the scree test visually indicates the number of factors to extract.

Extraction of Factors

a) *Factor loadings:* Factor loadings are described as the correlation between a factor and a variable. Let us assume that two factors are extracted. Specifically, let us look at the correlations between the variables and the two factors as they are extracted (see Table 6.21).

TABLE 6.21
Extraction of Factors Among Variables

Variable	Factor 1/Component 1	Factor 2/Component 2
env1	.654384	.564143
env2	.715256	.541444
env3	.741688	.508212
pov1	.634120	−.563123
pov2	.706267	−.572658
pov3	.707446	−.525602

It is evident from the table that usually the first factor is generally more highly correlated with the variables than the second factor.

b) *Rotating the factor structure:* Initial extracted components may not show a clear-cut demarcation, thus it become imperative that a rotational strategy is adopted. Researchers can plot factor loadings in a scatter plot wherein each variable is represented as a point. Factor loading/structure is then rotated by rotating axes to attain a clear pattern of loadings, which shall demarcate between the extracted components.

c) *Rotational strategies:* There are various rotational strategies, which can be used by researchers to obtain a clear pattern of loadings, that is, factors that are somehow clearly marked by high loadings for some variables and low loadings for others. Some of the most widely used rotational strategies are varimax, quartimax and equamax.

All rotational strategies are based on the assumption of maximizing variance due to rotation of the original variable space. To explain it further let us take the example of varimax rotation in which, the criterion for rotation is to maximize the variance of the new factor, while minimizing the variance around the new variable.

Even after deciding on the line on which the variance is maximal, there still remains some variability around the line. In principal components analysis, after the first factor has been extracted, that is, after the first line has been drawn through the data, researchers continue to do so to extract more line to maximize the remaining variability, around the line. In this manner, researchers can extract consecutive components/factors. Further, as each successive extracted factor tries to maximize the variability that is not captured by the preceding factor, the consecutive factors are independent of each other and orthogonal to each other. Table 6.22 presents factor loading of two components, extracted to maximize variance.

TABLE 6.22
Table Showing Factor Loadings

Variable	Factor 1/Component 1	Factor 2/Component 2
env1	.862443	.051643
env2	.890267	.110351
env3	.886055	.152603
pov1	.062145	.845786
pov2	.107230	.902913
pov3	.140876	.869995

Interpreting the factor structure: Now the pattern is much clearer. As expected, the first factor is marked by high loadings on the environment items, the second factor is marked by high loadings on the poverty items.

FACTOR ANALYSIS USING SPSS

Researchers can access factor analysis by selecting the Factor sub-option under the Data Reduction option in the Analyse menu option. Researchers can then click on the Factor option to open the Factor Analysis window (see Figure 6.8a). In the factor analysis window they can select all variables for factor analysis and move them to the variable box. The factor analysis window at the bottom has three important buttons named Descriptives, Extraction and Rotation, which provide important measures of factor analysis. Under the descriptive window, researchers need to select the initial option under statistics and coefficients, significance levels and KMO and Bartlett's test of sphericity under correlation matrix (see Figure 6.8b). The factor analysis extraction sub-window provides various options such as generalized least square, maximum likelihood and principal component as extraction methodology. Depending on the research methodology and extraction objective, researchers can select the appropriate extraction method from the drop down menu (see Figure 6.8c).

Further, under the rotation sub-window, researchers can select the appropriate rotation strategy from various rotation strategies provided such as varimax, promax and quartimax (see Figure 6.8d).

FIGURE 6.8a
Factor Analysis Using SPSS

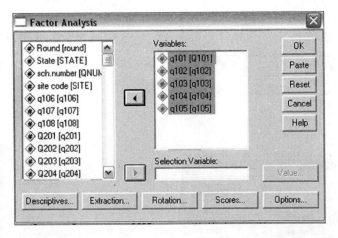

FIGURE 6.8b
Factor Analysis: Descriptive Window

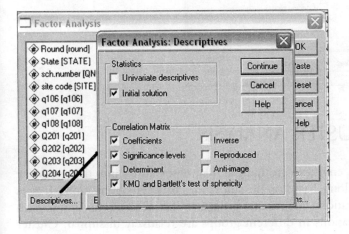

FIGURE 6.8c
Factor Analysis: Extraction Window

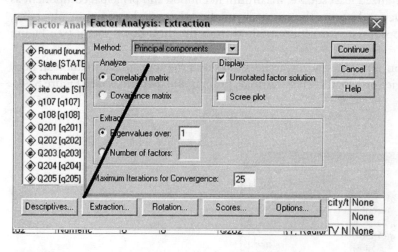

FIGURE 6.8d
Factor Analysis: Rotation Window

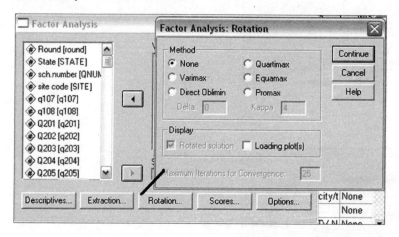

CLUSTER ANALYSIS

Cluster analysis, as the name suggests, envisages grouping similar observations into the respective clusters or categories to which they belong, based on the similarities between observations. It does so by dividing a large group of observations into smaller groups so that observations within each group is relatively similar and observations in different groups are relatively dissimilar. Cluster analysis like factor analysis and multidimensional scaling is an interdependence method where the relationship between subjects and objects are explored without identifying the dependent variable.

Most cluster analyses are undertaken with the objective of addressing the heterogeneity of data. It is important to keep in mind that separating the data into more homogenous groups is not same as finding naturally occurring clusters. Finding naturally occurring clusters requires that there be groups of observations with relatively high local density separated by regions of relatively low density.

The term cluster analysis[16] actually encompasses a number of different classification algorithms and there are three main clustering methods:

a) Hierarchical.
b) Non-hierarchical.
c) A combination of both.

HIERARCHICAL METHOD

Hierarchical methods combines data in two ways: (i) agglomerative methods, which begin with each observation as a separate cluster and then goes on to join clusters together at each step until one cluster of size n remains and (ii) divisive methods, which, quite in contrast, starts by assuming all observations in one cluster and then goes on to divide the cluster into two or more at each step of the process until m clusters of size 1 remain.

NON-HIERARCHICAL METHOD

Non-hierarchical cluster methods envisage combining observations into predetermined groups or clusters, using an appropriate algorithm. Non-hierarchical clusters are also known as k means clustering, wherein k specifies the number of predetermined clusters.

Non-hierarchical clustering combines observations into predetermined clusters based on certain methods such as (i) sequential threshold method, which groups all observations within a threshold of a predetermined cluster centre into a cluster, (ii) parallel threshold method, wherein observations are grouped parallel to each other into several predetermined cluster centres and (iii) optimizing partitioning method, wherein all observations, which are assigned initially, may be reassigned to optimize the partitioning criterion.

DISTANCE MEASURES: HIERARCHICAL METHOD

The hierarchical method of clustering is the most widely used approach; hence, we will concentrate on exploring the process of clustering in the case of the hierarchical method. Hierarchical clustering uses the dissimilarities or distances between objects while forming the clusters and these dissimilarities can be based on a single dimension or multiple dimensions. There are various ways of computing distances between objects in a multidimensional space, some of which are explained in brief:

a) *Euclidean distance:* Euclidean distance is the most used type of distance. It is an extension of the Pythagoras theorem and calculates the simple geometric distance in a multidimensional space. It is computed as:

$$\text{Distance } (x, y) = \{\Sigma_i\,(x_i - y_i)^2\}^{\frac{1}{2}}$$

Euclidean distances are simply geometric distances and thus are usually computed from the raw data. In Euclidean distances, the geometric distance calculated between any two observations is not affected due to other observations in the analysis. Euclidean distances can be greatly affected by differences in scale among the dimensions from which the distances are computed.

b) *Squared Euclidean distance:* Squared Euclidean distance is calculated to put greater weight on objects that are further apart, hence, the Euclidean distance measure is squared to derive the result. This distance is computed as:

$$\text{Distance } (x, y) = \{\Sigma_i\,(x_i - y_i)^2\}$$

c) *City-block distance:* City-block distance is also known as Manhattan distance. It calculates the distance based on the sum of absolute difference between coordinates of the observation or case. Further, in this measure, absolute difference is not squared, thus the effect of outliers is minimized as compared to Euclidean distance. The city-block distance is computed as:

$$\text{Distance } (x, y) = \Sigma_i\,|x_i - y_i|$$

d) *Chebychev distance:* It is used to compute distance between interval data. Chebychev distance computes the maximum absolute difference between variables. The Chebychev distance is computed as:

$$\text{Distance } (x, y) = \text{Maximum } |x_i - y_i|$$

e) *Power distance:* Power distance is used to increase or decrease the progressive weight that is placed on dimensions. The power distance is computed as:

$$\text{Distance } (x, y) = (\Sigma_i\,|x_i - y_i|^p)^{1/r}$$

Where r and p are user-defined parameters.

AMALGAMATION OR LINKAGE RULES

In hierarchical clustering, a critical question that arises is how does one compare distance between two observations and what are the options to link observations. The answer lies in amalgamation or linkage rules, which are used to combine clusters. Initially each object represents a cluster and thus distances between all objects or clusters are computed based on appropriately chosen distance measures. The distance measure provides a linkage or amalgamation rule determining when two clusters are sufficiently similar to be linked together. There are various linkages or amalgamation rules, which are used to determine the linkage of observations or clusters such as single link, average link or median method, etc.

a) *The single link method:* The single link method is based on the nearest neighbour method, where the observation is joined to another cluster after computing the shortest distance from any point in one cluster to another cluster. An observation is joined to a cluster if it gives a likeness to at least one member of a cluster.

b) *The complete link method:* The complete link method, quite in contrast to the single link method, is based on the farthest neighbour method. In the complete linkage method, observations are joined to a cluster if observations are closer to the farthest members of that cluster than the furthest member of any other cluster.

c) *The average link method:* In the average linkage approach, each time a cluster is formed, its average score is computed based on which they are joined together if the average scores are closer. Observations are joined to a cluster based on average distance calculated between all points in one cluster to another cluster.

d) *The weighted average link method:* Weighted average link method computes the average distance between all pairs of objects in two different clusters and uses size of each cluster as a weighting factor. In case the process does not take the relative sizes of the clusters into account in combining clusters, the process is known as unweighted pair group method using unweighted average.

e) *The median method:* The median method computes the distance between two clusters as distance between their centriods and uses the size of each cluster as the weighting factor.

f) *The centroid method:* The centroid method[17] assumes that the distance between clusters is the distance between their centroids. In a way it replaces a cluster, on agglomeration, with the centroid value.

g) *Ward's method:*[18] Ward's method uses the analysis of variance approach to compute distances between clusters and calculates the sum of squares of between clusters. An observation is joined in a cluster if that minimizes the sum of the squares between clusters.

CLUSTER ANALYSIS USING SPSS

Researchers can access both of the K-means and the hierarchical cluster analysis by selecting the Classify option under the Analyse menu option. Hierarchical method of clustering is the most used approach; hence, we will concentrate on exploring the hierarchical approach using SPSS. Researchers can open the hierarchal cluster analysis window by clicking on the Hierarchal Cluster option (see Figure 6.9a).

The cluster analysis window at the bottom has three important buttons named Statistics, Plots and Method, which provide the key option for doing cluster analysis. Under hierarchical cluster analysis: plot, researchers need to click on the Dendogram option and None Incase of Icicle option, in case they want to pictorially assess the way clusters are formed from each case (see Figure 6.9b). Further, the Hierarchical Cluster Analysis: Method window provides various options such as between group linkage, within group linkage and centroid for clustering method. It also provides various measures for computing distances based on level of data, that is, interval, counts and binary. Depending on the research methodology, researchers can select the appropriate clustering method and distance measure from the drop down menu (see Figure 6.9c).

FIGURE 6.9a
Cluster Analysis Using SPSS

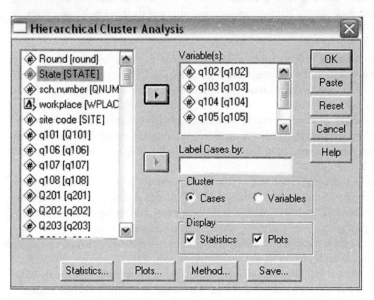

FIGURE 6.9b
Hierarchical Cluster Analysis: Plot Window

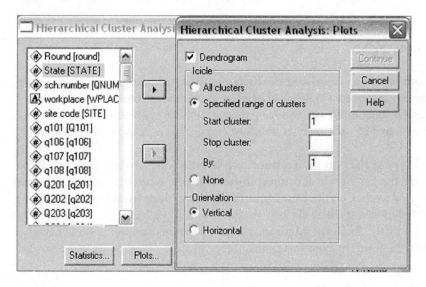

FIGURE 6.9c
Hierarchical Cluster Analysis: Method Window

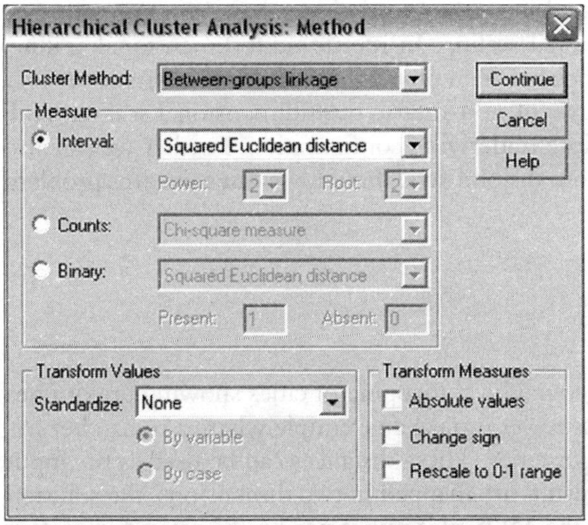

MULTIDIMENSIONAL SCALING (MDS)

Multidimensional scaling originated from the study of psychometrics. Torgerson[19] first proposed the term MDS and its method. Its development and initial application were to understand people's judgements or perceptions. But now, it is used widely in areas of psychometrics, sociology and even in market research.

Multidimensional scaling can be described as an alternative to factor analysis. It refers to a set of methods used to obtain spatial representation of the similarities or proximities between data sets. In certain cases, both principal component analysis and factor analysis are scaling methods, which we can use to depict observations in a reduced number of dimensions.

The goal of MDS is to use proximity or similarity between data sets to create a map of appropriate dimensionality such that the distances in the map closely resemble the similarities that is used to create it. Thus, MDS is also described as 'a set of multivariate statistical methods for estimating the parameters in and assessing the model fit of various spatial distance models for proximity data' (Davison, 1983).[20] It is also described as a decomposition approach that uses perceptual mapping to present the dimensions.

The first task in MDS is to ascertain that researchers have the similarity or dissimilarity data to plot. The best way to ensure that is to formulate the research schedule and questions in such a way that the respondents provide information about the similarities between a product and service attribute. Respondents can be asked to rate their preference of top schools based on the quality of education and cost of education. In case researchers do not have similarity/dissimilarity data to start with but have data in such a way that respondents have opined their view on certain products or services on certain indicators then certain statistical software such as SPSS provide the option to compute similarity data from such data to be used further for conceptual mapping.

Types of Multidimensional Scaling

Multidimensional scaling can be further classified into two broad classes based on the nature of data, i.e., metric and non-metric multidimensional scaling. In metric multidimensional scaling, similarity data is used to reflect the actual distance between physical objects in data sets to recover the underlying configuration; whereas in the case of non-metric multidimensional scaling, rank order of proximities is used as base data to explore underlying configuration. Further we can also use data depicting proximity between objects from disjoint sets, though we can solve this problem using non-metric MDS.

Multidimensional Scaling: Application

One of the most quoted examples of MDS is geographical mapping of cities showing proximities between cities. In a bid to further explore the issue, let us take an example where a researcher has a matrix of distances between a numbers of major cities. These distances can be used as the input data to derive an MDS solution and when the results are mapped in two dimensions, the solution will reproduce a conventional map, except that the MDS plot might need to be rotated in certain dimensions to conform to expectations. However, once the rotation is completed, the configuration of the cities will be spatially correct. Another example could be of product rating, wherein respondents assess their preference of a brand, say iodized and non-iodized salt, on parameters such as affordability and acceptability. After this, the researcher maps the observations to specific locations in a multi-dimensional space usually a two- or three-dimensional space such that the distances between points match the given similarity or dissimilarities as closely as possible.

Dimensions of this conceptual space along with proximity data need to be interpreted to understand the nature and extent of association between data. But like factor analysis, in MDS also the orientation of the axes in the final solution is arbitrary. Thus, the interpretation of axes is at the discretion of the researcher, who chooses the orientation of axes that are easily interpretable.

Multidimensional scaling as an approach has come a long way since its initial conceptualization by Torgerson. Now the latest version we are discussing is due to the work of Kruskal and he defined it in term of minimization of a cost function called stress, which is simply a measure of lack of fit between dissimilarities and distances. Kruskal's stress measure is a 'badness of fit' measure; which ascertain the best fit of observation in a multidimensional space; a stress percentage of 0 indicates a perfect fit and over 20 per cent is a poor fit. The dimensions can be interpreted either subjectively, by letting the respondents identify the dimensions, or objectively, by the researcher.

Multidimensional Scaling Using SPSS

The multidimensional scaling analysis option can be assessed in SPSS by going to the menu item 'analyse', 'scale' and 'multi dimension scaling'. As mentioned earlier, the objective of MDS is to identify and model the structure and dimensions from the dissimilarity data observed/collected, hence the type of basic data required is dissimilarities, or distance data.

In case researchers have objectively measured variables, MDS can still be used as a data reduction technique, as SPSS provides a procedure, which compute distances from multivariate data. Multidimensional scaling, as discussed earlier can also be applied to subjective ratings of dissimilarity between objects or concepts (see Figure 6.10). Further, the MDS procedure can also handle dissimilarity data from multiple sources such as questionnaire respondents.

FIGURE 6.10
Multidimensional Scaling Using SPSS

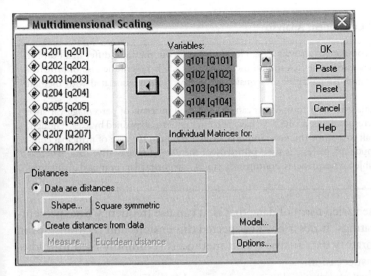

CORRESPONDENCE ANALYSIS

Correspondence analysis[21] is also known as perceptual mapping. It simply describes the relationship between two nominal variables in a perceptual map. It can best be described as a method of factoring categorical variables and displaying them in a space, depicting their associations in two or more dimensions.

Correspondence analysis helps researchers in analysing two-way tables whose cells shows measurement of correspondence between rows and columns. It is an appropriate method for summarizing categorical data through a visual representation of the relationships between the row categories and the column categories in the same space. However, unlike MDS, in correspondence analysis, both the independent variables and the dependent variables are examined at the same time.

Correspondence analysis[22] starts with analysing correspondence tables. A correspondence table is a two-way table whose cells contain measurements of correspondence between the rows and columns. The measure of correspondence could be due to association or interaction between row and column variables. Thus, the next question which arises is how is correspondence analysis different from the cross-tabulation procedure and the answer is simple. Cross-tabulation does not give any information about which categories of variables are similar or closer and also does not give any information about the extent of their closeness/association.

Correspondence analysis, like principal component analysis allows researchers to examine and depict the relationship/association between nominal variables graphically in a multidimensional space (see Box 6.8). It computes row and column scores and produces plots based on the score. In the end, categories which are similar to each other, appear closer and it becomes very easy to deduce which variables are similar to each other.

BOX 6.8
Correspondence Analysis and Principal Component Analysis

Correspondence analysis and principal component analysis have a lot in common but they also differ in a number of ways. Correspondence analysis depicts association in a multidimensional space, whereas in the case of principal component analysis, all points in multidimensional space are considered to have a mass associated with them at their given locations.

In the case of principal component analysis, each component can be described in terms of percentage variance expressed and similarly in the case of correspondence analysis we have percentage inertia explained by axes. Though, in the latter case, the values are too small to assume the same importance as they do in the case of principal component analysis. Further, principal component analysis is used primarily in the case of quantitative data, whereas correspondence analysis is recommendable for frequencies, contingency tables, categorical data or mixed qualitative/ categorical data.

Correspondence analysis can use varied form of data, that is, it can use frequency data, percentages, or even data in the form of ratings. It describes unexpected dimensions and relationships in keeping with the tradition of exploratory data analysis. This method is commonly used in studies of modern ecology and vegetation succession.

Correspondence analysis seeks to represent the inter-relationships of categories of row and column variables on a two-dimensional map. For example, consider a typical two-dimensional contingency table. Let us take the example of a study wherein eligible people (people in the reproductive age group) from different standards of living index (high, medium and low) were asked about the message they have received on birth spacing methods. Table 6.23 shows the correspondence table for both the variables.

TABLE 6.23
Correspondence Table

| Standard of Living Index (SLI) | Seen/Heard Any Message about Birth Spacing | | | |
	Yes	No	3	Active Margin
Low	137	58	3	198
Medium	292	82	6	380
High	268	30	4	302
Active margin	697	170	13	880

The first step in a correspondence analysis after making the correspondence table is to examine the set of relative frequencies. This concept is basic to correspondence analysis. Tables 6.24 and 6.25 give the row and column profiles for the data. The final row of the row profiles and the final column of the column profiles are labelled 'average'. These are the proportion of the number of respondents in the row or column.

TABLE 6.24
Correspondence Analysis: Row Profile

| Standard of Living Index (SLI) | Seen/Heard Any Message about Birth Spacing | | | |
	Yes	No	3	Active Margin
Low	.692	.293	.015	1.000
Medium	.768	.216	.016	1.000
High	.887	.099	.013	1.000
Mass	.792	.193	.015	

TABLE 6.25
Correspondence Analysis: Column Profile

| Standard of Living Index (SLI) | Seen/Heard Any Message about Birth Spacing | | | |
	Yes	No	3	Mass
Low	.197	.341	.231	.225
Medium	.419	.482	.462	.432
High	.385	.176	.308	.343
Active margin	1.000	1.000	1.000	

The column head 'proportion of inertia accounted for' shows that the first dimension explains 99 per cent of the total inertia, a measure of the spread of the points. The first two dimensions together explain 100 per cent and, therefore, a two-dimensional solution appears satisfactory. Further, an examination of the contribution to the inertia of each row and column point helps in the interpretation of the dimensions. Table 6.26 showing contribution to inertia can be produced by clicking on the option to show an overview of row and column points.

TABLE 6.26
Correspondence Analysis: Summary Statistics

| Dimension | Singular Value | Inertia | Chi-square | Sig. | Proportion of Inertia | | Confidence Singular Value | |
					Accounted for	Cumulative	Standard Deviation	Correlation 2
1	.188	.036			.999	.999	.031	.028
2	.006	.000			.001	1.000	.034	
Total		.036	31.289	.000[a]	1.000	1.000		

a. 4 degrees of freedom.

CORRESPONDENCE ANALYSIS USING SPSS

Researcher can access correspondence analysis by selecting the Correspondence Analysis sub-option under the Data Reduction option in the Analyse menu option. Researchers can then click on the

Correspondence Analysis option to open the Correspondence Analysis window (see Figure 6.11a) where researchers can select the row and column variable from the list to move into the row and column variable dialogue box. The correspondence analysis window at the bottom has three important buttons: Model, Statistics and Plots, which provide further options for selecting appropriate models and statistics.

FIGURE 6.11a
Correspondence Analysis Using SPSS

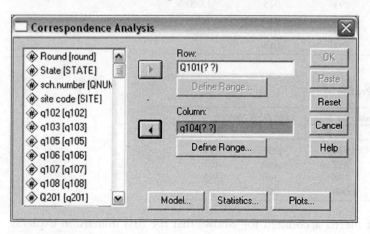

FIGURE 6.11b
Correspondence Analysis: Method Window

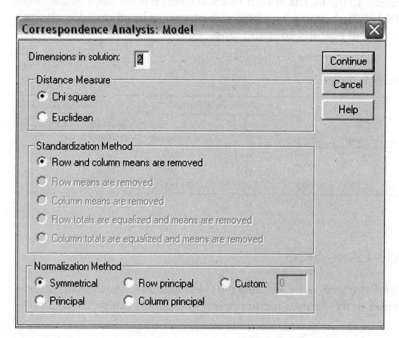

FIGURE 6.11c
Correspondence Analysis: Statistics Window

Correspondence Analysis: Statistics

☑ Correspondence table

☑ Overview of row points   ☐ Row profiles

☑ Overview of column points   ☐ Column profiles

☐ Permutations of the correspondence table

   Maximum dimension for permutations: 1

Confidence Statistics for

☑ Row points   ☐ Column points

[Continue] [Cancel] [Help]

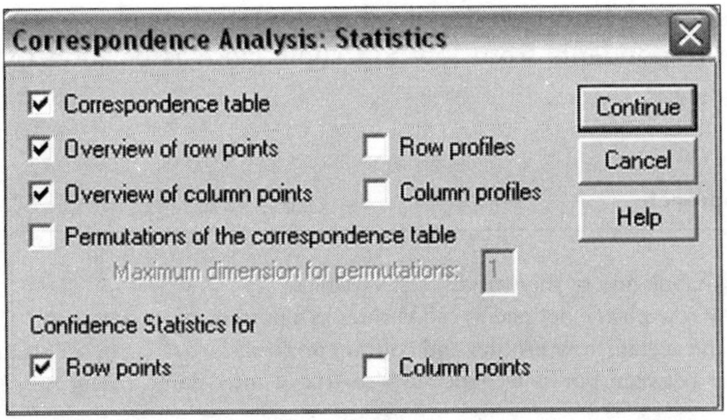

Researchers under Correspondence Analysis: Model window can specify the number of dimension they wish to have in the solution. Besides, researchers can select the appropriate distance measure, standardization method and normalization method (see Figure 6.11b). SPSS 10.0 offers five forms of standardization, which are known as normalization. Row principal is the traditional form and is used to compare row variable points. Column principle is the corresponding normalization for comparing column variable points. Principal normalization is a compromise used for comparing points within either or both variables but not between variables. Custom normalization spreads the inertia over both row and column scores to varying degrees. In case of symmetrical normalization, rows are the weighted average of column divided by matching value and columns are weighted average of row divided by matching value. Further, under Correspondence Analysis: Statistics window (see Figure 6.11c) researchers can select the correspondence table, row profile and column profile options for better understanding.

FIGURE 6.12
Figure Showing Correspondence Map

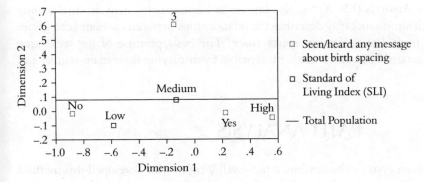

A correspondence map displays two of the dimensions, which emerge from normalization of point distances, and the points are displayed in relation to these dimension. In the present example (see Figure 6.12), symmetrical normalization is used to plot various categories. How satisfactory is this as a representation is explained by the inertia of each dimension. Total inertia is the sum of Eigen values and reflects the spread of points around the centroid.

In the example given in Figure 6.12, the respondents from high and medium SLI are closely associated with the message received while respondents from low SLI show close association to respondents who have not received the message.

BOX 6.9
Doing Correspondence Analysis: Stepwise Approach

Steps:
a) At the first stage, researchers shall do the cross-tabulation of the two discrete variables.
b) At the next stage, researchers shall compute the row profile defined as cell entities as a percentage of row marginal. Besides, researchers shall also compute the average row profiles and column profiles.
c) Researchers shall compute chi-square distance between points to generate a matrix of inter-point distances, which is the input data for normalization.
d) Inter-point data are put through normalization to generate dimensions to be used as axes in plotting correspondence maps.

DETRENDED CORRESPONDENCE ANALYSIS

Correspondence analysis usually suffers from two problem—the arch effect and compression. To remove these two effects, Hill and Guach (1980)[23] developed the technique of detrended correspondence analysis, which envisages removing arch effect and compression through detrending and rescaling.

Detrending removes the arch effect by dividing a map into two series of vertical partitions, whereas rescaling realigns the positions of samples along the primary axis as well as vertical axis.

MULTIPLE CORRESPONDENCE ANALYSIS

Multiple Correspondence Analysis (MCA)[24] is also known as homogeneity analysis, dual scaling and reciprocal averaging. It simultaneously describes the relationships between cases and categories by displaying them in a multidimensional property space. The basic premise of the technique is that complicated multivariate data can be made presentable by displaying their main regularities and patterns in plots.

PATH ANALYSIS

The popularization of path analysis can be attributed to Sewall Wright, who developed this method as a means for studying the direct and indirect effects of a variable where some variables are viewed as the cause and others as effects. Path analysis is a method for studying the patterns of causation among a set of variables and is also referred by some researchers as a straightforward extension of multiple regressions. Though path analysis diagrams are not essentially for numerical analysis, they are quite useful in displaying patterns of causal relationship among a set of observable and unobservable variables. This is best explained by considering a path diagram, which can be drawn by simply writing the names of the variables and drawing an arrow from each variable to any other variable it affects.

It is important here to distinguish between input and output path diagrams. An input path diagram is the result of an assumption made beforehand, which represents the causal connections that are predicted by our hypothesis. An output path diagram represents the results of a statistical analysis and shows what was actually found during analysis. Figure 6.13 presents an input diagram, showing assumption of predicted hypothesis.

FIGURE 6.13
Input Path Diagram

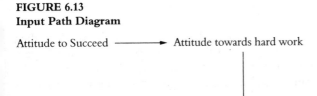

Path analysis is a framework for describing theories. It is particularly helpful in identifying specific hypotheses. Single-headed arrows represent a single direction of causation and double-headed arrows indicate that influence is in both directions.

It is helpful to draw the arrows so that their widths are proportional to the size of the path coefficients and if researchers do not want to specify the causal direction between two variables, a double-headed arrow[25] can be used.

The advantage of the path analysis model is the observation of latent variables. The variables we measure are called observed variables and hypotheses are conceptualized for unobserved variables. Path analysis can evaluate causal hypotheses and in some cases it can even be used to test two or more causal hypotheses, but it cannot establish the direction of causality.

STRUCTURAL EQUATION MODELLING

Structural equation modelling (SEM) tests specific hypothesis about the dependence relationship between a set of variables simultaneously. It represents a family of techniques, including latent variable analysis and confirmatory factor analysis. It can incorporate latent variables, which refer to the unobservable factors from our measurement models and structural equation refers to specific models of dependence between dependent and independent latent variables. For example, intelligence levels can only be inferred with direct measurement of variables like test scores, level of education and other related measures.

In a nutshell, structured equation modelling is a family of statistical techniques which incorporates and integrates all standard multivariate analysis methods. For example, SEM in which each variable has only one indicator is a type of path analysis. It assumes that there is a causal structure among a set of unobserved variables and that the observed variables are indicators of the unobserved or latent variables.

Structural equation modelling is used both for the purpose of confirmation and for testing. It can be used as a more powerful alternative to multiple regression, path analysis, factor analysis and analysis of covariance. It is defined as a confirmatory procedure, which uses three broad approaches.

a) *Strictly confirmatory approach:* The strictly confirmatory approach tests whether patterns of variance and covariance in data is consistent with the model specified by researchers.

b) *Alternative models approach:* In the case of the alternative models approach, researchers test two or more causal models to determine the best fit. However, in reality, it is very difficult to find two well-developed alternative models to decide the best fit.

c) *Model development approach:* The model development approach is the most common approach of finding the best fit. The models confirmed in this manner are post-hoc models and thus may not be very stable. But researcher can overcome this problem by using a validation strategy, where a model can be developed using a specific calibrated data sample and then it can be confirmed using an independent validation sample.

SURVIVAL ANALYSIS

Survival analysis can be defined as a group of statistical methods, which are used for analysis and interpretation of survival data. It is also known to be a technique for 'time to event' data or 'failure time data'. Survival analysis has applications in the areas of insurance, social sciences and, most importantly, in clinic trials. Survival analysis is applicable not only in studies of clinical trails or patient survival, but also in studies examining time to discontinuation of treatment or even in contraceptive and fertility studies, etc.

If you have ever used regression analysis on longitudinal event data, you have probably come up against two intractable problems of censoring and time-dependent covariate. Survival analysis is best suited to deal with these types of problems as discussed next:

a) *Censoring:* In an experiment in which subjects are followed over time until an event of interest occurs, it is not always possible to follow every subject until the event is observed. There are instances when we loose track of the subject due to several reasons before the completion of the event. This could happen due to the subject's withdrawal; dropout or even due to a situation where the data collection period may arrive before the completion of the event. Thus, in these situations, researchers have information on subject upto the time when the subject was last observed. The observed time to the event under such circumstances is censored[26] and collectively such cases are known as censored cases.

b) *Time-dependent covariate:* In certain situations, explanatory variables such as income changes in value over time and thus it becomes very difficult to put these variables in a regression equation. Survival methods are designed to deal with censoring and time-dependent covariates in a statistically correct way. For example, researchers can use the extended Cox regression model specifying time-dependent covariates. Researchers can analyse such a model by defining the time-dependent covariate as a function of the time variable or by using a segmented time-dependent covariate.

Thus, in nutshell, to deal with the problem of censoring and time-dependent covariate, it is imperative to use a time variable indicating how long the individual observation was observed, and a status variable indicating whether the observation terminated with or without the event taking place.

Survival analysis deals with several key areas such as survival and hazard functions[27] censoring, the Kaplan-Meier and life table estimators, simple life tables, Peto's Logrank with trend tests and hazard ratios. In survival analysis, researchers also deal with the comparison of survival functions such as logrank and Mantel-Haenszel tests, proportional hazards model, logistic regression model and methods for determining sample sizes.

The life table,[28] survival distribution and Kaplan-Meier survival function or Cox regression as mentioned earlier are descriptive methods for estimating the distribution of survival times from a sample, of which the Kaplan-Meier and Cox regression methods are described in brief.

a) *Kaplan-Meier procedure:* It is a widely used method of dealing with censored cases and thus estimating time-to-event models. It does so by estimating conditional probabilities at each time point when an event occurs and uses the product limit of probabilities of each such event to estimate the survival rate at each point.

b) *Cox regression:* It is another method, which estimates the time-to-event model in the presence of censored cases. It allows researchers to include covariates in the estimation model and provides the estimated coefficient for each covariate.

FIGURE 6.14
Survival Analysis Using SPSS

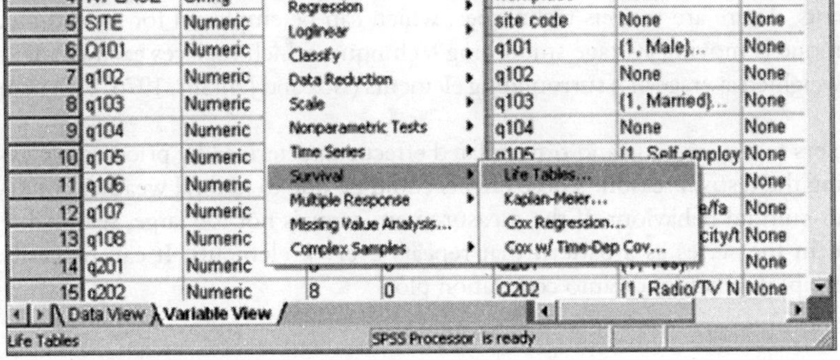

In experimental studies, the most commonly used survival analysis technique is likely to be the non-parametric Kaplan-Meier method, whereas in the case of epidemiology, the most popular one is the Cox regression model for further analysis.

Nowadays, survival analysis software available in the market has shown a major increment in functionality and is no longer limited to the triad of Kaplan-Meier curves, logrank tests and simple Cox models. Survival analysis can be done using SPSS through the menu items Analyse and Survival (see Figure 6.14). It has four options, namely, life tables, Kaplan-Meier, Cox regression and Cox time-dependent covariate.

TIME-SERIES ANALYSIS

Time-series is defined as a sequence of data collected over a period of time that tries to analyse the pattern in ordered data for interpretation and projection. It tries to identify the nature of the phenomenon represented by the observations and after identifying the pattern it tries to forecast the future values of the time-series variable. Thus, it is preemptive at the first stage to ensure that the pattern of observed time-series data is identified and described. After identifying the pattern of data, researchers can interpret and integrate it with other data.

IDENTIFYING PATTERN

The key concept is to identify the pattern in data, which is usually done through analysing and identifying various components such as trend, which may be cyclic, seasonal and irregular. Trend represents a long-term systematic linear or non-linear component, which changes over time and seasonality reflects the component of variation dependent on the time of year, for example, cost and weather indicators.

There are no well-established techniques to identify trend components in the time-series data but as long as the trend is consistently increasing or decreasing, a pattern can be established. There may be instances, when time-series data may contain considerable error. In such a case, the first step in the process of trend identification should be smoothing.

a) *Smoothing:* Smoothing, as the name suggests, involves some form of averaging of data to reduce non-systematic components. There are various techniques, which can be employed for smoothing. The most common technique is moving average smoothing technique, which replaces each element of the series by simple or weighted average of n surrounding elements (Box and Jenkins, 1976; Velleman and Hoaglin, 1981).[29]

b) *Seasonality:* Seasonality refers to a systematic and time-related effect characterized by price rise of essential commodities during the festival season. These effects could be due to natural weather conditions or even due to socio-cultural behaviour. If the measurement error is not too large, seasonality can be visually identified in the series as a pattern that repeats every k elements. It can be easily depicted by a run sequence plot, box plot or auto correlation plot.

FORECASTING

Time-series forecasting and modelling methods use historic values to forecast future values using identified, observed patterns. It assumes that a time-series is a combination of a pattern and some random error and thus attempts are made to separate patterns from errors.

In practical situations, patterns of the data are not very clear as individual observations involve considerable error. Thus, it becomes imperative to uncover the hidden patterns in the data to generate forecasts through a specified model. The forecasting model can be broadly classified into two categories of linear and non-linear models. Linear models includes (i) auto-regressive (AR), (ii) moving average (MA), (iii) ARMA and (iv) ARIMA model. Non-linear models include (i) threshold auto-regressive (TAR), (ii) exponential auto-regressive (EXPAR) and (iii) auto-regressive conditional heterescedastic (ARCH), etc. The next paragraph outlines the features of one of the most widely used linear models, that is, ARIMA, in brief.

ARIMA Model

Auto-Regressive Integrated Moving Average models (ARIMA) is also known as the Box-Jenkins model. An ARIMA model, as the name suggests, may contain only an auto-regressive term, only a moving average term or both. Auto-regressive parts of the model specify that individual values can be described by linear models based on preceding observations. This model is also known as ARIMA (p, q, d) model, where p refers to the auto-regressive part, q refers to the moving average part and d refers to the differentiation part.

SPSS provides the option for doing a time-series analysis (see Figure 6.15). It can be accessed via the menu items Analyse and option item Time Series. SPSS further provides the option for exponential smoothing, auto-regression, ARIMA and seasonal decomposition model.

FIGURE 6.15
Time-series Analysis Using SPSS

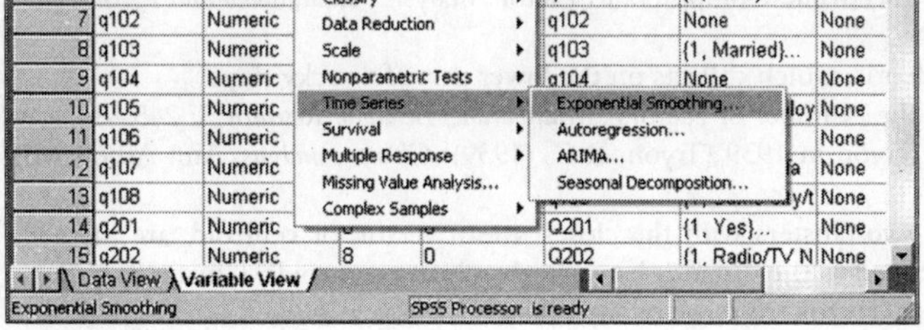

NOTES

1. The ordinary least square method tries to minimize residual value around the line of best fit.
2. R square can sometime overestimate the correlation. The adjusted R square, which is displayed by SPSS and other programmes, should always be used when your interest is in estimating the correlation in the population.
3. If one were to standardize all variables, that is, convert all raw scores to z-scores before carrying out multiple regression, the result would be the standardized regression equation:

$$Z . Y = \beta 1 Z1 + \beta 2 Z2 + ... + \beta pZp$$

When simple linear regression is carried out on standard scores rather than raw scores, the regression line passes through the point (0, 0). Thus, the intercept (a) is equal to zero, and can be left out of the equation. Similarly, in a standardized multiple regression equation, the intercept (b0) is equal to 0 and so can be left out.
4. In SPSS, MANOVA and MANCOVA are found under 'GLM' {(General Linear Model) and output is still similar, but with GLM, parameters are created for every category of every factor and this full parameterization approach handles the problem of empty cells better than traditional MANOVA.
5. Discriminant analysis may be used for two objectives. It can be used when we want to assess the adequacy of classification, given the group memberships of the objects under study. It can also be used when we wish to assign objects to one of a number of (known) groups of objects. Discriminant analysis may thus have a descriptive or a predictive objective.
6. Mathematically, MANOVA and discriminant analysis are the same; indeed, the SPSS MANOVA command can be used to print out the discriminant functions that are at the heart of discriminant analysis, though this is not usually the easiest way of obtaining them. The composite is determined in the same way, such that the groups maximally differ. The maximum number of dimensions, which can be calculated, is the smaller value of the following two: (i) the number of groups minus one, or (ii) the number of continuous variables. And, like before, each composite is formed from the residual of the previous, thereby making each orthogonal.
7. This technique has the fewest restrictions of any of the multivariate techniques, so the results should be interpreted with caution due to the relaxed assumptions. Often, the dependent variables are related and the independent variables are related, so finding a relationship is difficult without a technique like canonical correlation.
8. In general, almost all other multivariate tests are special cases of CVA. For example, when only one dependent variable exists, the calculation of CVA is identical to that of multiple regression. This is true for all techniques that assume linearity.
9. See Krüger (1999). *Kaliningrad Feasibility Study: Project Presentation Report*.
10. Factor analysis is a key multivariate technique which explains variance among a set of variables. It has its origin from psychometrics and is midely used in both social and market research.
11. Principal component analysis tries to extract te component based on the total variance of all observed variables. The first component, named principal, explains the maximum amount of total variance of all observed variables.
12. According to Afifi and Clark (1990: 372), one measure of the amount of information conveyed by each principal component is its variance. For this reason, the principal components are arranged in order of decreasing variance. Thus, the most informative principal component is the first, and the least informative is the last (a variable with 0 variance does not distinguish between members of the population).
13. See Kaiser H.F. (1960). 'The Application of Electronic Computers to Factor Analysis', *Educational and Psychological Measurement.* 20: 141–151.
14. 'Scree' is a geological term referring to the debris, which collects on the lower part of a rocky slope.
15. See Cattell R.B. (1966). 'The Scree Test for the Number of Factors', *Multivariate, Behavior Research*, I: 245–76.
16. The term cluster analysis was first used by Tryon in 1939 (Tryon, R.C. (1939). *Cluster Analysis*. Ann Arbor, MI: Edwards Brothers.
17. In the centroid method, at each stage, the two clusters with the closest mean vector, or centroid, are merged. Distance between clusters, thereafter, are defined as the distance between the cluster centroids. Cluster members, therefore, are closer to the mean of their own centroid to those of any other.

18. Refer to Ward (1963) for details concerning this method. In general, this method is regarded as very efficient, however, it tends to create clusters of small size. Ward, J.H., 1963, 'Hierarchical Grouping to Optimize an Objective Function', *Journal of the American Statistical Association*, 58: 236–244.
19. For details refer to Togerson, W.S., 'Multidimensional Scaling: I. Theory and Method'. *Psychometrika*, 1952, 17. 401–419.
20. Davison, M.L. 1983. *Multidimensional Scaling*, New York: John Wiley and Sons.
21. Correspondence factor analysis, principal components analysis of qualitative data and dual scaling are but three of a long list of alternative names presented by Nishisato (1980). See Nishisato, S., *Analysis of Categorical Data: Dual Scaling and its Applications*, Toronto: University of Toronto Press, 1980.
22. Correspondence analysis is an exploratory technique which analyses simple two-way and multi-way tables known as correspondence tables.
23. Hill, M.O., and H.G. Gauch Jr. 1980. 'Detrended Correspondence Analysis: An Improved Ordination Technique', *Vegetatio*, 42: 47–58.
24. Multiple correspondence analysis is an extension of correspondence analysis for more than two variables.
25. Some researchers will add an additional arrow pointing in to each node of the path diagram which is being taken as a dependent variable, to signify the unexplained variance—the variation in that variable that is due to factors not included in the analysis.
26. In general, censored observations arise whenever the dependent variable of interest represents the time to a terminal event, and the duration of the study is limited in time. Nearly every sample contains some cases that do not experience an event.
27. A similar and often misconstrued function related to hazard function is death density function, which is a time to failure function that gives the instantaneous probability of failure of an event. It differs from the hazard function, which gives the probability conditional on a subject having survived to time T.
28. In case of survival studies, life tables are constructed by partitioning time into intervals usually equal intervals and then counting for each time interval: the number of subjects alive at the start of the interval, the number who die during the interval and the number who are lost to follow-up or withdrawn during the interval.
29. For details, refer Box, G.E.P and G.M. Jenkins (1976), *Time Series Analysis: Forecasting and Control*, San Francisco, CA: Holden Day.

Chapter 7

Data Analysis Using Quantitative Software

The most critical step after collection of data is to perform data analysis. Though simple data analysis and descriptive statistics can be done using simple packages such as Microsoft Excel, detailed data analysis can only be done by using specialized software packages. This chapter presents an overview of the two of the most frequently used quantitative software, namely, Stata and SPSS in detail.

STATA: INTRODUCTION

Stata is one of the most powerful social research statistical software programmes, which provides the facility to enter and edit data interactively. It can be used for both simple and complex statistical analysis ranging from descriptive statistics to multivariate analysis.

Figure 7.1 illustrates the Stata main window, which has a Toolbar[1] at the very top of the window. In case after opening Stata you are not able to locate the Toolbar, then click on the window's menu to select Toolbar. In Stata, researchers should be aware of four important buttons, which serve as an important interface.

a) The Open Log button lets researchers record all Stata commands and result as they type them.
b) The Result button brings the Stata result window to the foreground. This contains the outputs.
c) The Editor button opens a spreadsheet window, where researchers can directly change or edit the data.
d) The Data Browse button opens a spreadsheet window, where researchers can read the data. In the Data Browse mode, researchers can only read the data, but cannot make any changes.

FIGURE 7.1
Overview of Stata

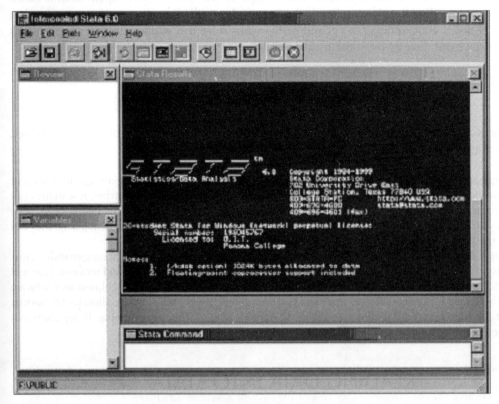

THE WINDOWS

The whole process of data analysis in Stata is pivoted around the following four windows:

a) Command window.
b) Review window.
c) Results window.
d) Variable window.

Researchers can enter commands in the Command window. They can record commands in the Review window, which can be activated/repeated by double clicking the Review window.

The Variable window lists the variables available in the current data set along with the variable labels. Another important window in Stata, which pops up when researchers open Stata, is called the Results window. The Results window is the log window and all of the results are reported in the Results window. Researchers can cut and paste results from this window to other applications but they cannot print directly from the results window.

ENTERING DATA INTO STATA

Programmers can enter data into Stata via the Command window or through the data spreadsheet, details of which are mentioned next:

a) *Entering data via the Command window:* Researchers can type the input format beginning with the input command, followed by the sequence of variable names separated by blanks. Further, researchers can enter the value for cases by hitting the Enter key. Researchers can enter a period for a numeric variable in case of a missing data or a blank for a string variable. After entering values for missing data, they can save the file by typing the command 'Save (filename)'.

b) *Entering data via the data spreadsheet:* Researchers can enter data very easily in the Stata spreadsheet just as they would do in any other spreadsheet, by simply typing Edit in the Command window. Edit will open a spreadsheet, where researchers can start entering data by treating each column as a separate variable. Stata[2] recognizes all data types and based on the data type, the software allocates the format itself. Further, by default it allocates var1 as the variable name for the first variable. Researchers can enter a variable name by double click on the variable name.

READING DATA INTO STATA

There are three basic ways of reading data into Stata, based on the data format the researcher is willing to read.

a) Researchers can use the Use command to read data that have been saved in Stata format.
b) Command Insheet can be used for spreadsheets that are in CSV file format.
c) Researcher can use Infile command for reading 'flat' files and 'dictionaries'.

USE

Researchers most frequently use the 'Use' command to read data that has been saved in Stata format. It is important to point out that '.dta' file extension is automatically appended to Stata files and researchers do not have to include the file extension on the use command. The only command researchers have to use is:

'use (filename)'

Where the filename is the name of the Stata file. For example, suppose the researcher has a Stata file named 'mine.dta.', he can read this file with the following command:

'use mine'

INSHEET

Stata uses the Insheet command to read data from Microsoft Excel. The researcher can read Excel data into Stata in two ways, first by way of simple copy and paste and second by importing the Excel data file. The following section discusses both the options in detail.

Copy and Paste:

a) Start Microsoft Excel.
b) After starting Excel, the researcher can either read previously saved file or enter data in rows and columns in case of a new file.
c) After reading file or entering data, the researcher can copy selected data.
d) Start data editor in Stata to paste selected data into editor.

Importing Excel data file:

a) Start Microsoft Excel to read Excel file.
b) After reading Excel file, save selected file as tab delimited or comma-delimited file. For example, if the original filename is mine.xls, then save the file as mine.txt or mine.csv.
c) Start Stata and type the command 'Insheet using mine.csv' where mine.csv is the name of the file saved in Excel.
d) Save data as a Stata dataset by using the Save command.

INFILE

Researchers can use the Infile command to read data that are in a special format. For example, when researchers have to download a data file from the web not having variable names in the first line, the Infile command is different as it assumes that blanks separate the variables whereas in the case of Insheet, commas separate the variables. Infile command also assumes that the variables have spaces between them but apart from that, there are no other blank spaces. Researchers can use the following command to read a file:

infile var1 var2 var 3 using data.raw

BASIC DATA FUNCTIONS

Saving Stata Files

Researcher can save a data file in Stata format by using the Save command as:

'save (filename)'

The Save command can save a Stata file in the working directory which researchers can access by using the 'Use' command. In case a researcher already has a file with a similar name, he can use the Save command with the Replace option as:

'save (filename), replace'

Variable and Value Labels

Variable labels and value labels provide very good options for tracking variables. Variable labels are nothing but an extended name for variables, whereas value labels define the different values a variable can take.

Researchers can assign a variable label by a simple command:

Label variable var1 'my variable'

Which would assign a label 'my variable' to the variable, var1, though it is important to point out that variable labels must be equal to or less than 31 characters. The value of a label refers to the actual value a variable may take, for example, in the case of gender, the variable can take only 'male' and 'female' values.

Variable Transformations

Stata provides the facility of storing data in either number or character formats, but most analysis require data to be in numeric form. Numeric variables are further categorized into various types based on the space they take up in the file—float, binary, double, long and int (integer). In Stata, researchers can use several ways to transform one variable into another variable. Variables may be renamed, recoded, generated, or replaced.

Rename

Researcher can use the Rename command to rename a variable, say 'age', to a variable called, 'age category' by simply typing: 'Rename age category'.

Encode

Researchers can also convert a character variable into a numeric variable by the 'Encode' command. It does so by assigning numbers to each group defined by the character variable. For example, suppose 'settlement' was the original character variable the new numeric variable is 'rural', then it would read:

encode settlement, gen (rural)

Generate

Researchers by using the Gen ... real command can transform a string variable into a numeric variable. The following command will create a new, numeric variable, var1n, by converting the string variable, var1:

gen var1n = real (var1)

Though often, researchers have to create new variables based on the existing ones, for example, computing total income by combing income from all sources. Researcher can use Generate and Egen as two of most common ways of creating a new variable. Researchers can use the following command to generate a variable called total:

gen total = var1 + var2 + var3

In this example, the variable total signifying total income is generated by combining income from three sources represented by var1, var 2 and var 3 respectively.

Extended Generate

Researchers can use the command Extended Generate or Egen, to create a variable in terms of mean, median, etc., of another variable, for all observations or for groups of observations. The command for creating such a variable is:

egen meanvar1 = mean (var1), by (var2)

In this example, the researcher has created a variable which is the mean of another variable for each group of observation designated by var2.

MISSING VALUE MANAGEMENT

Stata shows missing values as dots in the case of a numeric variables and blanks for string variables. Usually they are stored as very large numbers and can result in serious problems if they are not accounted properly.

Researchers can easily convert the values, which were missing before importation to Stata into Stata missing values by using the 'Mvdecode' command. Researchers can also convert missing values to new values by typing the 'Mvencode' command.

DROPPING A VARIABLE

In Stata, researchers can drop a variable from the data set by using the Drop command, for example, 'Drop x', would drop the variable x from the data set, keeping the other variables in the data set.

DATA MANAGEMENT/MANIPULATION

After getting all the files and variables in the desired format, researchers start the work of data management and manipulation which makes data easier to handle and use. Stata also provides the facility to save all operations such as commands or even mistakes during the course of data analysis through the Log and Do files (see Box 7.1). It is always recommended that researchers use this facility during data management, because of the critical nature of the task.

Based on the objective, researchers usually have to do several tasks such as sorting, appending, merging and collapsing.

BOX 7.1
Log and Do Files

Log files: Log and do files are very important and useful files. Logs keep a record of the commands issued by researchers and the output/results thus obtained during data analysis. Do files are very useful for recording long series of commands, which need to be modified before executing them. These files are quite useful to replicate things on new or modified data sets.

Researchers can very easily create a log file by using the command:

Log using filename

Where the filename is the name the researcher wishes to give to the file. It is usually recommended that researchers use names, which can help them remember the work they have done during that session. Stata automatically appends an extension of '.log' to the filename.

Do files: Do files record the set of commands the researcher issues during data analysis. Whatever command the researcher uses in Stata can be part of a do file. These files are very useful, especially in cases where a researcher simultaneously issues many commands, and later it becomes imperative that the commands are modified before executing them.

Researchers, after proper modification, can run this file in Stata by simply typing the command:

'do mydofile'

SORT

Researchers can use the Sort command to put the observations in a data set in a specific order. There are various statistical procedures, which require files to be sorted before further analysis. Researchers can sort a file based on one or more than one variable.

It is important to point out that Stata randomizes the order of the observations within the variables used to sort, thus it is always recommended to create a common or key variable. Researchers with the help of id variable can go back to the original order to start the process again. Id variable symbolizes identification variable, which uniquely identifies a record.

sort month

sort month year

APPEND

Researchers sometimes have more than one data file, which needs to be analysed. Thus to analyse both data simultaneously, it is imperative to combine both data files.

In a bid to explain the issue further, let us assume there are two data sets x.dta and y.dta that contain the same variables, but different cases. Then researchers can use the Append command to append cases of the second file to first file.

Researchers can first access the x data set by typing 'Use x' and when data set x is opened, cases of data set y can be appended just by typing 'Append using y'. The Append command completes the appending of the cases in data set y to those of data set x. Thus, as a result, the current data set would contain the observations of both data sets x and y, which can be saved under a different data set name.

MERGE

In case researchers have two files that have the same observations, but different variables, then it is imperative to use the 'merge' command instead of append to combine all the variables at once. Thus, in the case of merge, new variables are added to existing observations rather than adding observations to existing variables.

There are two basic ways in which data can be merged, i.e., a one-to-one merge and a match merge. In the case of a one-to-one merge, the software simply takes the two files and combines them together, regardless of whether the observations in each dataset are in the same order. It is important to point here that in case observations in both data sets are not in the same order then a one-to-one match can throw off the order of the data. In that case, the researcher has to do a match-merge, and users have to be able to check that all the observations are matched correctly.

Researchers need to follow some rules while doing a match-merge. Researchers need to decide about a key variable, by which the observations can be matched—serial number is a good example.

At the next stage, researchers need to sort both data sets by one identified key variable. Researchers can use more than one key variable such as month and year to merge historical data. It is important to point out that the key variables must be of the same nature in both data sets.

Further, researchers should take care of the presence of the same variable in both data sets, as then the values in the master data set will remain unchanged. In case the variables in the current data set have the same names as the ones in the master data set, then it is essential to rename one of the variables in the two data sets before performing the merge operation.

```
use a
sort sex

merge date using b
```

In this example, we simply match observations using the variable 'date' as the key.

DATA ANALYSIS

Like any other statistical analysis package, a number of elementary statistical procedures can be executed by Stata, some of which are detailed next.

DESCRIBE

All information related to variables in a data file can be described using a describe command. Researchers can use the 'describe' command, further abbreviated as *d* to list basic information about the file and the variables. The command is:

```
d using my file
```

Where my file is the name of the data file.

LIST

List command displays all information related to data lists. Researcher can use the List command, abbreviated as 'l' to display all of the data on screen as:

```
l var1 var2–displays just var1, var2
```

Researchers would have all data in a specified format, which allows them to check it before doing any analyses.

SUMMARIZE

Summarize, as the name indicates, provides researchers with the mean, standard deviation, etc., of the listed variables. In case researchers do not specify any variable then the 'summ' command would list all the information for all numeric variables. It provides very useful information about the variable nature, which is quite useful in planning a detailed analysis plan. The Stata command for summarization is:

   summ var1 var2

Further, researchers can use the Detail option to list additional information about the distribution of a specific variable.

   summ var1, detail

TABULATE

Researchers can use the 'Tab' command (short for tabulation), to generate frequency tables.[3] They simply need to specify two variables, after the Tab command to generate a cross-tabulation.

   tab var1 var2

Researchers can further use the command to compute the mean, standard deviation, standard error of the mean, for every specified variable by using the command:

   tabstat var1, stats (mean sd sdmean)

INFERENTIAL STATISTICS

T Tests

In case researchers wish to determine whether a mean of a sample is significantly different from some specified value, they can do a one-sample t test. Stata provides the facility of one sample, paired sample, and independent group's t tests.

   Let us take an example where the analyst wants to test the hypothesis that the average age at marriage in the data set is equal to, less than, or greater than 18 and researchers can do this by using a simple command for t test:

   t test am = 18

   where am is the variable name for age at marriage

Paired T Tests

Unlike one sample t tests, paired sample t tests compare the average pre-test score with the average post-test score for the sampled units. Stata, as mentioned earlier, provides the facility for a paired t test. Let assume we have two variable iq1 and iq2, which represent the intelligence level scores of respondents before and after the test, then the command for testing hypothesis using paired test would be:

    t test iq1 = iq2

Analysis of Variance (ANOVA)

Researcher can test hypotheses, which examine the difference between two or more means for two or more groups by using analysis of variance or ANOVA. The following section discusses the frequently used one-way ANOVA.

One-way ANOVA

Analysis of variance is used one-way, when one criterion is used and two-way, when two criteria are used. In the majority of cases, one-way ANOVA is used. The aim of the test is to ascertain whether there is a statistically significant difference between the means of the test variable between at least one of the several groups. Researchers can use the simple command given here for a one-way ANOVA:

    one-way response factor

Where the response signifies the response variable and factor signifies the factor variable. Let us take an example where literacy is the response variable and gender is the grouping variable then the command for the test would be:

    one-way literacy gender

REGRESSION

Stata provides the facility for estimating linear regression models by using the Regress command. Let us assume that the dependent variable is 'depvar' and the independent variable is listed in 'varlist'. Then the command researchers should use to run the linear regression is:

    reg depvar varlist

It is important to point out that in the regression command, the order of the variable is very important, as the first variable after the regress command is the dependent variable, which is followed by the relevant independent variables.

In regression, there are some additional regression analyses, which shall also be looked at to have a complete picture. Stata provides the facility of generating residuals with the help of the Predict command. Researchers can use the following command to generate residuals in the data set by specifying regit.

predict regit, residuals

Researchers can also generate standardized residuals called 'stdres', to adjust for standard error, by using the following command:

predict stdres, rstandard

OVERVIEW OF STATISTICAL PACKAGE FOR SOCIAL SCIENCE (SPSS)

Statistical Package for Social Science (SPSS) is the most popular quantitative analysis software used today in social research. It is a comprehensive and flexible statistical analysis and data management system. It can utilize data from almost every type of data set format to generate tabulated reports, distribution charts and trends to descriptive statistics and complex statistical analyses. Besides this, SPSS is compatible with almost every operating system such as Windows, Macintosh and UNIX.

Unlike other quantitative analysis software, SPSS provides a window user interface which makes the software very user-friendly. Researchers can use simple menus, pop-up boxes and dialogue boxes to perform complex analyses without writing even a single line of syntax. It is an integrated software which also provides a spreadsheet-like utility function for entering data and browsing the working data file. Its whole operation is pivoted around three windows:

a) A data window with a blank data sheet ready for analyses is the first window you encounter. It is used to define and enter data and to perform statistical procedures.
b) The syntax window is used to keep records of all commands issued in a Stata session. Researchers do not have to know the language for writing syntax, instead they can just select the appropriate option from the menu and dialogue box and can click a paste function. This would paste the equivalent syntax of the selected operation in the syntax window. Besides serving as a log for operations, it is possible to run commands from the syntax window.[4]
c) Whenever a procedure is run, the output is directed to a separate window called the Output window.

SPSS automatically adds a three-letter suffix to the end of the file name, that is, '.save' for data editor files, '.sop' for output files and '.saps' for syntax files (see Figure 7.2).

ENTERING DATA

Researchers can create data file by simply entering the data. The present section describes the step-by-step procedure for creating a data file by entering variable information[5] about subject/cases.

FIGURE 7.2
Overview of SPSS Data Editor

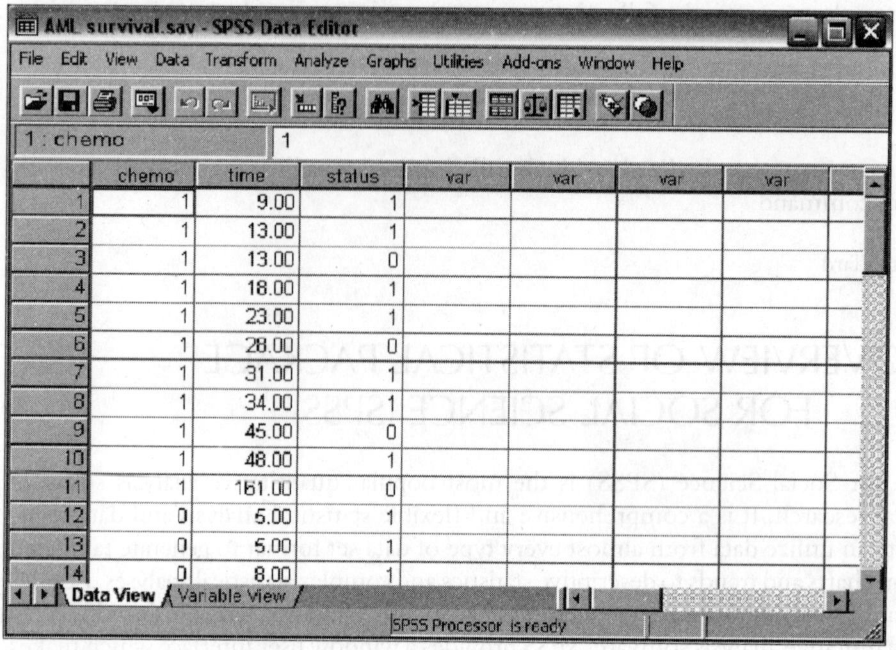

In SPSS, the main data window provides two options on the bottom left hand corner of the screen and researchers can access either the data view or variable view window (see Figure 7.3).

The variable view window depicts the characteristic of variables in terms of name, type and nature as mentioned next:

a) *Name:* The variable names in SPSS are not case sensitive, but they must begin with a letter. Further, the variable name should not exceed eight characters.

b) *Type:* SPSS also provides the facility to specify data type, that is, whether the data are in numeric, string or date format, though the default is numeric format.

c) *Labels:* SPSS also provides the facility of attaching labels to variable names. A variable name is limited to a length of eight characters (upto SPSS 12, but from SPSS 13 onwards it is possible to enter a variable name of more than eight characters); but by using a variable label, researchers can use 256 characters to attach a label to the variable name. This provides the ability to have very descriptive labels that appear at the output. Researchers can enhance the readability of the output by using the labels option.

d) *Values:* Researchers can assign variable values, for example, male and female can be coded as 1 and 2 respectively.

It is advised that researchers familiarize themselves with the data characteristic at the initial stages. SPSS, however, also provides the facility whereby researchers, at later stages of data analysis, can list information about the nature of the data, type and characteristic of the data by just selecting the Data Dictionary option (see Box 7.2).

FIGURE 7.3
Variable View Window

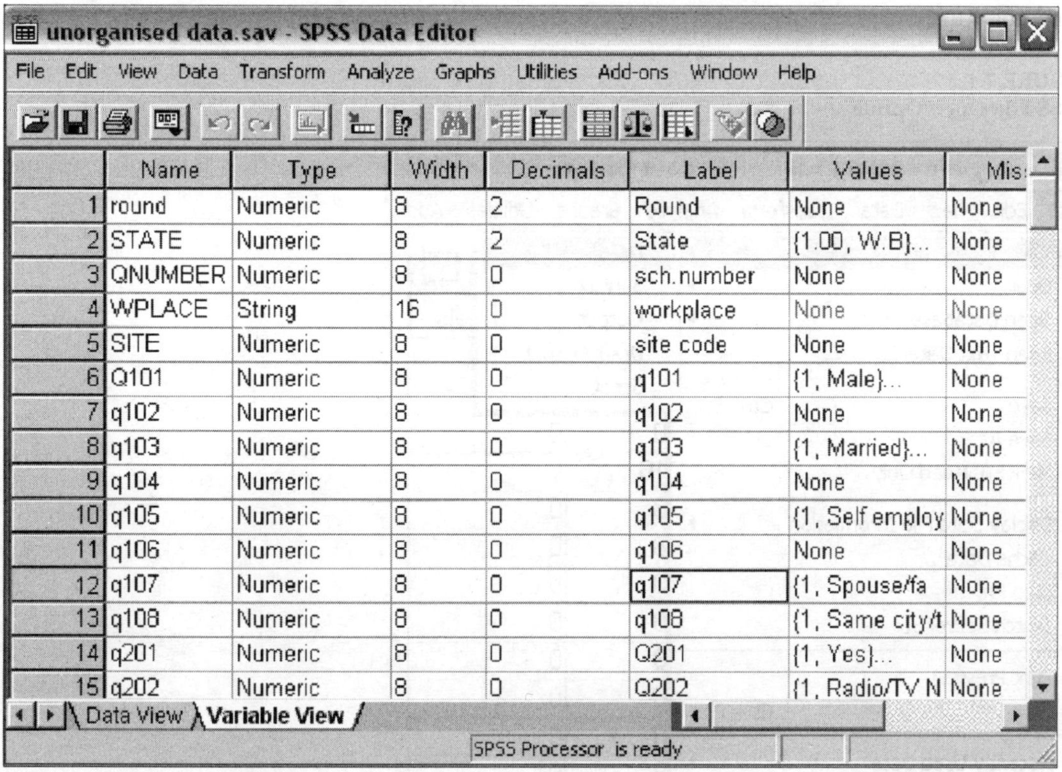

	Name	Type	Width	Decimals	Label	Values	Mis:
1	round	Numeric	8	2	Round	None	None
2	STATE	Numeric	8	2	State	{1.00, W.B}...	None
3	QNUMBER	Numeric	8	0	sch.number	None	None
4	WPLACE	String	16	0	workplace	None	None
5	SITE	Numeric	8	0	site code	None	None
6	Q101	Numeric	8	0	q101	{1, Male}...	None
7	q102	Numeric	8	0	q102	None	None
8	q103	Numeric	8	0	q103	{1, Married}...	None
9	q104	Numeric	8	0	q104	None	None
10	q105	Numeric	8	0	q105	{1, Self employ	None
11	q106	Numeric	8	0	q106	None	None
12	q107	Numeric	8	0	q107	{1, Spouse/fa	None
13	q108	Numeric	8	0	q108	{1, Same city/t	None
14	q201	Numeric	8	0	Q201	{1, Yes}...	None
15	q202	Numeric	8	0	Q202	{1, Radio/TV N	None

BOX 7.2
Data Dictionary

Data dictionary provides information about the nature of data, its type and characteristics. It provides all information, that is, variable name, type, variable label, value labels, missing value definition and display format for each variable in a data set. In other words, it documents how each variable in a data set is defined.

Researcher can easily produce a data dictionary by selecting the File Info option from the Utilities menu. The Data Dictionary first provides the list of variables on the working file, where the variable name appears on the left hand side and the column number of the variable appears on the right side of the Output window. The Data Dictionary also provides the print and write format after the variable name followed by special characteristics of the variable such as value labels.

EXPORTING DATA

Researchers can export data in several ways, though the simplest is the Open option. In this case, researchers can directly open the requisite database file by simply clicking on the Open option (see Figure 7.4). Second, researchers can import data files of other formats (dBase, Access) to SPSS through database capture. Researchers can also use the Read ASCII Data option, as the third option to read files that are saved in ASCII format, which further provides two options—freefield and fixed columns.

FIGURE 7.4
SPSS File Open Option

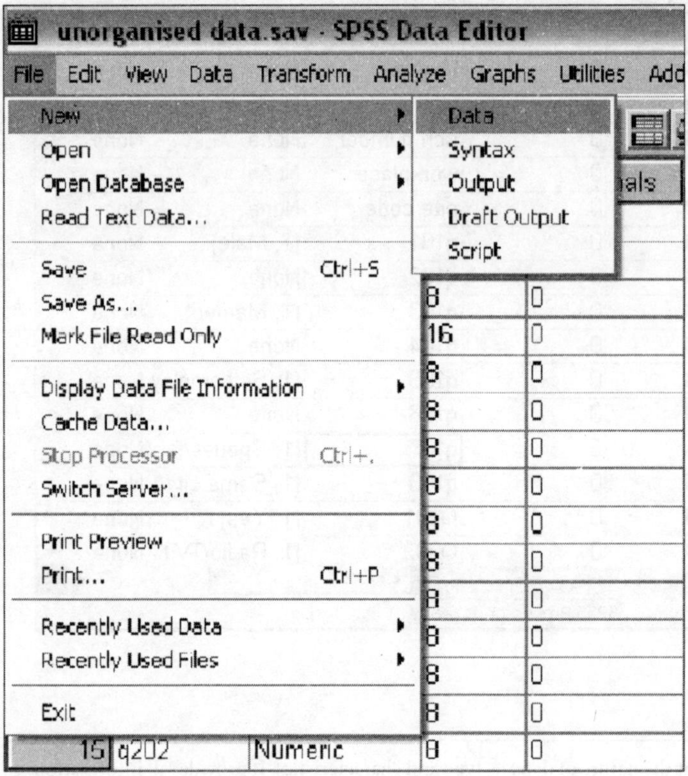

Opening a SPSS File

Researchers can open a SPSS file quite easily by just clicking on the menu item and option file > open > data. Researchers can select the SPSS files type (having a .sav extension). Similarly, researchers can open a SPSS output file by selecting file > open > output by selecting viewer document files type (having a .spo extension).

Opening an Excel File

Researchers can open an Excel workbook in the same way as in the case of opening an SPSS data file, only the file type needs to be changed to Excel (*.excel) as shown in Figure 7.5.

FIGURE 7.5
Option of Opening an Excel File: SPSS

After this, researchers can select the Excel workbook they wish to open by clicking on Open and Continue. This will open a screen similar to one shown in Figure 7.6.

It is important to point out that in case the first row of the Excel workbook contains the variable names, then researchers need to ensure that this option is ticked. In case data is not on the first worksheet, they need to change the worksheet using the down arrow to select the worksheet having data. SPSS also provides the facility to select the range from the worksheet, which you want to use, in case you are not interested in using all data in the worksheet.

Opening an Access File

In the earlier version of SPSS 10.0, researchers could have opened an Access file via the Open File option, But now, researchers have to go through a slightly more complex procedure, that is, they have to define a link to the database: file/open database/new query: In other words they have to define an ODBC (open database connection) connection to use with SPSS to define a new query. If this is the first time the researcher wants to do this, he has to add a new ODBC source[6] (see Figure 7.7).

FIGURE 7.6
Opening Excel Data Source: SPSS

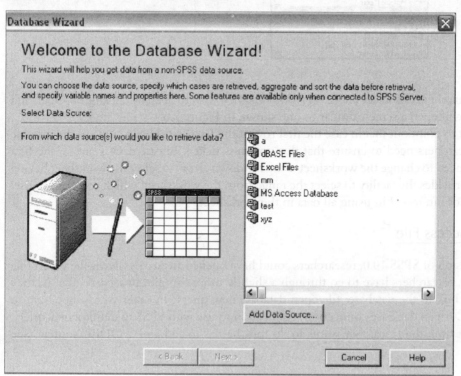

FIGURE 7.7
Welcome to Database Wizard Window: SPSS

After defining the database link, researchers can select the MS access database to add the access database in the ODBC data source administrator box. Further, to create a new data source, at the next stage, the researcher can highlight the Microsoft access driver. After finishing the selection of the driver the researcher should type in the name in the data source name in the ODBC Microsoft Access setup type as demonstrated in Figure 7.8.

FIGURE 7.8
ODBC Microsoft Access Setup: SPSS

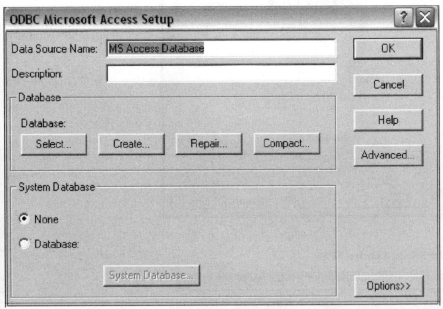

After typing in the name, the researcher can choose database from the list by clicking on the Select button in the database box. After selecting the database click Ok and wait until you see the screen: Welcome to the Database Wizard. In this option, the researcher can select the data source, which he has just added. After clicking on the added database and next button the researcher would come across a new window showing all tables and queries of the selected database. Now to see the field within each table, the researcher can click on the + to show the fields as demonstrated below in Figure 7.9.

In the next stage, researchers can drag the fields to the right hand box in the order they want to see them displayed in window[7] (see Figure 7.10).

Though in the present example we have selected all cases, the Database Wizard provides the facility to limit the cases researchers want to retrieve. Further, at the next stage researchers can edit the variable names. It is recommended that researchers edit variable names at this stage, but in case they do not want to do it at this stage, they can do it later in variable view. In the end, Data View displays the data and Variable View allows viewing and editing of variable names and other characteristics.

FIGURE 7.9
Retrieving Data from the Available Table: SPSS

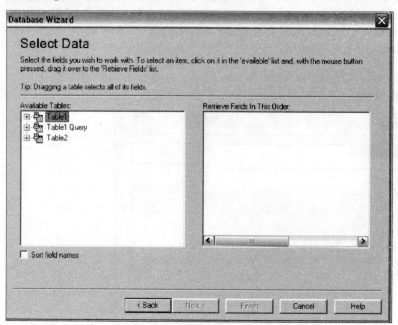

FIGURE 7.10
Retrieving Fields in the Selected Order: SPSS

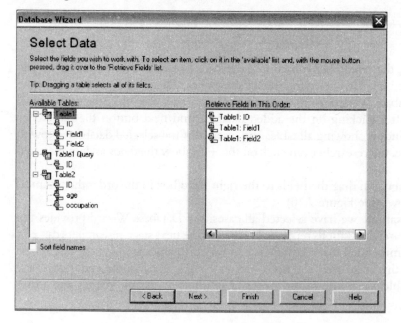

After finishing the process, researchers can save the query definition and then next time, while opening the Access data file in SPSS, they can just mention the open database/run query and choose the query saved in SPSS. This will update the Data View with the latest data in the database.

Importing Text File

SPSS provides the facility to import text files through the Text Wizard. Researchers can read text data files in a variety of formats:

a) Tab-delimited files.
b) Space delimited files.
c) Comma delimited files.
d) Fixed format files.

At the first stage, researchers can either specify a predefined format, or the remaining steps in the Text Wizard can be followed. The Text Import Wizard at the second step requests information about how variables are arranged, that is, whether variables are defined by a specific character (spaces, tabs or commas) or variables have fixed width, where each variable is recorded in the same column. This step also asks the researchers whether variable names are included at the top of the file as the file may or may not contain variable names. In case the file contains variable names of more than eight characters, then variable names will be truncated. Further, in case the file does not contain variable names, SPSS can allocate default names.

In the third step, the Text Import Wizard requests information about how cases are represented and the number of cases the researchers want to import. Usually, the first case begins with line 1 if no variable name is supplied and line 2 if variable name is supplied. Normally each line represents a case. At this step researchers are also requested to specify the number of cases they want to import, that is, whether they want to import all cases, the first *n* cases, or a random sample.

The fourth step of the Text Import Wizard requests information about the file, that is, whether it is comma delimited or space delimited file. In the case of delimited files, this step allows for the selection of the character or symbol used as a delimiter, whereas in the case of fixed width files, this step displays vertical lines on the file, which can be moved if required.

In step five, the Text Import Wizard requests information about variable specification. It allows researchers to control variable names and the data format to read each variable, which will be included in the data file. Values which contain invalid characters for the selected format will be treated as missing.

In the last step, that is, step six, the Text Import Wizard provides the facility to researchers to save the file specification for later use, or to paste the syntax.

Basic Data Management Function

Recoding Variables

Researchers, while analysing and reporting, require fewer categories than envisaged in a survey. They can use the option Recode Variable as a way of combining the values of a variable into fewer categories. One of the common examples is of recoding age of the respondent. In survey data we get actual age in years as reported by the respondent and data analysis would also present the information by actual age. But it would be very clumsy to present the information related to actual age so it is better if we group actual age into meaningful categories. In other words, data would be more useful if it was organized into age groups (for example, into three age groups of < = 18, 19–35 and 35+).

Researchers can use two options provided by SPSS for recoding variables, that is, Recode into Different Variables and Recode into Same Variables. Researchers, however, are strongly recommended to initially use only the Recode into Different Variables option, because even if they make an error, the original variable would still be in the file and they can try recoding again.

Researchers can recode data through several options. Researchers can change a particular value into a new value by entering the value to be changed into the Old Value Box and the new value into the New Value Box.

Creating New Variables Using Compute

In SPPS, researchers can very easily create a new variable by using the Compute command (see Figure 7.11). It can be easily done by typing the name of the variable that the researchers wish to create in the target variable field.

After typing the target variable, researchers need to specify the computation, which using the variables from the list, would result in the target variable. Researchers can use all of the operations listed at the bottom of this screen, though it is important to point out that the operations within parentheses are performed first.

Creating New Variables Using the If Command

Researchers can also use the If command to create new variables, out of old variables. Researchers can do this by selecting Transform and then clicking on the Compute function. They can further select 'Include if Case Satisfies Condition' in the dialogue box to select subsets of cases using conditional expressions.

In return, a conditional expression returns a value of true, false, or missing for each case. In case the result of a conditional expression is true, then the case is selected and if the result is false or missing, the case is not selected for data analysis.

Researchers can use several operators though in the majority of cases one or more of the six relational operators (<, >, < =, > =, =, and ~ =) are used. Generally, conditional expressions can include variable names, constants, arithmetic operators, numeric and other functions, logical

FIGURE 7.11
Creating New Variables Using 'Compute': SPSS

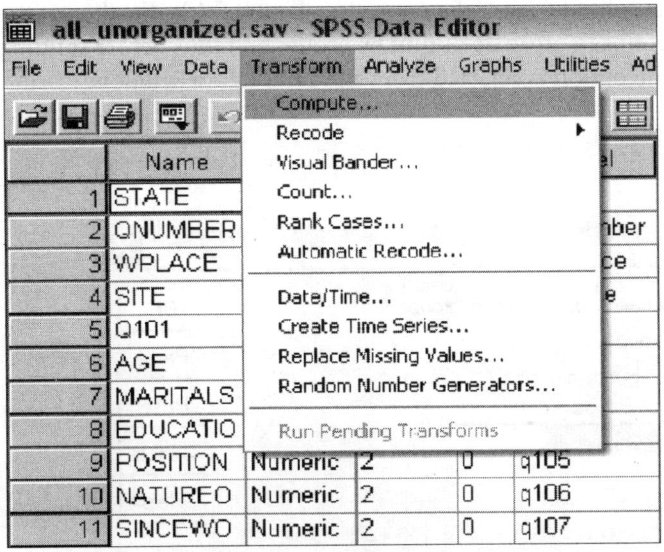

variables, and relational operators. Researchers can easily build expression by directly typing in the expression field[8] or by pasting component in field.

Spilt File Option

SPSS provides the facility of splitting a data file into separate groups for analysis based on the values of one or more grouping variables. In case researchers select multiple grouping variables, then cases are grouped by each variable within categories of first grouping variable based on the groups selected. For example, in case researchers select occupation as the first grouping variable and education as the second grouping variable, then cases will be grouped by education classification within each occupation category.

Researchers can specify up to eight grouping variables. Researchers then should sort values by the grouping variables, in the same order that variables are listed in the 'groups based on' list. If the data file is not already sorted, then researchers should sort the file by grouping variables.

Compare Groups

SPSS also presents the split file groups together for visual comparison purposes. For pivot tables, a single pivot table is created and each split file variable can be moved between table dimensions. For charts, a separate chart is created for each split file group and the charts are displayed together in the viewer.

Split a Data File for Analysis

Researchers can very easily choose 'data split file' from the menu (see Figure 7.12). Further, at the next stage, researchers need to select groups to organize output by groups and thus before splitting the file it is imperative that the Split File option is selected from the Data Editor window.

FIGURE 7.12
Splitting a Data File for Analysis: SPSS

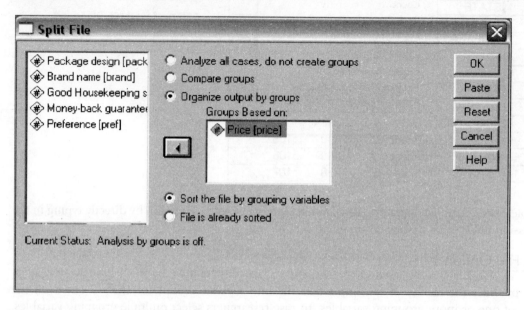

Researchers can turn off the Split File option by selecting Data and then the Split File option from the Data Editor window by clicking on the Analyse All Cases option.

Using Select Cases

SPSS also provides the facility to select subsets of cases for further analysis. Researchers can click on Data and then on Select Cases. This would open the Select Cases box and if researchers want to select a subset of these cases, they can select the option 'If Condition is Satisfied' to select subsets of cases.

Further, at the bottom of the window, a check box specifies that unselected cases are filtered,[9] which means that the cases researchers do not select can be used later if they click on the All Cases option. But in case the researcher had selected the Delete option, these unselected cases would be gone forever.

Weighting Cases

Researchers sometimes may want to weight some cases in the data more heavily than others. Take an example of a household represented in the survey that had an equal probability of selection. If there was more than one person eligible in the household and one of these individuals was randomly selected we can correct for this by weighting each case by the number of eligible people in their household. Let us take an example of a variable called eligible woman, which is defined as the number of women 18 years of age or older in the household and this is, of course, also the number of eligible people in the household. The number of eligible women in the household varied from one to five. Table 7.1 shows the distribution.

TABLE 7.1
Weighting Cases by Number of Eligible Women

	Weighting Cases by Number of Eligible Women	
Number of Eligible Women	Number of Cases	Weighted Number of Cases
1	45	45
2	105	210
3	225	675
4	540	2160
5	110	550
Total	1,025	3,640

The weighted number of women is just the number of eligible women multiplied by the number of cases. This means that each case with two eligible women has a weight twice that of each case with one eligible women, etc.

This problem can be solved by dividing weighted number of cases by actual number of cases and by getting the resultant fraction. The problem with this is that we started with 1,025 cases and ended up with 3,640 cases. This inflates the size of the sample, which researchers really do not want to do. There is an easy way to fix this. If we divide the weighted sum of cases by the actual number of cases we get 3.55. We can divide each weight by 3.55 to get an adjusted weight. This would produce the weighted data as shown in Table 7.2.

TABLE 7.2
Weighting Cases Using Adjusted Weights

Number of Eligible Adults	Adjusted Weight	Number of Cases	Weighted Number of Cases
1	1/3.55 = 0.281	45	12.64
2	2/3.55 = 0.563	105	59.11
3	3/3.55 = 0.845	225	190.12
4	4/3.55 = 1.12	540	604.8
5	5/3.55 = 1.40	110	154
Total		1,025	1,020.67

Now we want to weight the data using this variable we just created. Click on Data and then on Weight Cases. Click on the circle to the left of 'weight cases by' to proceed.

Missing Values

Missing data can be due to various factors such as interviewer fault in administering questions, leaving certain questions blank, or respondents declining to respond to certain questions, or due to some human error in data coding and data entry. There are three techniques to handle data with missing values: (i) complete case analysis (list-wise deletion), (ii) available case methods (pair-wise deletion), and (iii) filling in the missing values with estimated scores (imputation).

SPSS treats all blanks as missing values. Though it is important to note why the variable is blank, because it may be due to the fact that the question was not relevant to the case, or that the person refused to answer the question. Missing values must be appropriate for the data type of the variable, for example, a numeric value for a numeric variable and missing values for string variables must not be more than eight characters long.

In case a response is missing,[10] it is recommended that researchers use 999 as value so that it is known that data is actually missing rather than a data entry error. The default is no missing values, thus it is essential to specify the missing value, for example, usually 999 is imputed in place of the missing value. SPSS allows multiple missing value codes so that it is easy to distinguish (see Figure 7.13). Besides, researcher can use various functions and simple arithmetic expressions to extract missing values (see Box 7.3).

FIGURE 7.13
Defining Missing Value for Analysis: SPSS

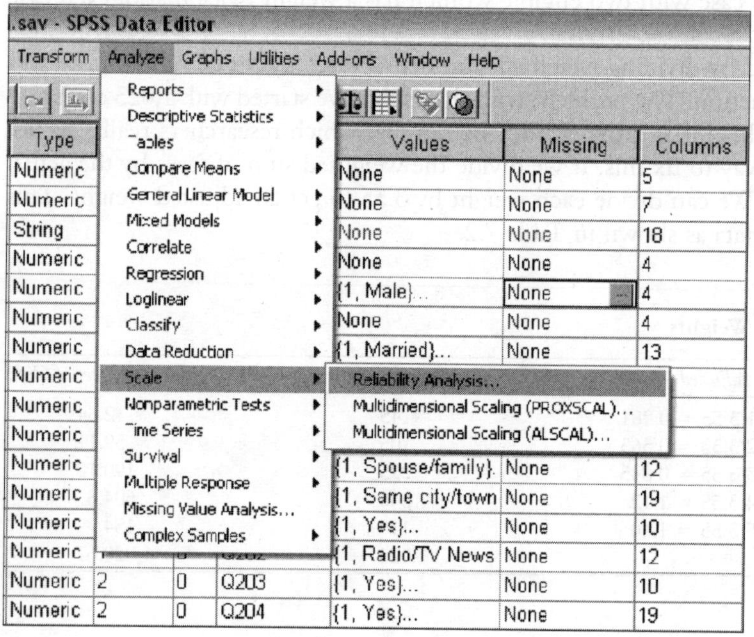

BOX 7.3
Functions Treating Missing Values

Researchers, while treating missing values, can use various functions and simple arithmetic expressions, which treat missing values in different ways such as:

a) Researchers can use the average expression such as (var1+var2+var3)/3, where the result is treated as missing only if a case has a missing value for any of the three variables.
b) Researchers can also use the expression MEAN (var1, var2, var3), where result is treated as missing only if a case has missing values for all three variables.
c) SPSS also provides the facility of specifying a statistical function, where researchers can specify the minimum number of arguments that must have no missing value, for example the function MEAN.2 (var1, var2, var3).

Reliability Analysis

Reliability signifies the issue of consistency of measures, that is, the ability of a measurement instrument to measure the same thing each time the instrument is used. Reliability inherently depends on three key elements, namely, stability, internal reliability and inter-observer consistency.

In case researchers want to construct an additive scale by adding various multiple items to come up with a score, the first thing they must determine is the internal consistency of the items, that is, whether individual items are positively correlated with each other or not. If they are correlated, researchers need to know whether the correlation is sufficient enough to justify their addition to measure the concept that the scale proposes to measure.

The SPSS package provides the facility of doing reliability analysis to assess the additive nature of individual items. Researchers can avail the option by going to Analyse > Scale > Reliability Analysis (see Figure 7.14). The procedure provides a large number of reliability coefficients for multiple-item scales. Its subcommands encompass many different approaches to reliability definition and estimation.

In a bid to explore further, let us take an example from a study conducted to assess the impact of a British Broadcasting (BBC) media campaign to increase awareness regarding symptoms and treatment of leprosy. Here various indicators related to awareness on symptoms of leprosy were combined to form an index on awareness of symptoms (see Table 7.3).

TABLE 7.3
Indicators Selected to Create Index

Q2A_1	Pale or reddish patches on skin
Q2A_2	Loss of sensation in any part of the body
Q2A_3	Weakness of muscles in hands, feet or face
Q2A_4	Itchy patches
Q2A_5	Deformity
Q2A_6	Pain in hands and feet
Q2A_7	Nodules (lump formation in parts of the body)
Q2A_8	Boils on the body
Q2A_9	Loss of parts of the body
Q2A_10	Body swelling
Q2A_11	Wrinkles on the skin of the face

FIGURE 7.14
Window Showing Option of Reliability Analysis: SPSS

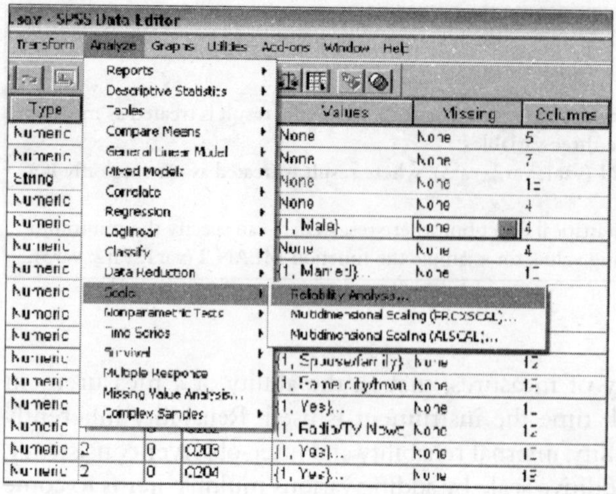

Researchers, at the next stage, shall enter these indicators as items to assess the reliability of scale. To do so, they need to have an idea about the scale mean, scale variance and the Cronbach alpha[11] for each item, in case that particular item is to be deleted from the scale. Researchers can very easily compute all these statistics by clicking on the 'Descriptive for Scale' and 'Scale if Items Deleted' options in the Reliability Analysis window (see Figure 7.15).

FIGURE 7.15
Reliability Analysis Statistics: SPSS

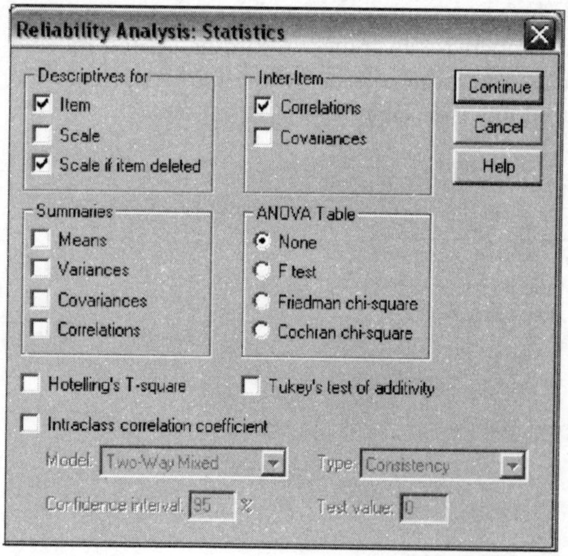

Reliability Analysis—Scale (Alpha)

Statistics for	Mean	Variance	Std. Dev	Variables
Scale	17.5190	15.9028	3.9878	11

TABLE 7.4
Item-total Statistics

	Scale Mean, if Item Deleted	Scale Variance, if Item Deleted	Corrected Item—Total Correlation	Alpha, if Item Deleted
Q2A_1	16.3437	14.6089	.2929	.7624
Q2A_2	16.2655	14.9074	.1687	.7742
Q2A_3	15.5651	12.0314	.6118	.7217
Q2A_4	15.9349	13.4892	.3662	.7563
Q2A_5	16.3267	15.0266	.1863	.7710
Q2A_6	15.5361	12.4215	.5577	.7303
Q2A_7	15.6743	12.3943	.5379	.7329
Q2A_8	15.8347	12.6276	.5298	.7344
Q2A_9	16.3637	15.4072	.0986	.7766
Q2A_10	15.6232	12.5881	.5195	.7357
Q2A_11	15.7224	12.4354	.5432	.7322

Reliability coefficients
N of cases = 998.0, N of items = 11, Alpha = .7672.

The output of Table 7.4 details the reliability coefficients for an awareness scale, which involves 11 awareness variables about symptoms of leprosy, having a high value of alpha (.7672). The rule of thumb is that an alpha value of 0.60 is considered low, while alpha values in the range of 0.70–0.80 are considered optimal. Further, Inter-item Correlation and 'Scale if Item Deleted' are also very important indicators to assess the reliability of the scale. Inter-item Correlation allows researchers to see if any of the items are negatively correlated with the other items in the scale, and the 'Scale if Item is Deleted' will reveal the alpha if each item were deleted from the scale.

DATA ANALYSIS

Univariate Statistics

Univariate analysis, as the name suggests, provides analytical information about one variable, which could be metric or non-metric in nature. The SPSS package provides the facility to carry out univariate analyses such as Frequencies, Descriptive and Explore, which are all located under the Analyse menu (see Figure 7.16).

Researchers can select Statistics, which offers a number of summary statistics and whatever statistic they select, the summarized information would be displayed in the Output window. The Frequency option generates frequency information in addition to measures of central tendencies and dispersion. Each time researchers select a statistical procedure like Frequencies[12] and Descriptive, the results are immediately displayed in an Output window.

FIGURE 7.16
Analysing Frequencies: SPSS

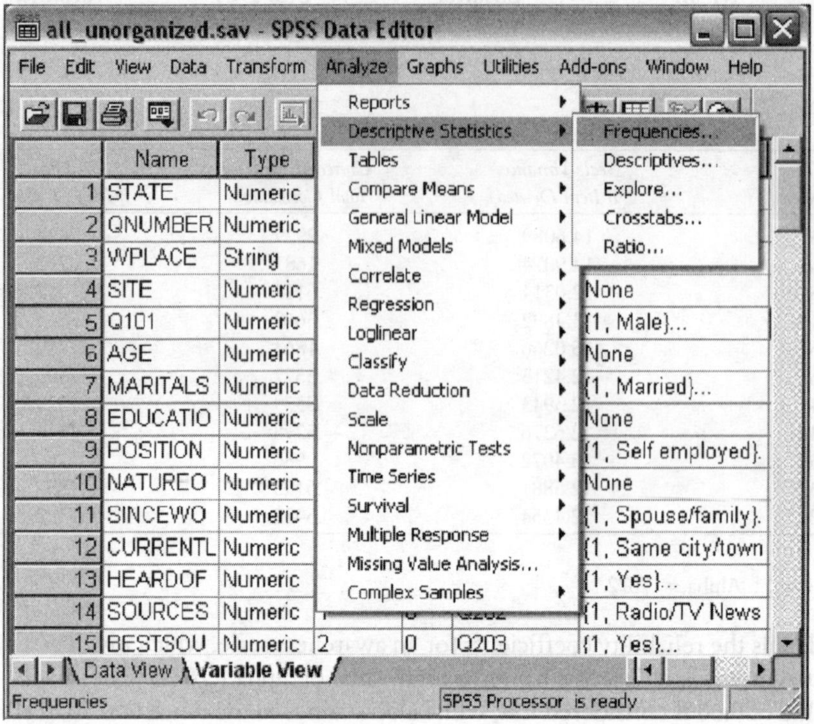

Frequencies

Researchers can use the Frequency option to list the detailed information on selected data. The option is extremely useful for nominal and categorical data such as in the case of gender where data is coded in two categories. The Frequency option provides a table, which shows counts, percentages and statistics including percentile values, central tendency, dispersion and distribution.

Descriptive

The SPSS package provides the facility to obtain summary information about the distribution, variability, and central tendency of continuous variables by using the Descriptive option. Researchers can select various measures such as mean, sum, standard deviation, variance, range, minimum, maximum, standard error (SE) mean, kurtosis and skewness by using the Descriptive option.

Explore

The SPSS package provides the facility to examine the central tendency and distributional characteristics of continuous variables by using the Explore option. Researchers can select statistics such as M estimators, outliers and percentiles by using the Explore option. It also provides the facility for grouped frequency tables, displays, as well as stem and leaf and box plots.

Cross-tabulations

Cross-tabulation, as discussed earlier, is the easiest way of summarizing data and can be of any size in terms of rows and columns. It generally allows us to identify relationships between the cross-tabulated variables based on the cell values.

The SPSS package provides the facility to generating bivariate cross-tabulations. A cross-tabulation helps in analysing the association of one variable with another variable and is extremely useful in cases where each variable contains only a few categories.

Researchers can select the cross-tab option by choosing Analyse from the menu and the Descriptive Statistics and Cross-tabs sub-options. Researchers can select the dependent variable and independent variable to generate cross-tabulation. Besides selecting Cross-tabs, researchers can click on the Statistics button to select the Chi-square test to obtain a measure of statistical significance, that is, Phi and Cramer's V (see Figure 7.17). In case both variables are dichotomous, the phi correlation coefficient should be used. Cramer's V should be preferred over phi-square coefficient in case of larger tables.

FIGURE 7.17
Cross-tabs Statistics: SPSS

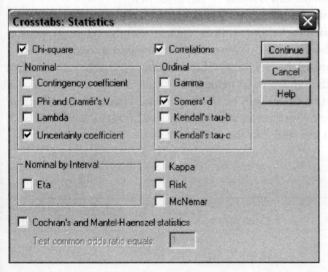

Means

Mean is a very important measure of central location of distribution, especially in the case of interval and numerical data. Researchers can use two methods in SPSS to produce means. Researcher can use the Frequencies sub-option from the Descriptive Statistics option.

Alternatively, they can select the option Compare Means from the Analyse menu option. They can select the variable, which they want to put into the Independent List box and the variable they want to put in the Dependent List box.

The Chi-square Test

The chi-square test is only used with measures that place cases into categories. The test indicates whether the results from the two measures are about what one would expect if the two were not related. Researchers can access the facility by selecting Analyse from the menu and Descriptive Statistics and Cross-tabs to open the Cross-tabs dialogue box. Further, in the Cross-tabs dialogue box, researchers can select variables, which they wish to be cross-tabulated. Researchers can select the Statistics option to open the Cross-tabs: Statistics box and can select the Chi-square box to continue.

Independent-samples T Test

The independent-samples t test procedure compares means for two groups of cases (see Table 7.5). In fact, there are two variants of unpaired t test based on the assumption of equal and unequal variances between two groups of cases. In case of unpaired t test, subjects should be randomly assigned to two groups, so that researchers, after employing significance test, can conclude that the difference in response is due to the treatment and not due to other factors.

Researchers can access the Independent-samples t test by clicking on Analyse and then pointing the mouse to the Compare Means option and clicking on Independent-samples t Test. To explain the test further, let us take an example where television viewership is compared across gender variables. Researchers can do the test by putting the TV viewership frequency variable into the Test Variable box and the gender variable in the Grouping Variable box.

Researchers, at the next stage, shall define the groups by clicking on the Define Groups button, which would open the Define Groups box. Since males are coded as 1 and females are coded as 2, researchers should type 1 in the Group 1 box and 2 in the Group 2 box.

TABLE 7.5
Independent Sample Test

		Levene's Test for Equality of Variances		T Test for Equality of Means					95% Confidence Interval of the Difference	
		F	*Sig.*	*t*	*df*	*Sig. (Two-tailed)*	*Mean Difference*	*Std. Error Difference*	*Lower*	*Upper*
TV	Equal variances assumed	34.915	.000	−8.4	878	.000	−1.13	.134	−1.390	−.865
	Equal variances not assumed			−8.4	868.501	.000	−1.13	.133	−1.389	−.865

Table 7.6 shows the results of two t tests. The table also gives the values for the degrees of freedom and the observed significance level. It is important to point out that this tests the null hypothesis that men and women have the same TV viewership frequency. The null hypothesis can be easily tested by comparing p value with the specified significance level. This significance value is the probability that the t value would be this big or bigger simply by chance if the null hypothesis were true. Since this probability is less than 0.05 (the significance level researchers use by convention in social studies), researchers can reject the null hypothesis and conclude that probably there is a difference between men and women in terms of TV viewership.

Paired-samples T Test

Paired t test is very similar to unpaired t test, except with the difference that paired t test is related to matched samples. It tests the difference between raw scores and is based on the assumption that data are measured in interval/ratio scale. The test assumes that observed data are from matched samples drawn from a population with a normal distribution.

The test statistic is t with $n-1$ degrees of freedom. If the p value associated with t is low (< 0.05), there is evidence to reject the null hypothesis. Thus, you would have evidence that there is a difference in means across the paired observations.

Researchers can access Independent-samples t Test by clicking on the Analyse menu option and then pointing the mouse at Compare Means and clicking on Paired-samples t test.

One-way Analysis of Variance

The method of analysis of variance is used to test hypotheses that examine the difference between two or more means. For example, researchers might want to see if the average monthly sale of Baragara (big crystal) salt type differs by traders' category.

Researcher can easily do this by using the 'one-way analysis of variance (ANOVA)'. They can easily access the option by clicking on the Analyse menu option and then pointing the mouse at the Compare Means option and then clicking on the Means options. Researchers at next stage shall move the average monthly sale into the dependent list and trader category into the factor list.

TABLE 7.6
One-way ANOVA: Descriptives

Average Monthly Sale—Baragara

	N	Mean	Std. Deviation	Std. Error	95% Confidence Interval for Mean		Minimum	Maximum
					Lower Bound	Upper Bound		
Wholesaler/ distributor/ stockist	201	51650.9	37290.500	2630.269	46464.25	56837.48	126	99999
Trader/repacker	467	16373.9	16857.198	780.058	14841.05	17906.78	50	99999
Retailer	539	2614.08	7098.876	305.770	2013.43	3214.73	0	99999
Total	1207	16103.9	25590.033	736.575	14658.81	17549.03	0	99999

TABLE 7.7
One-way ANOVA: Test of Homogeneity of Variances

Average Monthly Sale—Baragara

Levene Statistic	df1	df2	Sig.
566.274	2	1204	.000

TABLE 7.8
Model Statistics: ANOVA

Average Monthly Sale—Baragara

	Sum of Squares	df	Mean Square	F	Sig.
Between groups	3.52E+11	2	1.760E+11	484.324	.000
Within groups	4.38E+11	1204	363496035.5		
Total	7.90E+11	1206			

In this example, the independent variable trader has three categories. Table 7.7 also shows the average monthly sale for each of these groups and their standard deviations, as well as the analysis of variance table including the sum of squares, degrees of freedom, mean squares, the F value and the observed significance value.

The significance value for this example is the probability of getting an F value of 484.32 or higher if the null hypothesis is true (see Table 7.8). Here the null hypothesis is that the average monthly sale is the same for all three traders category. Since this probability is so low (< 0. 0005 or less than 5 out of 10,000), we would reject the null hypothesis and conclude that average monthly sale are probably not same.

Correlation

Correlation, as described in Chapter 4, is one of the most widely used measures of association between two or more variables. In its simplest form it signifies the relationship between two variables, that is, whether an increase in one variable results in the increase of the other variable.

Let us hypothesize that as education increases, the level of prestige of one's occupation also increases. Researchers can access the facility by clicking on the Analyse menu option and pointing to Correlate and Bivariate sub-option.

Though there are various measures of correlation between nominal or ordinal data, Pearson product-moment correlation coefficient is a measure of linear association between two interval-ratio variables. The measure, represented by the letter r, varies from –1 to +1. A zero correlation indicates that there is no correlation between the variable. The SPSS package includes another correlation test, Spearman's rho, besides Pearson correlation to analyse variables that are not normally distributed, or are ranked. Researchers can opt for both Pearson correlation and Spearman's rho. The output screen will show two tables: one for the Pearson correlation and the other for the Spearman's rho.

A correlation coefficient indicates both type of correlation as well as the strength of relationship. Coefficient value determines the strength whereas the sign indicates whether variables change in the same direction or in opposite directions.

Thus, if the coefficient is away from 0, regardless of whether it is positive or negative, it signifies a stronger relationship between the two variables. Thus, a coefficient of 0.685 is exactly as strong as a coefficient of –0.685. The only difference lies in the fact that positive coefficients tell us there is a direct relationship and as one variable increases, the other also increases. Negative coefficients indicate that there is an inverse relationship and when one variable increases, the other one decreases.

Regression

Regression is widely used in estimating the value of one variable based on the value of another variable. It does so by finding a line of best fit using ordinary least square method. The relation between variables could be linear or non-linear and thus the regression equation could also be linear or non-linear.

Further, depending on the number of variables, we classify regression techniques into simple regression and multiple regression. In simple regression, there is one dependent variable and one independent variable, whereas in multiple regression, there is one dependent variable and many independent variables. Researchers can compute beta values (partial regression coefficients) in case of multiple regression, which give an idea of the relative impact of each independent variable on the dependent variable.

The output will generate the R squared value, which is a summary statistic of the impacts of all the independent variables taken together. It is important to point out that regression is based on the assumption that the dependent variable is measured on an interval, continuous scale, though an ordinal scale can also be used. Another condition for multiple regression is to ensure normality, that is, distributions of all the variables should be normal.

Researchers can access regression analysis from SPSS by going to the menu option Analyse, Regression and Linear. Researchers can select the dependent variable from the variable list. After selecting the dependent variable from the list, they can click on Continue and then Options as shown in Figure 7.18, which shows the default options.

Researchers, at the next stage, can select the method of data analysis by click on the Method button right under the Independent(s) box. The SPSS package provides several choices for doing regression analysis though Stepwise is the one which is most frequently used.

GRAPHS

Graphical representation of data is a better visual medium of representing data, not only because of its visual appeal but also for interpretation by users. There are various ways in which data can be represented like bar graphs, line graphs and pie graphs. Researcher, in SPSS, can usually offer graphical presentations like bar graphs, stacked bar graphs, pie charts and line graphs. Though it is important to point out that not all graphic formats are appropriate for all data. Bar graphs and pie charts are permitted for all nominal, ordinal and ratio data types, whereas line graphs are only for the interval type data.

FIGURE 7.18
Regression by Stepwise Method

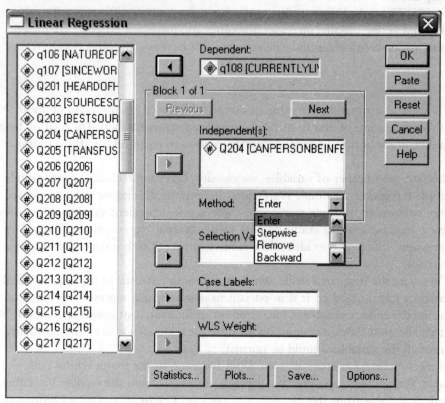

Bar Graphs

Researchers can select the bar graph option by selecting Graphs from the menu bar and option Bar > Single or > Stacked. At the next stage, researchers can select the independent variable to be placed on the vertical axes into the category box, and the dependent variable to be placed on the horizontal axes into the Y box.

Pie Charts

Researchers, after selecting the option Graph from the menu bar, can select the Pie sub-option. After selecting pie chart as graphical representation, they can select the variable.

Line Graphs

Like pie charts, researchers can easily select the Line Graph option from the menu bar option Graph and Line by selecting the variables.

WORKING WITH OUTPUT

Based on the commands or syntax researchers execute in SPSS, the result are displayed in the viewer window. Though when you run a series of commands, it generates a series of output, but you can easily navigate to whichever part of the output you want to see. The SPSS package also provides the facility of manipulating the output to create a document, which contains the requisite output in an arranged and formatted manner.

The SPSS package also provides the facility for researcher to:

a) Browse output results or show or hide selected tables and charts.
b) Change the display order of output by moving selected items up and down.
c) Access the pivot table editor, text output editor, or chart editor for modifying the output.
d) Move items between SPSS and other applications.

The output viewer window is divided into two panes, that is, a left pane, which depicts an outline view of all output contents, and a right pane, which contains statistical tables, charts and text output (see Figure 7.19). Researchers can also use the scroll bars to browse the results, or alternatively they can click an item in the outline to directly access the corresponding table or chart.

The SPSS package also provides the facility to copy the generated output into Microsoft Word or an Excel spreadsheet. Researchers should select the output they want to copy. After selecting the output to copy, they need to select Copy from the Edit menu option. They then need to switch to Microsoft Word or Excel, depending on which they want to use. In the selected window application, researchers should select either Edit/Paste or Edit/Paste Special from the menu. In case researchers want to paste the SPSS output as an embedded object then they should choose Edit/Paste Special. The pasted object can be activated in place by double-clicking then edited as in SPSS.

Manipulating Pivot Tables

The SPSS package presents much of its output in the form of pivot tables, which can be pivoted interactively to produce output. In pivot tables, researchers can rearrange the rows, columns and layers to a specific layout. Researcher can edit a pivot table by double-clicking the pivot table, which activates the Pivot Table Editor.

Further, researchers can choose the SPSS Pivot Table Object option and Open sub-option to open pivot tables. Researchers can edit the table and content in its own separate Pivot Table Editor window. The feature of editing content in its own separate Pivot Table Editor is extremely useful for viewing and editing a wide and long table that otherwise cannot be viewed full scale.

Creating and Modifying Pivot Tables

The facility of modifying pivot tables is provided in SPSS. Researchers have several options available to modify table size, look and structure.

a) *Delete data:* Researchers can delete data from a requisite cell, row, or column by selecting the respective cell or row/column and then pressing the delete key. Alternatively, researchers can click the Edit menu to choose Clear, which will leave the category but remove the data and headings.

FIGURE 7.19
Overview of Output Window: SPSS

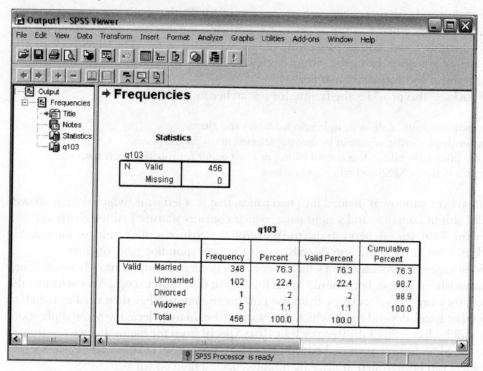

b) *Hide data:* The SPSS package also provides the facility to hide a row or column data, completely by selecting the View menu and choose Hide. Further, in case researchers want to show any rows or columns, which they have hidden in a table, they can double-click inside the table and then click on the View menu and show all.

c) *Rename a heading or title:* Researchers can rename a heading or title by double-clicking the text they want to change by typing in the new text.

d) *Add footnotes:* Researchers can also add footnotes to tables. To add a footnote to a pivot table researchers can double-click the table to select the table. At the next stage, they can click on the cell in which they want to insert the footnote. After selecting the cell, they can click on the Insert menu to select the Footnote option.

e) *Transpose rows and columns:* In SPSS researchers also have the facility of transposing rows and columns, which transforms the layout of a table by changing rows into columns and vice versa. Researchs can double-click table to select the requisite table. Further, they can click on the Pivot menu to select Transpose Rows and Columns option.

f) *Restructure a pivot table using pivoting trays:* If the pivoting trays are not already visible, double-click to select the table, click the Pivot menu and click on the Pivoting Trays option (see Figure 7.20).

To change the structure of a table, click and drag one of the icons. These can be moved from a row to a column or vice versa; from a row or column to a layer, which creates a layer in the table

FIGURE 7.20
Overview of Pivoting Trays: SPSS

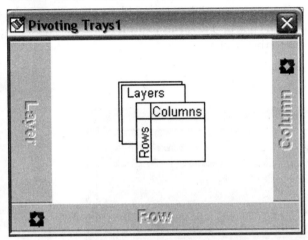

(that you can view in the table by clicking a drop-down menu); within a row or column to change the order in which categories are displayed.

Modifying Table Formatting

a) *Table looks:* SPSS provides several options for modifying the formatting of a pivot table to give it a different table look. The Table Looks option in SPSS presents the preset templates, which controls the appearance of a table.

b) *To apply a table look:* Double-click the table to select it. Click the Format menu and click on the Table Looks.

c) *Formatting tables manually:* Researchers can also manually format tables to set properties for tables and table cells. Researchers can select the area of a table, row, column, or cell they want to format and can use the tools on the formatting toolbar to change the fonts, font sizes and colours. Researchers can select the table, the Format menu and then on Table Properties. Alternatively, they can select the rows, columns or cells they want to format by clicking the Format menu and by clicking Cell Properties. After making all the necessary formatting changes to the table, researchers can save the changed settings as a Table Look to apply it to other tables by selecting the requisite table, and clicking on the Format menu and clicking on Table Looks then clicking the Save As button. Name the look as the .tlo file and click Save.

Printing the Output

Researchers, after doing the necessary analysis, can print the entire output on the viewer window, or delete the sections that are not needed. Further, researchers can also save the output to a diskette or hard drive to print it at a later stage.

Before giving the print command, researchers should the first go to the viewer window by selecting SPSS viewer from the window menu (see Figure 7.21). After going to the Output window, researchers can select the output they want to print. After selecting the output, researchers need to select the Edit/Options to make any changes before printing. Researchers need to choose the Infinite option for the length to save paper. Researchers can also control the page width by changing width. After making the necessary changes, researchers can click on File/Print to print file, after which the contents of the output window will be directed to the printer.

FIGURE 7.21
Overview of Available Options: SPSS

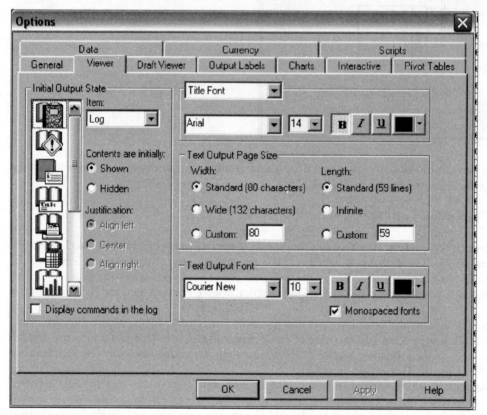

NOTES

1. In the header bar at the top of the screen is a list of topics: File, Edit, Prefs, Window and Help. The Help option in the header bar provides a contents option and a search option. The Contents option can be used by beginners unfamiliar with Stata commands. The Search option can be used by users who know the name of the command or the topic they wish to search for.
2. Stata will have designated the variable type a general numeric with eight digits and zero digits to the right of the decimal place.
3. It is possible to obtain univariate summary statistics on any variable. One can obtain these statistics with the Tabstat command where in order to obtain a frequencies analysis, the tabulate command is used.

4. The SPSS package has excellent contextual help while programming. Within the syntax file place your cursor in an SPSS keyword and click the syntax help menu bar button (▒). For example, placing your cursor in the Descriptives keyword and clicking the syntax help menu bar button opens the complete descriptives command syntax diagram.

5. The variable description area displays information about the variable. The default variable description is a numeric variable with a column width of 8, right justified, no decimal places, no labels and no missing values.

6. This technique imports an active copy of the data so that changes in the data in Access are viewed in SPSS; the SPSS data sheet is updated when Access is updated. Access is not updated when data in the SPSS data sheet is altered. This is useful because you only need to link the data once and can then continue to add or edit data in Access.

7. This also lists the queries, so if you want data from more than one table, develop a 'query' in Access (as explained earlier) to make sure it retrieves the data you want. This will still allow SPSS to read updates.

8. String constants must be enclosed in quotation marks or apostrophes. Numeric constants must be typed in American format, with the period (.) as the decimal indicator.

9. You can filter or delete cases that do not meet the selection criteria. Filtered cases remain in the data file but are excluded from analysis. Select 'cases' creates a filter variable, FILTER_$, to indicate filter status. Selected cases have a value of 1; filtered cases have a value of 0. Filtered cases are also indicated with a slash through the row number in the Data Editor.

10. There are three broad procedures that can be carried out—list-wise deletion, case-wise deletion and data imputation while carrying out data analysis.

11. Kuder-Richardson is a special case of Cronbach's alpha for ordinal categories which can also be used to asses reliability but is not available in SPSS.

12. Frequencies by themselves are seldom useful. Most people understand percentages better. To get SPSS to compute percentages, point your mouse at the button labelled Cells at the bottom of the screen and click on it. This will open the 'Cross-tabs: Cell Display' box. Find the box called Column Percentages and click on this box.

SECTION II

SECTION II

CHAPTER 8

POPULATION, HEALTH AND NUTRITION

POPULATION

The term population means different things to different people, but in demography it symbolizes the total number of human inhabitants of a specified area, such as a city, country, or continent, at a given time. Population study as an academic discipline is known as demography. It deals with the size, composition and distribution of populations. It studies changes in population patterns due to births, deaths and migration, and also analyses the determinants and consequences of such changes over time. The first section of this chapter deals with demographic transition and research issues related to demography.

DEMOGRAPHIC TRANSITION

The demographic transition model is a fundamental model, which is used widely to depict population dynamics. The model defines four stages to depict population dynamics in society.

a) High fertility, high mortality.
b) High fertility, declining mortality.
c) Declining fertility, low mortality.
d) Low fertility, low mortality.

The first stage of high fertility and high mortality prevailed all over the world initially. But, rapid population growth started in the second and third stages because of high birth rates in the first stage. Now there are regions, which are moving towards the stage of low fertility and low mortality.

The Industrial Revolution changed the whole scenario by facilitating the gradual mechanization of many tasks and activities, replacing human labour, meaning that people could lead a comfortable life. People also slowly acquired the knowledge and means to control disease. Further, around 1950, a new phase of population growth started when famine and disease could be controlled even in less developed areas that had not yet attained a high degree of literacy or technological capability. This happened as a result of the easy availability of cost-effective vaccines, antibiotics, insecticides and high-yielding varieties of seeds to the common people. As a result, life expectancy at birth in most developing countries increased from about 35–40 years in 1950 and to 61 years by 1990. The rapid decline in deaths among people who maintained generally high fertility rates led to annual population growths that exceeded 3.1 per cent in many developing nations—a rate that doubles population size in 23 years. Further economic and public health advances even in developing countries will decrease mortality rates and rapid population growth will occur until the society adjusts to the new realities after which fertility will decline.

The demographic transition model was based on the European experience, in which the decline in death rates was gradual. It remains to be seen how this model behaves in the developing world of today, in which the decline in death rates has occurred much more rapidly.

Demographic Balancing Equation

Demographic change is affected by three factors, namely, birth, death and migration. Population change in any country is primarily affected by the prevalent birth and death rates of that country, though the population in that particular region is also affected by net migration. Thus, birth, death and net migration are three key factors, which determine the demographic balancing equation—the increase or decrease in a population as the algebraic sum of births, deaths, immigration and emigration, which can be defined further as:

Starting population + births – deaths + immigration – emigration = ending population

Population Age Structure and the Population Pyramid

The population age structure, signifying the proportion of people in the younger age group and in the older age group is an important determinant, which shapes both demographic and economic dynamics. Population age structure shares a reciprocal relationship with the rate of natural increase and thus affects the growth rate of a population greatly, since both fertility and mortality vary greatly by age. As a result, a younger population has a higher rate of natural growth, which in turn lowers the median age of a population.

The Population Pyramid

The population pyramid represents the proportional age structure combination of a population with the age bands arranged from the lowest to the highest ages. Demographers display the age structure of a population by constructing a pyramid in which the population size in each age band is depicted by a horizontal bar that extends from a centreline to the left for one gender and to the right for the other gender. Population pyramid is a form of histogram having relative/absolute population on the x axis and the age/age group on the y axis.

Demographers use this pyramid to see how a growing population becomes younger and the transition to lower fertility makes it older. Researchers often describe population structure as an old age or a young age structure, depending on the higher proportion of young or old people in the population. Young population age structures are linked with high fertility, whereas ageing population structures are associated with declining fertility. The impact of decline of mortality on the age structure is much smaller than that of the decline of fertility, because a decrease in mortality affects all ages simultaneously. However, if mortality rate decreases at younger stages, population increases considerably.

It is estimated that if mortality and fertility remain constant over time and no migration takes place, then in the long run we can have a stable age structure. In the case of a stable age structure, the age distribution depends exclusively on age-specific fertility and mortality.

INFLUENCE OF POPULATION AGE COMPOSITION

Population age composition is influenced by various factors such as sex composition, median age of population and process of ageing. The following section illustrates the effect of these various factors on population age composition.

Ageing

Ageing is one of the various factors that affects population age composition. The most frequently used measures of the ageing process are:

a) Index of ageing.
b) Median age of population.
c) Dependency ratio of the elderly population.

Index of Ageing

Index of ageing is defined as the ratio of the number of elderly persons to the number of children in a population:

$$\text{Ageing index} = \frac{\text{Elderly population of 65 and over}}{\text{Children population below 15}} \times 100$$

In other words, ageing can also be defined as the process of the increase in the proportion of elderly people and the decrease in the proportion of children. This process has been evident in most of the developed countries where the population has become progressively older due to low mortality and low birth rates.

Median Age of Population

Median age of population divides the population into two equal groups. A median age of 25 years of a population denotes that one half of the population is aged below 25 years and the other half is aged above 25 years.

Old-Age Dependency Ratio

The old-age dependency ratio is defined as the ratio of the number of persons in the age group of 65 years and above to the persons in age group of 15–64 years, per 100 persons. It is a very useful indicator for looking at the proportion of the elderly within the population. The old-age dependency ratio in India has increased marginally from about 12.04 per cent in 1981 to 12.19 per cent in 1991, being somewhat higher for females than for the males.

$$\text{Dependency ratio} = \frac{\text{total number of old persons (aged 65 or above)} \times 100}{\text{number of persons in the age group of } 15-64}$$

Sex Composition

The sex composition of populations is often described by comparing the sizes of the sex categories with a ratio. Sex ratio, defined as number of females to 1,000 males, is one such indictor, which not only shows the present stage of India's demographic transition, but also provides the information about the prevalent gender equality scenario. It fluctuated between 927–934 during 1971 to 2001 at the national level, but there are some states such as Punjab and Haryana, where the sex ratio is even lower than 900. Sex ratio is measured as:

$$\text{Sex ratio} = \frac{\text{number of females}}{\text{number of males}} \times 1,000$$

It is important to point out that an unbalanced sex ratio affects the social, psychological, emotional and economic structure of society. It can severely affect the availability of marriage partners and thus can cause imperfection in laid down societal rules for marriage. An unbalanced sex ratio results from strong bias for one sex, like boy preference in India, or by means of large-scale migration, or unequal mortality rates in adults.

Ethnic and Religious Composition

India is a land of diverse cultures where people of diverse religions and castes cohabit together. In such diverse culture, population characteristics also vary due to beliefs, values, norms and practices of the various religious and caste sub-groups. It is imperative in these circumstances that planners have an idea about the variation in population characteristics due to existing norms and beliefs. Besides, the impact of population characteristics on factors such as economics, education and health also needs to be assessed.

DEMOGRAPHIC CONCEPTS, MEASURES AND TECHNIQUES

Demographic concepts and theories are centred on various demographic terms, concepts and measures, which are frequently used in common parlance but are rarely understood in their demographic sense. Most of the demographic indicators are expressed in rates and ratios. The computation and meaning of both rate and ratio are very different from each other and that is why certain indicators are expressed in rates while others in ratios (see Box 8.1).

BOX 8.1
Ratio, Proportion and Rate

Ratio, proportion and *rate* are often confused as one and the same thing, though they differ widely in their computation as well as application. *Ratio* is obtained by dividing the size of one of two non-overlapping groups possessing some common characteristics by that of other non-overlapping group.
Proportion is a relative number that expresses the size of one sub-group or one entity to the total of all sub-groups or total entity, which is equated to 1.
Rate is the most commonly used demographic term. It is expressed as the number of events say E that occur in a population in a given period of time, which is usually a year.

The following section attempts to explain the terms frequently used in demographic parlance.

Fertility

Fertility is defined as the actual birth performance of women. This is different from fecundity, that is, the biological capability to reproduce. A woman may be fecund but may not be sexually active, for example, in case certain socio-economic situations prevent her from marrying after physical maturity. In other cases, a woman may be fecund but may not produce a child, because of the adoption of contraceptive methods to prevent conception.

Thus, it is quite evident that high fecundity does not necessarily mean high fertility. The difference in population growth of developed countries and developing countries is not due to the difference in women's fecundity, but due to difference in women's fertility. In developed countries, women's fertility has declined to very low levels because of contraception use, though quite in contrast in developing countries, we observe high fertility levels due to low usage of contraception. Thus, fecundity and fertility are very different concepts. Fecundity in combination with low age at marriage and absence of contraception may cause higher fertility.

Researchers sometimes also use the term natural fertility, which signifies the fertility level that would have prevailed if family-planning methods had not been used. In other words, it is that fertility level which would prevail if women did not resort to any artificial intervention in the reproductive processes.

Fertility Analysis and Rate

Fertility rate is usually measured in two ways—in period perspective and cohort perspective. In cohort perspective, fertility status of a group of women which goes through the experience is studied over a period of time, whereas in the case of period perspective, fertility occurring in a given period of time is studied in relation to the duration of exposure of the population during that particular period. Cohort perspective tracks the fertility behaviours of a group of women in a longitudinal way, whereas periodic perspective looks at fertility rates in a cross-sectional way.

Periodic Measure of Fertility

Crude Birth Rate

The crude birth rate is defined as the number of births occurring during a stated period divided by the population size.

$$\text{crude birth rate} = \frac{\text{number of births}^x}{\text{mid-year population}^x} \times 1{,}000$$

Crude birth rate is typically calculated for the entire population, where the numerator is births, and the denominator is usually the mid-year population. Thus, crude birth rate for a year x is defined as the number of births in year x to the mid-year population in year x, multiplied by a constant of 1,000. It is important to point out that in case the number of birth is very few, then an average rate for several years should be calculated to have a precise estimate. For example, researchers can calculate the average number of births over three years to arrive at a three-year average birth rate.

As the name suggests, crude birth rate is a crude measure of fertility, because the denominator even includes men, young women under the age of 15 and women over the age of 50 who usually do not possess childbearing capacity.

General Fertility Rate (GFR)

Crude birth rate suffers from the limitation that its denominator includes the total population even though included members such as young children and men do not possess childbearing capacity. Thus, to modify the fertility indicator, a general fertility rate is introduced by including only women of reproductive age in the denominator. It helps in addressing the shortcomings of the crude birth rate by restricting the denominator to women of childbearing age. General fertility rate is expressed as:

$$\text{GFR}^y{}_f = \frac{\text{births}^y}{\text{mid-year population}^y{}_{f,15-49}} \times 1{,}000$$

Where the numerator is the number of births that occurred in year y and the denominator is the mid-year population of females aged 15–49 in year y. In general, for the calculation of the fertility rate, women in the reproductive age 15–49 years are considered as few women give birth before age 15 and after age 49.

Though GFR is a more refined indicator than crude birth rate, because of the use of mid-year population of females, aged 15–49, but it is a known fact that fertility varies remarkably by age; it is not practical to assume that fertility remains the same for females within the age range of 15–49. Thus, even the GFR indicator needs to be more refined to account for varying fertility rates determined by age.

Disaggregating by Age

A fertility rate, like any other demographic characteristic, is a function of a population's age and sex composition structure. Thus, it is imperative that a true measure of fertility is sensitive to the population's age and sex composition.

That, however, does not mean that overall 'crude' rates are not useful. They can be also be used for comparison purposes, but only across populations having similar composition. In a bid to account for different population characteristics such as age structure and sex composition, it is essential to use the attribute specific rate, that is, rates computed for a specific age or for a sub-group as a refined measure of fertility.

Further, as specific rates are calculated to account for varying characteristics of the population, these average rates can then be averaged, with some appropriate weighting, to obtain an overall rate for comparison. The specific rates calculated after appropriate weighting is known as weighted averages or standardized rates.

Age-specific Fertility Rate (ASFR)

Age-specific fertility rate is a refined measure of fertility, which accounts for fertility variation among females at different ages as demographers often measure fertility according to the age of the mother. The formula used for calculating ASFR for age group x to $x+n$ is:

$$\text{ASFR}_{\text{women, age } x \text{ to } x+n} = \frac{\text{births}_{\text{women, age } x \text{ to } x+n}}{\text{mid-year population}_{\text{women, age } x \text{ to } x+n}} \times 1{,}000$$

In most demographic analyses, demographers calculate ASFR by taking five-year age groups as one group. Usually, it is observed that age-specific fertility rates are low or moderate in the age group of 15–19 years, and is the highest in the age group of the 20s and then decline moderately in the age group of the 30s.

Total Fertility Rate (TFR)

The age-specific fertility rates are a very good measure of varying fertility rates and are very useful in comparing fertility rates for age groups across the population. But, most of time researchers need summative measures or summarized age-specific rates to compare fertility measures across the population.

Total fertility rate is one such summative measure, which signifies the average number of children a woman is expected to have during her reproductive life. The average number of children born to women can be simply calculated by averaging the number of live births, for women who have passed their reproductive years. But it is important to point out that TFR provides a projection into the future and thus cannot be calculated by taking an average but is calculated from a given set of ASFRs.

Total fertility rate is a standardized rate which summarizes ASFR and is calculated by summing the ASFRs and multiplying the result by the width of the age interval of the ASFRs. In the majority of cases, demographers use ASFRs based on five-year intervals. Thus, to calculate TFR, the sum of the ASFRs needs to be multiplied by five. The expression for calculating total fertility rate is:

$$\text{TFR} = \Sigma(_n\text{ASFR}x)\, i$$

Where i = the width in years of the age interval.

In a way, TFR summarizes the fertility rate at each age by projecting the fertility experience of a cohort of women as they go through their age band. Unlike crude birth rate, general fertility rate and age-specific fertility rate, the total fertility rate is a standardized measure because it is computed by multiplying ASFR at each age by a standard population (usually of 1,000 persons). In other words, TFR estimates the total number of live births a group of 1,000 women would have if all of them lived through their entire reproductive period. Though while calculating TFR, we usually ignore the determinants which inhibits fertility, but in reality these determinant exist and that is why TFR in the real scenario may be different from that experienced by a cohort of women (see Box 8.2).

BOX 8.2
Determinants Inhibiting Fertility

> It is an established fact that delayed marriage, use of contraception, induced abortion and postpartum infecundability are four principal reasons, which inhibit fertility. In case the effects of these factors are controlled then fertility levels will increase significantly based on the factor controlled.
>
> In case we are able to negate the effect of delayed marriage and marital separation without any other changes in fertility behaviour, then fertility level will be equal to total marital fertility rate. Further, if we can negate the effect of contraception and induced abortion, fertility will rise to a level of total natural fertility rate. In case we are able to remove the practice of lactation and therefore the resultant postpartum infecundity, fertility levels will rise to the level of total fecundity rate.

Gross Reproduction Rate (GRR)

Gross reproduction rate as a measure of fertility estimates tries to assess the population growth in terms of replicability. It tries to answer whether a given set of fertility rates suggest that the population will grow, decline or would replace itself.

GRR, like TFR is a standardized rate, the only difference lies in the fact that GRR is the sum of age-specific rates, which includes only live female births in the numerator. But as the number of female live births by age of mother may not always be known, the proportion of female births is used as a multiplication factor for the age-specific rates to compute GRR. The GRR is mathematically expressed as the proportion of female births out of total births multiplied by TFR, as depicted in the following formula:

$$GRR = \left(\frac{\text{female births}}{\text{births}} \right) \times TFR$$

Net Reproduction Rate (NRR)

Gross reproduction rate as a measure of assessing a population's replicability measures only the production of females. It is based on the assumption that no woman is going to die during the childbearing years. Net reproduction rate (NRR) is widely used as a more accurate measure and it measures replacement of mothers by their daughters in a hypothetical cohort.

Net reproduction rate measures the number of female births given by a hypothetical cohort of 1,000 mothers, accounting for the mortality of the mothers from the time of their birth. Thus, NRR estimates the average number of daughters who will replace a cohort of 1,000 mothers, if age-specific fertility and mortality rates remain constant. If the rate is above 1,000, then the population will increase and if it remains less than 1,000, the population will decrease, provided that the age-specific rates remain constant.

The formula for NRR is:

$$NRR = \frac{\sum({}_n ASFR_{x*} * {}_n L_x)}{5L_o}$$

METHODS FOR FERTILITY ESTIMATES

Demographic studies calculating fertility estimates first need to assess the total number of births given by a mother. Estimates of fertility from NFHS-1 (National Family Health Survey-1) and NFHS-2 (National Family Health Survey-2) are derived using two methods: (i) the birth-history method and (ii) the own-children method.

Birth-History Method

In the birth-history method, as the name suggests, interviewers ask women to provide information on the total number of births they have given. Interviewers then cull out the information on the number of sons and daughters that are still living with them, living elsewhere and the number who have died.

While requesting this information, the interviewer obtains a birth history for each woman, including details of each live birth separately, recording month and year, sex and survival status of each live birth. Further, in case of children who had died at a later stage, their age at death is also recorded.

In the birth-history method, researchers simply count the births by age of the mother as reported in the birth histories for each calendar year up to a specified time before the survey. In case researchers wish to calculate a robust measure ASFR, it is advised that they take birth history information up to 15 years before the survey.

After counting the number of births to a woman, at the next stage, researchers count woman-years of exposure to the risk of birth by woman's age, for each year up to a specified time before the survey. Then, at the next stage, for each year or a group of years, researchers divide the number of births that occurred to women in each five-year age band by the number of woman-years of exposure among women in the same age group to calculate an ASFR.

Own-children Method

The own-children method[1] uses a reverse survival technique for estimating ASFRs for 15 years preceding a census or household survey. In case of the own-children method, researchers first collect information about the total number of children in households. Then based on demographic information collected, researchers try to match children with the line number of mothers in the household listing. A reverse survival method is then used to estimate numbers of births by age of mother in previous years. All matched children (age group of 0–14 years) with mothers (age group of 15–64) are referred to as own-children.

Let us now discuss some terms commonly associated with fertility estimates.

a) *Cohort measurement:* Cumulative fertility is a commonly calculated measure of cohort fertility, which is simply computed by summing up the cohort's childbearing experience from the start to the end.

b) *Parity progression ratio:* Parity progression ratio is the probability of a woman having another child given that she has already had a certain number. It is normally calculated for marriage or birth cohorts of women who have already completed childbearing.

c) *Birth interval:* Parity progression ratio gives the probability of a woman having another child given that women have had their first, second or higher order births, not their timings. But timing of birth is also a very crucial indicator and should be taken into account while calculating fertility estimate. Birth interval accounts for timing of birth and is usually analyzed from survey data complied in the form of birth history.

In order to have an idea about the fertility estimates, it is necessary to have a basic understanding of three basic terms—fecundity, fecundability and fertility. Fertility by definition refers to actual births, while fecundity refers to the biological ability to have children.

The next section explains the basic terms further:

a) *Fecundity:* Fecundity is defined as the biological capacity of a woman to reproduce. According to biologists, fecundity is a function of various factors such as density of population, protein intake and diet and even stress. But still demographers have not come to any conclusion regarding the impact of socio-economic development on fecundity, that is, whether with an improvement in socio-economic situation, fecundity rises or falls linearly.

Further, some women, for definite biological reasons, cannot produce children and are said to be suffering from primary sterility. Primary fecundity characterizes the lack of childbearing capacity of a woman, who has never been able to bear children. Some aspects of primary sterility can be removed if appropriate medical facilities are available but some are still incurable and not properly understood. Secondary sterility, on the other hand, characterizes the lack of childbearing capacity of a woman before reaching the end of her reproductive span, though the woman may have earlier produced a child.

b) *Fecundability:* Fecundability is defined as the measure of fecundity. It is obvious that not every act of sexual intercourse would result in conception even in the absence of contraception and further not all conceptions result in successful childbirths. Fecundibility is defined as the probability of conceiving during a month or a menstrual cycle, in case of a sexually active women not using any contraception. As it is a probability measure, its value should lie between 0 and 1. It is one of the most important parameters for studying fertility patterns in different societies.

c) *Natality:* Natality signifies the role births plays in human reproduction. Thus, in a way it also reflects the measures of fertility.

d) *Family size:* Family size signifies the number of children a woman or a couple has at a specific point of time. The complete family size signifies the total number of births given by a woman up to the end of her reproductive life, that is, up to 49 years of age.

e) *Birth order and parity:* Birth order, as the name suggests, refers to a particular point of time when population is classified according to birth occurrences. In the case of family planning studies, data is presented according to the number of children born to a woman referred as parity. Thus first parity women are those who have given birth to one child; second parity women are those who have given birth to two children.

f) *Fertility and reproduction:* Fertility analysis signifies the childbearing capacity of a population whereas reproduction signifies the ability of a population to replace itself.

g) *Sterility:* Sterility or infecundity signifies the lack of childbearing capacity of a woman or a couple. It can be further classified into primary sterility and secondary sterility based on the lack of childbearing capacity of a woman vis-à-vis her reproductive period.

h) *Nuptiality:* Nuptiality analysis is the analysis of all processes related to marriage, separation, widowhood and remarriage.

i) *Reproductive period:* Reproductive period is defined as the period between menses and menopause, when a woman possesses childbearing capacity. Usually, the reproductive period of a woman starts at the age of 15 or at the minimum age at marriage, and ends between 45 to 49 years of age or at the dissolution of marriage due to divorce, separation or death of her husband.

LIFE TABLE

Demographers' interest in mortality and cohort attrition is reflected in life tables, which provide a description of people's lives as they die and quite optimistically are called life tables and not death tables.

A life table is composed of a number of columns showing values of different life-table functions at each age, starting from birth. The basic column shows mortality rates at each age and probabilities of dying between successive years. There are other columns, which show other characteristics, such as one column shows the number of people that would be there at each age if deaths occurred according to life table, that is, if fertility balances mortality. It has another column for life expectancy that shows the average number of years left to be lived by people. Another important column shows the number of people who survived and hence come out from the original cohort.

There are two main types of life tables in common use: period life table and the cohort life table.

Period Life Table

The period life table is based on mortality rates of a calendar year. The mortality rates are obtained by relating counts of death at particular ages to estimate of the population alive at those stages. The periodic life table incorporates the experience of mortality by different ages of population during a given period of time. Unless specified otherwise, life table signifies current life table.

Cohort Life Table

The simplest life table is the cohort life table, a registered birth cohort that is followed until all members die. This life table is constructed by relating to the number of individuals who survive to a particular birthday and the number of deaths that occur during the following year or period of years.

A life table characterizes mortality in a period of years by showing what would happen to a hypothetical cohort if the current age-specific death rate at each age did not change during their life time. The periodic life table uses risks derived from recent death rates at each age and life expectancies are simply calculated by taking a simple average of age-specific death rates. Though in real situations, age-specific death rates are likely to change, hence results may vary. The cohort life table is constructed to account for changing death rates, though the process of calculation and observation of death rates of cohorts takes quite a long time (see Box 8.3).

BOX 8.3
Cohort Effects

> The life table and the total fertility rates are based on the experience of a group of cohort who goes through same experience over a period of time, assuming that age-specific rates remain same over that time. But, in reality, populations consist of innumerable number age of such cohorts and age-specific rates also changes over time. Moreover as age, time and cohorts are linked to each another it is very difficult to decipher whether an association with one of these aspects results in change in other aspects.

The standard life table has many applications as its mortality rates are used as inputs for population projection. The standard life table also has many variants like the segregated life table by gender as men generally suffer from higher mortality than women.

Though age distribution of population is an important factor in shaping social structure, mortality does not play a major role in this. The proportion of population above 65 is defined as affected fertility rates, which determines the rate of number of children to number of persons of childbearing age.

LIFE EXPECTANCY: COMPUTATION FROM LIFE TABLE

Life expectancy is simply defined as the average age at the time of death in a lifetime. It is expressed as the number of years the person is expected to live if the prevailing age-specific mortality rates remain true. It is a general measure of mortality that captures prevailing mortality rates of a population at different age groups.

A life table represents mortality over a period of years by showing what would happen to a group of cohort if the current age-specific death rate holds true. The expectation of life at birth or life expectancy is the average age at death. For example, if life expectancy as per the life table is 75 years then it means that only about 25 per cent of a hypothetical cohort would die when they cross the age of 75. The value of life expectancy is pulled down by the number of individuals who die at a young age.

The importance of life expectancy increases because often the age-specific mortality rates are not well correlated. This is particularly true of the infant mortality/child mortality rates and other age-specific mortality rates.

Life expectancy is a summative measure of a set of age-specific mortality rates and thus it can be computed for any particular age. Life expectancy at birth provides a summarization of mortality rates across all ages, whereas life expectancy from age 65 summarizes mortality rates after the age of 65 years. That is why life expectancy at birth can be influenced by changes in infant mortality. It is because of this factor that reductions in mortality at early stages of life add many more years of life than reductions in mortality rates for later stages of life.

Life expectancy and total fertility rate both depend upon cohort measure for prediction. Putting it in another way, both life expectancy and total fertility rates are based on the experience of a group cohort who go through the same experience over a period of time. As life expectancy is also a prediction, it involves judgement about the future. Thus, in all probability, the majority of the people would live beyond their life expectancy.

The explanation for this interesting paradox is that life expectancy is a representation of age-specific death rates as they are at the present time. But as we are moving towards better medical care technology, better knowledge about health and diseases, and better conditions of living, death rates are bound to come down significantly. Further, as death rates for 40–90-year-olds represent the experience of people who were born during about 1900–1960 (remember we are using cohort data), conditions with respect to death rate are going to be much better. Thus, in all probability, most of us can hope to live beyond the predicted life expectancy.

HEALTH

The dictum that a healthy mind lives in a health body underlines the importance of health to a healthy mind. This emphasis is not new, especially in India, where environmental sanitation programmes such as the provision of underground drains and public baths were an integral part of cities even in ancient times. Since ancient times, key aspects of health including personal hygiene, health education, exercise, dietary practices and treatment of minor ailments and injuries have been given emphasis in India. More than that, concepts which emphasize on total health care through health promotion are well-documented in Ayurveda. Ancient India made great advances in curative medicine and surgery. The works of Charak and Sushrut also testify to the advances made by Ayurveda—a stream of medicine that is practiced even today. In the present day scenario, health concerns and issues remain the same though we have better technological options and methods to deal with the problems. The next section presents an insight into health issues and prevalent methods available to deal with them.

MORTALITY AND MORBIDITY

Birth and death are the two most vital events in the life of an individual, family or community. Thus, these event, which form the basis of fertility and mortality estimates, determine population growth, size and structure. In case the death rate is greater than the birth rate, the population growth will decline and if the death rate is less than the birth rate, the population growth will increase. In case the birth rate equals the death rate, then the population becomes stationery and if the growth rate (difference between birth rate and death rate) becomes constant, the population is called stable population.

Mortality, as described earlier, is an important factor in influencing the age-structure of the population. Even in case of equal fertility levels, different mortality schedules may affect age structure as usually mortality affect young and old populations. The next section describes some of the basic ratios related to mortality:

a) *Foetal deaths:* A foetal death is defined as a death prior to birth. However, according to the recommendations of World Health Organization (WHO) experts, a foetal death is a 'death prior to the duration of pregnancy. The death is indicated by the fact that after such separation, the foetus does not breathe or show any other evidence of life such as beating of the heart, pulsation of the umbilical cord or definite movement of voluntary muscles'(WHO, 1992).

b) *Foetal death ratio and rate:* The loss through foetal death may be assessed through foetal death ratio and foetal death rate. The foetal mortality rate,[2] that is, the number of foetal deaths per 1,000 total births in the same year is defined as:

$$Foetal\ death\ ratio = \frac{FD}{B} \times 1,000$$

Where FD is foetal deaths in a year and B is the number of live births in the year.

$$Foetal\ death\ ratio = \frac{FD}{B+FD} \times 1,000$$

If FD relates to stillbirths, then this ratio and rate become stillbirth ratio and stillbirth rate.

$$Foetal\ death\ rate = \frac{SB}{B} \times 1,000$$

$$Foetal\ death\ rate = \frac{SB}{B+FD} \times 1,000$$

Mortality During Infancy

There are various indicators of infant and child mortality. The more commonly used ones are discussed next.

Neonatal and Post-neonatal Mortality Rate

Neonatal death refers to the death of an infant before completing 28 days of life and neonatal mortality rate (NMR) is defined as the number of deaths in the first 28 days of life per 1,000 live births. It is primarily assessed to reflect the quality of in-hospital care and after adjusting for case mix risk, a higher than expected NMR suggests that attention be directed to the quality of in-hospital obstetric and neonatal care. It is proven by studies that in developing countries most neonatal deaths are caused by birth asphyxia or birth trauma, prematurity and infections, though the rate varies across regions.

It is important to point out here that within India, the NMR varies from a high of over 60 per 1,000 live births in states like Orissa and Madhya Pradesh to a low of around 11 per 1,000 live births in Kerala (SRS, 1998–99; NFHS, 1998–99), explaining the disparity in quality of in-hospital obstetric and neonatal care among states.

Post-neonatal mortality rate is defined as the number of deaths between the 28th and 365th day of life among all infants who live more than 27 days. It reflects the availability and quality of primary health care facility at the village/town or community level. Post neonatal mortality provides important information regarding the health services that need to be upgraded at the community level. Its correlation with socio-economic development of the community is also well established. Post-neonatal deaths reflect poor health of mother and lack of access to health services. Post-neonatal mortality can be prevented more easily as compared to neonatal mortality.

It may be noted here that the overall infant mortality rate is the sum of the neonatal and post-neonatal mortality rates as the denominators of all the concerned rates during infancy are the same, i.e., number of live births during a specified calendar year.

$$Neonatal\ mortality\ rate\ (NMR) = \frac{NND}{B} \times 1,000$$

Where NND is the number of neonatal deaths

$$Post\text{-}neonatal\ mortality\ rate\ (PNMR) = \frac{PNND}{B} \times 1,000$$

$$= \frac{ID - NND}{B} \times 1,000$$

Where PNND is number of deaths in the post-neonatal period.

The neonatal and post-neonatal mortality, mentioned earlier, are normally used to separate out roughly the biological and environmental components of infant mortality. Neonatal mortality is primarily influenced by biological and genetical factors, whereas post-neonatal mortality is affected by environmental factors. Thus, it is imperative to adopt a different approach to reduce neonatal and post-neonatal mortality taking into account the access to primary health care facilities and prevalent socio-environmental conditions. Post-neonatal mortality can be controlled by improving socio-environmental conditions such as creating awareness in the community regarding immunization, personal hygiene and child care, or by initiating measures to improve socio-economic situations. Though to reduce neonatal mortality, it is essential to tackle the causes of the majority of neonatal deaths such as birth asphyxia or birth trauma, prematurity and infections.

Perinatal Mortality Rate (PMR)

Perinatal mortality rate[3] is defined as the ratio of all foetal and neonatal deaths observed per 1000 births. It can be calculated by adding the counts of foetal deaths and neonatal deaths and dividing it by the total births and multiplying the result with 1,000.

Observed PMR = 1,000 × ((foetal deaths + neonatal deaths) / total births)

Infant Mortality Rate (IMR)

It refers to the number of deaths per 1,000 live births in the first year of a child's life. It reflects the probability of a child dying before attaining the age of one year. As per the 1981 Census, IMR is estimated at 115 per 1,000 live births. It was 122 for males and 108 for females. The IMR declined to 77 infants per 1,000 live births by 1991. While there was an absolute decline in the IMR in 1991 as compared to 1981, unlike 1991 the infant mortality for females was lower than for males in 1981.

The number of deaths within the first year of birth or under one year of age is called infant deaths and infant mortality rate is defined by the number of infant deaths occurring in an area within a calendar year per 1,000 live births in the same area during the same calendar year.

$$IMR = 1,000 \times ((\text{neonatal deaths} + \text{post neonatal deaths}) / \text{live births})$$

Under-Five Mortality Rate

Under-five mortality represents the probability of a child dying before his fifth birthday. It is a very important indicator to ascertain the access to key health services. Unlike the life expectancy indicator, which is slow moving, the infant and child mortality indicators are much more sensitive to changes, which affect access to health services or quality of life, particularly, to the health and longevity of people.

The sudden change could be due to a change in availability of critical public health and life support services. Thus, to keep a check on high infant and child mortality it is imperative that changes in health attainments of a population are tracked and reviewed at more frequent intervals, particularly when the population is yet to complete its demographic transition. In India, the under-five mortality rate was 152 children per 1,000 live births in 1981 as compared to 94 children per 1,000 live births in 1991. The decline in the case of males was from 147 to 91 and for females from 157 to 101, during this period.

Besides, it is also essential to desegregate the under-five mortality rate into infant and child mortality to assess the true situation (see Box 8.4).

BOX 8.4
Infant and Neonatal Mortality Data

It is a known fact that infant mortality accounts for the bulk of under-five mortality. This is also corroborated by the 1981 and 1991 census figures that show that nearly three-fourth of the under-five mortality is accounted for by infant mortality. The NFHS 1 and 2 estimated the proportion of infant mortality to be around 72 per cent of under-five mortality.

Further, as per the sample registrations system, neonatal mortality accounted for the bulk of infant mortality, that is, 60–65 per cent of infant mortality during last two decade. Desegregated results across rural and urban areas showed that neonatal deaths were marginally lower in urban areas than in rural areas.

Among other mortality indicators, the age-specific mortality rate for the age group 0–4 or 5–9 years, maternal mortality rates, that is, the number of maternal deaths per 100,000 women in the age-group 15–49 years and the death rate defined as the number of deaths per 1,000 persons can also be used as indicators to track premature mortality of infants, children as well as the young and middle-aged adults.

Maternal Mortality

Maternal mortality represents all deaths of women attributed to the complications of pregnancy, child birth and the puerperium occurring within 42 days after the termination of pregnancy[4] (excluding abortion-related mortality). A death is considered a maternal death if it is caused directly by the pregnancy (including those deaths that result from treatment of complications) or if the pregnancy aggravates another condition. It is important to point out that 'accidental and incidental deaths' are generally not included.

The maternal mortality rate is defined as the number of female deaths due to puerperal causes among the residents of a community during a specified year per 10,000 live births.

Symbolically it is represented as:

$$MMR = \frac{FD}{B} \times 10,000$$

Where FD is the number of female deaths due to maternal causes, and B is the number of live births during the same year

It is a well-known fact that one of the most important initiatives to reduce maternal mortality and under-five mortality is to immunize pregnant mothers and newborn children against infectious diseases through vaccination. The following section lists the effectiveness of immunization in reducing mortality rates (maternal mortality and under-five mortality). It also describes the immunization schedule for pregnant mothers and the new born.

IMMUNIZATION AND HOW IT WORKS

Immunization is a way of protecting the human body against infectious diseases through vaccination. Immunization works on the basis that if a body is exposed to an infective agent, it develops capacity to fight infection. Thus, in this way, it prepares our bodies to fight against diseases in the future. Children, though, are born with some natural immunity, which they get from their mothers through breast-feeding. But that immunity is not sufficient to protect a child from infectious disease and thus providing immunization to children gives them extra protection against illnesses.

Immunization in India: Programmes, Levels and Inequalities

Immunization is one of the most cost-effective public health interventions that can drastically reduce under-five mortality. But still, a large proportion of infants and children in India are beyond the reach of this simple intervention. As a result, out of the total number of children who die before the age of five, a significant proportion die of vaccine-preventable diseases such as measles and neonatal tetanus.

It is not that efforts have not been taken to initiate an immunization programme. BCG immunization was started in 1948 and by 1951 it was organized on a mass scale to cover all those below 25 years of age. The Indian government's Fourth Five-Year Development Plan (1969–74) included plans for DPT immunization of infants and pre-school children and also adopted EPI in 1977–78 to provide free vaccines to all eligible children (Kanitkar, 1979). Measles vaccination was added to the Indian programme in 1985 (R.N. Basu, 1985), and in 1985–86, to provide a further impetus to im-munization, the government started a special programme called the Universal Immunization Programme (UIP). The objectives of the UIP was to cover at least 85 per cent of all infants by 1990 against the six immunizable diseases and by 1989–90, the goal was that it should reach all districts in the country (IIPS, 1995; Sokhey et al., 1993).

Immunization Schedule

The immunization schedule as prescribed in the immunization programme of the Government of India is mentioned in Table 8.1.

TABLE 8.1
Immunization Schedule

Whom	*When*	*What*	*Route*
Pregnant women	Early in pregnancy	TT 1	Intramuscular
	One month after TT 1	TT 2	Intramuscular
Infant (<1 Year)	At birth*	BCG & OPV O	Intradermal and oral respectively
	At 6 weeks	BCG, DPT 1,OPV 1	Intradermal, intramuscular and oral respectively
	At 10 weeks	DPT 2, OPV 2	Intramuscular and oral respectively
	At 14 weeks	DPT 3, OPV 3	Intramuscular and oral respectively
	At 9 months	Measles	Subcutaneous
Children (above 1 year)	At 16–24 months	DPT booster and OPV booster	Intramuscular and oral respectively
	At 5–6 years	DT	Intramuscular
	At 10 years	TT	Intramuscular
	At 16 years	TT	Intramuscular

Source: Handbook for Vaccine Administration, Child Health Division, Ministry of Health and Family Welfare, Nirman Bhavan, GoI, 2005.
Note: *In case of institutional delivery.

FAMILY PLANNING

India was the first country to adopt a family-planning approach and has experienced significant growth and adaptation over the past half century since its inception in 1951. The programme has broadened its spectrum since its inception and its services now include immunization, pre-natal and ante-natal care, preventive and curative health care and, of late, the programme has been integrated with the broader Reproductive and Child Health Programme.

The Family Welfare Programme in India was launched with the objective of reducing fertility to stabilize population. But despite concerted efforts and innovative approaches, we have not succeeded in bringing down fertility to replacement levels for India. This could be due to the fact that initially family planning was considered more a mechanism to improve the health of mothers and children than a method of population control (Visaria and Chari, 1998). The programme later shifted focus away from vertical family-planning services towards the provision of comprehensive integrated reproductive health care at all levels of the health sector (Pachauri, 1999).

The integrated programme envisaged a multi-pronged strategy, wherein different national level programmes were adopted with a different focus and target segments. The maternal and child health programme was one such programme that focused on promoting the health of mothers and children, whereas the safe motherhood programme focused on the need to ensure that the pregnant woman received adequate and timely prenatal care, safe delivery and post-natal care. In a bid to combine these programmes, the Reproductive, Child, Health (RCH) programme was conceptualized in 1994 to incorporate all these aspects in a broad and comprehensive manner. It was launched in 1996 at the national level.

Besides the RCH services, the programme has also concentrated on increasing awareness and services for a range of family-planning options and as a result, the range of contraceptive products delivered through the programme has widened. Multiple stakeholders, including the private sector and non-governmental sector, have been engaged in providing contraceptive services. The couple protection rate has quadrupled from 10 per cent in 1971 to 44 per cent in 1999 (MOHFW, 2000). Notwithstanding these achievements, several issues continue to daunt the programme and many goals remain under-achieved: a significant proportion of pregnancies continue to be unplanned; the contraceptive needs of millions of women remain unmet; several sub-population groups including adolescents and men continue to be neglected and under-served; contraceptive choice remains conspicuous by its absence and the quality of care within the programme is also a cause for concern. The immediate objectives of the National Population Policy are to address the unmet need for contraception, the limitations in health care infrastructure and the shortages in health personnel, and to provide integrated service delivery for basic reproductive and child health care.

CONTRACEPTION

Contraception is defined as a woman's ability to plan her reproductive life. It epitomizes women's quest to have the right of reproductive self-determination. Though in a real sense, the majority of women in developing countries do not have much say in their reproductive lives.

The right to plan one's family gives rise to a governmental duty to ensure that women and men have equal access to a full range of contraceptive choices and reproductive health services. Besides that, it is also imperative to ensure that users have accurate information about sexual and reproductive health rights and issues.

The full range of contraceptive methods includes: male and female condoms, vaginal barrier methods, oral contraceptives, implants, injectables, intrauterine devices and male and female sterilization. Consistent and correct use of modern methods of contraception can prevent many unwanted pregnancies. In order to meet their international commitments, governments must improve access for men, women and adolescents to high-quality family-planning information and services that offer a range of freely chosen contraceptive methods.

Contraceptives

As per the official statistics, around 87 million eligible couples, out of an estimated total of 171 million eligible couples, were effectively protected against conception by various contraceptive methods in the year 2000 (MOHFW, 2003). The NFHS-2 also indicate that nearly one-half of currently married women were using some method of contraception in 1998–99. This figure, however, is far from satisfactory, as in many states like UP, MP and Bihar, fertility rates are quite high as compared to other states, emphasizing the need to provide a whole range of contraceptive options to eligible couples. The following section lists the contraceptive methods into two broad categories: (i) spacing methods and (ii) terminal methods available for men and women.

Spacing Methods/Temporary Methods

Spacing methods, as the name suggests, is for people who wish to space out or delay pregnancies. The contraceptive action of these methods is meant to last for a single act of sexual intercourse or for a specific period of time (for example, for several days, months or years, or for as long as one continues to use the method).

Condom

a) *Male condom:* The male condom is a thin sheath made of latex or other materials. It not only protects against unwanted pregnancies but also protects against sexually-transmitted diseases and <u>HIV infection</u>. Though it is important to point out that male condoms are effective only in case they are used correctly every time during sexual intercourse.

b) *Female condom:* The female condom is a thin, loose-fitting covering, which can be fitted inside the vagina. It forms a pouch lining the vagina. It has two flexible rings and its inner ring is at the closed end of the condom, which eases insertion into the vagina, holding the condom in place, whereas the outer ring remains outside the vagina. The female condom provides a useful contraception option to woman and prevents pregnancies by blocking the passage of the sperms to the egg.

Oral Contraceptive Pill   The oral contraceptive pill inhibits pregnancy by stopping ovaries from releasing eggs. Oral contraceptive pills are usually a combination of estrogen and progestin hormones and the dosage is usually one pill per day.

Progestin only pill (POPs) are pills, which use progestin to prevent pregnancy by stopping the release of eggs from the ovaries. Unlike the combined oral contraceptive pills (COCs), POPs do not contain the hormone estrogen. The hormone thickens the cervical mucus thus making it difficult for the sperm to enter the uterus. The dosage is usually one pill every day.

Intrauterine Device (IUD)   Intrauterine device (IUD) is a device, usually made of plastic and copper, which if placed in the woman's uterus prevents pregnancy by stopping sperms from meeting the egg. Unlike, a condom and the oral pill, it is a long-acting contraceptive method intended to be used for several months or years.

It is usually placed by a doctor or trained health care worker. The most commonly used IUD is the Copper T380-A, whose physical presence in the uterus, keeps the sperms from moving normally inside the uterus and fallopian tubes.

Cervical Cap   A cervical cap is just like a soft rubber cup, which is fitted over the cervix. Further, the inner rim grove helps in improving the seal between the inner rim of the cap and the surface of the cervix. The cervical cap prevents pregnancy by blocking the entrance of the cervical canal to sperms.

Diaphragm   A diaphragm, like a cervical cap is a rubber cup, which is placed in a women's vagina after applying a contraceptive jelly (spermicide) on it. The diaphragm and the spermicidal jelly together prevent pregnancy by keeping the sperms out of the woman's uterus.

Injectables   Injectables are hormones, which prevent pregnancy by inhibiting the release of eggs from ovaries every month. It is usually delivered to the woman through an injection and that is why the method is known as injectables.

Lactational Amenorrhea Method (LAM)   It is an established fact the breastfeeding can also be used as a temporary contraception method for up to six months if a woman's periods have not returned after delivery. When breastfeeding is used as a contraception method, then the exclusive breastfeeding pattern is specified as the lactation amenorrhea method (LAM). It effectively prevents pregnancy by inhibiting the release of eggs from the ovaries. Though it is important to point out that for LAM to work effectively, the baby must be exclusively breastfed on demand.

Norplant Implants   Norplant implants are placed under the user's skin of the upper arm by making a small cut. It usually consists of six plastic capsules. Like the IUD, it is a long-acting contraceptive method intended to be used for several years. The capsules may remain in the user's arm for up to five years. They have to be removed at the end of five years, but in case the need arises, they can be taken out at any given time before the five-year period.

Norplant implants usually work by releasing the hormone progestin levonorgestrel, which keeps the ovaries from releasing eggs. It also prevents pregnancy by thickening the cervical mucus, making it difficult for sperms to enter the uterus.

Natural Method   Natural methods such as rhythm and withdrawal are traditionally used methods for contraception.

a) *Rhythm:* The rhythm method is based on the concept of safe period. As we know, ovulation takes place two weeks before menses. But the menses cycle in women does not start on the precise day every month, hence the calculation of the safe period is done on the basis of the duration of the previous 12 cycles. Based on the duration of the previous cycles, the shortest and longest cycle can be computed, to calculate the first and last fertile day of the cycle. The first fertile day is calculated by subtracting 18 days from the shortest cycle and the last fertile day by subtracting 11 days from the longest cycle.

b) *Withdrawal:* Withdrawal, as the name suggests, is an old practice of withdrawing just before ejaculation. It is considered very safe and simple and does not involve any extra cost. But, in the withdrawal method, the contraception decision is in the hands of the male partner and the female partner does not feature in the decision-making process.

Permanent Methods

The contraceptive action of these methods is meant to last forever and is not meant for a single act of sexual intercourse or for a specific period of time.

Male Sterilization   Vasectomy or male sterilization is a simple, minor surgical procedure that is performed by entering the scrotum through a small incision or puncture and blocking the vas deferens, the tube that carries the sperms from the testis to the penis. In conventional vasectomy, the clinician uses a scalpel to either make one midline incision or two incisions in the scrotal skin, one overlying each vas deferens, whereas 'no-scalpel' vasectomy (NSV) is performed through a small puncture and sutures are not needed.

Female Sterilization   Female sterilization is usually done by a simple operation, which closes the tubes between the ovaries and the uterus. In this operation the two fallopian tubes are blocked through a small incision made in the abdomen. Since the tubes are blocked off, the sperms cannot reach the eggs. Female sterilization is further classified into laparoscopy and minilaproscopy based on the way the doctor reaches the tubes.

a) *Laparoscopy:* This method is named after a long, thin instrument, the laparoscope, which is put in the body through a very small cut right below the abdomen. It lets the doctor see the fallopian tubes and close them.

b) *Minilaparotomy (Minilap):* The difference between a laparoscopy and minilaparotomy lies in the size of the incision. In minilaparotomy, the doctor reaches and closes the fallopian tubes through a smaller cut in the lower part of the body, just above the pubic hairline.

Contraceptive Prevalence Rate

Contraceptive prevalence rate is defined as the percentage of currently married couples[5] (which includes couples in union) in the age group of 15–49, who are using any form of contraception. Besides the contraceptive prevalence rate, there are some other indicators, which are used frequently to assess fertility behaviour. These are discussed next.

Couple Year of Protection

Couple year of protection is defined in terms of estimated contraceptive protection required during a one-year period to prevent pregnancy. It is based on the volume of contraceptives used by eligible clients during that period.

Couple year of protection is computed by multiplying the quantity of each family planning method used by clients by a conversion factor. The result thus obtained provides an estimate of the duration of contraceptive protection provided per unit of method.

Mean Desired Family Size

Mean desired family size is represented as the average number of children a woman would wish to have if she could have the same number as she desires. Mean desired family size indicator can also be analysed for an age cohort, to infer important information about future demands.

Wanted Birth Rate

Wanted birth rate corresponds to the proportion of births occurring during a specified period, which were planned in advance by a couple/family. Technically speaking, births are classified as 'wanted' when couples report that they had desired to have a child at the time of becoming pregnant and 'unwanted' births are births that couples did not desire at the time of becoming pregnant.

Unmet Need

Unmet need signifies the need for contraception, which could not be fulfilled due to lack of availability of contraception methods. It thus represents a gap between fertility preferences and contraceptive use. Researchers usually consider currently married women who do not want any more children, but are not using any contraceptive method as having an unmet need for family planning. Findings from NFHS-2 reveal that 16 per cent of currently married women have an unmet need for contraception (spacing—8.3 per cent and limiting—7.5 per cent).

MORBIDITY INDICATORS

Morbidity in social science refers to health experience in terms of sickness. It is defined as the study of issues related to sickness, its incidence and duration. Morbidity indicators or rates such as the incidence and prevalence rate of any disease provides an idea about exposure to sickness (see Box 8.5). Findings from Fifty-second Round of the NSSO, clearly states that around 6 per cent of rural people and 5 per cent of urban people reported ailments during the 15 day-period prior to the survey.

Morbidity tries to assess the quality of life by analysing how sickness occurs and how it affects individuals and society, because loss of life and sickness are, perhaps, equally important for individual and social well-being. Episodes of sickness or morbidity are usually categorized into (i) short-term or acute morbidity resulting from infectious diseases such as measles, influenza and diarrhea, (ii) long-term morbidity with limited duration such as in the case of tuberculosis and (iii) permanent or chronic morbidity because of diseases such as diabetes or arthritis, etc.

Mortality and morbidity are related to each other as prolonged sickness often results in death. But it does not mean that high morbidity results in high mortality and vice versa. For instance, Kerala, which has the lowest mortality rate, has the highest incidence of morbidity in the country for acute, as well as chronic ailments. It thus becomes preemptive at low levels of mortality to see that indicators for morbidity are reflected in the assessment of health attainments.

BOX 8.5
Incidence and Prevalence Rates

> *Incidence rate (IR)* is defined as the rate of new occurrences or disease over a period of time. It is computed as the ratio of new occurrences or cases to overall population at risk. It is important to point out that the incidence rate accounts for only new cases and excludes cases that have already developed the disease.
> *Prevalence rate (PR)* measures the number of cases or occurrences at a given point of time. It provides a snapshot of the situation. It is computed as the ratio of the number of present cases to the population at risk at that specified period of time. The incidence rate would be equal the prevalence rate if the prevalence rate is computed over a period of time, that is, PR = IR. D (duration).

In morbidity study, researcher envisage to reduce the number of sickness episodes to lessen the duration of sickness individuals experience. It is important to note that though over the years the likelihood of death has declined sharply, the likelihood of falling sick has declined at more gradual pace. Put in a different way, the likelihood of dying from sickness has changed for diseases.

Disabilities: Nature and Magnitude

Disability signifies any restriction due to which a person cannot perform an activity in the manner or within the range considered normal for a human being. The NSSO survey covered the various types of disabilities such as visual, hearing, speech, hearing and/or speech. It also coveres loco-motor disability, referring to the inability of an individual to execute activities associated with moving himself and objects from one place to another. As per the NSSO survey, the number of people having some sort of physical disability increased from nearly 12 million in 1981 to 16 million in 1991.

The NSSO survey findings further concluded that in 1981, the number of disabled people was just 1.8 per cent of the total population of which males accounted for 57 per cent of the total disabled people and 41.5 per cent of the visually disabled.

NUTRITION

Human nutrition deals with nutrients and other food substances and how the body assimilates them. It plays a key role in determining overall health and human development making it impera-tive to realize the importance of providing optimal nutrition for the entire population suffering from malnutrition.

Over the years, the country has made considerable progress on social and economic fronts, as indicated by improvements in indicators such as life expectancy, IMR and MMR and even the literacy rate, but still a lot needs to done to improve the nutritional status of the populace especially women and children. India today is a country of one billion people, but remarkably food grain production is still not a problem. The problem lies in access and entitlement of food as still millions suffers from chronic poverty and hunger. Despite several initiatives taken by the government to build buffer stock, i.e., improve food security through the food for work programme, the public food distribution system, food subsidy, complementing nutritional requirements of the vulnerable population through the Integrated Child Development Scheme (ICDS) and the mid-day meal programme, micronutrient deficiencies are still widespread. A substantial proportion of children and women are anaemic and reduction in cases of Vitamin A deficiency and iodine deficiency disorders (IDD) are also not up to the desired level, highlighting the gravity of the situation. In order to explore the issue further, the next section lists the nutritional requirement scenario and research issues frequently discussed while studying nutrition.

PROTEIN ENERGY MALNUTRITION (PEM)

Malnutrition which results from the deficiency of energy and protein is commonly known as protein energy malnutrition or (PEM). It is most commonly assessed by growth monitoring as usually initially it is not visible. It is important to point out that researchers use the term malnutrition synonymously with PEM.

According to the NFHS-2 survey, around 47 per cent of children under the age of three are underweight and 46.5 per cent are stunted. A comparison of malnutrition status from NFHS-1 survey (1991–92) and NFHS-2 survey (1998–99) has shown very little change. Surveys conducted by NFHS[6] in 1991–92 showed that the proportion of children who were underweight, stunted and wasting[7] were 52 per cent, 47 per cent and 19 per cent, respectively. The percentage of proportion of children who were underweight, stunted and wasting[8] as per the NFHS-2 survey (1998–99) were 47 per cent, 46 per cent and 16 per cent, respectively. Further, the malnutrition status varies across regions and the conditions are much worse in states like MP, UP, Bihar and Orissa.

Malnutrition starts with under nutrition of the mother and as a result, around 30–40 per cent of infants born in India have low birth weights (birth weight less than 2.5 kg). Further, two-third of children are small because they did not get adequate nourishment while they were in the womb.

MICRONUTRIENT MALNUTRITION

Apart from the PEM, three micronutrient deficiencies, namely, iodine, iron and vitamin A deficiency, are well-documented in India. They affect all age groups, some more than others. The next section discusses the status of micronutrient malnutrition in India.

Iodine Deficiency

One of the commonest micronutrient deficiencies is that of iodine. Iodine is an essential element required on a daily basis for proper mental and physical well-being of human beings (see Box 8.6). Iodine deficiency can cause irreversible brain damage before birth and is the main cause of mental retardation and increasing levels of deaf-mutes born in certain parts of the country. Though required in very minute quantities (150 microgram per day), its deficiency results in a wide array of preventable disorders collectively known as iodine deficiency disorders (IDD).

BOX 8.6
Essentiality of Iodine

Iodine is an essential for the synthesis of the thyroid hormones and lack of it affects a variety of vital physiological processes such as early growth and development of the brain and body. These are commonly known as iodine deficiency disorders (IDD). The consequences of IDD include goitre, mental retardation, stillbirths/abortions and infant deaths.

Further, iodine does not occur naturally in specific foods; rather, it is ingested through foods grown in the soil. The deficiency of iodine in a particular place is a result of deficiency of iodine in the soil of that place. Earlier in India it was believed that the problem of IDD was limited to hilly areas, but later it was established that it exists in every part of the country.

Iodine deficiency disorders exist in most regions of the world. The deficiency of iodine leads to goitre, reduced mental function, increased rates of stillbirths/abortions and infant deaths. Even mild iodine deficiency has been reported to reduce intelligence quotients by 10–15 points. Further, it is the single greatest cause of preventable brain damage and mental retardation in the world.

IDD in India

In India, IDD constitutes a major public health problem. The country has emerged as one of the major endemic iodine deficient countries in the world. In fact, prior to 1989, the prevalence of goitre and cretinism was believed to exist only in the broad Himalayan and sub-Himalayan belt. However, a multi-centric study by the Indian Council of Medical Research (ICMR) revealed the prevalence of goitre outside the traditional goitre belt as well.

In 1998, the Government of India reported that 200 million people were at risk of IDD while the number of persons suffering from goitre and other IDDs was about 70 million. One of the sample surveys conducted in 25 states and four Union Territories by the IDD Cell of the Government of India did reveal that 235 of the 275 sample districts in India were IDD endemic.

Salt as a Vehicle for Micronutrients: Universal Iodization of Salt

Salt is the most commonly accepted vehicle for iodine for a number of reasons. All the people universally consume it in fairly uniform quantities almost daily and the production of salt is limited to a few regions/centres, which makes it feasible to monitor the quality effectively. Moreover, iodization does not impart any colour, taste or odour to salt. Thus, it is considered as an ideal vehicle to deliver iodine to the population at large. It has been realized that prevention, control and eventual elimination of IDD requires the establishment of a salt iodization programme in which all salt for human and animal consumption is fortified with iodine.[9] The technology is low cost and well established. Daily iodine supplementation, through iodine-fortified salt, has been successfully applied in several developed countries, resulting in the total elimination of goitre several decades ago. Thus, in India also, iodization of salt is considered a proven intervention for the elimination of IDD and to ensure universal salt iodization (USI), which is both a preventive and a corrective measure vis-à-vis iodine deficiency.

State Initiatives Towards the Elimination of IDD

In one of the pilot studies conducted in the Kangra Valley between 1954 and 1972 by Sooch and Ramalingaswami (see Sooch and Ramalingaswami, 1965), it was found that regular consumption of iodized salt had a positive impact on iodine nurture. Salt fortified with potassium iodate (34–66 grams of potassium iodate per kg of common salt) was proven effective in prevention and control of iodine deficiency.

Following the experiment in the Kangra Valley, the Government of India introduced the programme of iodized salt in 1962–65 with the establishment of 12 iodization plants in the country with assistance from UNICEF. The initiatives of the Government of India since then can be classified as:

a) Phase I (1962–82): Implementation of National Goitre Control Programme (NGCP).
b) Phase II (1983–89): Focus on universal iodization of salt by 1992.
c) Phase III (1989–91): Sustaining production and creating the demand for iodized salt.
d) Phase IV (1992–98): Intensification of universal salt iodization (USI) activities and implementation of the National IDD Control Programme, (NIDDCP)
e) Phase V (1998–99): Evaluation and Re-planning of USI (Vir, 1994).

Iron Deficiency

Iron deficiency anaemia[10] is another major micronutrient deficiency that affects very large proportions of children, adolescent girls and women in the reproductive age group. Anaemia is a very widespread and a much-neglected problem. In India, the prevalence of anemia is higher because of low-dietary intake, poor bio-availability of iron in phylate fibre-rich Indian diet.

India was the first developing country to start a National Nutritional Anaemia Prophylaxis Programme to prevent anaemia among pregnant women and children. Screening of anaemia and iron-folate therapy in appropriate doses and route of administration for prevention and management of anaemia in these vulnerable groups have been incorporated as essential components of antenatal care.

Studies conducted by the ICMR and National Nutrition Monitoring Bureau (NNMB) shows that the prevalence of anaemia is high among pregnant women[11] (50–90 per cent) and children (50–70 per cent). The NFHS 2 also revealed that nearly three out of four children below three years of age are anaemic and over half of the women in the child-bearing age group are iron deficient. Further, an evaluation by the ICMR found that the current strategy of combating anaemia of pregnancy through distribution of iron and folate tablets during the last trimester of pregnancy has had only a limited impact.

Vitamin A Deficiency

Vitamin A is another micronutrient, the deficiency of which not only contributes to night blindness but also results in increased morbidity and poor protection against severe forms of respiratory and skin infections.

Vitamin A is essential for the health of epithelial cells and for normal growth. Diet surveys have shown that the intake of Vitamin A is significantly lower than the recommended dietary allowance in young children, adolescent girls and pregnant women. Vitamin A deficiency leads to skin changes, night blindness and the failure of adaptation to the dark due to adverse effects on the retina.

Later, xerophthalmia, an eye condition characterized by dryness and thickening of the surface of the conjunctiva and cornea, may develop; untreated, xerophthalmia can lead to blindness, especially in children.

Vitamin A can be obtained directly in the diet from foods of animal origin such as milk, eggs and liver. In developing countries like India, most Vitamin A is obtained from carotene, which is present in green and yellow fruits and vegetables. Carotene is converted to Vitamin A in the body.

In 1970, the National Prophylaxis Programme against blindness was initiated as a centrally-sponsored scheme. Further, in an attempt to improve the coverage, especially of the first two doses of Vitamin A, a decision was made to link Vitamin A administration to the ongoing immunization programme during the Eighth plan period. In India, Vitamin A control programmes cover children from nine months to three years with high dose supplements through primary health centres and sub-centres. Vitamin A deficiency in childhood is mainly due to inadequate dietary intake of Vitamin A.

Studies in certain countries have also demonstrated that Vitamin A has a role in decreasing childhood and maternal mortality as well. The National Survey of Blindness (1986–89), suggested that the prevalence of night blindness in children under six years was around 6 per cent with Bitot's spots having been observed in 0.7 per cent of children through another survey during the same period. Taking Bitot spots as an index of Vitamin A deficiency (VAD), the prevalence showed a reduction from 1.8 per cent in 1975–79 to 0.7 per cent in 1988–89. Keratomalacia, due to severe VAD, is reportedly not seen often and is observed only in pockets suffering from extreme poverty.

CONSTRAINTS AND ACTIONS FOR THE FUTURE

It is true that India still has one of the highest proportions of malnourished children in the world. But, the conditions have improved due to concerted and integrated efforts. Severe forms of malnutrition and under-five mortality have decreased during the last few decades in the country. But still a lot needs to be done to realize the goal set out in the National Nutrition Policy.

During the Tenth Five-year Plan, the government announced the setting up of the National Nutrition Mission to reduce both protein energy and micronutrient malnutrition. The Tenth Plan has envisaged bringing down the prevalence of under weight children less than three years from 47 per cent to 40 per cent. The plan also envisages reducing the prevalence of severe undernourishment in children in the 0–6 year's age group by 50 per cent. The Plan also aims to reduce the prevalence of anaemia by 25 per cent, IDD to less than 10 per cent and completely eliminate Vitamin A deficiency. But to achieve the target set out, various interventions like ICDS and mid-day meal programmes need to be implemented with vigour, besides being reviewed and strengthened.

Further, as per a World Bank study, around 15–25 per cent of the poor in rural areas covered by the ICDS do not have access to services provided by the ICDS. Thus, there is an urgent need to ensure that programme reaches to all targeted segments. Besides, it is imperative to ensure that the nutrition programme helps in improving food security, strengthening the public distribution system and improving community participation.

Further, as pointed by Amartya Sen, food insecurity and hunger is a function of loss of purchasing power/entitlement set. The purchasing power of poor people needs to be strengthened through employment generation programmes in drought/extreme conditions. Besides, there is an urgent need for better coordination among the three ministries of health and family welfare, women and child development and education for implementing the major nutrition-related programmes in the country.

Anthropometric Approach to the Study of Nutrition

Malnutrition remains a widespread problem in developing countries, in particular among the poorest and most vulnerable segments of the population. Malnutrition is typically caused by a combination of inadequate food intake and infection, which impairs the body's ability to absorb or assimilate food. It is an important cause of low birth weight, brain damage and other birth defects. It also contributes to developmental retardation, increased risk of infection and death and other problems in infants and children.

One approach to studying nutrition is to assess nutritional status on the basis of anthropometrics indicators. These are based on physical body measurements such as height or weight related to age and sex of the individual. From an anthropometrics perspective, nutritional status can be seen as the output of a health production function, where nutrient intake is one input, but where other individual, household, and community variables also feature. Anthropometrics indicators are useful both at the individual and at the population level. Some of indicators frequently used in anthropometrics analysis are discussed next.

Weight-for-Height (W/H)

Weight-for-height measures body weight relative to height and has the advantage of not requiring age data. Weight-for-height is normally used as an indicator of current nutritional status, and can be useful for screening children at risk and for measuring short-term changes in nutritional status.

Low W/H relative to the child of the same sex and age in a reference population is referred to as thinness and extreme cases of low W/H are commonly referred to as wasting. Wasting may be the consequence of starvation or severe disease but it can also be due to chronic conditions. It is important to note that a lack of evidence of wasting in a population does not signify the absence of nutritional problems.

Height-for-Age (H/A)

Height-for-age reflects cumulative linear growth. Deficits indicate past or chronic inadequacies in nutrition and/or chronic or frequent illness, but cannot measure short-term changes in malnutrition. Low H/A relative to a child of the same sex and age in the reference population are referred to as shortness and extreme cases of low H/A, where shortness is interpreted as pathological, is referred to as stunting. It is primarily used as a population indicator rather than for individual growth monitoring.

Weight-for-Age (W/A)

Weight-for-age reflects body mass relative to age. It is, in effect, a composite measure of height-for-age and weight-for-height, making interpretation difficult. Low W/A relative to a child of the same sex and age in the reference population is referred to as 'lightness', while the term 'underweight' is commonly used to refer to severe or pathological deficits in W/A. It is commonly used for monitoring growth and to assess changes in the magnitude of malnutrition over time. However, W/A compounds the effects of short- and long-term health and nutrition problems.

Mid Upper Arm Circumference (MUAC)

This is a measure of the diameter of the upper arm and it gauges both fat reserves and muscle mass. It is primarily used for children, but can also be applied to pregnant women to assess nutritional status. The measurement is simple and requires minimal equipment. It, therefore, has been proposed as an alternative index of nutritional status, in particular in situations where data on height, weight, and age are difficult to collect. For children, a fixed (age-independent) cut-off point has sometimes been used to determine malnutrition. However, this risks over-diagnosing young children and under-diagnosing older people.

Body Mass Index (BMI)

Body mass index is the most widely used measure for assessment of nutritional status in adults as it reflects the affect of both acute and chronic energy deficiency/excess. It is defined as the weight in kilograms divided by the square of height in meters. In developing countries, the BMI is primarily used with age-independent cutoffs to identify chronic energy deficiencies in adults.[12] According to the currently used norms, BMI of less than 18.5 indicates under-nourishment and a person with a BMI of more than 25 is considered overweight. These norms were evolved on the basis of data from developed countries. Although there is some scope for using BMI for adolescents, the index varies with age for children and teens and must, therefore, be interpreted in relation to BMI-for-age reference charts.

ANTHROPOMETRIC INDICES: CONSTRUCTION AND COMPARISON

Anthropometric indices are constructed by comparing relevant measures with those of comparable individuals in terms of age and sex in the reference[13] data. It is important to point out that the international reference standard that is most commonly used and recommended by the WHO is based on data on the weights and heights of a reference population of healthy infants and children in the United States.

It is further assumed that as these reference standards[14] are from well-nourished and healthy children, the observation will have a similar distribution of height and weight in case of the US reference population, regardless of their country and ethnic background they live in and belong to. Though it is a debatable issue as there are bound to be some variations in growth patterns across countries due to the differences in socio-economic factors. Nevertheless, most of the researchers use these indicators worldwide and there are three ways of expressing these comparisons based on indices:

a) *Z score:* Z score provides the distribution spread in terms of standard deviation above or below the median value. It is mathematically defined as the difference between an individual observation and the median value of the reference population for the same variable, divided by the standard deviation of the reference population.

b) *Percentage of median:* Percentage of the median is defined as the ratio of an individual observed value to the median value of the reference data for the same variable expressed in terms of percentage.

c) *Percentile:* Percentile indicates the percentage of a distribution that is equal to or below a given reference distribution. It can be thought of as the percentage of children in the reference population below the equivalent cut-off.[15]

Out of these three measures, z scores are the most preferred and widely used way of expressing anthropometric indices. Z scores have a number of advantages, such as z scores can be used to construct summary statistics like mean and standard deviation, which cannot be meaningfully done with percentiles. Z scores provide information in terms of deviation from the median value, which enables us to give percentages, corresponding to different z scores depending on the age or height of the individual. Percentages of median do not provide such information about an individual's location in the distribution.

Cut-off to Assess Malnourishment

All anthropometric indices are calculated by comparing observed value with reference value, thus it is imperative to decide on the cut-off/minimum level below which an individual can be described as malnourished. The most commonly used cut-off to define with z scores is −2 standard deviations, irrespective of the indicator used, for example, a child who's height for age z score is less than −2 is considered stunted. Similar cut-offs are decided for percentile and percentage of median (see Box 8.7).

BOX 8.7
Malnutrition Classification Systems

The WHO classification and Gomez classification are the two most important and widely used malnutrition classification systems. The WHO classification uses z scores as cut-off points for malnutrition classification, whereas the Gomez classification uses percentage of median. The Gomez system was widely used in the 1960s and 1970s, but nowadays the WHO classification is used widely in every country. It is important to point out here that analysis results can vary based on the classification system used, especially in the case of severe malnutrition cut-offs between the WHO method and the Gomez method. As can be seen from the classification system discussed later in the text, mild, moderate and severe is different in each of the classification systems, thus it is important to use the same system to analyse and present data. Nowadays, the WHO method is recommended for analysis and presentation of data.

Comparison of Mean Z scores

Though there are other indicators to compare malnourishment status such as percentage of median and percentile, researchers prefer to compare mean z score change to evaluate the change in a nutritional index. For comparison of mean score, it is imperative that data is collected at the baseline and endline of a project. The mean and standard deviation data is compared across baseline and endline data with the same project area. Researchers use mean z score because it has the advantage of describing the entire population, without resorting to a subset of individuals below a set cut-off. The cut-off varies for different indicators like per cent of median, percentile and z score for various classifications such as moderate and severe. But, in the majority of cases, researchers use a –2 standard deviation cut-off (or –3 standard deviation) to depict a change over a period of time. A presentation of the mean reflects all children whereas comparison of mean reflects the community shift or improvement.

Researchers need to use significance tests such as t test or chi-square statistical test while making a comparison of mean z scores over time. This would help in showing statistical significance of comparison results.

Cut-off Malnutrition Classification

WHO	< –1 to > –2 z score	mild
	< –2 to > –3 z score	moderate
	< –3 z score	severe
Gomez		
	> 90% of median	normal
	75% –< 90% of median	mild
	60% –< 75% of median	moderate
	< 60% of median	severe

The use of a cut-off for malnutrition classification provides results, which groups individuals into a malnutrition sub-population. It helps in identifying those children, who suffer from severe malnutrition or are a special case of stunting and wasting. The proportion of such children in each classification system provides important policy direction and strategies. The most commonly used cut-off with z scores is –2 standard deviation,[16] irrespective of the indicator used. This means children with a z score for underweight, stunting or wasting below –2 standard deviation are considered moderately or severely malnourished. For example, a child with a z score for height for age of –2.56 is considered stunted, whereas a child with a z score of –1.78 is not classified as stunted. A comparison of cut-offs for percentage of median and z scores illustrates the following:

90% = –1 z score
80% = –2 z score
70% = –3 z score (approx.)
60% = –4 z score (approx.)

Cut-off Points for MUAC for the 6–59 Month Age Group   MUAC has been used as surrogate measure of assessing wasting, when collection of height and weight data is difficult. A cut-off point is fixed at 12.5 cm for identifying moderately and severely malnourished children under five.

Besides, all these indicators, cut-off for global acute malnutrition and severe acute malnutrition are also used widely to assess malnutrition status (see Box 8.8).

BOX 8.8
Global Acute Malnutrition

> Global acute malnutrition is defined in relation to the weight for height index. It signifies the percentage of children (age 6–59 months) with weight-for-height below –2 z scores or presence of an edema.
>
> It is different from severe acute malnutrition, which signifies the percentage of children (age 6–59 months) with weight-for-height below –3 z scores or presence of an edema.

CONSTRUCTING AND ANALYSING ANTHROPOMETRIC INDICATORS

The easiest way to construct anthropometric indicators is to use designated anthropometric software, which contains the relevant reference data and has easy procedures for constructing the indicators of interest. This section provides a brief overview of the most popular anthropometric software packages and a step-by-step guide to use one of these pieces of software to construct key anthropometric indicators.

Software for Anthropometric Analysis

The anthropometric software uses raw measurement data to calculate anthropometric indices using reference data, though their analysis function and power is not limited to anthropometric analysis only. Many of the available software packages also have more advanced functions, including statistical and graphical analysis. Anthro and Epi-Info are the two most popular software packages for anthropometric analysis.

ANTHRO
The Anthro software package is based on the 1978 NCHS/CDC/WHO growth reference data of healthy infants and children in the US. It was developed especially to cater to the demand of researchers who use dBase file and can use dBase files for batch processing.

Anthro calculates anthropometric z values, percentiles and percent of median from raw data having variables such as sex, height, weight and age of children. In a nutshell, it performs the following basic tasks:

a) It performs a batch processing of existing dBase files.
b) It performs standard anthropometric analyses, such as calculating z score and centile distributions.
c) It also has an anthropometric calculator.

Epi-Info
Epi-Info statistical software was developed by the Centre for Disease Control and Prevention (CDC) especially for epidemiologists and other public health and medical professionals. It is an integrated software, which provides the facility to develop a questionnaire, data entry programme, customizes

the data entry process and analyses data. Epi-Info like Anthro calculates anthropometric indices by comparing raw data with reference standards. Besides doing anthropometric analysis, researchers can use it to generate tables, graphs, maps and even correlation with simple commands. It does so through a series of microcomputer programmes known as modules for different functions such as the Analysis module, which can perform cross-tabulations, stratified analysis and regression and can also create graphs and scatter plots.

Epi-Info calculates anthropometric indices through a special module called NutStat, which is used for data analysis by comparing raw data on height, weight, age, sex with international reference standards for assessment of nutritional status. Like Anthro, it also calculates z scores, percentiles and percent of median based on the sex-specific CDC/WHO normalized version of the 1977 NCHS reference curves for height-for-age, weight-for-age and weight-for-height reference data.

It is important to point out that anthropometric data analysis involves three basic stages. At the first stage, researchers enter data in the computer. After this, researchers need to combine the entered data to compute a nutritional status index such as weight-for-age, height-for-age or weight-for-height. Third, the programme should transform these data into z scores so that the prevalence of nutritional conditions, such as being underweight and stunted, can be calculated.

These analyses can be done easily in Anthro and EpiInfo, but if you are familiar with SPSS/Stata and want to do analysis in both these software, it entails three steps:

(i) exporting data from Stata or SPSS, (ii) reading and processing the data in Epi-Info or Anthro and re-exporting the constructed variables to Stata or SPSS.

a) *Exporting Data in Stata or SPSS:* Epi-Info and Anthro, as mentioned earlier, compares raw data with reference data through batch processing to construct anthropometric indicators. However, in order to calculate the desired anthropometric indicators, it is imperative that the appropriate information on variables such as sex, age and weight are entered. Thus, it is imperative to take note of important points such as for how many anthropometric indicators, age-specific reference data are used. When the data permits it, it is always preferable to calculate age as the difference between date of measurement and date of birth. To calculate 'biologic' age, anthropometric software calculates the number of days between the two dates. Second, for younger children, height is normally measured with the child in a recumbent position.[17] This measurement is sometimes referred to as length, which is contrasted with standing height measurements, referred to as stature.[18]

The first step is to construct a data set with all the relevant variables in the appropriate format, if we have data on the birth date, measurement date, sex, weight and height of children under five years of age.

b) *Reading and Processing Data in Epi-Info/NutStat:* Depending on the Epi-Info version, researchers can read and process data in Epi-Info and Nutstat in a variety of ways. Epi-Info version 6 (DOS version) can even read SPSS, besides reading dBase files and we can import data by simply going to the Import Data menu and giving the file location and type. Though, in the case of Epi-Info (Windows version) it is better if we have an Access file.

There are two ways of importing external data into NutStat. We can simply do it through the Add Statistics feature which processes the data from a Microsoft Access Data file and adds the results of calculations to the file. In contrast, the Import Data feature can be used to import data from an existing table into a new table that has the data structure that is required by Nutstat.

After importing data, researchers need to link variables in the imported data file with fields that Epi-Info requires to calculate the anthropometric indicators, and, for some fields, select the unit of measurement. Finally, the user needs to select the statistics or anthropometric indicators to calculate, that is, z scores, percentiles and percentage of median for weight-for-age, height-for-age and weight-for-height.

c) *Exporting the Data for Analysis in Stata or SPSS:* After the variables of interest have been constructed, we can export data in a format such as Excel or Microsoft Access database, which can be easily converted into a format that can be read by Stata or SPSS before the variables can be merged with the original data, for example, z scores, percentiles and percentage of median for weight-for-age, height-for-age and weight-for-height can be merged with the main data (see Box 8.9).

BOX 8.9
Precautions to be Taken Before Exporting Data in Stata or SPSS

It is important to point out that while adding data care must be taken of some issues. The first issue is related to the problem of missing values. In most surveys, interviewers are not able to collect all the relevant data for all sampled individuals. The most common problem concerns the age of the child, where the parent and birth records may not be able to provide the precise birth date.

The second problem is concerned with the calculated z scores, where errors in measurement, reporting of age, coding, or data entry sometimes result in out of range values. The WHO recommends that, for the purpose of analysis, values outside a certain range should be treated as missing values and these problems can be explored by looking at descriptive statistics, scatter plots and histograms.

Analysing Anthropometric Data

Analysis of anthropometric data tries to identify the malnourishment in a population or sub-population. However, in many cases, researchers go beyond establishing prevalence to try to understand the causes of malnourishment and how the malnutrition problem can be addressed.

As the first step in anthropometric analysis, researchers analyse the distribution of appropriate indicators such as z scores and overall prevalence. Researchers can easily compute the statistics from either Epi-Info or Anthro software and can also depict the distribution graphically. Epi-Info or Anthro computes the statistics by comparing the observed data with the distribution in the reference population, thus providing different dimensions of nutritional status in the population.

Further, while reporting anthropometric data, it is imperative that data is presented according to age and sex groups. This is imperative because patterns of growth vary with age and it also facilitates the identification of determinants of malnutrition. Another important point to consider is the result of irregularities in the reference curves. Wasting tends to be exaggerated for children in the 12–24 month age group. Thus, the WHO recommends that at least two age disaggregations should be used, that is, for the under 24 months and for the 24 months and over age groups.

Anthropometric data in itself may not provide all information, thus, it is advised that descriptive analysis of anthropometric data should also be accompanied to assist in the interpretation of findings. Information such as general characteristics of the population, sample design and size, method of determining age, proportion of data missing along with standard errors or confidence intervals for estimates should also be provided for better understanding.

NOTES

1. It should be noted that the own-children fertility estimates are not affected much by errors in the mortality estimates used for reverse-survival. One reason is that the reverse-survival ratios used to back-project children and women are both fairly close to 1.00, and the other reason is that errors in the reverse-survival ratios used to back-project births from children in the numerators of age-specific fertility rates cancel to some extent errors in the reverse-survival ratios used to back-project women in the denominators (Cho et al., 1986).

2. The foetal mortality rate is thought to reflect prenatal care, and, to a lesser extent, hospital-based perinatal care. But higher than expected risk-adjusted foetal mortality may not reflect the quality of hospital care in that a foetal death is attributed to a hospital even for women who present to the hospital for the very first time with a foetal demise. World Health Organization (1992). *International Statistical Classification of Diseases and Related Health Problems*. Tenth Revision. Vol. 1. Geneva: WHO.

3. The perinatal mortality rate is a measure of the combined foetal and neonatal mortality. It can be misleading to attribute to a facility the responsibility for unavoidable foetal deaths, for example, those due to severe congenital anomalies or foetal deaths resulting from deficient prenatal care not provided by that facility.

4. A maternal death is also defined as the death of a woman who is currently pregnant or who has been pregnant in the last six weeks.

5. Depending on the country context, women of reproductive age currently married or in union could be used instead of all women of reproductive age to calculate this indicator; however, one or the other must be used consistently throughout the equation.

6. The ICMR established the National Nutrition Monitoring Bureau (NNMB) in 1972 to conduct nutritional studies and is now the source for most nutrition related data.

7. NFHS has obtained anthropometric data on children under four years of age. Children who fall below –2 standard deviation weight-for-age NCHS median are considered to be undernourished.

8. Underweight refers to weight-for-age, stunting is related to height-for-age and wasting refers to weight-for-height anthropometric measurement.

9. The iodine compound used in India for salt fortification is potassium iodate, which is highly stable in tropical weather conditions. However, it undergoes partial decomposition due to the presence of moisture in salt. Hence higher levels of iodine (30 ppm of iodine or 50 ppm of potassium iodate) are prescribed at the production level to take care of storage and transportation losses to ensure availability of a minimum of 15 ppm of iodine at the consumer level.

10. Anaemia is defined as a haemoglobin concentration that is below normal, usually defined as two standard deviations below the median haemoglobin values observed for a reference population of healthy individuals of the same gender, age and physiological status.

11. Pregnant women with haemoglobin less than 8g/dl show functional decompensation and constitute a high risk group.

12. More than one out of three women is undernourished according to the BMI indicator, an indicator derived from height and weight measurements. Chronic energy deficiency is usually indicated by a BMI below 18.5 kg/m^2.

13. References are used to standardize a child's measurement by comparing the child's measurement with the median or average measure for children of the same age and sex.

14. Notwithstanding this empirical regularity, there is a long-standing debate about the appropriateness of the US reference standard for children in developing countries, in particular concerning the extent to which growth paths will depend on feeding practices. While these are important issues to address, analysts are currently recommended to use the NCHS/WHO reference data. The reference population chosen by NCHS was a statistically valid random population of healthy infants and children.

15. Approximately 0.13 per cent of children would be expected to be below –3 z score in a normally distributed population. A comparison of cut-offs for percentage of median and z scores illustrates the following:

z score   percentile
–3   0.13
–2   2.28
–1   15.8

16. In the reference population, by definition, 2.28 per cent of the children would be below –2 standard deviation and 0.13 per cent would be below –3 standard deviation. In some cases, the cut-off for defining malnutrition used is –1 standard deviation (for example, in Latin America). In the reference or healthy population, 15.8 per cent would be below a cut-off of –1 standard deviation. The use of –1 standard deviation is generally discouraged as a cut-off due to the large percentage of healthy children normally falling below this cut-off.

17. This is almost always more accurate than age reported by survey respondents. The reference curves are based on 'biologic' age rather than calendar age. Biologic age in months divides the year into 12 equal segments as opposed to calendar age in which months have from 28 to 31 days. Although this makes little difference in older children, it can have an effect on the anthropometric calculations for infants.

18. While using the recommended 1978 CDC/WHO reference in Epi-Info, recumbent length is assumed from birth to age 24 months, and standing height 24 months and older. However, in Epi-Info it is also possible to use a 2000 CDC reference standard. If this option is chosen, the user must indicate if the measurements are recumbent length or standing height for children in the age group of 24–36 months.

CHAPTER 9

EDUCATION

In today's knowledge management era, the key to growth and development of any economy is enshrined in the development of its knowledge assets and if India wants to spearhead this knowledge management era, it has to achieve the objective of providing universal education[1] to all as early as possible. The Indian Constitution has made the provision for free and compulsory education for all children until they complete 14 years of age in Article 45 of the Directive Principles of State Policy. The government has also formulated policies to provide education for all, the priority being on free and compulsory elementary education, with special emphasis on coverage of children with special needs, vocational training, women's education and education of socially disadvantaged sections. Unfortunately, the result has not been commensurate with the targets. Nevertheless, efforts are on through a three-pronged strategy concentrating on all aspects of elementary education, secondary education and adult education. The subsequent section looks at the efforts and impact of strategies in detail.

ELEMENTARY EDUCATION

Elementary education has been the focus of both the central and the state governments since independence. The aim has been to realize the goal of Universal Elementary Education (UEE) and the emphasis was clearly reinforced in the National Policy on Education (1986) and Plan of Action (1992). In consonance with the stated objective, the government laid emphasis on: (i) universal access and enrollment (ii) universal retention of children up to 14 years of age[2] and (iii) a substantial improvement in the quality of education to enable all children to achieve essential levels of learning.

The government has taken several initiatives in the field of elementary education to provide infrastructure facilities, which have resulted in manifold increase in institutions, teachers and students. This has also translated into a better enrolment ratio, indicated by the NFHS-2 (1998–99), which states that 79 per cent of children in the 6–14 years age group are attending school. The real boost has been provided by various initiatives launched by the central and the state governments. As a result, national literacy rates increased from 43.7 per cent in 1981 to 52.2 per cent in 1991 (male 63.9 per cent, female 39.4 per cent) and 65.38 per cent in 2001, that is, an increase of around 13 per cent in the last decade. However, despite these laudable efforts, there are still wide regional and gender variations in the literacy rates. For example, in 2001, the southern state of Kerala, with a literacy rate of about 89.8 per cent, was ranked first in India in terms of both male and female literacy, whereas Bihar was ranked lowest with a literacy rate of only 39 per cent (53 per cent for males and 23 per cent for females).

Besides regional and gender variations in the literacy rates, there are wide variations in literacy rates among different strata of society. Though there has been considerable improvement in the participation of children belonging to Scheduled Castes/Scheduled Tribes, but dream of universal education still seems to be far fetched. They are still excluded from the mainstream education system due to lack of access, lack of adequate facilities, poor quality of education, inhibition and social stigma. The right to education still remains a forbidden dream for children from poor and disadvantaged communities such as children belonging to Scheduled Castes, children with disabilities, girl children, children of unorganized and migrant labourers, landless poor, etc.

In India, childhood education status signifies two extremes, on one hand there are millions of young children belonging to poor and disadvantaged communities (especially rural and girl children) constituting nearly 40 per cent of first class entrants, who never complete primary school. On the other hand, there are millions of children who are enrolled in public schools and have access to the best education system in the best possible environment.

Further, in the case of government primary schools, teachers' absence from school, poorly-qualified teachers, high student–teacher ratios, inadequate teaching materials and out-dated teaching methods result in a low quality of education, which results in high drop-out ratios. The most important aspect of the approach is the attitude of the teacher, which should be that learning is a form of play, which fosters the blossoming of the child's natural development.

Learning should and can be made interesting, enjoyable and fun. Lack of toilets, hygienic conditions including safe drinking water at the school is an additional lacuna. Therefore, availability of potable water within walking distance and access to health care from properly qualified health workers should also be available. Primary health care is the other side of this coin of the right to primary education. Thus, it is imperative that investment is made in health and nutrition of the children to ensure that they have the physical energy and spirit for learning.

It has been established through research that there is a positive correlation between levels of household income and literacy. Thus, it is mostly the poor and disadvantaged who are facing the brunt of illiteracy. In order to keep all children aged 6–14 years in India at the existing level of quality, government's investment in education is required to be up against the current outlay of about 1.5 per cent. Further, state funding of the education sector, despite best efforts, has been inadequate and has not reached the goal of 6 per cent of the gross domestic product (GDP) and efforts are on to enlist the support of all stakeholders to mobilize extra budgetary support. Initiative like 'Bharat Shiksha Kosh' is being constituted to receive donations/contributions/endowments from individuals and corporates, central and state governments, non-resident Indians (NRIs) and people of Indian origin (PIOs) for various educational purposes.

It is not that the government has not initiated programmes. Several innovative steps have been taken to improve the efficiency and coverage of the existing schemes of elementary and secondary education, especially targeted for the educational uplift of Scheduled Castes and Scheduled Tribes.

The central government along with the state government has launched various interventions to improve the quality of primary and secondary education since the introduction of the National Policy on Education. The various intervention programmes include Operation Blackboard, District Primary Education Programme, Sarva Shiksha Abhiyan[3], Education Guarantee Scheme, Alternation and Innovative Education, Mahila Samakhya, Teacher Education, Mid-day Meal Scheme, Lok Jumbish, Shiksha Karmi and Janshala (see Box 9.1).

BOX 9.1
The Government's Initiatives for the Universalization of Education[4]

Operation Blackboard: Operation Blackboard was launched in 1987 to improve the school environment. It aimed to enhance the retention and learning achievement of children by providing essential facilities in all primary schools.

District Primary Education Programme (DPEP): The DPEP was launched in November 1994, as an attempt to overhaul the primary education system in India. The programme aims at operationalizing the strategies for achieving UEE through decentralized district-level planning and target setting. The DPEP was launched in the early 1990s, to achieve the aim of universal primary education. Since then, it has since become the world's largest education programme, reaching 60 million children. It is supported jointly by the World Bank (the single largest contributor to this initiative), the European Commission, UNICEF and the governments of the Netherlands and Sweden. The programme focuses on providing four or five years of primary education to children between the ages of six and 14. The project also aims to reduce the number of school dropouts and improve the overall quality of primary education. It puts special emphasis on girls who were formerly prevented from attending school and children with mild to moderate disabilities and working children.

Bihar Education Project (BEP): The Bihar Education Project launched in 1991, was designed to bring both quantitative and qualitative improvement in the elementary education system of Bihar. It focused especially on the education of deprived sections of society, such as Scheduled Castes, Scheduled Tribes and women.

Uttar Pradesh Basic Education Programme: The Uttar Pradesh Basic Education Programme was launched as a project, which envisioned providing education for all. The project was implemented by the Government of Uttar Pradesh with the financial support of the International Development Agency (IDA) in June 1993. Initially the project was launched in 12 districts, but later the coverage was expanded to 15 districts under DPEP II.

Community Mobilization and Participation—Lok Jumbish and Shiksha Karmi Project: The Lok Jumbish (LJ) and Shiksha Karmi Project (SKP) were both based on the core strategy of community mobilization and participation. The projects identified community mobilization as a key tool to ensure that the village community takes responsibility for providing quality education for every child in their efforts to universalize primary education and deliver quality education.

Andhra Pradesh Primary Education Project (APPEP): The Andhra Pradesh Primary Education Project, with assistance from the Overseas Development Administration (ODA), was launched with the twin objective of improving the classroom-learning environment by training teachers and boosting school construction activities.

INDICATORS TO REFLECT EFFORTS IN LITERACY AND EDUCATION

In a bid to assess the impact and efficacy of education interventions, it is imperative to conduct an education survey/research to have an idea about the direction and impact of the interventions. The following section lists some of the commonly used education indicators for assessing the effectiveness of education programmes.

a) *Ever enrolment rate:* Ever enrolment rate is defined as the proportion of children aged 6–14 years ever enrolled in a school at any level at any time of the survey.

b) *Enrolment in schools:* The enrolment of children in schools is an important measure of the spread as well as the quality of education and there are various measures that are commonly used to assess enrolment of children in schools. Among the more commonly used measures are gross enrolment ratio, age-specific enrolment ratio, net enrolment ratio, dropout rates and school attendance rates for capturing both the quality and spread of education.

c) *Gross enrolment ratio:* Gross enrolment ratio is defined as the total enrolment of students in a grade or level of education, regardless of age. It is expressed as a percentage of the corresponding eligible age-group population in a given school year. For example, gross enrolment ratio at the primary school level would be the percentage of children in classes I to V to total number of children in the age group of 6–11 years. It provides an indication about the spread of education among the corresponding official age-group populations and captures accessibility and capacity of the education system to enrol students.

d) *Age-specific enrolment ratio:* Age-specific enrolment ratio is a simple measure of the percentage of children enrolled in a particular age group to the total population of children in that age group. Though like the gross enrolment rate, a higher ratio indicates a higher educational participation, but it suffers from the limitation that it does not indicate the schooling level/class in which the students are enrolled. The age-specific enrolment ratio for the age group 6–14 years registered an increase from 48.3 per cent in 1981 to 55.3 per cent in 1991 as per the census figures.

e) *Net enrolment ratio:* Net enrolment ratio is defined as the number of students enrolled in an education level say the primary level, belonging to a particular age group as a percentage of the total population in that particular age group.

The net enrolment ratio measure is a refinement over the gross enrolment ratio, especially in cases where a comparison needs to be made across states and countries having education systems of different lengths. Unlike the gross enrolment ratio, it also takes into account the age group of the students and thus truly captures the age-specific enrolment of students in the classes they ought to be as per the prevailing norms for school enrolments.

Net enrolment ratio is considered as a better indicator of efficiency as it captures the large proportion of students who start early or late as per school enrolment norms, which is the usual norm/practice in the developing countries. Further, in developing countries like India, information regarding actual age of a child, especially in rural areas is often either not available or is inaccurate. In such circumstances, the use of net enrolment ratio as an indicator for school enrolments may not be reliable.

f) *Average discontinuation rate (ADR):* The average discontinuation rate is defined as the percentage of ever-enrolled children who discontinued studies at any time during primary school or between the ages of 6–14 years.

   The non-attendance rate is another related indicator. It refers to the percentage of students in the age group 6–14 years not attending school for a period of more than 7 days in the month preceding the date of survey.

g) *Teacher–student ratio:* The teacher–student ratio is an important indicator to assess both quality and efficiency of the education system. It is an established fact that one of the key reasons for the high dropout rate and poor quality of education in rural areas is the low teacher–student ratio. As per a UNDP report, the number of registered teachers at the elementary level was 2.3 million in 2000–2001, though the percentage share of female teachers to total teachers was only 36.7 per cent. Despite an increase in the number of teachers and the teacher–student ratio, we have not seen any significant impact on the primary education level. The reason could be the phenomenon of absenteeism among teachers posted in rural areas.

h) *Dropout Rate:* Dropout rate is defined as the percentage of students who dropout of a class in a year. Dropout rate along with repeaters or failed students gives an indication of the quality of the education system.

   It is important to point out that the dropout rate or school attendance rates are very important indicators, which provide very important information about enrolment status to capture the flow aspect of educational attainment in any context. Further, though the dropout rate at the national level for India has been declining, there is considerable regional disparity.

In a report released by Ministry of Education[5] in 1985, findings showed that nearly 60 per cent children dropped out between class I and V. The findings further elucidated that out of 100 children enrolled in class I, only 23 reached class VIII.

The key question which needs to be answered is: what are the reasons for the high dropout ratio and what could be the probable solution to minimize the dropout ratio? The reasons are evident, as nearly 20 per cent of habitations still do not have schools in their vicinity. The situation is further compounded by the fact that around 60 per cent of the schools have no drinking water facilities and around 90 per cent of schools lacked proper sanitation facilities. The problem is further aggravated by low teacher–student ratio. There are primary schools that have only one teacher. Further, it is not unusual for the teacher posted in rural areas to be absent most of the time and sometimes they even subcontract the teaching work to some other person.

ASSESSING DROPOUT RATE: COHORT ANALYSIS

Cohort analysis is a frequently and most commonly used technique in education research to assess the retention and dropout rate. A cohort is defined as a group of persons who experience a series of specific events over a period of time. Thus, we may define a 'school cohort' as a group of students who join the first grade in the same school year and subsequently experience the events of promotion, repetition, dropout or successful completion of the final grade.

Cohort analysis reports results based on tracking of a group of students who pass through the same classes in a similar way. It provides opportunity for programme leaders to monitor progress as students pass through rather than observing pass rates. It tracks the progress of students throughout a continuum template to assess changes in repeaters and dropout patterns and also look out for ways in which the programme can be compared to other programmes and how it can be improved.

A cohort analysis has three main elements:

a) A continuum template, which pictorially depicts student progress over the years as he/she moves through the classes.
b) An input measure, which takes into consideration all new enrolment for a year at all stages.
c) An output measure, which reports the result as students leaves or complete a year.

BOX 9.2
Coefficient of Efficiency

Coefficient of efficiency is a measure of the internal efficiency of an education system. It is obtained by dividing the actual number of years a student requires to complete an educational level by the total estimated number of years a student actually spends to complete the same educational level. It is calculated for the same cohort of students and is inversely equal to the input–output ratio.

There are three ways to analyse educational internal efficiency (see Box 9.2) by means of the cohort student flow method, namely, the true cohort, apparent cohort and reconstructed cohort[6] methods.

a) *True cohort method:* The true cohort method is generally used in longitudinal studies to track the progress of a cohort of students through the educational cycle. Though it can also be used in retrospective study, where school records of past years are traced to track the flows of students through successive grades. Though the true cohort method provides good estimates, it is very time consuming and given the state of school records that are available in government schools in India, it is also not very reliable.

As mentioned, records available in government schools are inadequate to apply the true cohort method. Thus, researchers in these conditions often resort to either the apparent or the reconstructed cohort methods.

b) *Apparent cohort method:* In case of apparent cohort method, enrolment data of a particular grade in a particular year is compared with enrolment data in successive grades during successive years and it is assumed that the decrease from the previous grade to the next grade is due to wastage. The apparent cohort method provides good estimates in the absence of data on repeaters, as it assumes that students are either promoted or else they dropout.

c) *Reconstructed cohort method:* The reconstructed cohort method,[7] as the name implies, tries to construct the cohort method by using enrolment data by grade for two consecutive years and data on repeaters by grade from the first to the second year. It thus calculates the promotion, repetition and dropout rates and can successfully analyse patterns of repetition and students dropping out.

Assumptions Behind the Cohort Reconstruction Model

Like the apparent cohort model, the reconstructed cohort model also assumes that once students are enrolled in a class, then there are three possibilities that could arise—some of them would be promoted to the next class, some would dropout from school and the remaining students would remain in the same class.

Thus, in case of the reconstructed cohort method, researchers can simulate a data of selected students, let us say a cohort of 1,000 students, through an education cycle. But this simulation exercise is based on certain important assumptions such as: (i) no new students would be enrolled in any education year during the cohort's simulation time other than students whose education progress is being tracked, (ii) the number of times a student is allowed to repeat a class is fixed, (iii) the students' movement for all grades remains the same as long as members of the cohort are still moving through the cycle and (iv) for any given class, the same rate of repetition, promotion and dropout are applied both for students who have moved directly to the next class or have moved after repetition.

In developing countries, it is very difficult to get accurate data on promotees and dropouts, hence often researchers encounter problems in calculating the flow rates. The common problems which researchers may encounter are listed next:

a) *Over-reporting enrolment/repeaters:* Over reporting is one such problem, which is deliberately done by school authorities/parents to avail some scheme or incentive. In developing countries, where incentive schemes are offered for enrollment, parents have a tendency to register their children at school at the beginning of the school year, but a large number of those registered students do not attend school or only attend for a very brief period.

b) *Confusing records of new entrants and repeaters:* Often while collecting data, it is very difficult to segregate the records of new entrant and repeaters. This confusion may lead to an under-reporting of repeaters in a particular class and an overestimation of dropouts from this grade.

c) *Complete data:* The most challenging and arduous task in collecting education data is to ensure that the data is complete in all respect and can be used as base data for cohort analysis. In most cases, researchers may find data for one or two years but data for successive years may not be available. This kind of in- complete data often results in underestimation of the promoted students and repeaters and over- estimation of dropouts in case data is not available for that particular year.

In case complete data set is available for more number of years, then this implies that some of the promotees and repeaters that year were not a part of the enrolment process in the previous year. This kind of problem results in overestimation of the promotion and repetition rates and underestimation of the dropout rates.

It is important to minimize the error mentioned here to estimate the flow rates. Though over- reporting and confusing data problems are expected to affect the flow rates for the first class of primary education, incomplete data would distort the flow rates for all classes.

SECONDARY EDUCATION

It is well-known that the quality of primary education shapes a student's interest in education and motivates him/her in continuing with education. But it is secondary education, which acts as a bridge between primary and higher education and is expected to prepare young persons in the age group of 14–18 years for higher education. The secondary education process starts with classes IX and X and leads up to higher secondary classes.

India has made considerable improvement in providing secondary education facilities. The number of secondary and senior secondary schools increased from 1,16,000 in 1999–2000 to 1,21,951 as on 30 September 2002, with a student enrolment of 28.8 million. But a lot still needs to be done on the quality front. If we consider the progress since the First Five-year Plan, it is laudable that the percentage of primary school-age population attending classes has increased threefolds. The number of schools and teachers has also increased dramatically.

The number of primary schools increased by around 300 per cent between 1951 and 2000, how-ever, during that period, the number of middle schools increased about tenfolds. The numbers of teachers showed similar rates of increase. But the situation has not improved considerably, even while the numbers of trained teachers in primary and middle schools increased by up to 90 per cent in 1987.

ADULT EDUCATION

Adult education plays a key role in educating adults who have either discontinued their education or have not attended school at all. It is thus defined as an organized and sustained learning programme designed for and appropriate to the needs of adults.

The educational needs of adults as well as the approach to teach them is quite different. The approach should take into consideration their domestic and work responsibilities as they study voluntarily.

Adult education envisages covering all types of education and training activities for adults. It covers formal, informal and vocational education offered by schools, colleges, universities, voluntary organizations and private bodies. In order to achieve the envisaged objective, the government constituted the National Literacy Mission with the approval of the Union Government on 30 September 1999, to attain total literacy, that is, a sustainable threshold literacy rate of 75 per cent by 2007. It can be achieved by imparting functional literacy to non-literates in the 15–35 years age group by increasing the adult literacy rate (see Box 9.3).

Further, the government has now wished to adopt an integrated approach to the total literacy campaign and the post literacy campaign, which signifies that basic literacy campaigns and post literacy programmes will be implemented under one literacy project called the 'Literacy Campaigns

BOX 9.3
Adult Literacy Rate

Adult Literacy Rate: Adult literacy rate is defined as the proportion of literate population aged 15 years and above. Adult literacy rate is a robust indicator of educational efforts in a social environment over a period of years. Such a measure is relatively insensitive to the current spread of education among children and underplays the importance of social investment in educating the young in a society. The adult literacy rate depends on various indicators such as coverage of the non-formal education system and the social environment.

---

and Operation Restoration'. This would help in maximizing the effort and would also ensure continuity and efficiency while minimizing unnecessary time lag. The integrated approach would also ensure that resources are utilized in the best possible way to achieve the best possible results.

The adult education programme is implemented through district literacy societies which act as the nodal agencies for the programme. Further, at the grass-roots level, district literacy societies involves voluntary agencies, community organization, Mahila Mandals, Small-Scale Industries in the literacy campaigns. It is important to point out that the total literacy programme has been initiated in almost all the 600 districts of the country. Further, even the programme of continuing education has been initiated in more than half of the total districts.

The adult literacy rate has also shown a consistent improvement as the proportion of adult literates in the population has increased from about 49 per cent in 1991 to 57 per cent in the year 1998 (NSSO 54th Round). Further analysis of findings segregated by gender reveals that the increase in proportion of female adult literates during 1991–2001 was marginally more than that of males, thus, reducing gender disparity in adult literacy.

In a nutshell, if we analyse the progress on the literacy front, it is evident that India has made significant progress in the field of literacy during the last decade, that is, 1991–2001 as reported by the 2001 Census figures. The literacy rate increased significantly from 52.21 per cent in 1991 to 65.38 per cent in the year 2001, that is, the literacy rate showed a considerable increase of around 14 percentage points, which is the highest increase in any decade.

Findings also show that for the first time during the last 10 years, even the absolute number of non-literates shows a decline. The total number of non-literates has come down from 320 million in 1991 to 296 million in 2001. During 1991–2000, the population in the seven plus age group increased by 171.6 million while 203.6 million additional persons became literate during that period. Out of 858 million people above the age of seven years, 562 million are now literates. Three-fourths of our male population and more than half of the female population are literate. This indeed is an encouraging indicator for us to speed up our march towards the goal of achieving a sustainable threshold literacy rate of 75 per cent by 2007.

LITERACY: CAUSE AND IMPACT

As per the definition of the Census of India, literacy rate is defined as the proportion of literates to total population in the age group of seven years and above. In 1951, it was merely 18.3 per cent but it grew up to 43.6 per cent in 1981 and is 65.2 per cent as per the 2001 Census. Though the literacy level has increased consistently, but still there is long way to go to attain the dream of universal education.

One major and consistent preoccupation that has remained at the centre of all literacy activities has been the concern for gender equality and women's empowerment (see Box 9.4). Literacy has been sought to be used as a major tool to educate women about their rights and duties and to bring them more and more into the mainstream of national life.

BOX 9.4
Gender Inequality in Education

Despite the earnest effort by the government, gender inequality in literacy levels is still a cause of concern. As per the 2001 Census, around 50 per cent of the women were literate, as compared to only 25 per cent of male who were illiterate. It is a well-known fact that low level of literacy, especially among women has a negative impact not only on their lives but also on generations to come. A woman's lack of education also has a negative impact on the health and well-being of her children. Further studies have also shown that illiterate women have high levels of fertility and mortality. They also suffer from poor nutritional status and low earning potential.

Illiteracy has adverse affects on the socio-economic development of the household, village and even country. Illiteracy affects the freedom and welfare of the people, Literacy could help bring about social change, population control and better health care and weed out the problems of large-scale female infanticide, acute poverty, economic disparity, discrimination based on caste and sex, child marriage, child labour etc. To achieve this, quality education must be provided to all, without discriminating on the basis of gender and caste.

NOTES

1. Education is divided into pre-primary, primary, middle, secondary and higher levels. Primary school includes children of age 6–11 studying in classes I through V. Middle school students aged 11–14 are organized into classes VI through VIII. High school students' ages range from 14–17 and they are enrolled in classes IX through XII. Higher education includes vocational education, technical schools, colleges, and universities.
2. The central government has introduced the 93rd Constitution Amendment Bill, 2001 for enacting the Fundamental Right to Free and Compulsory Education for children in the age group of 6–14 years.
3. Government of India launched the Sarva Siksha Abhiyan (SSA) in the year 2000–2001 as a key programme through which the goals of elementary education sector are going to be met. It is a significant step towards providing elementary education to all children in the age group of 6–14 years by 2010.

4. For more details please refer to Ministry of Human Resource website or link http://www.education.nic.in/htmlweb/eleedu1.htm.
5. The Ministry of Education was incorporated into the Ministry of Human Resources in 1985 as the Department of Education. In 1988, the Ministry of Human Resources was renamed the Ministry of Human Resource Development.
6. A comparison of the apparent cohort and reconstructed cohort methods shows that neglecting the repetition factor leads to an underestimation of survivals and an overestimation of dropouts.
7. Even the number of secondary and senior secondary schools increased from 1,16,000 in 1999–2000 to 1,21,951 as on 20 September 2002.

CHAPTER 10

WATER AND SANITATION

In all likelihood, the next world war is going to be over the control of the world's water resources. The future availability of water supplies poses serious challenges for governments amidst increasing populations and demands. Governments and societies are facing the danger of resource scarcity and resource degradation, especially in developing countries like India, where the growing demand for water to provide for domestic supplies, feed the population and service agriculture, industry and commerce is causing increasing scarcity and pollution of water resources.

Today, an increasing number of the rural poor are coming to view access or entitlement to water as an equally critical problem as access to food, primary health care, and education. In fact, increased usage and scarcity of water resources have resulted in conflicts both at the macro level, that is, between different states, between neighbouring countries, as well as at the micro level, that is, between villages and households.

Further, in several regions, the physical unavailability of water is exacerbated by regular droughts, which results in failure of natural resource economy. This chapter looks at the issues affecting water and the sanitation sector and discusses the prevalent water management practices.

WATER RESOURCES

India possesses about 16 per cent of the global population, but its water resources are just 4 per cent of the world's average annual runoff from rivers. As per the assessment (National Water Policy, 1993) for India, the total water resources are estimated to be around 4000 billion cubic metres (BCM) in the country, the availability from surface water and replenishable groundwater is put at 1869 BCM, out of which only around 690 BCM from surface water and 432 BCM from groundwater, can be used beneficially (see Box 10.1).

BOX 10.1
Water Resources Classification[1]

Internal renewable water resources of a country are defined as the sum total of average annual flow of rivers and groundwater recharge generated from within the country.

Surface water: Surface water is the sum total of average annual flow generated from rivers and base flow generated by aquifers. It is measured by assessing the total river flow occurring in a country in a year.

Groundwater recharge: Groundwater recharge is defined as the sum total of water resource, which enters aquifers from surface water flow and precipitation.

Overlap: Overlap, as the name suggests, is defined as the water resources, which is common to both surface water and groundwater recharge. It is usually created due to an aquifer's contribution to surface flow and recharge of aquifers by surface run-offs.

Total internal renewable water resources (IRWR): Total internal renewable water resources is the sum of surface water and groundwater recharge minus overlap, that is:

IRWR = surface water resources + groundwater recharge − overlap.

Per capita internal renewable water resources (IRWR): Per capita internal renewable water resource is an important indicator for measuring water availability and is usually computed as cubic meters per person per year (m³/person/year).

Natural renewable water resource: Natural renewable water resource is defined as the sum total of renewable water resources inside a country and water resources (due to natural flow) originating outside the country.

Water Withdrawals and Desalination: Water withdrawal is defined as the total water, which is removed for human use in a year and is measured in million cubic meters. It does not count evaporative losses from storage basins.

Water Withdrawals as a Percentage of Renewable Water Resources:[2] Water withdrawal as a proportion of renewable water resources helps in assessing the total availability of water resources. It is defined as the proportion of renewable water resources withdrawn on a per capita basis. It is important to point out that the share of water withdrawals[3] is expressed as a percentage of one of three purposes: agriculture, industry and domestic uses.

Another key issue is erratic rainfall distribution. The distribution of rainfall is uneven in India and varies from 100 mm in Jaisalmer, to over 11,000 mm in Cherapunji in the northeast. Thus, water availability varies from basin to basin or from region to region. The uneven distribution of water in the country can be gauged from the fact that Rajasthan accounts for 8 per cent of the population but has access to only 1 per cent of country's water resource.

India is the second largest consumer of water in the world after China. India's water consumption is approximately 20 per cent of world's consumption and per capita consumption is more than the world average per capita consumption. The National Commission for Integrated Water Resource Development in September 1999 adopted a norm of 220 litres per capita per day for urban areas and 150 liters per capita per day for rural areas. According to these norms, the national water requirement for domestic and national water requirement for the years 2010, 2025 and 2050 were calculated as 43 BCM, 62 BCM and 111 BCM. India's total annual renewable fresh water resources were estimated at 2085 BCM. However, the average annual availability is estimated at 1086 BCM comprising 690 BCM of surface water and 395 BCM of groundwater. Thus, it is essential that water is efficiently stored and used. Traditionally rainwater has been stored in village ponds, irrigation tanks and reservoirs.

According to the International Water Management Institute even if an equitable water use efficiency of 70 per cent were to be attained by 2025, there would be a 17 per cent increase in the demand for water. Further, it is estimated by the National Commission for Integrated Water Resources Development that the country's total water requirement by the year 2050 would exceed the estimated utilizable water resources. Although there is no need to panic or take an alarmist view or imagine a scarcity scenario,[4] there is definitely a need to have an integrated approach to development and management of water resources in the country.

It is essential to devise a policy framework to ensure efficient utilization of water resources at each level and across every part of the country, considering that often conflict arises over the use and control of resources between states or between states and the centre (see Box 10.2). Only then we would be able to strike a comfortable balance between requirement and availability of water resources. Quite importantly, there is an immediate need to ensure that availability and requirement match across regions, states and between various social strata of society.

BOX 10.2
Water: Use and Control of Resources

Water as a resource falls in the state subject list and state governments have been entrusted with the responsibility of controlling it. The administrative control and responsibility for development of water resources lies with the various state departments and corporations.

The Ministry of Water Resources at the central level is responsible for the development, conservation and management of water resources. The Ministry of Urban Development handles urban water supply and sewage disposal, while rural water supply comes under the purview of the department of drinking water under the Ministry of Rural Development.

Hydroelectric power and thermal power are the responsibility of the Ministry of Power and Pollution and environment control comes under the purview of the Ministry of Environment and Forests.

Besides looking at availability and requirement, it is imperative to ensure that the quality of water is also as per standards. Rampant pollution of water resources and lack of adequate measures to ensure that quality water is available further compounds the problem. It is estimated that 200 million Indians do not have access to safe and clean water. An estimated 90 per cent of the country's water resources are polluted by untreated industrial and domestic waste, pesticides and fertlizers. According to a report, about 1.5 million children younger than five years of age die annually from water-borne diseases (Parikh, 2004). The country also loses over 200 million workdays due to water-borne diseases.

WATER RESOURCE PLANNING, USAGE AND PRACTICES

The key objective of all water resource planning process is to bring all available water resources within the category of utilizable resources to the maximum possible extent. In order to do so, it is imperative to adopt an integrated approach utilizing both non-conventional and traditional methods. Non-conventional methods such as inter-basin transfers and artificial recharge of ground-water need to be adopted on a large scale. Besides non-conventional methods, traditional water conservation practices like rainwater harvesting also need to be practiced and popularized among the masses to increase the utilizable water resources.

To improve utilizable water resources, it is necessary to maximize optimum utilization of water resources by minimizing wastage. In India water is primarily used for three purpose: (i) agricultural use, which includes water used for irrigation and livestock, (ii) domestic use, which includes water used for drinking, water used in homes, commercial establishments and for public services and (iii) industrial use, which includes water used for cooling, boiling and mixing in industrial plants.

It is estimated that out of the total water resources available and used, around 92 per cent is used in agriculture, roughly 3 per cent is used by industries and only 5 per cent is used for domestic purposes like drinking water and sanitation (WRI, 2000). Thus, water used for agriculture and domestic purposes forms the bulk of the water consumed and the demand is bound to increase with the growth of the population, urbanization and industrialization. The next section lists the prevalent water usage practices, issues and approaches.

AGRICULTURE

Agriculture has played a dominant role in strengthening India's economy, contributing to 29 per cent of its GDP and is a primary source of livelihood for 70 per cent of the population. Thus, it is imperative that irrigation facilities are strengthened for rural economic development. The rapid expansion of irrigation and drainage infrastructure has been one of India's major achievements. From 1951 to 1997, the gross irrigated areas expanded fourfold. However, a lot still needs to be done to provide irrigation facilities in inaccessible areas.

Irrigation

Irrigation projects are classified into three broad categories, namely, major, medium and minor based on the command area of the project. Projects having a cultivable command area (CCA) of more than 10,000 ha are termed as major projects whereas projects having a CCA in the range of 2,000–10,000 ha are termed as medium projects and those with a CCA of less than 2,000 ha are classified as minor projects.

The key objective of irrigation planning should be to extend the benefits of irrigation to large number of farmers, including marginal farmers, to maximize production. It should also take into account the nature of land that needs to be irrigated, the area that needs to be irrigated, devise cost-effective irrigation options and appropriate irrigation techniques for optimizing water efficiency. Besides, we need to have special programmes for areas that are drought prone (see Box 10.3).

BOX 10.3
Drought-prone Area Development

Drought-prone area development programme is a special programme, which emphasizes reducing the vulnerabilities in drought-prone area. The programme devises strategies centred on the principle of soil moisture conservation, water harvesting and groundwater development

The emphasis is on encouraging farmers to plant drought-resistant species and adopting other such modes of development that are relatively less water demanding.

Reforms in irrigation institutions have already taken significant steps to incorporate farmer's participation and devolve management responsibilities to water users but water rights need to be more clearly defined and negotiated. Growing competition for water has intensified the urgent need for improving institutional arrangements for water allocation.

Watershed Management

Out of a total 329 million hectares (mha) of the country's geographical area, it is believed that only around 200 mha have the potential for production, which includes 143 mha of agricultural land. Millions of India's poor live in rural areas without irrigation and are dependent on the rains for agriculture production. It is no surprise that rain-fed farming still prevails in 67 per cent of the cultivated area, which produces 44 per cent of the foodgrains and supports 40 per cent of the population. Further, it is estimated that even with the development of irrigation capability to a maximum, half of the cultivated acreage will remain rain-fed in the near future.

Despite the prevalence of rain-fed farming, there has always been an effort to devise ways to concentrate on the development in rain-fed areas. Until the 1980s, no such new technology was available to farmers in rain-fed areas. In a bid to look out for such technology, the government initiated the Pilot Project for Watershed Development in rain-fed areas in 1984. The emphasis of the programme was on devising mechanisms for increasing agricultural production in rain-fed areas through land and crop management, moisture conservation and production of fuel and fodder.

The watershed approach has provided a new lease of life to rain-fed areas. The watershed approach is defined as an integrated rural development approach, centred on water as the key development source. It is defined as strategy for conserving, protecting and restoring aquatic ecosystems. This strategy is based on the assumption that the problems of water availability can be best solved at the watershed level in rural areas, rather than at the individual water body level. It is based on simple logic that water should be made available to water-short areas by transfer from other areas or storing water in water-short area for future use.

The watershed protection approach, as an integrated approach emphasizes on solving water resource related problems by promoting a high level of stakeholder involvement. It focuses on common lands through community participation to ensure a sustainable livelihood stream for villagers. Watershed management planning envisages protecting water resources through construction of check-dams. Planning is based on measures of extensive soil conservation, catchment area treatment and preservation of forests.

Industrial Purpose

The industrial sector accounts for only 3 per cent of the consumption of total water resources and thus does not put much pressure on water availability, but it contributes significantly to water pollution especially in urban areas.

Even in the case of consumption, it is estimated that consumption will grow at a rate of 4.2 per cent per year (World Bank, 1999) and demand for industrial, energy production and other uses will rise from 67 BCM to 228 BCM by 2025. Increased industrial water consumption coupled with the water pollution problem due to industrial usage poses serious challenge for water resources planners. Despite all this, there are some sectors, which have huge potential, for example, hydroelectric generation. In India, the potential for hydroelectrical generation has been estimated at 84,000 MW (equivalent to about 450 billion units of the annual energy generation by taking a 60 per cent load factor), of which only 22,000 MW is currently being harnessed (MOWR, 2001). The huge untapped potential and ever-increasing demands for electricity shall ensure that development of this activity continues in the coming years.

Domestic Purpose

The domestic sector accounts for only 5 per cent of the total annual freshwater withdrawals in India (World Resources Institute, 2000), but like industrial water usage, domestic water use will increase with an increase in the population. It has been estimated that over next 20 years, the demand will double from 25 BCM to 52 BCM.

Though the domestic sector accounts for only 5 per cent of the total water withdrawal but even then, the availability of safe drinking water is a huge problem. The central government made a commitment to improve access to water in rural and urban areas in the National Water Policy[5] adopted in 1987. Access to potable water and adequate sanitation services vary between states. As of 2001, over 73 per cent of the rural population and 90 per cent of the urban population had access to potable water. Though the figures do not tell us how frequently and in what quantity people get potable water and, even more importantly, what is the quality of water? In a bid to review the situation, the next section discusses the drinking water scenario in urban and rural areas.

Drinking Water

It is shameful that even after more than 50 years of independence, availability of potable water to the entire population in urban and rural areas is still a problem. The proportion of the population with access to safe drinking water, as mentioned earlier, is 70 per cent in rural areas and 90 per cent in urban areas.

Public piped systems are the major source of water supply in the urban areas, whereas in the rural areas, more private hand pumps are being installed to substitute for the public system and to improve the service level. But still a lot needs to be done to improve the service aspect. According to a national survey, about one-fourth of the total surveyed households reported breakdown of taps/hand-pumps once in three months. Further, when enquired about the satisfaction regarding availability and quality, only 27 per cent of the households were fully satisfied with the quality of water and 20 per cent were satisfied with water availability (Paul et al., 2004).

Regarding urban water supply, the service levels are far below the desired norms. Most municipalities[6] do not have any system for monitoring the availability or quality of water and water contamination problems are there even in metro cities like New Delhi and Kolkata.

In order to the solve the problem of drinking water availability in urban areas, the central and state governments launched the Accelerated Urban Water Supply Programme (AUWSP) in towns having a population less than 20,000. The programme envisages involving the community from the planning stage itself, in the supply facilities and their subsequent maintenance and in sharing the maintenance costs. Besides this, there have been initiatives such as Swajaldhara, which aims to boost water supply in a big way (see Box 10.4).

BOX 10.4
Swajaldhara

> The government scaled up its reforms initiative programme throughout the country in 2002 as the *Swajaldhara* programme. It addresses the basic reform principles of being demand responsive and community led. Further 10 per cent of capital costs and the full operation and maintenance (O&M) costs are borne by the users and thus the community/*Gram Panchayat* is free to levy a water tariff.

Rural Water Supply

The availability of safe drinking water supply is a basic necessity of life. The government has made several efforts to ensure availability of drinking water in rural areas under the Minimum Needs Programme (MNP). Access to potable water and adequate sanitation services vary between states.

At the begining of the Eighth Five-year Plan, there were about 3,000 'no source' villages out of a list of 162,000 'problem' villages. Besides there were about 150,000 villages that were only partially covered. Though the number has come down substantialy, a lot still needs to be done to ensure availability of safe drinking water for all.

The main constraints with regard to water supply are inadequate maintenance of rural water systems, lack of finances and poor community involvement. Thus, future actions should look into all these aspect for a better implementation plan. It is because of a lack of innovativeness and concerted approach that several good initiaves have not achieved the goals they have desired.

The Accelerated Rural Water Supply Programme (ARWSP), launched by the department of drinking water supply in 1972–73 sought to accelerate the pace of coverage of rural populations with access to safe and adequate drinking water supply facilities with the help of financial assistance[7] from the centre. Government allocation under the ARWSP has increased substantially from Rs 171.5 million in 1999–2000 to Rs 290 million in the year 2004–05.

The programme emphasizes on ensuring coverage of all rural populations, especially the people living in inaccessible area. The government should also ensure sustainability of the water resources to tackle the problem of water quality by institutionalizing water quality monitoring and surveillance.

The programme has been revamped to push reforms vigorously by institutionalizing community participation in rural water supply. It envisages shifting from the government-oriented, centralized, supply-driven policy to a people-oriented decentralized, demand-driven and community-based policy. The emphasis is on ensuring equity in coverage, sustainability of water sources and to sort out the emerging water quality problems.

India has been ranked among the worst countries in terms of quality of water. It is estimated that around 90 per cent of the total water resources are polluted with industrial and domestic waste. The next section discusses the quality problem persistent in India.

WATER QUALITY PROBLEMS

Developing countries, especially India, not only suffer from a scarcity of water, but also face the problem of poor quality of water. Availability of safe drinking water is still one of the major problems because of a variety of reasons. Water pollution is a serious problem in India. According to the estimates of the ministry of water resources, almost 70 per cent of India's surface water resources and a bulk of its groundwater reserves are contaminated by biological, organic and inorganic pollutants (MOWR, 2000). Water quality is primarily affected by two kinds of contaminants: (i) chemical contaminants and (ii) biological contaminants.

Chemical contamination occurs mostly due to the presence of fluoride and arsenic. Fluoride[8] is a commonly occurring contaminant in drinking water in many regions of the world. Though at low levels, say 1 mg/l, it is found to be beneficial in preventing dental caries, but exposure to high levels of fluoride can even cause skeletal damage. Arsenic is another chemical, which in the case of prolonged exposure can cause serious health problems. Its prolonged exposure can result in skin lesions, cardiovascular diseases, neurological diseases, hypertension and even lung cancer or cancer of the kidneys. In high concentrations, arsenic poisoning[9] can result in serious health problems characterized by an acute condition called arsenicosis.

Water quality is further affected by biological contamination such as (i) Bacteria/viruses contamination, (ii) discharge of untreated/partially treated effluents, sewage and (iii) excessive use of fertilizers.

Ways to Maintain Efficient Supply and Good Quality of Water

Water is one of the most crucial resources for survival. Thus, every possible effort should be made to develop, conserve, utilize and manage this important resource. There is an urgent need to devise ways to develop groundwater resources, ensure soil conservation, and develop water-sharing mechanisms in an integrated manner. The real challenge is to maintain a sufficient supply of good quality of water over a period of time.

The government instruments to develop water resources by restructuring water rights in a way, which may be counter productive unless changes are carefully negotiated. One of the most important directions for improving allocation is recognizing and enhancing the capacity for self-governance of water as a common property resource.

Water resource utilization and exploitation must be carried out within the capacity limits of the resource available. Over-exploitation of aquifers pose serious threats to sustainable water resource utilization. High dependence on groundwater (85 per cent) and neglect of traditional practices and systems, including rainwater harvesting and inadequate integrated water management and watershed development has compounded the problem. Further, the problems of water quality only add to the misery of the people. The solution lies in groundwater development.

GROUND WATER DEVELOPMENT

It is estimated that out of the total amount of rainwater received, only one-third is recharged into aquifers, while two-thirds is lost as run-offs. It is imperative in this situation that a periodical assessment of groundwater potential is done to devise policies for groundwater development.

Rapid depletion of groundwater levels is a cause of great concern for India as agriculture depends on this water source. According to one estimate, groundwater sources account for as much as 70–80 per cent of water resources utilized for irrigation.

The reservoir of groundwater is estimated at 432 BCM and it has been declining at a rapid rate of 20 cm annually. Unregulated extraction of water has led to a fall in groundwater table by about 25 m in the last 25 years in backward blocks of the country. Thus, it is high time to ensure regulations to control the exploitation of groundwater resources and to ensure equitable distribution of water resource across space and time. Besides, controlling overexploitation, it is imperative in these conditions to adopt strategies to enhance artificial recharge of groundwater to build on existing groundwater resources.

Artificial recharging is defined as the process in which groundwater reservoirs are augmented either by spreading water on the surface, by using recharge wells, or by altering natural conditions to replenish an aquifer. Based on the way in which groundwater is augmented, the recharge process is classified as direct and indirect artificial recharge. It is also defined as a way to store water underground in times of water surplus to meet demands in times of shortage. Rainwater harvesting is one such approach, which if used appropriately, can solve the water supply problems to some extent (see Box 10.5).

BOX 10.5
Rainwater Harvesting

Rainwater harvesting, as the name suggests, involves collecting and using precipitation from a catchment surface. It gains importance because surface water is inadequate to meet our demand and we have to depend on groundwater.

There are two main techniques of rainwater harvesting: (i) storage of rainwater for future use and (ii) recharge to groundwater. The storage of rainwater is a traditional technique. It is usually done with the help of underground tanks, ponds, check-dams, weirs, etc. The second method of recharging groundwater is an emerging concept of rainwater harvesting. It is usually done through such means as pits, trenches and dug wells.

Management of water resource is as critical to survival as management of natural resources. It is very important to sustain the needs of more than a billion people. It is critical for the functioning of both agriculture and the industrial sector as well as for all domestic work. It is thus essential to devise a comprehensive policy framework focusing on rational and equitable allocation of water resources, especially among the poor and disadvantaged people.

The government also has a big part to play in pushing the measures of water conservation, water quality and equitable water consumption with vigour. Water should be perceived of as a precious commodity for which one has to pay and thus should be equitably used. There is a need to devise a common water policy among states regarding utilization of river water and sharing of water resources, as often states use water resource as a tool to settle political scores. Further, in the majority of cases, water supplying public sector agencies are not efficient enough in ensuring availability of water and are not even able to collect the dues. There is a shortage of funds to replace or renovate the existing water transfer facilities. It is high time that policy-makers and people look at water as an economic good and not merely as a social good.

IS WATER A SOCIAL GOOD OR AN ECONOMIC GOOD

Traditionally, water has been viewed primarily as a social good. It has been viewed as an open access resource, which is not taxed heavily. The supply of water, like other basic needs, has been viewed as the sole responsibility of the government. The government has framed policies and frameworks to ensure that water is available to all, but it costs money and even today government public agencies are in a financial mess as the government continues to finance the running costs of most of these systems. The government has subsidize water supply because it is a social good.

Water can also be viewed as an economic good, because it has monetary value. Researchers often use various demand estimation techniques to illustrate the value users are willing to pay for a service. This willingness to pay shows the extent to which users value the benefits gained from an increased supply of water or improved quality of water. There is debate over the issue whether users should be charged more for increased supply or for quality of water or whether users are ready to pay the charges. Today, however, largely due to funding shortfalls, many governments are open to the idea that users pay some of the cost of the supply and this requires water supply to be viewed in economic terms.

DEMAND ASSESSMENT TECHNIQUE

The greatest challenge a welfare state face today is to ensure that the water is available to all, especially for the poor and disadvantaged communities not simply for consumption, but also to combine with other assets in order to furnish sustainable livelihoods. To ensure this it is imperative that we understand the necessity of a good water management regime. A good water management regime should always be pivoted around the dynamics of demand and supply streams. So it is of paramount importance that an assessment of demand is done vis-à-vis the supply options and facilities. While assessing demand and supply, another dimension, that is, the willingness to pay for improved water supply and services also needs to be assessed in order to promote water as an economic good.

Different social/market research and socio-economic research techniques can be used for assessing the demand for improving water supplies and even for improving water treatment and sanitation. These techniques induce users to volunteer information regarding the maximum sum of money they would be willing to pay for water as a non-market good, that is, the price they would be willing to pay for water if water was available in the market for sale.

Some of the most widely used techniques are:

a) Contingent valuation method.
b) Hedonic pricing method.
c) Conjoint analysis method.
d) Random utility method.

Contingent Valuation Method

The contingent valuation method works on a framework of a hypothetical market or contingent method, through which it tries to elicit valuation directly from individuals. These studies try to elicit people's preference and perception on a variety of issues ranging from improvement in water quality to reduction in air pollution levels. It is based on the assumption that the consumer is the best judge of his interests and the consumer has the ability to rank preferences in a rational way.

The method involves setting up a carefully worded questionnaire, which asks people their 'willingness to pay' (WTP) and/or 'willingness to accept' (WTA) through structured questions. The method involves devising various forms of 'bidding games' eliciting 'yes/no' response to questions and statements about maximum WTP and at the next stage econometric analysis of the resulting survey data is done to derive the mean values of WTP bids.

The contingent valuation technique is the most commonly used valuation technique because it is the only means available for valuing non-use values and estimates obtained from well-designed, properly-executed surveys. It gives results which are as good as estimates obtained from other methods.

The contingent valuation method presents a hypothetical scenario describing the terms and conditions under which the good or service is to be offered to the respondent. A carefully worded questionnaire provides information on when the service would be provided and how the respondents are expected to pay for it. It also provides detail about the institutional arrangement for the delivery of the service, the quality and reliability of the service.

Respondents are then asked about the value of goods or services provided under the specified terms and conditions. The question describe various bidding options and ask respondents to select the bidding option, which they find appropriate. These bids are further analysed to reveal the willingness to pay and the willingness to accept. Econometric models or regression equation, depending on the relationship between variables can be used to infer their WTP for the change.

In order to understand this method better, let us look at a case study done on contingent valuation for the Barbados Sewer System.[10] It is a well-known fact that the installation of a sewer system potentially creates three kinds of direct services: (i) easier disposal of waste water, (ii) cleaner water for swimming, beach use and expected healthier reefs and (iii) a healthier marine environment.

The study concentrated on the indirect effects of assessing the impact of the sewer system on tourist activity. In case marine waters gain a reputation of being severely polluted, tourist activity, essential to the economy, may be reduced, bringing a decline in employment. To estimate the benefits of the sewer system, the study envisaged calculating the total willingness to pay for a cleaner environment.

The study provided two sets of options: one for respondents who lived outside the sewer district and the other for those who lived in the proposed sewer system area. Respondents living outside the sewer system area were asked only about the environmental aspects of the sewer system. They were offered two options: (i) pay a randomly varied increase on the quarterly water bill to achieve the aims of the sewer system or (ii) not pay anything and continue on the path of potentially polluting the beaches and face the other environmental consequences of private disposal of waste water.

In responding to these questions, households that were not in the proposed sewer system area were asked to assess the effect of continued disposal of waste water into the ground, and the impact of this disposal on marine water quality. Their response, that is, the probability of answering yes to the question was modelled in the form of an equation:

$$p \text{ (yes to the question)} = a0 + a1d + a2age + a3c_{tv} - byw$$

Where

   a = coefficient
   d = 1 if household visited relevant beaches more than 15 times a year
   0 = otherwise
   age = age of respondent
   c_{tv} = 1 if household had seen a television show about the relation between the sewer system and pollution
       of the beaches of Barbados
   0 = otherwise
   w = 4 (increment to quarterly water bill)

The c_{tv} variable represents an increment to knowledge about the sewer system and its impact on the marine environment. This model was then used to calculate the willingness to pay for constructing the sewer system. The general expression used for measuring mean willingness to pay (E_w) was represented by:

$$E_w = (a0 + a1d + a2age + a3c_{tv})/by$$

Thus, expected willingness to pay was calculated by using estimates from the first equation.

Further, the second set of respondents, who lived in the proposed sewer system area, were given a similar option, but one that included the services of public waste water disposal. The randomly chosen households were offered two options, that is, either (i) pay a randomly varied quarterly addition to their water bill and receive the services of waste water disposal or (ii) not pay the increment to the water bill and continue the private method of waste water disposal that affects the environment.

Similar to the equation mentioned earlier, respondent's probability to answer yes was represented in the form of a model for households, who had the potential to connect:

P (yes to the question) $= c0 + c1d + c2age + c3c_{tv} - dyw$

Where the variables are the same as mentioned for the households outside the district except that $d = 1$ for households who visit the relevant beaches anytime during the year and 0 otherwise; and c is the coefficient.

The survey results and findings showed that the estimated model for respondents living in the proposed sewer system area was stronger than the model for households outside the proposed sewer district. In this case also, the mean willingness to pay was calculated using a similar expresion:

$$E_w = (c0 + c1d + c2age + c3c_{tv})/dy$$

Hedonic Pricing Method

The hedonic price model tries to monetize basic environment amenities by assessing impact of amenities on prices of related goods and economic services. It is most widely used in assessing the impact of environmental pollution on residential housing value.

It is based on the premise that the price of a market good, let us say, for example, a house is a combination of various attributes such as size, location, structural qualities and environmental amenities that makes up the marketed good. Researchers then, using econometric techniques, can calculate a hedonic price function relating property price to various attributes of property. Researchers can further derive separate expressions for environmental attributes, assessing how the price would change if the level of an environmental attribute were changed. It is important to point out that it does not measure non-use value and is confined to cases where property owners are aware of environmental variables and act because of them.

To explore the concept further, let us take a case study done in the Philippines (North and Griffin, 1993). This case study illustrates that it is feasible to use an indirect, non-market valuation technique to estimate the economic benefits that result from an improved water supply project. The study used the hedonic property valuation method to determine how rental values of households in one rural area of the Philippines reflects the households' willingness to pay for the different types of water supply services, that is, private connection, a tap, or a community source and distance to the source.

The hedonic model was based on the idea that households choose to rent or purchase a house based on the dwelling and community characteristics. Thus a bid-rent function was formulated to analyse the trade-offs each household was willing to make between attractive characteristics of house and community and increased payment for dwelling and community characteristics.

The study then used the regression equation having monthly rental value of a dwelling as the dependent variable and its characteristics, such as water source, construction materials, number of rooms and lot size as the independent variables to estimate the hedonic price function. Further, marginal willingness to pay for each characteristic was calculated using the derivative of the hedonic price function with respect to that particular characteristic.

The model, however, assumes that all consumers are alike, which in reality is not a practical assumption. Thus, to solve this problem, the sample was divided into three different income groups, and it was assumed that the households in each income group had similar tastes while estimating the bid-rent function directly for each group.

The study formulated the problem as a random bidding model in which the bid-rent parameters were estimated by predicting the type of respondents likely to occupy a particular house. The advantage of this bid-rent function was that it allowed researchers to directly estimate the bid-rent function without having to recover the parameters of the utility function.

The study estimated the households' willingness to pay in terms of the capitalized value of improvements to water situations. It was based on the premise that households pay monthly costs associated with the use of different sources and costs were estimated in the form of water charges, electricity and household members' time. Further, the coefficients in the regression equation represented marginal willingness-to-pay for each housing characteristic, assuming that tastes were similar within each of the three income groups.

The study results, interestingly, showed that low-income households were willing to pay more, for distance characteristic, that is, to be nearer to the main town. However, middle-income groups did not want to pay anything to be closer to town and, quite in contrast, the higher-income group showed its willingness to pay to be farther away from the town. The study also analysed the tradeoffs between other characteristics and findings revealed that all income groups were willing to pay more for better construction. Surprisingly, the findings showed that willingness-to-pay for a closer water source was statistically significant only for lower-income households and even for high-income households, the magnitude of the effect of distance on willingness to pay was small.

Conjoint Analysis

Conjoint analysis is concerned with measurement of psychological judgements such as consumer preference. It is based on the assumption that consumers do not make choices based on a single attribute of a product, but on combining various attributes. Consumers make judgements or trade-offs between various attributes to determine their final decision.

In conjoint analysis, researchers try to deconstruct a set of overall responses so that the utility of each attribute can be inferred. It is based on the economic utility theory and has proven successful in market research. In this process, a part worth, or utility, is calculated for each level of attribute. Though conjoint analysis was developed as a market research technique, nowadays it is also used extensively in social research. It is the recommended approach to determine the willingness to pay for changes in service levels.

Conjoint analysis as stated preference survey method is the most reliable method to assess the willingness to pay for future services or non-use benefits. It minimizes the risk of strategic answers as the consumers are asked to choose the preferred option among two or more alternatives.

Researchers can estimate the total utility function from answers to stated preference questions. Respondents are asked to choose an alternative between two alternatives, A and B and if U represents the utility function, respondents will choose the alternative that implies the highest utility. Besides calculating the total utility function, part utility can also be estimated from the function to evaluate the alternatives by tariff and service characteristics.

Random Utility Model

The probit model is an alternative log-linear approach to handling categorical dependent variables. It deals with the problem of predicting a dependent variable, which is nominal, or ordinal. In the case of the probit model, the response is assumed to be normally distributed. These models can be used to explain a households' decision to connect to a piped water system as a function of various factors such as cost of connection, socio-economic and demographic characteristics of the household, respondents' attitudes and the households' existing water supply situation.

The random utility model relies on predefined options and it assumes that respondents have the perfect capability to discriminate between options and are extensively used in assessing water connection.

It is established that the cost of providing water utilities is quite huge and thus it requires a high percentage of households to connect to a piped water supply system so that revenues are sufficient to cover capital and operating costs.

In developed countries, the majority of households use piped water supply as the exclusive source of supply. Hence, revenues are much more than the cost of providing facilities. But, in many developing countries, the scenario is quite different. In developing countries, households decide not to connect to piped water systems for a variety of reasons. Further, even those who are connected to piped water supply use other sources. Thus, it is imperative that before devising a plan to provide piped water supply, planners should have an understanding of the factors that influence a household's decision to connect to a piped water system. As in most cases, they simply assume that a household will connect to a piped water system if the monthly tariff is less than 3–5 per cent of the income. Planners can take this indicator to be the base for all planning processes. The random utility model can guide planners in assessing the willingness to pay for connecting to piped water supply.

To explain the procedure and usage of the random utility model in detail, let us examine a case study, which studied the willingness to connect to a piped water system. The study was done in five villages of Punjab (Pakistan) and covered 378 household respondents.[11] Though all five villages had piped water systems, only some households had decided to connect to it and others had decided against getting a connection. The surveys collected information on the tariff, the connection fee paid at the time of connection and the cost of bringing water from the distribution line into each house.

The survey results showed that in the surveyed area all three components of costs—the tariff, connection fee and linking costs—were statistically significant and had negative influences on the connection decision. Results corroborated the fact that one-time costs had a smaller effect on the likelihood of connection than the tariffs, which strongly suggested that variable and progressive tariff option might have been a good option to provide affordable piped water supply for all.

The study also offered interesting results for demographic and attitudinal variables. Education and family size were found to be positive and generally significant determinant of the connection decision in both the districts.

Further analysis showed that household's labour supplies available to collect water from sources outside the home had quite different effects on the connection decisions in the two districts. In the brackish district both the proportion of women and the proportion of children variables were found to have negative influences on the connection decision, but only the proportion of children variable was found to be statistically significant. In contrast, in the sweet water district, both proportion of women and proportion of children variables were found to be positively correlated with the connection decision.

The findings proved the utility of the random utility model in modelling household demand for piped water supplies. The survey results also showed that both one-time connection costs and monthly tariffs were found to influence the connection decisions. The study also indicated a difference in the effect of one-time connection costs and monthly tariffs on household connection decisions. It is noteworthy to mention here that all demand assessment techniques showed the correlation of willingness to pay with price and income determinants (see Box 10.6).

BOX 10.6
Price and Income Effects

Demand assessment techniques are used to ascertain how changes in price and income affect the water consumption and willingness to pay. Demand assessment is necessary because it is demand that ultimately influences the optimal utlization capacity of water. Researchers usually considers two types of effects:

a) Increase in income over time may result in high willingness to pay or higher demand for water resources signifying higher revenues for the supplying organization.
b) Increase in water tariff structure may result in lower water demand (considering that income does not increases proportionately), resulting in lower revenues for the supplying organization.

Estimation of Elasticity

Sensitivity analysis can measure the elasticity. It is defined as the percentage change in water demand due to one percentage point increase in water tariff. Elasticity in this case is expected to be negative, because higher water tariffs may result in decrease in water consumption. Further, it is expected that the elasticity would be less than 1, signifying that total water consumption decreases by less than 1 per cent when water tariff is increased by 1 per cent.

SANITATION

Sanitation facilities in rural India are in dismal state and as per the Census of India, 2001 a staggering 71 per cent of households in Indian villages do not have toilet facilities. The problem is further compounded by the fact that only 15 per cent of primary schools have toilets. The time has come to take up this issue on a priority basis since it affects the all-round development of the majority of the country's people, especially women in the lower strata of society.

Poor hygienic and sanitation conditions are detrimental to children's health. In India, rural infant mortality rate has remained very high and a major cause of mortality is diarrhoeal diseases due to oral faecal infection. It has been proven beyond doubt that lack of sanitation and hygiene is the primary cause of almost all infectious diseases. Thus, it is high time that efforts were made to improve sanitation facilities, especially for poor and disadvantaged people in rural areas.

It is not that efforts have not been made to improve sanitation facilities. The ministry of rural development launched the Rural Sanitation Programme in 1986 to improve the sanitary conditions in rural areas. All rural sanitation aims at supplementing the efforts made under different central and state sector programmes for improving sanitary facilities in the rural areas with the overall objective of improving the quality of life in rural areas. Further, the Central Rural Sanitation Programme (CRSP) was restructured in 1999 to provide adequate sanitation facilities to the rural poor to generate awareness about health education and hygiene.

TOTAL SANITATION CAMPAIGN—STRATEGIES AND PRINCIPLES

Total Sanitation Campaign (TSC) launched in 1999 is a programme that emphasizes on a demand-driven participatory approach, where greater emphasis is on attitudes and behavioural change through awareness generation. It also signifies a shift from high to low subsidy, with a range of technological options and is implemented with the district as a unit also focusing on school sanitation and hygiene education. It aims to create a synergestic interaction between the government organization and NGOs.

Integration holds the key for the successful completion of Swajaldhara and TSC (see Box 10.7). Even the implementers have to plan in an integrated way to move ahead to provide solutions to water and sanitation problems.

BOX 10.7
The Way Forward

> Integration of drinking water, sanitation, health and hygiene programmes through *Swajaldhara* and TSC as vehicles of reforms in the water and sanitation sectors has been a key innovation. The review of funding patterns of the schemes, the allocation criteria of central assistance, restructuring of rural water supply departments in the states and capacity building of PRIs and community-level organizations have been the key strategies.

NOTES

1. For more information please refer to 'Water Resources, Development and Management Service', October 2001. Statistics on Water Resources by Country in FAO's AQUASTAT Programme available online at http://www.fao.org/ag/agl/aglw/aquastat/water_res/index.stm and http://earthtrends.wri.org/text/water-resources/cp_notes.html.
2. The value is calculated by dividing water withdrawals per capita by actual renewable water resources per capita; data are usually from different years.
3. Evaporative losses from storage basins are not considered; it should be keep in mind, however, that in some parts of the world up to 25 per cent of water that is withdrawn and placed in reservoirs evaporates before it is used by any sector.
4. As per the water barrier concept of sustainability indicators, which is the most widely cited measures of water sufficiency (Falkenmark, 1989; Falkenmark et al., 1989; Falkenmark and Widstrandt, 1992; FAO, 1993; Gleick, 1993a) any situation of water availability of less than 1,000 m³ per capita per year is considered as a scarcity condition.
5. The National Water Policy is the primary document stating the position of the Government of India (GoI) on water resources issues ranging from drought and flood management to drinking water provisions.
6. Most urban areas are serviced by a municipal water distribution system. Usually, the municipal water supply originates from local reservoirs or canals, but in some cases, water may be imported through inter-basin transfer.
7. Over Rs 400 billion ($ 8.9 billion) were invested in 3.7 million hand pumps and 145,000 piped water supply schemes.
8. It is estimated that in India, over 66 million people, including 7 million children, in 17 states out of the 32 states and union territories are afflicted with endemic fluorosis. There is no specific treatment for endemic fluorosis apart from drinking water free from fluoride.
9. If the proposed new World Health Organization guideline (0.01mg/l) are adopted, then a further 20–25 million people are likely to be included. The scale of the disaster in Bangladesh is greater even than the accidents in Bhopal and Chernobyl (WHO, 2000). For details see http://www.nytimes.com/2005/07/17/international/asia/17arsenic.html
10. For more details on the case study refer to Darling et al. (1993).
11. For more details on the case refer to Altaf Mir et al, (1993).

CHAPTER 11

POVERTY, INEQUALITY AND RURAL DEVELOPMENT

India being a welfare state embodies the spirit of well-being of individuals. The planning process and all development policies are pivoted around the core issue of improving the quality of life of the people. To deconstruct the issue further, let us juxtapose the spirit of well-being of individuals and quality of life with the present situation where millions of people, especially in rural areas, still live below the poverty line and are entangled in a downward spiral of developmental backwardness and a vicious circle of poverty. It is shameful that even after more than 50 years of independence, gross inequality, poverty and widespread hunger are major development issues, which still need to be addressed. It is widely believed that the unequal distribution of assets and the low level of wealth are the main causes of poverty. But the key question that needs to be answered is whether society has always been like this, where we have a rich and elite class, which enjoys power and luxury and a poor class, which has no means of livelihood. There are vast inter-regional differences and disparities that still plague millions of people, especially in rural areas, where opportunities for personal and social advancement for people are limited.

In terms of magnitude as well as severity, the problems of poverty lies in the rural sector as three out of four of India's poor live in the rural areas, making it quite evident that the key to reducing poverty in India is agricultural growth, accompanied by strong non-agricultural growth that reaches the rural poor (which is discussed in detail in the present chapter) besides the need of developing the non-farm sector economy as a measure to remove inequality.

Economic growth is the single most important factor in reducing inequality. It generates additional goods and services in the economy, which in an equitable and just society should translate into better social opportunities, especially for disadvantaged people. In reality, however, economic growth does not always translate into better development prospects for the poor and disadvantaged people and inequality still remains a major problem that needs to be assessed and tackled. The following section lists some key measures of inequality and techniques to measure them.

MEASURING INEQUALITY

The overall level of inequality not only exacerbates the quality of life of individuals but also affects the welfare of groups, society and the country. Thus, it is essential that strategies are devised to reduce inequality.

CRITERIA FOR INEQUALITY MEASURES

The Anonymity Principle

As per the anonymity principle, it does not matter who is earning an income and hence permutation of income among people do not matter, for example, if two people swap their income levels, this should not affect the overall income distribution measure.

The Population Principle

The population principle states that inequality measure should not be a function of population size and the key consideration while measuring inequality should be proportions of the population that earn different levels of income.

Relative Income Principle

The relative income principle states that relative and not absolute level of income matters while measuring inequality. Thus, if everybody's income rises in the same proportion, the overall inequality measure should not be affected. Relative income criteria is measured by the following measures:

a) *Percentile distributions:* In case of percentile distribution, one percentile is compared with another variable. For example, researchers can compare the income of the top 10 percentile to the bottom 40 percentile.
b) *Standard deviation of income:* Standard deviation of income measures income deviation by assessing the deviation from the mean.
c) *Relative poverty line:* Relative poverty line tries to assess the individual's or household's position in society as compared to others.

The Pigou-Dalton or Dalton Principle of Transfers

The Dalton principle of transfers assess transfer from an individual to one who is initially equally well off.

The Lorentz Criterion

The Lorentz criterion states that in case one Lorentz curve lies above another Lorentz curve, then the curve that lies above represents more equal distribution of income than the other curve. In case two curves intersect at some point, then researchers need some more information before commenting on the equality of income.

Absolute Income Criteria

Absolute income criteria defines an absolute standard and calculates the number or percentage of individuals below a specified absolute income criteria. The absolute income criteria is a very useful method for determining the absolute poverty in a society. Some of the absolute income criteria frequently used are:

a) *Poverty line:* Poverty line tries to measure the level of income which is necessary to meet the minimum specific standard needed for survival. It varies from place to place and from time to time depending on the cost of living and people's expectations (see Box 11.1).

b) *Poverty index:* The poverty index measure was developed by Amartya Sen to sum up poverty in an index numbers approach. The index takes into account both the number of poor and the extent of their poverty. Sen defined the index as:

$$I \ = \ (P/N)((B-A)/A)$$

where:

P = number of people below the poverty line
N = total number of people in society
B = poverty line income
A = average income of those people below the poverty line.

BOX 11.1
Poverty Lines

Poverty lines, based on the way measurements are made, can be broadly classified into two types—absolute poverty lines and relative poverty lines.

Relative poverty line: The relative poverty line, as the name suggests, is based on how individuals or households perceive their position in society as compared to others. It is determined by deciding on a percentage cut-off point in the welfare distribution measured by income or consumption level below which, say, a particular percentage of the population is located.

Absolute poverty line: The absolute poverty line is linked to a specific welfare level. It defines a minimum standard and then calculates the number of percentage of individuals below the specified standard to calculate the poverty line. There are two ways in which the absolute poverty line can be calculated. In the first case we can calculate the set of people whose actual consumption basket is less than the desired consumption basket. This method is known as the direct method of calculating poverty. In the alternate method, known as the income method, researchers can calculate the number of people whose income is less than the specified income that is required to meet basic needs.

The food poverty line: The food poverty line can be easily estimated by using either the least-cost approach or the expenditure-based approach. In the case of the least-cost approach to calculating the food poverty line, first a specific baskets of food items is selected and then calculation is done to see which basket yields the specified caloric minimum at the lowest cost. In the expenditure-based approach to calculating the food poverty line, actual food consumption patterns of some segments of the population are studied. The foods consumed by this group are included in the basket to reach the minimum calorie level, after weighing for food expenditure and quantity.

INEQUALITY MEASURES

LORENTZ CURVE

The Lorentz curve is named after Max O. Lorentz, who first used it as a graphical representation of income inequality.[1] The Lorentz curve depicts observed income distributions and compares this to a state of perfect income equality by plotting percentage of households on the x axis and percentage of incomes on the y axis. It does so by plotting the cumulative percentages of total income received against the cumulative percentages of individuals or households receiving incomes, starting with the poorest individual or household. Nowadays, the Lorentz curve is not only related to measurement of income inequality but is also used extensively to depict social inequality.

The Lorentz curve plots cumulative percentages of incomes against cumulative percentages of individuals or households; hence, at the first stage, the income levels of all the individuals or households are ranked, from the poorest to the richest. Then at the next stage, all of these individuals or households are divided into five quintiles of 20 per cent each, or 10 quintiles of 10 per cent each, depending on the spread of income inequality desired from the graph. After dividing individuals/households in groups, the cumulative percentage of income received by these groups is plotted against the income share of the poorest 20 per cent of the population, and subsequently, the income share of the fourth quintile is plotted against the cumulative 40 per cent of the population, and so on, until the aggregate share of all five quintiles is plotted against cumulative individuals households receiving income (see Figure 11.1).

FIGURE 11.1
Lorentz Curve Showing Income Inequality

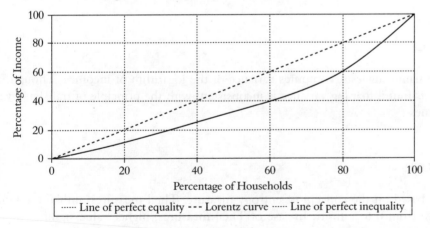

In case of perfect equality, the Lorentz curve would be a straight diagonal line, called the line of equality, signifying that the bottom 20 per cent of individuals or households receive 20 per cent of income, that is, every person has the same income. If there is any inequality in size, then the Lorentz curve falls below the line of equality and a perfectly inequal distribution, by contrast, would be one in which one person has all the income and everyone else has none.

The Gini Coefficient

The Gini coefficient[2], denoted by 'G', is a measure of the extent of inequality, which is calculated from the Lorentz curve. It represents the percentage of area between the line of perfect equality and the Lorentz curve. Let us assume that the area between the line of perfect equality and the Lorentz curve is x, and the area underneath the Lorentz curve is y, then the Gini coefficient for distribution represented by the Lorentz curve would be

$$x/(x+y)$$

It ranges from a minimum value of 0 to a maximum value of 1. A Gini index of 0 per cent represents perfect equality signifying that all individuals are equal. In case of perfect equality, the Lorentz curve coincides with the straight line of absolute equality. A Gini index of 1 implies perfect inequality, that is, all individuals are unequal and the Lorentz curve coincides with the x axis.

The Coefficient of Variation

The coefficient of variance is measured as the standard deviation of the income distribution divided by the mean. The coefficient of variance is Lorentz-consistent.

The Log Variance

Log variance, as the name suggests, computes variance of the logarithm of incomes. Though in certain situations, it is found that log variance is inconsistent with the principle of transfers over some range of incomes.

The Theil Measures

Theil statistics T is based on the concept of entropy measure. Theil measures, unlike the Gini coefficient can range from 0 to infinity. In case of Theil measures, higher value signifies more equal distribution and lower values denote unequal distribution.

THE KUZNETS RATIOS

Kuznets ratios ascertain the share of income owned by x per cent of rich over y per cent of poor. In other words, it measures the ratio of the income of people in the top quintile to those in the bottom quintile.

THE CONCENTRATION INDEX

The Lorentz curve measures income inequality by plotting the cumulative percentage of incomes against the cumulative percentages of individuals or households. The concentration curve follows the same principle and provide a means of quantifying the degree of income-related inequality in a specific health variable. The concentration curve and index are widely used nowadays to depict social and health inequality. The statistical software STATA provides the facility for plotting the concentration curve and also calculating the concentration index.

The concentration curve plots the cumulative percentage of the sample, ranked by living standards on the x axis and plots the corresponding cumulative percentage of the selected health variable for each cumulative percentage of the living standard variable on the y axis. The concentration index is defined with reference to the concentration curve in a similar way as the Gini index is defined in relation to the Lorentz curve. The concentration index is defined as twice the area between the concentration curve and the line of equality. Though the concentration index is calculated in the same way as the Gini coefficient, but unlike the Gini coefficient, it varies between a range of –1 and +1.

The concentration index takes a negative value when the distribution curve of the health variable falls above the diagonal. It takes a positive value when the health variable distribution curve is under the diagonal. Further, in relation to the Gini coefficient, it is important to point out that if the results do not vary due to sorting of socio-economic and health variables, then the concentration index will have the same absolute value as the Gini coefficient. So, in that case, when there is no income-related inequality, the concentration index would be 0.

The concentration index can be used to quantify the degree to which health subsidies are better targeted towards the poor in some countries than others, or the degree to which child mortality is more unequally distributed to the disadvantage of poor children in one country than another, or the extent to which inequalities in adult health are more pronounced in some countries than in others (see Figure 11.2).

After discussing inequality and measures of inequality, the key question to answer is whether equal distribution of incomes is good or bad for a country's development? There are different opinions and views about inequality and its impact on a country's development.

Some researchers argue that an excessively equal income distribution can be bad for economic efficiency and in reference they cite the example of socialist countries, where forced low inequality

FIGURE 11.2
Concentration Curve Showing Ill-health

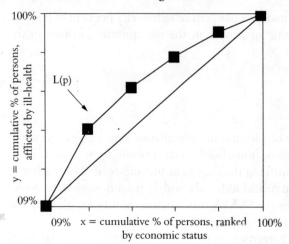

with no private profits killed the entrepreneurial spirit of people and even minimal differences in wages and salaries and lack of incentives for hard work harboured inefficiency among workers. This resulted in poor discipline and low initiative among workers, poor quality of goods and services, slow technical progress and slower economic growth leading to more chronic poverty. But does that mean that excessive inequality is good. Researchers argue against excessive inequality as it adversely affects people's quality of life, leading to a higher incidence of poverty and thus impeding progress in health and education. The majority of researchers agree that excessive inequality rather than equality of assets and income generated by growth results in widespread poverty.

POVERTY

Poverty as a concept is not multidimensional in its construct but also in the ways it manifests itself. Neither poverty nor the poor are same anywhere, they vary greatly in the way they adapt and cope with poverty, in the way they try to break from poverty and in the way they succumb to poverty. But underlying these variations are the common causes, which result in widespread poverty. India since its independence has come a long way in realizing the dream of an equitable society free from poverty, but a lot needs to be done to really fulfill that dream.

Poverty data in India are subject to considerable uncertainty and is measured by expenditure data collected by the Indian National Sample Survey Organization (NSSO) approximately every five years, from a large sample of Indian households. Nevertheless, we stick to the official data to portray the poverty trend across rural and urban area. Table 11.1 shows that poverty has reduced significantly and now stands at 26 per cent. But 27 per cent of the rural population lies below the poverty line. This coupled with the fact that more than 60 per cent of the population lives in the rural area, we can have an idea about the gravity of the situation.

TABLE 11.1
Distribution of Poverty Ratio (rural and urban) 1973–74 to 1999–2000

Year	All India	Rural	Urban
1973–74	54.9	56.4	49.0
1977–78	51.3	53.1	45.2
1983	44.5	45.7	40.8
1987–88	38.9	39.1	38.2
1993–94	36.0	37.3	32.4
1999–2000 (30 day recall)	26.10	27.09	23.62

Source: Economy Survey (2000–2001).

Further, rural poverty in India does not have a uniform face. Many of the poor manage to provide a steady subsistence level of income for themselves and their families. Whereas others, the poorest of the poor are often without any means of livelihood, highlighting the need of broadening livelihood options by strengthen both the farm and non-farm sectors of rural economy.

RURAL ECONOMY

Agrarian economy/rural economy is a resource-driven economy and the majority of poor people are dependent on natural resources for survival. Natural resources determine the course of development, especially in a country like India. The rural economy can be further segmented into the farm sector economy and non-farm sector economy. The next section discusses the characteristics of the farm sector economy, and the non-farm sector economy (which is still at very fledgling stage) is discussed in the section on alternative employment.

FARM SECTOR

Poverty, essentially is a problem of the rural sector as three out of four of India's poor live in rural areas, making it quite evident that the key to reducing poverty in India is agricultural growth, accompanied by strong non-agricultural growth that reaches the rural poor. The agriculture sector provides livelihood to around 70 per cent of the total population and accounts for about 18 per cent share of the total value of the country's exports. It supplies the bulk of wage goods required by the non-agricultural sector and raw materials for a large section of industry. But still marginal farmers owning very small amounts of land and labourers living in rural areas make up the large majority of India's poor.

In a bid understand the basic paradigm of rural poverty, it is imperative to understand the difficulties faced by agriculture to sustain its role of as the major source of livelihood. It is imperative to investigate the failure of agriculture as an economic sector to absorb rural populations, who have to search for livelihoods in urban areas, and reasons why agriculture no longer can fulfill its traditional role.

LAND UTILIZATION AND FOOD PRODUCTION

Agriculture was the mainstay of the Indian economy at the time of independence and the planning process at that time was aimed at improving agricultural production and sustainability. In the 1960s and 1970s, though India adopted the path of industrialization, measures for sustained food production were pushed with vigour. This emphasis led to an agricultural improvement called the Green Revolution followed by other programme such as the public distribution system and price supports for farmers. Today, India is self-sufficient in foodgrain production. Agricultural production today is matched to the food demand of the growing population.

As per available land utilization records, it is estimated that the net sown area has increased considerably over last three decades and as a result production has also increased substantially. It is noteworthy that per capita net availability of foodgrains[3] went up to a level of 467 g per day in 1999–2000 as compared to that of 395 g in the 1950s. To continue with this trend, we need to focus on sustainable agricultural production combined with the judicious use of natural resources. Thus it is imperative to combine natural resources, capital resources, institutional resources and human resources.

It is clear from this discussion that agricultural production has increased substantially over a period of time and has always exceeded the demand. Thus, agriculture production per se is not an area of concern, though equity, efficiency and sustainability of the current agricultural production approach are questionable. To introspect further, we analyse the impact of the marginalization of farmers and unemployment in rural areas on widespread poverty in rural area.

Marginalization of Farmers

The poverty ratio in itself does not reveal the micro-level situation. It also does not reveal the profile of people who are trapped in poverty. Marginalization of farmers coupled with the lack of alternative employment options has contributed in a large way to rural inequality and poverty. Food and Agricultural Organization (FAO) studies have shown that small farms constitute between 60–70 per cent of total farms in developing countries and contribute around 30–35 per cent to total agricultural output (Randhawa and Sundaram, 1990). At the onset of globalization, over 40 per cent of rural households were landless or near landless. Result and studies prove that over time more and more people became landless and shifted to the agriculture labourers and other workers category. Correlating these findings with the poverty ratio and employment figure in the agrarian economy reveals the causal linkage between poverty and environment—natural resource degradation. As though the poverty ratio has declined, the absolute number of people lying below the poverty line has increased and has shown a detrimental effect on workforce composition. Poor people living in abject poverty have been forced to sell agricultural land to become agricultural labourers.

RURAL EMPLOYMENT SCENARIO

Though agriculture constitutes only one-fourth of GDP; it sustains around three-fourth of the population, putting immense pressure on rural economy. The situation is further compounded by the agricultural sector's vulnerability to the vagaries of the monsoon, which causes relatively large fluctuations in the employment scenario from one year to the next. To understand the employment scenario it is necessary to take stock of rural employment and the rural work force involvement scenario. The sector-wise breakdown of the 388 million employed workers in rural areas in 1999–2000 is presented in Table 11.2.

TABLE 11.2
Breakdown of Rural Employment, 1999–2000

Sector	Total Workers (million)	% of Total
Agriculture, animal husbandry, fisheries and forestry	238	60
Unorganized non-agricultural sector	133	33
Organized sector	28	7

Source: Radhakrishna (2002).

As can be seen from the table, employment in the organized sector increased slowly from 24 million in 1983 to 28 million in 1999–2000. But since it is coming close to its saturation point, a major portion of newcomers to the labour force will have to be absorbed in the unorganized agricultural and non-agricultural sectors. Further, the composition of employment, that is, self-employment, regular salaried employment and casual employment has also been changing. The percentage of self-employed people as part of the rural workforce declined from 62 per cent in 1977–78 to 56 per cent in 1999–2000, whereas casual labour showed an increase of 7 percentage point during the same time. Regular employment figures also showed a marginally decline of about 1 percentage point in the same period. (Radhakrishna, 2002).

The problems of widespread poverty, growing inequality, rapid population growth and rising unemployment all find their origins in the stagnation of economic life in rural areas. Non-agricultural rural households are gradually withdrawing from cultivation to look for alternative sources of employment generation. But what is the scope of alternative source of employment generation in the rural sector, which has immense potential to sustain the non-farm sector economy. In the next section we will discuss governmental and non-governmental initiatives for employment generation.

GOVERNMENT'S INITIATIVE TO GENERATE EMPLOYMENT: RURAL DEVELOPMENT SCHEME

The government has made various efforts, especially in rural areas, to provide subsistence income to poor people through a series of anti-poverty programmes. These programmes aim to reduce the vulnerabilities of millions of poor people, who are facing the brunt of acute poverty.

The government felt the need for initiating an anti-poverty programme in the early 1960s and since then it has launched various schemes targeting various marginalized sections of society. Some of the early anti-poverty programmes that focused on generating employment were the

National Rural Employment Programme and the Rural Landless Employment Guarantee Programme. The National Rural Employment Programme, launched in the 1980s, replaced the earlier Food for Work Programme that used unemployed and underemployed workers to build productive community assets.

The Rural Landless Employment Guarantee Programme was also launched in the 1980s to generate rural employment through the construction of rural infrastructure. The programme aimed to provide employment for the rural poor in addition to providing a boost to rural economy. But, like several other programmes, the programme was novel in ideas but poor in their implementation. In order to improve the effectiveness of the National Rural Employment Programme, it was combined with the Rural Landless Employment Guarantee Programme in 1989. This came to be known as the Jawahar Rozgar Yojana.

Besides employment generation programmes, programmes were launched to provide food security, building capacity of labourers and workers, but due to obvious reason none of these programmes has been successful in meeting its targets. One of the key reasons is lack of coordination among various government departments or even between the states and the centre.

State governments are important participants in anti-poverty programmes. In the Indian Constitution, the Directive Principles of State Policy entrusts state governments with the responsibility of providing all basic amenities to their people. State governments implement most of the central government programmes concerned with land reforms or employment generation.

The central government formulates programmes and norms but the implementation is often left to the lower bureaucratic levels, which results in implementation problems. Thus, it is high time that planners thought of a development planning process (see Box 11.2) integrating the different department and ensuring better coordination among the various stakeholders of the project.

BOX 11.2
Development Planning

Development planning has been at the core of the planning process of India. Even the British government before independence, had established a planning board, which formulated development plans. Independent India followed the same path. After independence, the country adopted the formal economic planning process as an effective way to intervene in the economy to foster growth and social justice.

The Planning Commission was established in 1950 and since then development planning has been the key instrument of the development process. The first few five-year plans were based on the Russian model of development planning. The First Five-year Plan (FY 1951–55) emphasized on balanced economic development focusing on agricultural development as the key thrust area. The Second Five-year Plan continued in same way, though it strongly emphasized industrialization in the public sector. The Second Five-year Plan also stressed on the need of generating social goods for the poor ensuring equal distribution of income and by extending the benefits of economic development to the poor and disadvantaged people.

Successive five-year plans also stressed on the need of having people-centric development planning and fostering rural development. But experience has shown that planning has not worked so far and thus actual results are not as per the plan targets.

ALTERNATIVE EMPLOYMENT

It is well established now that the agrarian economy alone cannot provide livelihood to around 70 per cent of the rural populace. Natural resource degradation and population pressure have further compounded the problem for millions of people living on the fringes. The next section discusses (i) credit in rural areas and (ii) sustainable livelihood options available to rural people.

MICROFINANCE

One of the key strategies to help millions of people break the vicious circle of poverty is to provide microfinance to provide impetus to their microentrepreneurial spirit in a way to broaden livelihood options in a sustainable way.

Microfinance or provision of credit facility for poor and disadvantaged communities for self-employment without any collateral is a fast growing phenomenon spreading its roots across all parts of India. The Small Industrial Development Bank of India (SIDBI) defines microfinance as 'provision of financial services delivery to poor women, at their door steps, in a sustainable and profitable manner, which includes loans, savings and insurance products, on time, in user friendly manner at affordable cost to the clients, reaching out in large number of people formed in groups or severally consisting of small value products' (SIDBI, 2000).

Propounded and prophesied by NGOs, microfinance is well supported by the central and state governments as a tool to reduce poverty. In the recent years, a number of microfinance institutions have been catalyzing growth in the non-farm sector economy. Much of the success of microfinance can be credited to innovative lending methodologies, which are specifically developed to cater to large numbers of poor client. These methodologies are backed by strong management efforts to maintain high repayment rates.

Microfinance Institution

A microfinance institution[4] (MFI) is an organization that offers financial and other related services to poor and disadvantaged communities, especially women for self-employment. Most MFIs are NGOs though off late some private companies and banking institutions have also pitched in to support the effort.

Different Lending Modalities

Microfinance derives its strength from different and unique lending methodologies. Their lending approach is different from traditional bank lending, which tends to be based on assets, relying heavily on collateral and guarantees to ensure payments. Microfinance lending, on the other hand, is based on trust and operates without any guarantee. The group selection and loan approval process is based more on willingness and ability of the clients to pay.

The operation of MFIs relies on graduated loan sizes. Initially an MFI provides a small loan to take stock of a group's functioning, dynamics and willingness to pay and larger loans are extended to the group only if the MFI is satisfied with the repayment status and functioning of the group. The group's motivation to repay lies mainly in an implicit option for future services: they expect a long-term relationship with an MFI for larger loans.

Types of Microfinance Lending Methodologies

Microfinance lending methodologies can be roughly divided into two broad models, that is, the individual lending model and the group-based lending model. The majority of MFIs provide group-based lending without collateral, but some MFIs also lend directly to individuals without any sort of guarantees, but the risks are high in the case of individual lending. Thus, individual loans are more likely than group-based loans to require collateral to cover the risks.

Most microfinance institutions use some form of group lending. In the most prevalent model, an MFI ask members to form themselves into small groups of four to six people. Members of the group then start by contributing some of their savings in a small way, and the groups are picked up at a later stage by the MFI for lending. Group lending has a distinctive advantage over the individual lending methodology because in the case of group lending, members can provide cross guarantees for each others loans. This sort of peer pressure and group dynamics adds to the MFI's confidence about receiving repayment of the loan amount.

Groups supported by MFIs, also known as self-help groups, are common in rural areas and are specifically oriented to provide women with employment opportunities. Though these group start on a small scale with an initial group size of five to six and savings of a few hundred to thousand rupees, well-managed and successful groups deal in lending amounts running into lakhs and have 20 to 50 borrowers.

Microfinance: Tool to Reduce Poverty

The key objective of MFIs is much more than just being a loan-disbursing agency. It strives to catalyze societal change to help millions break the vicious circle of poverty in the long term.

Thus it is paramount to assess/determine how well an institution performs financially and operationally, how strong the management team is and in which direction the organization is heading in achieving its objective. Assessments include institutional appraisals, rating exercises and other activities aimed at determining how well an institution performs financially and operationally.

PROMOTION OF SUSTAINABLE LIVELIHOOD OPTIONS

One of the key strategies to help millions of people break the vicious cycle of poverty is to broaden their livelihood options in a sustainable way so that they can receive a stream of income in a sustainable way. Sustainable livelihoods[5] as a strategy encapsulate two broad concepts, 'sustainability' and 'livelihood'.

Sustainability

The definition of sustainability offered by the World Commission on Environment and Development (WCED) is broadly accepted and seems to have intuitive appeal. It defines sustainability as: meeting the needs of the present without compromising the ability of future generations to meet their needs. Sustainability as a concept has two dimensions—those of space and time. The first dimension characterizes optimum utilization of resource and equitable distribution of benefits among stakeholders in the current generation and the second dimension, that of time, means access to resources for future generation.

Livelihood

Livelihood options or entitlement set as conceptualized by Amartya Sen are basically the same concept (see Box 11.3). Diversification of livelihood options aim to affect the livelihood pattern, that is, the nature in which livelihoods needs to be changed, transformed and diversified. The emphasis is on analysing how rural people exercise their entitlement to arrange for livelihood for goods required for a means of living (Sen, 1981).

BOX 11.3
Entitlement Approach by Amartya Sen

According to Amartya Sen, the entitlement approach is built on three interrelated basics (i) the endowment set, (ii) the entitlement set and (iii) the entitlement mapping.

The endowment set is defined as the combination of all resources legally owned by a person. In this definition, resources includes both tangible assets, such as land, equipment and animals, and intangibles such as knowledge and skill, labour power, or membership of a particular community. The entitlement set is defined as the set of all possible combinations of good and services that a person can legally obtain by using the resources of his endowment set. The entitlement mapping is simply the mapping of the endowment set, on one hand, and the entitlement set, on the other.

It is a well-known fact that in rural areas, livelihood options are often determined by natural endowments, availability of land, irrigation facility, rainfall, or proximity to forest goods and probable market. In the case of agricultural livelihood, diversification option depends on availability of natural resource and dependence on natural resource for survival. Thus, pressure on the natural resource base is critical to understanding institutional and technological change and the resultant viability of the livelihood system (Hayami and Kikuchi, 1981; Wiggins, 2000).

Livelihoods analysis may be done at the household level, or may involve pooling together resources of a number of families, such as in an organization or even at the intra-household level and works on three basic premises listed next.

a) *Sustainability, in the long run, should reduce vulnerability:* Sustainable livelihood option, in the long run, should reduce vulnerability. One of the key constructs to measure reduction in vulnerability is increase in income. Respondents are asked about their perceived notion of vulnerability before and after group formation to assess whether broadening of livelihood option has resulted in reduction of vulnerabilities.

b) *Broadening of the security net and improvement in the quality of life is integral to the goal of sustainable livelihood:* Foremost in the conduct of many livelihood projects is the target of increasing income. However, it is a fact that the sustenance of life is not merely financial or economic, but involves building and maintaining social networks, stretching support systems and accessing public goods and services. Thus, sustainable livelihood interventions must target not only increasing incomes or expanding financial opportunities, but also assure that the basic necessities of a healthy, decent and secure standard of living are met. During the exercise, respondents/participants will be probed on the issue of perceived basic needs of the households and achieving an 'average' quality of life to assess whether the intervention has widened the security net.

c) *Changes in the quality of life and reduction in vulnerability shall ultimately lead to empowerment:* Livelihood choices are determined by factors such as economic status and access to credit and other resources. Social relations, norms and patterns of relationships shape the livelihood strategies possible at a household level or within the household. Sustainable livelihood interventions will usher in new kinds of relations, or transform and challenge existing ones.

NOTES

1. Lorentz curve can also be used to measure inequality of assets or other distributions.
2. The Gini coefficient is a measure of income inequality developed by the Italian statistician Corrado Gini.
3. There are three main crop seasons, namely, kharif, rabi and summer. The major kharif crops are rice, jowar, bajra, maize, cotton, sugarcane, sesame and groundnut. The major rabi crops are wheat, jowar, barley, gram, linseed, rapeseed and mustard. Rice, maize and groundnut are grown in the summer season also.
4. Different legal forms of microfinance institutions are trusts, private or charitable, societies, Section 25 companies, companies other than those under Section 25, co-operative banks, local area banks licensed by the Reserve Bank of India, banking companies licensed and treated as a scheduled bank by the RBI, informal bodies such as self-help groups, village-level organizations, federations, etc.
5. Besides assessing the options available for sustainable livelihood, data shall be analysed in such a way as to have an idea of the vulnerabilities. Vulnerability assessment frames the external environment in which people exist. People's livelihoods and the wider availability of assets are fundamentally affected by critical trends as well as by shocks and seasonality over which they have limited, or no control.

CHAPTER 12

ENVIRONMENT AND NATURAL RESOURCE MANAGEMENT

India has made considerable progress, since independence, in the areas of food security, industrial development and energy generation and to some extent even in socio-economic conditions. However, issues pertaining to environment and natural resource management remain unnoticed and hence unsolved. Developing countries, especially India, today face an uphill task of conserving natural and environmental resources amidst rapid population growth and environment degradation. Environmental degradation and depletion of natural resources not only threatens the resource base but is also a serious cause for concern for the millions of people who are dependent on natural resources for their livelihoods. It is high time that a concerted approach linking issues related to poverty, health, development and environmental concerns is devised to counter threats to the natural resource base. This chapter, which is divided into two sections, tries to explore the linkage between various facets of the environment and to establish linkages with poverty, health and development. The first section explores basic environmental concepts and tries to explain the link between environment, poverty and health, while the second section explores the link between development and growth.

PART I

The following section lists the priority issues pertaining to the environment in areas of (i) natural resources (ii) biodiversity conservation (iii) pollution (air and water pollution), and (iv) waste management.

THE NATURAL RESOURCES SCENARIO

The existence or absence of favourable natural resources can facilitate or retard the process of economic development. Natural resources determine the course of development, especially in a country like India. In order to embark on a programme of economic development, it is imperative to concentrate on the development of locally-available natural resources as an initial condition for lifting the local levels of living and purchasing power and for setting in motion the development process.

Natural resources, in its broadest sense, includes water, air, atmosphere and land, but when we speak in terms of livelihood, agriculture and forest are the two major uses of land that determine the livelihood patterns of millions of poor people. In India, the population has grown from 361 million in 1951 to more than a billion and under this burgeoning pressure of population, the area under agriculture has increased from 118 mha in 1951 to more than 150 mha at present putting enormous pressure on the country's natural resources. Even today, natural assets are of the utmost importance as often they are the only source of livelihood for the poor.

Degradation of natural resources, characterized by deforestation, contributing to the loss of precious topsoil, soil erosion and flood irrigation that lead to salinity and water logging, excessive use of chemical fertilizers, insecticides and pesticides has rendered more than 13 mha of irrigated land unfit for agriculture and another 125 mha is estimated to be generally degraded. Thus, in today's scenario, beside conservation, it is necessary to actually invest in the regeneration of natural capital, making it amply clear that natural capital holds the key to curb poverty to provide sustainable livelihoods. Essentially, the first step in the economic uplift of the poorest of the poor is to ensure that they have the capacity to rebuild and regenerate natural resources on which their livelihoods depends.

AGRICULTURE

Agriculture forms the mainstay of India's rural economy and though it contributes only a quarter to India's GDP, it supports more than 60 per cent of the populace. Ownership of land is an important determinant of livelihood among rural households. In India, for example, the average size of an operational holding had already declined from 2.5 ha in 1961 to 1.82 ha in 1981, and is even lower today. Studies by the FAO have shown that small farms constitute between 60–70 per cent of the total farms in developing countries and contribute around 30–35 per cent to total agricultural output (Randhawa and Sundaram, 1990) and India is no exception. The average holding in the mid-1990s was about 1.5 ha and about half the land in India is cultivated by farmers owning more than 4 ha and only few farms are larger than 20 ha because of limited land reforms.

The Green Revolution played an important part in spurring agricultural growth by using high-yielding crop varieties, fertilizers and carefully managed irrigation, but its benefits were limited to only certain sections of farmers in northern India.

India is one of the world's largest food producers with an annual production of around 600 million tonnes. India's most important crops include sugarcane, rice, wheat, tea, cotton and jute as well as cashews, coffee, oilseeds, and spices.[1] Milk production and distribution increased dramatically in the 1990s because of a nationwide, government-supported cooperative dairy programme.

It is necessary to ensure that new initiatives such as agribusiness, food processing, contract farming and export-oriented policies[2]/vision are pushed forward to unleash the potential of the agriculture sector to realize the dream of providing sustainable livelihood options to more than three-fifths of the population, which is dependent on agriculture.

FOREST

The total forest cover of the country according to an assessment made in 2001 is 675,538 km^2 and this constitutes 20.55 per cent of the geographic area of the country. Out of this, 416,809 km^2 (or 12.68 per cent) is dense forest cover while 258,729 km^2 (or 7.87 per cent) is open forest. The non-forest area includes scrubs estimated to cover an area of 47,318 km^2.

The National Forest Policy, 1998, envisages bringing one-third of the geographical area of the country under forest/tree cover to maintain ecological balance and environmental stability. It is unlikely to happen as agriculture land would not be available for the expansion of forest cover. It is only the 'culturable wasteland' and part of the 'fallow land and other than current fallows' which seems to be the potential areas on which forest cover can be expanded through afforestation.

According to The State of Forest Report, 1997, India's total forest cover has dropped from 63.96 mha during the period 1991–93 to 63.34 mha during the period 1993–1995 and remained so in year 1997 (see Figure 12.1). Though, according to a 1999 assessment, the total forest cover was 637,293 km^2 (dense forest cover:[3] 377,358 km^2, open forest: 255,064 km^2, mangroves: 4,871 km^2) while in the year 2001 it has been estimated as 675,538 km^2 (dense forest: 416,809 km^2, open forest: 258,729 km^2). Comparison of the two assessments show an overall increase of 38,245 km^2 or 6.0 per cent in the forest cover of the country.

Forests play a very important part in the lives of millions of poor as it determines their livelihood and income. It is the dependence of the poor people on forests for their survival that has triggered the need of having a people-centric approach to forest management in the form of the Joint Forest Management (JFM) and Sustainable Forest Management (SFM) programmes.

FIGURE 12.1
Status of Forest Cover in India

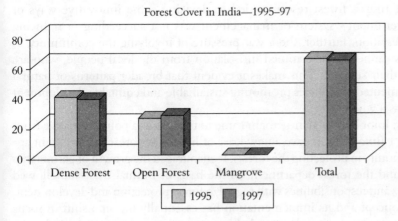

Forest Management: From JFM to SFM

It is true that only a fraction of the world's natural forests are managed in ways which allow current yields of all goods and services to be sustained and as a result the overall trend remains towards deforestation. Any long-term deforestation trend has worrying ecological consequences, and in a country like India it also triggers loss of employment and income for rural settlements.

The forest cover of the country has been estimated to be 675,538 km^2, which is 20.6 per cent of the geographical area of the country. Among the states, Madhya Pradesh accounts for 20.68 per cent of the forest cover of the country followed by Arunachal Pradesh (10.80 per cent), Orissa (7.38 per cent), Mahrashtra (7.32 per cent) and Andhra Pradesh (6.94 per cent) (The State of Forest Report, 2001).

India's forest cover is under tremendous pressure from growing demand for fuel, fodder, grazing, timber and non-wood forest produce from an increasing human and livestock population, prompting us to realize the need of sustainable forestry.

The actual uses of the forests have tended to reflect the economic[4] and political powers of particular forest stakeholders, and their support from government agencies and policies. They also reflect beliefs, policies and political intentions that express how society wants to organize itself, divide its wealth, consume the products of wealth and embark on what it believes are the best paths for development.

Forests form an inseparable part of the lives of millions of people who live in proximity of forests and hence there has always been clashes between the forest department and people living around forest about ownership of the forests. More importantly, clashes tend to have more to do with the various forest goods and ownership as management[5]/ownership of forest is also a serious issue. It is beyond doubt that forest management regime in a way defines the boundary between the public functions of forests and private benefits, highlighting the need of a management regime, which can resolve the issue of private benefits and ownership.

Joint Forest Management

The increasing depletion of India's forest resources led to devising some innovative ways of managing forests as the government's system of management was not succeeding in reducing forest degradation and deforestation. Further, there was pressure of involving the community, as forest conservation priorities cannot be determined in isolation from the local people, who are dependent on the forest for their survival. This makes it evident that broader patterns of natural resource use must be complimented by policies promoting sustainable and equitable development of the natural resource base as a whole.

In response to these issues, Joint Forest Management came to the fore as a policy initiative from the Government of India on 1 June 1990. It gave a new lease of life to the forest management approach by involving the community in protecting the forests. It encouraged the growth of partnership between forest user groups and the forest department on the basis of mutual trust and allowed them to jointly define the roles and responsibilities with regard to forest protection and development. The evolution of the JFM concept and its implementation has essentially meant a shift in focus with the objectives of managing forests. People's needs have now taken centre stage. Under the JFM programme, the government encourages participation from people living on the fringes of forests in managing forests in their proximity and in return the government allow them the right to collect, use or sell most of the non-timber forest produce (NTFP) and receive a percentage share of the final timber harvest.

Sustainable Forest Management (SFM)

Sustainable forest management as a concept is considered by many as new wine in an old bottle. It talks of the principle of sustainable forestry but with an added emphasis on developing broad consensus on principles, guidelines, criteria and indicators for sustainable forest management on an international governmental level. It talks of forest certification issues wherein each country shall develop, in a broad multi-stakeholder process, its own national standard for sustainable forest management based on the agreed guidelines.[6]

BIODIVERSITY CONSERVATION

India is known not only for its rich and varied cultural heritage but also for its rich and varied bio-diversity. India is one of the 12-mega centres of biodiversity having over 45,000 plants and 65,000 animal species. India also has an abundance of wild varieties of food crops, cereals, leguminous crops, vegetables, oil seeds and spices, but around 60 of the 250 wild crop relatives in India are either rare or threatened. It is high time that the value of biodiversity resource is realized as resources once lost cannot be replaced at any cost.

The government has tried various innovative approaches and has invested a lot for the conservation of threatened animal species, but still poaching present a major threat. Biodiversity conservation cannot be an act in isolation; a lot needs to be done to promote biodiversity conservation. Conservation of biodiversity is both an investment and an insurance to build the genetic pool to improve production of natural resources.

AIR QUALITY

The WHO has rated Delhi as the fourth-most polluted city in the world. Delhi is not the only polluted city, pollution levels are just as high in other metropolitan cities in the country. It is all due to ineffective air quality/environmental management system. Heavy industrial growth coupled with an unprecedented spurt in the number of vehicles is the key factor that contributes to the deteriorating quality of air in urban India.

It is a well-known fact that outdated and inefficient refining processes in India are largely responsible for high vehicular emissions and it is no surprise that diesel in India contains very high levels of sulphur as compared to diesel available in developed countries. Though initiatives such as the introduction of compressed natural gas (CNG) vehicles in Delhi have contributed to an improvement in air quality, such efforts need to be replicated with vigour in other parts of the country as well.

Further, the focus so far has only been on a few pollutants such as sulphur dioxide, nitrogen oxides and suspended particulate matter. Other harmful pollutants also need to checked upon on a regular basis. Besides this we need to have an enforcing mechanism for enforcing punitive charges against polluters, otherwise the whole effort would be nothing more than academic exercise.

WATER QUALITY

Increasing industrialization and urbanization has severely affected water quality. There are various factors that affect water quality such as water quality degradation due to discharge of agro-chemicals into waters, industrial and domestic pollution, groundwater depletion, soil salinization and siltation. Water quality is also affected by an overdose of pesticides and fertilizers in the soil. While some of these may become inert over a period of time, traces end up in the closest water body in the form of irrigation or monsoon run-offs.

The gravest danger of water contamination is posed by fertilizer wastes and industrial effluents, as they pollute rivers and rivers are the primary source of drinking water. Despite the Ganga Action Plan (GAP), the bulk of fertilizer waste and industrial effluents still enter the river without being treated and the condition has not improved considerably after the initiation of the plan.

Thus, the problem persists not only due to scarcity of water but also due to poor quality of water and in both cases, it is the poor and disadvantaged people who face the brunt of the problem. The problem is compounded further by the prevalence of water-borne diseases. Controlling wastage and pollution and providing clean and safe drinking water has emerged as a major challenge, especially in rural areas and the time has come to consider water not only as social good but also as an economic good.

UNDERSTANDING LINKAGES AND REASONS

The environment affects every realm of life in some way or the other and it is no surprise that it has major effects on the health, poverty and development prospect of people, especially the poor. The various linkages between environmental management and other aspect of development need to be assessed and looked into to have a better understanding of how to devise strategies to ensure the health of the people and reduce poverty.

ENVIRONMENT AND POVERTY

In India, poverty is officially linked to a nutritional baseline measured in calories (food energy method). These poverty lines correspond to a total household per capita expenditure sufficient to provide a daily intake of 2,400 calories per person in rural areas and 2,100 in urban areas. Despite splendid achievements, India is still among the poorest nations in the world in per capita terms. It has managed to reduced poverty over that period, but only since 1975 the decline has become fairly steady.

Poverty, whether it is rural or urban does not have a uniform face and varies considerably across geographical regions and affects various realms of life. Whilst the link between poverty and other socio-economic conditions are clearly established and debated, important dimensions of rural poverty and scarcity of natural resources are often missed out. It is imperative that all dimensions related to rural poverty and its link with environmental degradation[7] are discussed as majority of the rural people depend on natural resources for their survival. In this scenario, it is imperative that models of truly sustainable development take into account the equality of opportunities for all section of society especially the disadvantaged and poor communities, who depend on natural resources for their livelihood. Community mobilization and participation of poor people should be the defining model as they are the worst affected.

Whilst the link between the social, economic and environmental dimensions of sustainable development are clearly acknowledged and studied, it is imperative that aspects of these linkages are carried forward into integrated development programmes. The reason for this incoherent approach is that despite the linkage of poverty and environmental concerns at the level of macro policy, at local level there is lack of consensus that the interests of the poor and of the environment are mutually compatible.

It is a well-known fact that unequal access to basic necessities and other environmental resources are the foundation of relative poverty, especially in a resource-driven economy. In addition to being excluded from access to natural resources, the poor are also most likely to be subjected to the degrading or polluting impacts of the consumption patterns of others. All of these are directly associated with worsening health profiles and morbidity levels amongst the poorer populations.

Poor people are often not concerned about the need to have a sustainable natural resource base as their immediate concern is to arrange a livelihood for themselves, housing and clothing for their children and care in their old age. Thus, both production and consumption of the natural resource base is determined by immediate needs rather than a consideration of their longer-term impact. Thus, often poor people adopt methods, which are unsuitable and even illegal. It is high time that alternative employment generation options are made available to the poor for their sustenance and livelihood so that they do not fall into the poverty trap and do not resort to unsustainable actions.

It is not that poor people are not attracted to environmentally-sustainable activities. They are conscious of the fact that sustainable use of resources would benefit them in the long term. But, chronic poverty, hunger and lack of social and political voice, prompts them to opt for a myopic view. In order to make them more accountable towards sustainable resource usage, significant changes needs to be made in the current distribution of resources and power, including gender relations in households and in the community. The challenge for the promoters of sustainable development is to involve all stakeholders' especially the poor and disadvantaged people to make them accountable for sustainable resource production and consumption.

HYPOTHESIS RELATING NATURAL RESOURCE DEGRADATION AND POVERTY

The two popular beliefs/hypotheses discussed widely by researcher is assessed next.

The first hypothesis states that poverty and the environment are linked in a downward spiral in which poor people are compelled by the situation to overexploit environmental resources for their livelihood. As a result, they are further affected by degradation of these resources.

According to the second hypothesis, poverty should be the first priority, especially in developing countries, before taking up the cause of environmental protection.

Environment and Health

Sustainable development nowadays is the buzzword in the environment and development scenario. Researchers have argued in detail about the domain and linkages between different components/facets of sustainable development. Some areas and linkages have received more emphasis whereas some areas have been left untouched.

Environment and health is one such area. Changes in the environment are affecting health and already the majority of the population in developing countries are attempting to survive in deteriorating environmental conditions. The majority of the poor and disadvantaged people are not able to adapt to such circumstances, while others are forced to do so. This is the antithesis of sustainable development. The ultimate objective of sustainable development can only be achieved if rudiments of basic environmental health interventions are ensured even to the poorest of the poor, who lack the most basic sanitary necessities.

It is imperative at this point to differentiate between the concept of 'environmental health' and the health consequences of socio-economic development. 'Environmental health' signifies the efforts and initiatives specifically undertaken to make the environment more conducive to human health wherein health consequences of development include effects of environmental degradation due to development processes such as deforestation, urbanization, irrigation, which are also defined as side effects of social and development changes.

It is shameful that even today a substantial portion of the world population does not have access to basic environmental conditions. They lack adequate supply of safe domestic water and adequate facilities for the disposal of human wastes. Further, they are exposed to pollutants such as lead, industrial effluents and pesticides, unprotected food and indoor air pollution from cooking fuels. Provision of these basic facilities for all must be a preliminary to sustainable development.

Researchers have been trying for a very long time to draw attention to the direct and indirect health consequences of these developments and to persuade policy-makers and implementing organizations to insist on adequate provisions to limit the adverse health effects. In a bid to explore the issue further, the next section tries to understand the link between environmental health and health effects caused by environmental change.

ENVIRONMENT HEALTH: CONCEPT

Environmental health can be broadly defined as activities to prevent health risks through control of human exposure to: (i) biological agents, such as bacteria and virus, (ii) chemical agents such as suspended particulate matter, pesticides, and fertilizers, (iii) disease carriers, such as mosquitoes and (iv) physical and safety hazards, such as traffic accidents and fires. The WHO does not include traffic accidents and disease carriers in its definition (Listorti and Doumani, 2001). In such a situation, it is imperative to set priorities to devise ways to measure the magnitude of the problems and some tools to measure the level of improvement due to interventions.

Disability-adjusted Life Years (DALYs)

Disability-adjusted life years is defined as a measure of the burden of disease inflicted on human beings due to the environment. It takes into account the life years lost due to premature death and life years lost because of illness or disability. Thus, while combining the total life years lost, researchers use a weighting function to assign different social weights for life years lost due to illness and premature mortality at different ages. The combination produces the result, which shows the pattern of DALY lost by a death at each age.

Air Pollution and Health

It is a know and established fact that health problems result from changes in the environment. At least a million deaths in India occur every year because of rampant water pollution and air pollution.

The conditions are much worse in metropolitan cities like Mumbai, Kolkata and Delhi, where cases of hospital admissions and sickness requiring medical treatment due to air pollution have increased sharply during the last decade. The main reason is the presence of suspended particulate matter (SPM) in the air. (Suspended particulates refer to smoke, soot, and dust, which remains suspended in the air.) Particulate levels[8] indicate the air quality that people are forced to breathe and the current state of a country's technology and pollution controls (see Table 12.1).

TABLE 12.1
Status of Suspended Particles

City	Total Population	Total Suspended Particles
Bombay	15,138	240
Calcutta	11, 923	375
Delhi	9,948	415

Source: Centre of Science and Environment. *State of India's Environment: The Citizens Fifth Report, Part I: National Overview.* New Delhi: Centre for Science and Environment. October 2002 (reprint).

The key questions that need to be answered are (i) what are the sources of SPM and (ii) why are we not able to control pollutants levels. Suspended particulate matter is a result of outputs from industrial units and auto emissions. It is important to point out that particulate matter less than 10 micrometers in diameter (PM10) and particulate matter less than 2.5 micrometres in diameter (PM2.5) can penetrate the lungs very easily and are quite detrimental to human health.

Climate Change and Human Health

Global climate change affects health in many ways and its effects are beginning to be seen everywhere. This includes both direct and indirect affects like illness due to increased temperatures and impact on health due to air pollution respectively.

Climate change has resulted in wide season fluctuation, which results in increased water-borne and vector-borne disease. The impact of global climate change is not the same everywhere in the world, as some countries fare worse than others. The problem is compounded by the fact that some of the countries that are worst affected are not even prepared to deal with issues such as global climate change and health.

Understanding the Causal Relationship

The causal relationship between environment and its health impact needs to be analysed in detail, especially in a country like India, where millions are dying slowly due to various environment-related causes. There are various studies that have revealed that water and sanitation quality is closely related to child survival and child malnutrition problems. But no study seems to have studied the integrated impact of the environment on health.

It is important to remember the complex interactions between health outcomes and factors such as water supply. For example, access to safe water may affect a mother's choices about breast-feeding. If water is available, she may choose either not to breastfeed or to breastfeed for a shorter period of time. Hence, health interventions need to anticipate behavioural responses to changes in infrastructure and may need to combine such measures with a health education component.

It is important to point out that health benefits from improving the quality of drinking water are less visible than those from sanitation (Klees et al., 1999). Improved sanitation is the first step towards health and benefits from water occur only if sanitary conditions are up to the mark. Further, even in the case of water, quality is an important consideration once optimal quantity of water is ensured. Increases in water quantity do more to improve health than improvements in water quality, because of the improved hygiene that goes along with it. Hygiene education is often required, though, before communities can realize the potential health benefits (Klees et al., 1999).

Small measures such as washing hands can go a long way in reducing incidents of water-borne diseases. This has been corroborated through analysis of 144 water and sanitation interventions worldwide, which revealed that improved water and sanitation services were associated with a median reduction of 22 per cent in diarrhoeal incidences and 65 per cent in deaths from diarrhoea. Improved excreta disposal and hand washing can reduce under-five mortality rates by 60 per cent, cases of schistosomiasis by 77 per cent, intestinal worms by 29 per cent and trachoma by 27–50 per cent (Esrey et al., 1988b).

Development Consequences and Health

Environmental health and the health consequences of socio-economic development are two different concepts. Environment health emphasizes on understanding and correlating environment. The next section is pivoted around the underlying approach of understanding the effect of change in socio-economic development, that is, growth and trade on health.

Health Impacts of Trade Liberalization

There is consensus on the relationship of environment and health but the linkage between trade, development and health still needs to be analysed. It is widely argued by a section of economists that trade liberalization would help poor countries in utilizing their capacities and hidden potential and help them catch up with rich countries, thus alleviating poverty and improving health. There are, however, large sections of economists, who feel quite the opposite and suggest that trade liberalization is dragging millions of poor people into conditions far worse than that they were in earlier.

They argue that trade liberalization has led to the erosion of hard-won health and environmental standards. They indicate that liberalization would result in shifts of public services into private control with little regulation and an increase of income inequalities.

ENVIRONMENT KUZNETS CURVE: LEARNING AND SPECIFICATION FOR INDIA

Simon Kuznets tried to correlate the prevalent environment conditions and economic growth in his presidential address in December 1954 on 'Economic Growth and Income Inequality'. According to Kuznets, as per capita income increases, income inequality also increases at first but after some point, it starts declining (Kuznets, 1955: 23–24).

Over the years, Kuznets curve has been widely accepted as an instrument for describing the relationship between environmental quality and per capita income of a country or region. The environmental Kuznets curve (EKC) follows an intuitive logic, based on the premise that initially pollution conditions worsen because of economic growth led by heavy industrialization but conditions improve as economies become rich. This has come to be known as the environmental Kuznets curve (EKC)[9] hypothesis.

The EKC is also referred as the 'inverted U' relationship between the level of economic development and the degree of income inequality. This relationship and its importance was realized due to a World Bank World Development Report (1992), which debated the cause for such regularity in environmental quality and the merits of the evidence.

The EKC relationship indicates that with development and industrialization, exploitation of natural resources has increased significantly, resulting in damage to environmental resources. But despite the alarming signals, the world is still operating on less efficient and relatively dirty technologies coupled with the fact that high priority is given to increasing material output while the environmental consequences of growth are usually neglected.

But as economic growth continues and life expectancies increase, cleaner water, improved air quality and a cleaner living place becomes more valuable to people. A study conducted by Munasinghe also substantiated that cleaner technology and a shift to information and service base activities coupled with a willingness to enhance environmental quality would bring a turning point in environmental resource quality (Munasinghe, 1999).

Methodologies: Environment Kuznets Curve

Though the EKC hypothesis was the work of Simon Kuznets, it came to the fore through an influential paper (1995) by Princeton's Gene Grossman and Alan Krueger. They analysed the water pollutants and air pollutants situation between the late 1970s and late 1980s. Their pioneering study involved measuring levels of 14 different water and air pollutants at multiple locations in 66 countries.

After analysis, they concluded that there was an inverted U relationship between a country's income and the levels of air and water pollutants. It was observed that relatively low and high levels of income are associated with relatively low levels of pollution, whereas pollution tends to be highest at intermediate income levels.

Grossman and Krueger after testing a structural model of the determinants of pollution concluded that a poor underdeveloped country does not contribute substantially to increased pollution. However, as a country develops economically, pollution grows due to increased industrial activity. Pollution continues to grow till the pollution problem becomes bad enough to spur collective action to control pollution. At the same time, incomes rise enough for residents to be prepared to pay for pollution abatement technologies. Simultaneously, there is a shift toward low-polluting products and as a result, pollution falls as income grows.

In terms of the notation used in the paper, the specification used by Grossman and Krueger (1995) are given next:

I = measurement station
P_{it} = measure of pollution level at that station
Y_{it} = per capita GDP of the country in which the station is located
$Y_{it}-$ = average GDP per capita over the prior three years

P_{it} = $\gamma_{it}\beta_1 + \gamma_{it}^2\beta_2 + \gamma_{it}^3\beta_4 + \bar{\gamma}_{it-}\beta_4 + \bar{\gamma}_{it-}^2\beta_5 + \bar{\gamma}_{it-}^3\beta_6 + X'_{it}\beta_7 + \varepsilon_{it}$

X_{it} = a vector of covariates

Grossman and Kruger's specification was modified later by Bradford, Schlieckert and Shore, who proposed that pollution level is a function of two key economic indicators of a country, namely, income level (y) and growth rate (g) reduced to single numbers. They argued that increase in the pollution rate depends on income level and growth rate of a country.

Building on the hypothesis, Bradford, Schlieckert and Shore arrived at the alternative functional form, based on the premise that if the Kuznets curve phenomenon exists then it might relate more to the long-term growth trends in countries at different levels of development than to year-to-year variations in income. This led them to the following schematic model:

$dP/dt = \alpha (y - y*)g$

P refers to the mean level of pollutant at a particular location
y and g are the income level and economic rate of growth, respectively
t signifies the reference time period
α and $y*$ are constants.

For the cross-sectional estimation of the parameters of the mentioned equation, they, in effect, integrate it to obtain change in pollution levels as a function of growth.

$$P = \alpha\,(\gamma - \gamma^*)gt + \beta$$

The equation describes a locally linear relationship between pollution and income level and growth over a period of time at a specific location.

The trend rate of increase in pollution depends upon the level of development of the country in which the measuring station is located and the rate of growth, g, of that country's economy. If α is less than 0 and γ greater than γ^*, then pollution decreases with increase in economic growth of a country. Further, if γ is less than γ^*, then pollution increases with an increase in economic growth in a country. Thus, if a country's economic growth rate is negative, pollution would decrease if the country is poor and would increase if the country is rich.

It has been established through research that though economic growth is important, to be effective it should be accompanied with institutional reform. Further, improvement of the environment with income growth depends on policies formulated and effective implementation by institutions.

If economic growth is complemented by effective institutional mechanism, then GDP growth creates the conditions for better environmental improvement by raising the demand for improved environmental quality. The institutional arrangement in the case of forests shows that joint forest management and social awareness has helped a lot in sustaining the forest cover. Whereas, in the case of air and water pollution, no effective institutional arrangement has taken shape. Moreover, the issue of forming networks, social capital, awareness and willingness to pay for better environmental quality also comes into play

IMPACT ASSESSMENT, MANAGEMENT AND VALUATION

In a bid to assess the state of the environment at the national, sub-regional, and regional levels it is necessary to have a system in place for environmental assessment, valuation and monitoring. The objectives of impact assessment and valuation are to have an understanding of environmental trends and conditions and to provide a foundation for improved decision-making at all levels and to facilitate the measurement of progress towards sustainability.

ENVIRONMENTAL IMPACT ASSESSMENT

Environmental impact assessment[10] (EIA) process is a method, which is used widely to predict the environ-mental consequences of a decision to introduce legislation, to implement policies and plans, or to undertake development projects.

The environment impact assessment methodology has also been modified and applied in other sectors such as health impact assessment and social impact assessment. Of late, the emphasis has been on cumulative effects assessment and strategic environmental assessment (which tracks environmental assessment at the policy and programme level). Sometimes, environmental assessment is used as broader term for various approaches. In some cases, social and economic impacts are also assessed as part of the assessment, though in other cases, these issues are considered separately. It is important to point out here that the term environmental audit, often used along with environment assessment, is applied to the voluntary regulation of an organization's practices in relation to predetermined measures of environmental impact.

Environment impact assessments typically consist of a sequence of steps, which start with the screening of a project to decide if a project requires assessment and if so then to what level of detail. After screening, a preliminary assessment is done to identify key impacts, their magnitude and importance. Then, at the next stage, scooping is done to ensure that the environment impact assessment focuses on key issues to determine the area where more detailed information is required and at the last stage, detailed investigations are done to predict and/or assess impacts.

In a nutshell, the process usually encompasses examining alternative options, proposing mitigatory measures and based on options and mitigatory measures, makes recommendations in the form of a report, often called an environmental impact statement. After finishing a project, a post audit is done to determine the accuracy of the EIA predictions vis-à-vis the observed/real impacts. Nowadays, there is a growing interest among industrialist to have an assessment of the environmental situation, which can immensely help in setting performance targets, particularly with regard to waste disposal and energy use.

ENVIRONMENT MANAGEMENT SYSTEM

Growing environmental concerns and pressure from the community have resulted in affirmative government action in formulating stringent laws to minimize land, water and air pollution. These laws and regulations are backed by severe penalties on organizations and managements that break the laws. These laws and regulation are encapsulated in the form of an Environment Management System, which provides guidelines through ISO (International Organization for Standardization) rules for managing business entities without affecting the environment adversely.

The ISO14000 provides a framework for organizations to establish laws in a legal sense for management responsibility towards the environment. It is a group of standards encompassing Environmental Management Systems (14001, 14002, 14004), Environmental Auditing (14010, 14011, 14012), Evaluation of Environmental Performance (14031), Environmental Labelling (14020, 14021, 14022, 14023, 14024, 14025) and Life-cycle Assessment (14040, 14041, 14042, 14043).

In fact, ISO 14001 is the only standard intended for registration by third parties and all others are for guidance. The underlying purpose of ISO 14001 is that companies will improve their environmental performance by implementing ISO 14001, but there are no standards for performance or the level of improvement. It is a process for managing company activities that impact the environment. Some unique and important characteristics of ISO 14001 are:

a) Environment management system states that all members of the organization shall participate in environmental protection.
b) It focuses on forward thinking and action instead of reacting to command and control policies.

c) Its emphasis is on improving environmental protection by using a single management system across all functions and echelons of the organization.

Environmental management systems provide a framework for organizations that aspire to manage their environmental affairs. It envisages to establish a link between business and environmental management for all the companies regardless of their turnover, size or area of operation. It provides the industrial sector with a system, which can help them track, manage and improve environmental performances, without conflicting with their business priorities or operations.

Implementing an Environment Management System

After agreement on the release of international standards for the implementation and auditing of environmental management systems—the ISO14000 series—there is now a recognized, comprehensive and auditable basis for companies and organizations around the world to put in place and to measure their environmental performance against an agreed international benchmark. Organizations may use the ISO14001 as a standard or blueprint to implement and audit their environment management systems.

In a nutshell, EMS involves three basic steps: first, to measure the existence level of adherence; second, to identify the gaps; and finally implementation of environmental strategy/policy as per the gap analysis.

Measure the Existence Level

The first step is to measure the existence level, that is, to measures the status quo of environmental indicators formulated in company's environmental policy. Though the answer is simple it depends on clarity of objectives set and statistical procedure and mathematical programming used in measuring the current level of environment indicators.

Identify the Gaps

Gap analysis will help in identifying the areas that need improvements by analysing existing levels of environment indicators vis-à-vis the standards laid down in ISO 14000.

Implementation

Implementation consists of the following:

a) Effective implementation strategies.
b) Planning and executing process improvement projects.
c) Getting the most out of your Management Information System (MIS).
d) Integrating quality, safety and environmental management and other business systems.

ENVIRONMENTAL VALUATION

Environmental degradation and depletion of natural resources not only threatens the extinction of the resource base but also poses a serious challenge to millions of people who depend on natural resources for their survival. Thus, it is imperative to understand the importance of natural and environmental resources to thwart extinction of the resource base. Economic valuation ascertains value of natural resources and reveals the true cost of using up scarce environmental resources. It can help in the decision-making process and policy formulation to minimize pollution of land, water and air and can ensure that the principle of sustainable development is followed as a pragmatic approach not as theoretical concept.

The economic approach involves the monetary valuation of changes in environmental quality. The valuation task is to determine how much better or worse off individuals are as a result of a change in environmental quality. Total economic value ascertains the monetary measure of a change in an individual's well-being due to change in environmental quality. It is not environmental quality that is being measured. It is people's preferences for changes in that quality which is assessed.

Total economic value of a resource can be disaggregated into constituent parts consisting of use value (UV) and non-use value (NUV). Use values can be further segregated into (i) direct use value, (ii) indirect use value and (iii) option value. Direct use values though are straightforward in concept but they are not necessarily easy to measure in economic terms.

Indirect use value is based on the relationship of demand of a marketed good and supply of environmental goods. Now from this assumption, valuation for non-marketed good is obtained by collecting data on how demand of marketed good changes with the availability of environment resources. For example, a forest helps in protecting watersheds and thus removing forest cover may result in water pollution and siltation. Option values signify the amount individuals would be willing to pay to conserve a resource for future use. It is, therefore, also defined as an insurance premium to ensure the supply of resource benefit for future use.

Non-use values is not only difficult to define but also to measure. Non-use values can be further segregated into (i) existence value, which measure willingness-to-pay for a resource for some attachment, affiliation or other reason and is unrelated to use or option value and (ii) bequest value (BV) which measures an individual's willingness-to-pay to ensure that their future generations can use resources in the future.

Total economic value can be expressed as:

$$TEV = UV + NUV = \text{direct use value} + \text{indirect use value} + \text{option value} + \text{existence value} + \text{bequest value}$$

VALUATION TECHNIQUES

There are basically two broad approaches to valuation: (i) direct and (ii) indirect valuation approaches, which further comprises several techniques. The direct valuation approach consists of techniques that attempt to elicit preferences directly by the use of survey and experimental techniques such as contingent ranking and contingent valuation. Whereas the indirect approach takes its cue from actual, observed market based information and includes techniques like hedonic price and wage techniques, travel cost method, avertive behaviour and conventional market approaches.

Direct Valuation Techniques

Contingent Valuation Technique

The method involves setting up a carefully worded questionnaire, which asks people about their WTP and/or WTA through structured questions. The method involves devising various forms of 'bidding game' eliciting 'yes/no' response to questions and statements about maximum WTP. At the next stage econometric analysis of resulting survey data is done to derive mean values of WTP bids.

Contingent valuation technique is most commonly used valuation techniques because it is the only means available for valuing non-use values and estimates obtained from well-designed, properly executed surveys gives results which are as good as estimates obtained from other methods.

Contingent Ranking

In contingent ranking, individuals are asked to rank several alternatives in order of preference rather than expressing willingness to pay and options differ as per risk characteristic and price. Contingent ranking can also be used to do a ranking of house characteristics vis-à-vis house price to convert rankings into WTP.

Contingent ranking is very useful in situation when the good is rather difficult to value or not very familiar to the respondent, for example, in case of air pollution abatement. In contingent ranking, the respondents are asked to rank the options according to their preferences. Contingent rating and contingent choice are two other variants of this technique. In case of contingent rating, respondents are asked to rate all options in order, whereas in the case of contingent choice, respondents are asked to pick only the most preferred option.

Indirect Valuation Techniques

Indirect valuation techniques try to infer an implicit value for a non-market good from observable, market-determined prices of market goods and services in an indirect way. Indirect valuation envisages formulating an explicit relationship between the demand for a market good and the supply of environmental goods. It is based on the premise that given a change in level of some environmental good, demand of market goods would also change and more marketed goods would be demanded as better environmental quality increase additional demand for good. Indirect valuation techniques can be further classified into surrogate market approach and conventional market approach.

Surrogate Market Approach

Surrogate market approach, as the name suggests, looks at available markets for private goods and services, which are related to the environmental commodities. Thus, respondents are asked to reveal their preferences for both private goods and environmental goods though they may be purchasing the private goods. It further comprises hedonic techniques and household production function approach.

Household Production Functions: Averting Expenditures   Averting behaviour techniques, as the name suggests, ascertains how by investing in certain technology can result in averting adverse environmental effects. If the respondent is willing to invest in such technology then the researcher can estimate the value he is willing to pay to avert an adverse environmental impact. This is quite useful in analysing expenditures undertaken by households in offsetting some environmental risks.

It is important that the averting behaviour must be between two perfect substitutes otherwise an underestimation of the benefits of the environmental good may occur. Examples include air pollution abatement, noise pollution abatement, purchase of monitoring equipment, etc. This technique is not used very frequently as it usually requires significant econometric modelling.

Household Production Functions: Travel Cost Method   Travel cost methods are one of the earliest methods of environmental valuation, which works on weak complementarities. It has been widely used to measure the value of natural resources as a source of recreational activities.

It is based on the premise that consumers reveal their valuation of the natural resources through their actual travel cost behaviour. Thus, researchers can compute the value of time spent in recreational activities, the cost of travel and entrance and other expenditure at site. Based on the assumption that this value is due to people's access to a natural resource or park, computed value can be considered as value of the natural resource or park. The computation requires detailed sample survey of travellers, together with their costs of travel to the site, wherein information on money and time spent by people in getting to a site is used to estimate willingness to pay for a site's facilities or characteristics.

Hedonic Property Pricing   Hedonic price model tries to monetize basic environment amenities by assessing the impact of the amenities on prices of related goods and economic services. It is most widely used in assessing the impact of environmental pollution on residential housing value.

It is based on the premise that price of market goods, or let us say a house, is a combination of various attributes such as size, location, structural qualities and environmental amenities that makes up the marketed good. Researchers then using econometric techniques can calculate a hedonic price function relating property price to various attributes. Researchers can further derive separate expression for environmental attribute; assessing how price would change if the levels of the environmental attributes were changed. It is important to point out that it does not measure non-use value and is confined to cases where property owners are aware of environmental variables and act because of them.

Hedonic Wage: Risk Estimation   In consonance with the principle of hedonic price approach, hedonic wage approach uses multiple regression to predict change in wages/salaries due to various environmental factors influencing them including the determining factor, that is, measure of the risk of accident. The technique is based on the assumption that the wage one gets on a job can be broken down into the price of relevant attributes that define the job, one of which is the degree of risk involved. Thus, it states that workers in riskier jobs must be compensated with higher salaries.

Conventional Market Approach

Conventional market approach is used in situations when the output of goods or services is measurable, wherein market price/shadow price is used to value environmental damage. It comprises dose-response technique, replacement cost technique and opportunity cost technique.

Dose-response Technique   Dose-response technique, also known as cost of illness method, is used to estimate economic gains from improved health. It can be used in situations where there are markets or where shadow prices can be easily estimated.

It estimates the change in private and public expenditure on health care and the value of production lost due to morbidity, mortality and ambient pollution levels. A dose-response function relates ill health due to the level of pollution as well as other variables. Though it is important to point out that these expenditures do not necessarily measure everything a household is willing to pay to avoid poor health.

The technique is used specifically in cases where the dose-response relationship between some causes of damage such as pollution and output/impacts are known. Examples include health impact due to air pollution, crop failure due to pollution, productivity lost due to soil erosion and sedimentation.

Replacement Cost Technique   Replacement cost, as the name indicates, ascertains environmental damage to value the cost of operation, which shall restore the environment to its original state. It is especially used in situations where the objective is to assess costs related to achieve specified environmental standards.

The tricky part in estimating replacement cost is to collect information on replacement costs. Researchers usually collect information either by observing actual spending on restoring damaged assets or from estimates of costs incurred in restoring the damaged environmental assets.

Opportunity Cost Technique   Opportunity cost technique ascertains functions of displaced land use and estimates the usage value in terms of kind and money incomes from those uses. Like other valuation techniques, the opportunity cost technique also requires a household survey to assess economic and leisure activities in the area. It is especially used in situations where a policy or rule precludes access to an area. In that situation it is quite useful in estimating opportunity cost from construction of a protected area.

PART II

GROWTH AND SUSTAINABLE DEVELOPMENT

Developing countries today faces one of the gravest challenges of sustaining environmental and natural resources. Though some of the linkages among sustainable development, natural resource conservation, population growth, poverty and the environment have received attention from researchers and policy-makers, the dream of chalking out a sustainable framework seems to be far-fetched. Policy-makers need to understand the ways in which use of natural resources, economic growth and development are interrelated in order to formulate a coherent and concerted approach towards sustainable development. The following section lists the rudiments of sustainable development, importance of natural resource management and accounting regime and reasons of resource degradation.

SUSTAINABLE DEVELOPMENT

The Brundtland Report defines development as sustainable if it ensures 'that it meets the needs of the present without compromising the ability of future generations to meet their own needs ... and extending to all the opportunity to fulfill their aspirations for a better life' (World Commission on Environment and Development, 1987: 8). Sustainable development envisages optimum utilization of resources for each generation with sufficient resources to generate its own wealth. The concept of optimum utilization ensures that current generation utilizes resource for maximum satisfaction besides leaving enough for future generations.

QUADRANGLE APPROACH TO SUSTAINABILITY

Sustainable development encompasses all facets of development and thus cannot be discussed in isolation. It has to be discussed as a function of socio-demographic factors, namely, population, natural resource dependence, socio-demographic pressure, poverty, and institutional establishment. Sustainable development[11] includes everything that changes welfare and is defined as the resultant of ecological, economic, institutional and social sustainability (Bartelmus, 1999). According to Barrelfuls, the issues to be looked into in ecological sustainability are natural resource depletion and increase in defensive expenditures, whereas economic sustainability is influenced by consumption, utility and capital accumulation. Social sustainability is measured by unemployment, health and education expenditure, literacy rate and life expectancy, and institutional sustainability is pivoted around the key issue of organizational and institutional rules and norms. To achieve sustainable development, each aspect of the sustainability quadrangle must in itself be sustained including four different kinds of capital: natural capital, human capital, social capital and human capital.

CONCEPT OF WEAK SUSTAINABILITY/STRONG SUSTAINABILITY

Some researchers also define sustainable development in the form of weak and strong sustainability. Goodland and Daly went so far as to differentiate four degrees of sustainability: weak sustainability, intermediate sustainability, strong sustainability, and absurdly strong sustainability (Goodland and Daly, 1996). Weak sustainability requires overall capital maintenance, thus, if natural capital depletion is substituted by an increase of social capital, then overall capital would remain unchanged and would satisfy the condition for weak sustainability. However, this assumes natural and social capital to be perfect substitutes, which in not true as degradation of any natural capital can be replaced by any form of social capital. In the case of strong sustainability, it is essential that every type of capital is maintained, which means, capital depreciation must not extend the regeneration rate for the same sort of capital.

SUSTAINABILITY AS A CONCEPT OF DYNAMIC EFFICIENCY AND INTERGENERATIONAL EQUITY

Sustainability is also defined as a concept combining both dynamic efficiency and intergenerational equity, which is defined best in terms of meeting the needs of the present without compromising the ability of future generations to meet their needs. In the absence of efficiency, constant consumption at no more than a subsistence level could satisfy this requirement, yet it would surely not be accepted as a reasonable social goal or target for public policy. That is, a meaningful definition of sustainability, which has normative standing, as a social goal ought to include dynamic efficiency, expressed formally as the maximization of W (t), that is, welfare function against time. The important point here is that W (t) must capture total welfare. Omitting contributions to welfare of any kind of capital will lead to an underestimation of the total value of W (t), and neglecting any form of capital depreciation will lead to an overestimation.

INTERGENERATIONAL EQUITY

Dynamic efficiency is argued to be a necessary condition for sustainability but it is not the only condition for sustainability. The condition of intergenerational equity also needs to be met. It is also essential for consistency that the maximized total welfare function does not decrease over time or to put it in other words, an optimized consumption path fulfills the condition of intergenerational equity if it is non-declining over time.

MEASURE OF SUSTAINABLE DEVELOPMENT

Governments around the world calculate economic data known as national income accounts to calculate macroeconomic indicators such as gross domestic product. The primary purpose of national accounts is to record economic activity, not to measure aggregate well-being in the nation. Nevertheless, national accounts are widely used as indicators of well-being and national aggregates such as GNP/GDP are widely construed as measures of development and growth.

Gross National Product (GNP)

Gross national product and gross domestic product (GDP) are well-known indicators of measuring economic growth and development. Gross domestic product is calculated as the value of the total final output of all goods and services produced in a single year within a country's boundaries and GNP is computed as GDP plus incomes received by residents from abroad minus incomes claimed by non-residents.

Gross national product is widely accepted as measure of economic growth by economists, politicians and people in general (Daly and Cobb, 1994) and even the International Monetary Fund (IMF) and the World Bank use it as evidence of economic growth. Gross national product is seen as a popular indicator of economic success, but in reality it cannot be justified as a measure of development especially in developing country like India. The definition of GNP is:

GNP= Σ factor income earned from economic activities occurring in one nation

As can be seen from this definition, GNP is a measure of income rather than welfare. Jacobs further elaborates on the issue: 'There is little virtue in high income if it is achieved simply by running down reserves or productive capacity.... When capital runs out there will be no income at all' (Jacobs, 1991: 224). Now the key question is while measuring economic growth and development are we accounting for implicit cost due to resource degradation as every percentage increase in GNP/GDP has an implicit cost due to environmental degradation. It affects GNP and GNP is less than it otherwise would be if at least some environmental damage were avoided. Second, it generates costs, which are not recorded as part of GNP hence GNP accounts needs to be modified to reflect comprehensive measures of aggregate well-being rather than economic activity. In order to modify the GNP account, capital depreciation is subtracted from the GNP to get the net national product (NNP).

Hicks Measure of Sustainable Income

Hicks made the first step towards a sustainable economic measure. He defined a measure of sustainable income known as Hicksian income. According to Hicks, 'a person's income is what he can consume during the week and still expect to be as well off at the end of the week as he was at the beginning' (Hicks, 1946: 176). This definition takes into account capital stock along with pure income flow; however, Hicksian income is still not an income measure and says nothing about wealth or welfare in general.

Daly and Cobb argued that Hicksian income (HI) is a better estimate and measure of sustainable development. Hicks subtracted defensive expenditures (DE), which were expenditures to avoid negative impacts of environmental damage and the depletion of natural capital (DNC) from NNP to arrive at Hicks income as defined by the formula:

$$HI = NNP - DE - DNC$$

Hicksian income still could not be defined as a measure of welfare, as there was expenditure in the NNP, which did not lead to growing welfare. Nordhaus and Tobin then introduced the concept of measure of economic welfare and concluded that though welfare is highly correlated with the GNP, its growth rate is less than GNP. But, Daly and Cobb criticized the measure of economic welfare concept arguing that one goal of Nordhaus and Tobin was to demonstrate that it is correct to accept the GNP as an overall measure of welfare.

NATURAL RESOURCE MANAGEMENT

In a developing country like India, natural resource management is critical for providing livelihood to millions of poor people. One of the key questions though is ownership management of natural resources.

There are two streams of theories. One suggests that the government should be the owner and manager of critical natural resources such as land, water, forests and fisheries. The other believes that the community that depends on natural resources for survival should manage the resources. In many cases, the government took over land or other resources that had historically been the property of local communities. Though recently, through initiative such as JFM, there has been an increased emphasis on people's participation. Some argue that the move was driven by the reality that very few governments had adequate financial and manpower support to monitor the use of forests and rangelands areas.

Irrespective of the reason, it is established that natural capital hold the key to curb poverty. Thus, it is imperative to maintain natural resources above critical sustainability levels in order to facilitate the task of sustaining livelihoods. The problem of widespread poverty and degradation of natural resources essentially reflects two sides of the same coin. The poor in India cannot possibly improve their lot in life if they have to cultivate the soil, which is highly degraded, use water that is inaccessible or polluted and provide fodder for their cattle from areas where nothing grows. Essentially, the first step in the economic uplift of the poorest of the poor is to ensure that they have the capacity to rebuild and regenerate natural resources on which their livelihood depends.

Further, in the case of natural capital, property rights are often very difficult to establish and because some natural resources/assets fall in the category of open access such water and the atmosphere, are very difficult to tap. The situation is further compounded by the lack of any accountability of the people who use these resources.

NATURAL RESOURCE ACCOUNTING

How green is our GDP or our national accounts? Have you ever asked such questions to yourself, if you have not then its time to ask such questions. We have flogged our natural resources to such an irrevocable extent that it is high time to take a stock of the situation, otherwise it will be too late. It is imperative to make policy-makers and implementers aware of the fact that the national accounts or GDP do not capture the essence of the green economy. In their assessment of costs and capital, national accounts neglect the scarcity of natural resources that threaten the sustained productivity of the economy and degradation of environmental quality. Thus national accounts and GNP accounts need to be modified to reflect comprehensive measures of aggregate well-being rather than economic activity.

The primary purpose of national accounts is to record economic activity, not to measure aggregate well-being in the nation. National aggregates such as GNP/GDP are widely construed as measures of 'development' though these measures need to be adjusted to take into account resource degradation such as the degradation of forests.[12] In their assessment of cost and capital, national accounts have neglected the scarcity of natural resources that threaten the sustained productivity of the economy and the degradation of environmental quality.

A consensus emerged from the workshop organized by the UNEP to develop the links between environment accounting and unite the system of national accounts (SNA). Parallel to revision, the statistical division of the United Nations has developed methodologies for a system of integrated environmental and economic accounting.

NATURAL RESOURCE ACCOUNTING[13]

There have been various approaches to natural resource accounting, based on the accounting system, which capture changes in natural resources. Its process is similar to the system of national accounts, though the only difference is in the type of asset used. Natural resources accounting uses data on stocks of natural resources and track changes in them caused by nature and human use. Further, it includes the stock of all natural resources like agricultural, forests, fisheries, and water.

The basic principle is to ascertain the monetary value of the natural resource base in order to track changes in income as a function of change in resource base. It allows valuation of natural resource usage and depletion, besides estimating expenditures needed for environmental protection. It helps countries in maintaining accounts of annual resource use and depletion. Besides, natural resource accounting, the other approach is to integrate environmental accounts with the traditional system of national accounts. But, for integration to be effective, countries have to modify their existing system of national accounts to incorporate environmental assets. Another problem in the integration process is the inclusion of only marketed natural resources such as oil and timber and it still does not account for all environmental aspects, particularly environmental pollution.

The other approaches that are in use are discussed next.

Green GDP

Green GDP tries to adjust the GDP for environmental resource utilization and depreciation. It is a very useful indicator with which policy-makers can assess the real GDP or economic growth. The methodology is still not widely accepted as it may not be comparable across countries.

Desegregation of Conventional National Accounts

Conventional accounts data are desegregated to identify expenditures specifically related to the environment. Researchers while using this data can observe links between changes in environmental policy and cost of environmental protection.

Valuing Environmental Goods and Services

Researchers, economists and even academicians agree that the time is ripe to integrate environmental accounts with the traditional system of national accounts. They are, however, still not sure about what to do with the non-marketed value of goods and services in national accounts like the benefits of unpolluted water. It is often argued that it is very difficult to standardize the value of such services. Efforts have been made, however, to devise accounting systems which include all environmental resources as stocks.

Emission Accounting

National Accounting Matrix including Environmental Accounts (NAMEA) has developed a matrix, which prepare accounts on the basis of identified pollution emission by economic sector. It is based on the premise that if emissions are valued in monetary terms then these monetary values can provide an indication about the cost of avoiding environmental degradation.

Heuting propounded this approach by highlighting the fact that valuing in monetary terms the loss of environmental functions due to competition among different uses required the estimation of prices for those functions.

Based on shadow prices, a demand supply and curves for environmental functions can be constructed. But, estimating demand curves of environmental functions based on individual preferences is very difficult to determine. Thus, it became necessary that some standard for the availability of the environmental function were devised, which could be based on the sustainable use of the environment. Thus, Heuting proposed his approach that consists of calculating the cost of measures required to shift the level of economic activity to a sustainable level.

He defined the type of costs that included cost of restoration measure, cost of devising alternate option for resource usage, cost of shifting from environmentally adverse activities to environmentally favourable activities that are essential to estimate. However, it is not easy to calculate correct shadow prices based on individual preferences. Thus, true economic valuation of the environment is very difficult to estimate. All valuations require that preferences for environment and sustainability be explicitly stated.

System of Integrated Environmental and Economic Accounting (SEEA)

In a bid to devise a concerted and integrated system, the UN Statistics Department coordinated some of the ongoing efforts and in 1993, the UN published the *System for Integrated Economics and Environment Accounting* as an annexure to the 1993 revisions of the SNA. The SEEA, as the name suggests, integrates different approaches in natural resource and environment accounting. It envisages linkage of physical resource accounts with monetary environment accounts and balance sheet. The other objective is to have an estimation of all flow and stocks of asset related to the environment to permit the estimation of the total expenditure for the protection of the environment. It also tries to do an assessment of environmental costs and benefits by extending the concept of capital to include natural capital.

The SEEA is derived from the overall national accounts framework, the recently revised 1993 SNA. This has been achieved by the incorporation of produced and non-produced asset accounts in the 1993 SNA, which are further elaborated and expanded in the SEEA. The system integrates environmental issues into conventional national accounts. Researchers using SEEA, can easily develop green indicators to complement traditional economic indicators such as eco-domestic product (EDP). The eco-domestic product (EDP) is an environmentally adjusted measure of net domestic product. It helps in accounting for resource depletion and serves as an effective tool for policy makers to take more informed decision-making regarding resource allocation and economic development.

Integrated accounting introduces three categories of monetary valuation of natural assets and thus three different basic versions of SEEA have been proposed. One version is that of market valuation approach. The second version uses maintenance valuation, which estimates the costs needed to keep the natural environment intact. The third version combines the first version of market valuation with a contingent valuation approach to assess the environmental cost. The handbook suggests the first two measures for valuation.

As per the SEEA approach, a market value of natural resources can be easily calculated by using the price of goods or services provided by those assets as future sales value. But, estimate would require information on availability of future stocks, prices and interest rates which are usually available at the macroeconomic level. The whole exercise involving consideration of the costs of depletion of natural resources and changes in environment quality helps in calculating the environment adjusted net domestic product. Two valuation methods for the maintenance of natural capital as a production factor were proposed in the SEEA.

The first was the net price method, which neglects future losses of net returns from resource depletion. The value of natural resources thus calculated is a product of natural resource stock and net price, wherein net price of an asset is defined as the actual market price of raw material minus marginal exploration cost. It is based on hotelling rent assumption, which claims that in a perfectly competitive market, the price of natural resource rises at the rate of interest of alternative investment. Though there is evidence to prove that the net price method could reflect upper limit on economic depreciation. As natural resources reflect different qualities and marginal exploitation cost increase with lower quality resource extracted and rents would increase at a lower rate than interest rate. Thus, hotelling rent would overstate natural resource depreciation.

The second approach was the user cost allowance proposed by El Serafy of the World Bank, the use of which has been proposed while dealing with an exhaustible resource. It is based on the concept of converting a time bound revenue stream from the sale of an exhaustible natural resource into permanent income by investing a part of the revenue, defined as user cost allowance. Computation of user cost allowance requires two additional parameters, namely, discount rate and lifespan. But, the dispute over the use of discount rate and availability of appropriate investment of user cost allowance act as hindrances in the validity of this approach.

Though there are various plus points in the SEEA approach, there are also limitations to valuation techniques. The SEEA takes in account immediate damages linked to economic activities, but further environmental damages to human health or the ecosystem are not addressed.

THREATS TO THE NATURAL RESOURCE BASE

In a bid to achieve a convergence for growth and sustainable development, it is imperative to have an understanding of reasons that are threatening to make extinct the natural resource base. This section tries to assess the threats to the natural resource base.

INSTITUTIONAL FAILURE

Natural resource degradation, especially in a country like India, is triggered by violation of established norms and behaviour laid down by formal and informal institutions. Some researchers also believe that the poor degrade environmental resources because poverty forces them to discount future incomes at unusually high rates (Bardhan, 1996: 62).

Poor people are the most disadvantaged people in every aspect; they suffer from poverty but cannot raise their voices as they do not have a voice of their own. They do not have a collective voice because they lack social capital or affiliations to formal and informal institutions. This makes it important to assess how formal and informal institutions affect their access to opportunities. They lack assistance and mutual support and suffer from poverty of social relations. For those with extensive social capital, these networks can open opportunities for investment or employment and they can protect their households against the economic shocks that may plunge the most vulnerable into destitution.

Further poor people are subject to more risks than the non-poor. This is compounded by the fact that they have few assets to rely upon in the face of a crisis. Thus, in order to lessen the hardships of the poor, one needs to develop and maintain social networks and funds for the poor. There is need for strategies/policies on the lines of rural risk management and insurance. Second, social protection recognizes that the most vulnerable to risk maybe the poorest among the poor and emphasizes the need to provide support to the poorest. Moreover, social services and anti-poverty programmes do not perform effectively as there is also poverty of access to public goods and services. Also, the poor do not participate extensively in networks of informal institutions.

It is imperative that both formal and informal networks and institutions are strengthened and further participation of poor and disadvantaged people are ensured. When we talk of formal institutions, PRIs are such institutions that can make an immense contribution in lending a voice to the poor. The decentralized decision-making process coupled with the reservation of seats for members of the disadvantaged community is one such step that should have ensured participation of poor people in the decision-making process. Further, PRIs, which have been the basic conduit for funds for rural development and rural poverty alleviation should have served as an ideal platform for the participation of the poor. But the results are not that encouraging as even today PRIs in most cases serve the cause of the rich and candidates from the reserved and disadvantaged communities participate in the PRIs only in name. The real power is still in the hands of the rich. Besides the PRIs, there are a lot of organizations and committees under the government that protect resources such as the FMC, etc., though still a lot needs to be done to ensure the participation of poor people in decision-making and benefit sharing.

Natural resource degradation can also be due to government policy. Binswanger in his study in Brazil (1991) proved that the government's policy of tax exemption from virtually all agricultural income provided strong incentives to the rich to acquire forestland and to then deforest it and use it for agricultural purposes. Forests are not a localized resource, and deforestation has its impact on neighbouring countries and areas.

In developing countries, natural resource degradation is a major cause of concern as it affects the livelihood of millions of people dependent on the natural resource economy. Failure of the natural resource economy results in chronic poverty. Though there is evidence to prove that poverty itself can be a cause of environmental degradation (Dasgupta and Mäler, 1991; Ehrlich et al., 1995). Social norms, which determine long-term economic relationships, tend to break down and as a result it is the disadvantaged and marginalized people who become poorer. In certain cases, due to the breakdown of social norms, local resources become open access resources.

It is essential to point that in the natural resource economy, the functioning and failure of micro-institutions such as households is as important and critical as the functioning of any other formal or informal institution. In developing countries, especially in India, typically men are in control of the decision-making process and all decisions are guided by male preferences, not female needs. Thus, on matters of afforestation in the drylands, women are expected to favour planting for fuelwood and men fruit trees, but as decisions are usually taken by men, sources of fuelwood continue to recede, while fruit trees are increasingly planted (Dasgupta, 1993a).

FAILURE IN MANAGING THE COMMONS

Common property resources, as per conceptualization, act as a buffer for the majority of the population who are dependent on natural resources for their survival. But as communities are entrusted with the responsibility of managing the resource base, these resources suffer from the problem of becoming 'everybody's responsibility, nobody's accountability', that is, everyone wants to share the resource but nobody want to take care of it. This phenomenon, popularly known as the tragedy of the commons is another key factor that triggers resource degradation and economic disenfranchisement among the poor.

Common property resource management emphasizes collective action by a group or community in managing the resource. Jodha (1995), in his very famous study, in the drylands of India, noted that over a 20-year period, there had been a 25–60 per cent decline in the area covered by the commons. The decline was due to privatization of land, the majority of which was awarded to non-poor people. In an earlier study, he stressed that rise in the profitability of land from cropping and grazing had triggered desertification in the northern state of Rajasthan. Jodha concluded that the process was triggered by government's initiative of land reform programmes which was not accompanied by investment in improving the natural resource productive base.

Ostrom (1996b) in his pioneering work in Nepal noted that systems that had been improved by the construction of permanent head works were not only in a bad state of repairs, but that they delivered substantially less water to the tail-end than to the head-end of the systems and had lower agricultural productivity than the temporary, stone-trees-and-mud headworks that had been constructed and managed by the farmers themselves.

Ostrom explains that, unless it is accompanied by counter-measures, the construction of permanent headworks alters the relative bargaining positions of the head- and tail-enders, resulting in so reduced a flow of benefits to the latter group that they have little incentive to help repair and maintain the headworks, something the head-enders on their own cannot do. Head-enders gain from the permanent structures, but the tail-enders lose disproportionately. Ostrom (1996a) also notes that traditional farm-managed systems sustained greater equality in the allocation of water than modern systems managed by such external agencies as the government and foreign donors.

It has been confirmed by several studies that privatization of village commons and forest lands, can have a disastrous effect on the disadvantaged and poor people, as in the majority of cases common land is their biggest source of sustenance. Various studies have indicated that privatization of village commons and forest lands can have a disastrous effect on poor people. It is a well-established fact that there is a close link between environmental protection and the well-being of the poor.

MARKET FAILURE

Market failure, especially in the case of natural resources is a key factor, which results in natural resource degradation, the reason being the absence of measures to ascertain the value of natural resources and the services they provide. Some may ask about the need of having markets to ascertain the value of natural resources and why market-regulated mechanisms are required to decide on the importance of natural resources, as for many natural resources markets simply do not exist.

Markets do not exist in some cases, as usually the costs of negotiation and monitoring are too high, while in some cases, unprotected property rights prevent their existence, or make markets function imperfectly even when they do exist. Thus, it is also said that environmental problems are often caused by market failure.

There is no market to ensure intergenerational equity, that is, there are no forward markets for transactions between the present generation and future generations. Sustainable development as a principle talks of both dynamic efficiency (maximizing current output) and intergenerational equity (leaving enough for future generations). In the absence of markets it is very difficult to ensure that the current generation is leaving enough for the future. In short, market failure involves not only misallocation of resources in the present, but also misallocation across time.

Market prices of goods and services fail to reflect their social worth and usually, they are less than their social worth. These situations compel researchers to often resort to shadow prices.

It is imperative to decide about the price of resource. The accounting price of a resource is the increase in social well being, which would be enjoyed if a unit more of the resource were made available cheaply. But, presence of externalities distorts prices and results to a difference between market prices and accounting prices. Accounting price also depends on the access of resource. For example, if there is free access to a resource base, then the market price of the resource would be zero.

Market failure typically results in an excessive use of the natural resource base, which results in a livelihood issue for millions of poor people. Economic growth is important but not a solution to all problems of income inequality. There is no significant relationship between the level of growth and the decline in poverty. At the most the relationship is weak and does not take into consideration the households who were not poor but become poor in high growth regions (Krishna et al., 2003). Markets are indifferent to the needs of the majority of the people. More importantly, there is no relationship at all between market-driven growth and the level of human development and that is precisely because these markets are not driven by the wishes and aspiration of more than 70 per cent of the population. Thus, there is a need to do develop markets that can operate in the realm of rural India.

Marketing of natural resource products is an altogether different proposition. In the case of agriculture products, the government has some control over trade and market mechanisms and most of the state governments have enacted legislations necessary for the regulation of agricultural produce markets. Agricultural marketing is linked to a network of cooperatives at the primary, state and national levels and marketing cooperatives function in the area of fruit and vegetable processing, sugarcane and cotton ginning, etc. But, in the case of other natural resource products, markets simply do not exist. Thus, it is the need of the hour that initiatives are taken to integrate rural markets in such a way that farmers can have access to markets without bothering about logistic issues such place to stock products and marketing of products.

NOTES

1. India is amongst the top three producers in the world of rice, wheat, liquid milk, poultry products, fruits and vegetables, coconut, tea, spices, and marine and fresh water products including fish and shrimp.
2. It is estimated that 30 per cent of India's agriculture relies on traditional methods of farming, thus the potential for organic produce exports to the developing countries is very high.
3. Forests having a crown density of 40 per cent or more are referred as dense forests.
4. Income from forest resources is aggregated under the head of 'Forestry and Logging'. Forestry and logging includes income from the sources such as (i) industrial wood—timber, roundwood, match and pulpwood, (ii) firewood and (iii) minor forest products—bamboo, fodder, lac, sandalwood, honey, resin, gum, and tendu leaves (GOI, 1999).
5. The governance of forest resources in India may be divided into three categories, namely, (i) governance by the state, (ii) joint governance by the state and civil society and (iii) governance by civil society.
6. The Ministerial Conference on the Protection of Forests in Europe guidelines or national laws and regulations or core International Labour Organization (ILO) conventions and other international conventions ratified by the country in question such as the Convention on Biological Diversity, Kyoto Protocol, Convention on International Trade on Endangered Species of Wild Fauna and the Flora and Bio-safety Protocol.
7. India contains 172 species of animals considered globally threatened by the IUCN, or 2.9 per cent of the world's total number of threatened species (Groombridge, 1994). These include 53 species of mammals, 69 species of birds, 23 species of reptiles and three species of amphibians. India contains globally important populations of some of Asia's rarest animals, such as the Bengal fox, Asiatic cheetah, marbled cat, Asiatic lion, Indian elephant, Asiatic wild ass, Indian rhinoceros, markhor, gaur, wild Asiatic water buffalo, etc. (Groombridge, 1994).
8. The Central Pollution Control Board (CPCB), which is India's national body for monitoring environmental pollution, undertook a comprehensive scientific survey in 1981–82 in order to classify river waters according to their designated best uses. This report was the first systematic document that formed the basis of the Ganga Action Plan (GAP). The plan was formally launched on 14 June 1986. The main thrust was to intercept and divert the wastes from urban settlements away from the river.
9. It is widely believed by resource researchers that three broad reason, that is, institutional failure, lack of proper governing of commons and market failures are the probable reason behind the downward spiral linkage between environment and poverty.
10. EIA was first introduced in the United States in 1969 as a requirement of the National Environmental Policy Act (NEPA). Since then, an increasing number of countries have adopted EIA, introducing legislation and establishing agencies with responsibility for its implementation.
11. Sustainable development includes all components of community development, environmental protection, natural resource conservation and local economic development.
12. Gross domestic product (GDP) and net domestic product (NDP) from forestry and logging are calculated as: GDP = value of output – repairs, maintenance and other operational costs and NDP = GDP – consumption of fixed capital. The depreciation in natural capital is, however, not taken into account while calculating NDP.
13. The effort to correct the national accounts in order to calculate NNP or the related 'green GDP', known as natural resources accounting, has been a lively research area in the last decade. Two basic methodologies have been proposed in the literature to value the loss of natural assets, the net price or depreciation method and the user cost approach.

APPENDIX A

BASIC MATHEMATICS THEORY

ALGEBRA

Algebra is a branch of mathematics that may be defined as a generalization and extension of arithmetic. It is divided into (i) elementary algebra, where the properties of the real number system are recorded and the rules governing mathematical expressions and equations involving these symbols are studied, and (ii) abstract algebra, where algebraic structures such as fields, groups and rings are axiomatically defined and investigated, and (iii) linear algebra studies the specific properties of vector spaces.

Elementary algebra is the most basic form of algebra that deals with basic principles of arithmetic. While in arithmetic only numbers and their arithmetical operations occur, in algebra researchers uses symbols (such as a, x, y) to denote numbers. Algebra is quite useful because (i) it allows the conceptualization of arithmetical laws (such as $a + b = b + a$ for all a and b), and thus is the first step to a systematic exploration of the properties of the real number system, and (ii) it provides the facility for the formulation of equations.

Further, in algebra, the expression contain numbers, variables and arithmetical operations. Examples are $a + 3$ and $x^2 - 3$. An 'equation' is the claim that two expressions are equal. Expressions or statement may contain many variables, from which you may or may not be able to deduce the values for some of the variables. For example,

$$(x - 1) \times (x - 1) = y \times 0$$

After some algebraic steps (not covered here), we can deduce that $x = 1$; however, we cannot deduce the value of y.

NUMBER THEORY

Number theory is the mathematical study of integers and their generalizations. A number is an abstract entity used to describe quantity. We shall denote all real numbers by R.

The most familiar numbers are the natural numbers {0, 1, 2, ...} used for counting and denoted by N. If the negative whole numbers are included, one obtains the integers Z. These are given by, N = {1, 2, 3,...} and Z = {..., −3, −2, −1, 0, 1, 2, 3, ...}.

Ratios of integers are called rational numbers or fractions; the set of all rational numbers is denoted by Q. To put it simply, this is the collection of all fractions. If all infinite and non-repeating decimal expansions are included, one obtains the real number R. Further, all real numbers which are not rational are called irrational numbers. Any irrational number, when expressed in decimal notation, has non-terminating and non-repeating decimals, for example, the number π. It is known that $\pi = 3.14159....$ Further, the real numbers are in turn extended to the complex numbers C in order to be able to solve all algebraic equations.

Prime numbers and composite numbers: A prime number is an integer n with no divisors other than 1 and n. A composite number is an integer, which is not prime. The first few prime numbers are 2, 3, 5, 7, 11, 13,.... though there are infinitely many prime numbers.

Two integers are relatively prime if they have no prime factors in common. For example, 101 and 17 are relatively prime, but 12 and 100 are not as they are both divisible by 2. The greatest common divisor (GCD) of two numbers a and b is the largest number dividing both a and b.

FUNCTIONS AND TRANSFORMATIONS OF FUNCTIONS

DEFINITION OF A FUNCTION

Let A and B be sets. Let us say A is a function of B and x and y are values of sets A and B. Whenever we write $y = f(x)$ we mean y is the value of f at x or the image of x under f. We also say that f maps x to y. To put it simply, y is a function of x and any changes in x reflects a corresponding change in y.

In terms of set theory, set A is called the domain of f. The set of all possible values of $f(x)$ in B is called the range of f. Here, we will only consider real-valued functions of a real variable, so A and B will both be subsets of the set of real numbers.

Examples: $f(x) = x^2$, x real.

$f(x) = \sin(x)$, x real.

Even/Odd Functions

A function f is said to be even if and only if, $f(-x) = f(x)$ for all x belonging to A. A function is said to be odd if and only if $f(-x) = -f(x)$ for all x belonging to A.

The graph of an even function is symmetric about the x axis, while the graph of an odd function is symmetric about the origin. Most functions are neither even nor odd. Out of the functions in the earlier examples, $f(x) = x^2$ is even, $f(x) = \sin(x)$ is odd.

Functions: Exponential and Logarithm

Exponentials: Exponentials are powers of e having mathematical numbers as 2.718282.... It is written as e^x or exp (x). Negative exponentials follow the same rules that all negative powers do: $\bar{e}^x = 1/(e^x)$. Further, Taylor expansion of e^x around 0 is $1+x+x^2/2+x^3/3!+ -$ in particular, when x is small (sometimes expressed as $x << 1$, read as 'x is much less than 1').

Logarithms: Logarithms are the solutions to equations like $y = e^x$ or $y = 10^x$. Natural logs, ln or $\log_e$, are logarithms base e ($e = 2.71828$.); common logs, $\log_{10}$, are typically logarithms base 10. When you see just log it is usually in a context where the difference does not matter. The section below lists some of the properties of logarithms:

1. If $x > 1$ then $\log(x) > 0$, and vice versa.
2. $\log (ab) = \log(a)+\log(b)$.
3. $\log(a^n) = n \log(a)$.
4. There is nothing you can do with log $(a+b)$.
5. In logarithms bases can often be converted, that is,
   $\log_x(a) = \log_y(a)/\log_y(x)$.
   $\log_{10}(a) = \log_e(a)/\log_e(10)$ and $\log_e(a) = \log_{10}(a)/\log_{10}(e)$.
6. The derivative of the logarithm, d $(\log x)/dx$, equals $1/x$. This is always positive for $x > 0$ (which are the only values for which the logarithm means anything anyway).

Logarithmic and Exponential Functions: Logarithmic and exponential functions are inverses of each other: $y = \log_b x$ if and only if $x = b^y$ and $y = \ln x$ if and only if $x = e^y$.

CALCULUS

Calculus[1] as a branch of mathematics developed from algebra and geometry. Unlike, the latter, calculus focuses on rates of change, such as accelerations, curves, and slopes. Calculus as branch of mathematics is based on the fundamentals of derivatives, integrals and limits.

There are two main branches of calculus:

a) *Differential calculus* is concerned with finding the instantaneous rate of change (or derivative) of a function's value, with respect to changes within the function's arguments.

b) *Integral calculus:* It studies methods for finding the integral of a function. An integral is also defined as the limit characterizing summation of terms corresponding to areas under the graph of a specified function. Thus, it allows the user calculate the area under a curve.

DIFFERENTIAL CALCULUS

Differential ($df(x)/dx$) is the derivative of a function f (which depends on x) with respect to x. The derivative of a function is usually written as $[df/dx]$. Further, users can also use the notation f' for the first derivative (f'' for the second derivative, etc.) in case he is sure about the function.

Consider the function $f(x) = 3x^4 - 4x^3 - 12x^2 + 3$ on the interval $[-2, 3]$. We cannot find regions on which f is increasing or decreasing, relative maxima or minima, or the absolute maximum or minimum value of f on $[-2, 3]$ by inspection. We can use the first derivative of f, however, to find all these things quickly and easily.

Now recalling a function $y = f(x)$, the derivative $f'(x)$ represents the slope of the tangent. It is easy to see from a picture that if the derivative $f'(x) > 0$, then the function $f(x)$ increases; in other words, $f(x)$ increases in value as x increases. On the other hand, if the derivative $f'(x) < 0$, then the function $f(x)$ decreases; in other words, $f(x)$ decreases in value as x increases.

Let us introduce the second derivative $f'(x)$ of the function $f(x)$. This is defined as the derivative of the derivative $f''(x)$. Similar to the concept of first derivative function $f''(x)$ instead of the function $f(x)$, users can conclude that if the second derivative $f''(x) > 0$, then the derivative $f'(x)$ increases.

In words, the derivative is the slope of the line tangent to a curve at a point, or the 'instantaneous' slope of a curve. The second derivative, d^2f/dx^2, is the rate of change of the slope, or the curvature. Some of the differential properties are mentioned next in brief:

a) Derivatives of polynomials: $[(d(x^n))/dx] = n\, x^{n-1}$.
b) Derivatives of sums: $[(d(f+g))/dx] = [df/dx] + [dg/dx]$.
c) Derivatives times constants: $[d(cf)/dx] = c[df/dx]$, if c is a constant ($[dc/dx] = 0$).
d) Derivative of a product: $[d(f(x)g(x))/dx] = f(x)[dg(x)/dx] + g(x)\,[df(x)/dx]$.
e) Derivative of the exponential: $[d(exp(ax))/dx] = a\exp(ax)$.
f) Derivative of logarithms: $[d(\log(x))/dx] = [1/x]$.

INTEGRAL CALCULUS

The fundamental theorem of calculus states that derivatives and integrals are inverse in operational value. It also allows users to compute integrals algebraically, by finding antiderivatives. It also allows users to solve some differential equations which relate an unknown function to its derivative.

There are two classes of (Riemann) integrals: definite integral, which has upper and lower limits such as:

$$\int_a^b f(x)dx$$

and indefinite integral which does not have an upper and lower limit such as:

$$\int f(x)dx$$

The first fundamental theorem of calculus allows definite integrals to be expressed in terms of an indefinite integral. Let f be a function that is Riemann integrable on $[a, b]$, let c belong to $[a, b]$. For x from $[a, b]$, define

$$F(x) = \int_c^x f(t)dt$$

Then F is a continuous function on $[a, b]$. Function can also be defined as a Riemann sum function.

BASIC INTEGRAL FUNCTION

a) One of the basic theorems of integration states that sum of an integration function can also be expressed as individually. In these a, n, c are constants and u, v functions of a single variable.

$$\int (du + dv) = \int du + \int dv$$

The integral of a sum is equal to the sum of the integrals of its parts. Integration, like differentiation, is thus a distributive operation.
Example:

$$\int (4x + 5x^2)\, dx = \int 4x\, dx + \int 5x^2\, dx$$

b) Another important theorem of integral calculus states that a constant factor can be transferred from one side of the integral sign to the other side.

$$\int a\, du = a\int du.$$

It should be noted that a variable cannot be transferred in this way. Thus,

$\int x\, dx$ is not equal to $x \int dx$.
Example:

$$\int 3\, x^3\, dx = 3 \int x^3\, dx$$

c) $$\int [f(x) \pm g(x)]dx = \int f(x)dx \pm \int g(x)dx$$

d) $$\int x^n dx = \frac{x^{n-1}}{n+1} + C, n \ne 1$$

NOTE

1. The development of calculus, is credited to Archimedes, Leibniz and Newton; lesser credit is given to Barrow, Descartes, de Fermat, Huygens, and Wallis.

APPENDIX B

PROBABILITY THEORY AND DISTRIBUTION

PROBABILITY THEORY

All statistical methods and techniques hinge on one key concept—probability theory. Probability is the likelihood or the chances that a given event will occur. Thus, probability tells us how likely it is that the data we gather is due to random fluctuations among participants, or due to an actual treatment effect.

If the event is A, then the probability that A will occur is denoted by P (A). The probability of an event A, P (A), is the proportion of times the event occurs in a long series of experiments. The probability of an event always lies in the range of 0 to 1. Thus, probability of an impossible event is 0. For example, if you roll a normal dice, then the probability that you will get a seven is 0. In case of a sure event, probability is 1. For example, if you roll a normal dice, then the probability that you will get a number less than 7 is 1.

THREE APPROACHES TO CALCULATING PROBABILITY

a) *Classical probability:* In this approach, outcomes are assumed to be equally likely; for example when you flip a coin, the probability of it landing on its heads face is equal to the probability of it landing on its tail face, so heads and tails are equally likely outcomes.

b) *Relative frequency:* If the outcomes for an experiment are not equally likely, we cannot use the classical probability rule. Instead, we perform the experiment repeatedly to generate data. We use the relative frequencies from this data to approximate the probability. If n is the number of times you repeat the experiment and f is the times an event A is observed then $P(A) = f/n$.

c) *Subjective probability:* Subjective probability, as the name suggests is the probability, which is assigned to an event based on judgement, perception, information and belief.

PROBABILITY: SOME DEFINITIONS

a) *Simple event:* An event that includes one and only one of the final outcomes for an experiment is called a simple event.

b) *Compound event:* An event having more than one outcomes for an experiment is called a compound event.

c) *Mutually exclusive events:* Mutually exclusive events are events that cannot occur together. For example, a card is chosen at random from a standard deck of 52 playing cards. Consider the event 'the card is a 5' and the event 'the card is a king'. These two events are mutually exclusive because there is no way for both events to occur at the same time.

d) *Independent events:* Two events can be classified as independent events if the probability of happening of one event does not affect the probability of the occurrence of the other event. It can be easily checked by researchers by assessing the relationship $P(A|B) = P(A)$ or $P(B|A) = P(B)$.

e) *Dependent events:* Two events are dependent if the occurrence of one affects the occurrence of the other event.

f) *Multiplication rule for independent events:* This is the probability of two independent events A and B occurring together: $P(A \text{ and } B) = P(A) * P(B)$.

g) *Multiplication rule for dependent events is denoted as:* $P(A \text{ and } B) = P(A)P(B|A)$.

h) *Union of events:* The union of events A and B is the collection of all outcomes that belong either to A or to B or to both A and B; it is denoted as: 'A or B' or 'A U B'.

The probability of the union of two events is denoted by:

$$P(A \text{ or } B) = P(A) + P(B) - P(A \text{ and } B).$$

Probability of the union of two mutually exclusive events is denoted by:

$$P(A \text{ or } B) = P(A) + P(B).$$

PROBABILITY DISTRIBUTIONS

Probability distribution is a theoretical model that indicates the probability of specific events happening for a phenomenon distributed in a particular manner. In statistics, numerous probability distributions are used to describe, explain, predict and assist in decision-making. Probability distributions can be further classified into discrete distributions and continuous distributions.

DISCRETE DISTRIBUTIONS

Discrete distribution signifies the probability distribution of a discrete random variable. A discrete probability function is different from continuous distribution as it can only take a discrete number of values. There is no hard and fast rule that discrete probability functions are only integers, but generally that is adopted as practice. It is also sometimes called the probability function or the probability mass function. The probability that x can take a specific value is $p(x)$.

$$P[X = x] = p(x) = p_x$$

1. $p(x)$ is non-negative for all real x.
2. The sum of $p(x)$ over all possible values of x is 1, that is

$$\sum_j p_j = 1$$

where j represents all possible values that x can have and p_j is the probability at x_j.
One consequence of properties 2 and 3 is that $0 <= p(x) <= 1$.

Types of Discrete Distribution

a) *Poisson distribution:* Poisson distribution is a discrete probability distribution, which was developed by a Frenchman, Simeon Poisson (1781–1840). It happens in cases where the chance of any individual event being a success is small. The distribution is used to describe the behaviour of rare events. The probability distribution form of Poisson variates is:

$$p(k) = \frac{\mu^k}{k!} \exp(= \mu)$$
$$k \geq 0$$

b) *Bernoulli distribution:* This function returns either a 0 or 1, the result of a Bernoulli trial with probability p. The probability distribution for a Bernoulli trial is:

$$p(0) = 1 - p$$
$$p(1) = p$$

c) *Binomial distribution:* This function returns a random integer from the binomial distribution, the number of successes in n independent trials with probability p.

d) *Negative binomial distribution:* Negative binomial distribution functions returns a random integer from the negative binomial distribution. It is generally used in case of a number of failures occurring before n successes in independent trials with probability p of success.

e) *Pascal distribution:* Pascal distribution depends on two parameter (p, k). The function returns a random integer from the Pascal distribution. The Pascal distribution is simply a negative binomial distribution with an integer value of n.

$$p(k) = \frac{(n + k = 1)!}{k!(n = 1)!} p^n (1 = p)^k$$
$$k \geq 0$$

f) *Geometric distribution:* Geometric distribution depends on parameter (p). The function returns a random integer from the geometric distribution, the number of independent trials with probability p until the first success.

g) *Hyper geometric distribution:* The hyper geometric distribution returns a random integer from the hyper geometric distribution.

h) *Logarithmic distribution:* The logarithmic (p) function returns a random integer from the logarithmic distribution. The probability distribution for logarithmic random variates is:

$$p(k) = \frac{-1}{\log(1-p)}\left(\frac{p^k}{k}\right)$$

$$k \geq 1$$

CONTINUOUS DISTRIBUTIONS

Continuous variable/measurement means every score on the continuum of scores is possible, or that there are an infinite number of scores. In this case, no single score can have a relative frequency because if it did, the total area would necessarily be greater than one. For that reason probability is defined over a range of scores rather than a single score.

For continuous outcome experiments, the probability of an event is defined as the area under a probability density curve. It is a function giving the probability that the random variable X is less than or equal to x, for every value x.

1. The probability that x is between two points a and b is

$$p[a \leq x \leq b] = \int_a^b f(x)dx$$

2. It is non-negative for all real x.
3. The integral of the probability function is 1, that is:

$$\int_{-\infty}^{\infty} f(x)dx = 1$$

Types of Continuous Distribution

a) *Gaussian distribution:* Gaussian distribution results when many independent random factors act in an additive manner. The data will follow a bell-shaped distribution. The distribution does occur frequently and is probably the most widely used statistical distribution, because it has some special mathematical properties, which form the basis of many statistical tests. The probability distribution for Gaussian random variate is:

$$p(x)dx = \frac{1}{\sqrt{2\pi}}\exp\left(-\frac{(x-\mu)^2}{2}\right)dx$$

$$\infty < x < \infty$$

b) *Standard normal distribution:* This function returns a Gaussian normal random variate, with mean 0 and standard deviation 1. The probability distribution for a normal random variate is:

$$p(x)dx = \frac{1}{\sqrt{2\pi}}\exp\left(-\frac{x^2}{2}\right)dx$$

$$\infty < x < \infty$$

c) *Exponential distribution:* This function returns a random variate from the exponential distribution with mean μ. The distribution is:

$$p(x)dx = \frac{1}{\mu}\exp\left(-\frac{x}{\mu}\right)dx$$

$$x \geq 0$$

d) *Laplace distribution:* The Laplace (a) function returns a random variate from the Laplace distribution with width a. The distribution is:

$$p(x)dx = \frac{1}{2a}\exp\left(-|\frac{x}{a}|\right)dx$$

$$\infty < x < \infty$$

e) *Exponential power distribution:* The exponential power (a, b) function returns a random variate from the exponential power distribution with scale parameter a and exponent b. The distribution is:

$$p(x)dx = \frac{1}{2a\gamma\left(1+\frac{1}{b}\right)}\exp\left(-|\frac{x}{a}|^b\right)dx$$

$$x \geq 0$$

f) *Cauchy distribution:* The function Cauchy (a), returns a random variate from the Cauchy distribution with scale parameter a. The probability distribution for Cauchy random variates is:

$$p(x)dx = \frac{1}{a\pi\left(1+\left(\frac{1}{b}\right)^2\right)}dx$$

$$-\infty < x < \infty$$

g) *Rayleigh distribution:* The Rayleigh distribution is a special case of the Weibull distribution. Rayleigh distribution is widely used in radiation physics, because of its properties of providing distribution of radial error when the errors in two mutually perpendicular axes are independent. The distribution is:

$$p(x)dx = \frac{x}{\sigma^2}\exp\left(-\frac{x^2}{2\sigma^2}\right)dx$$

$$x > 0$$

h) *Rayleigh tail distribution:* The function Rayleigh tail (a, sigma) returns a random variate from the tail of the Rayleigh distributions with scale parameter sigma and a lower limit of a. The distribution is:

$$p(x)dx = \frac{x}{\sigma^2}\exp\left(-\frac{a^2-x^2}{2\sigma^2}\right)dx$$

$$x > a$$

i) *Gamma distribution:* Gamma distribution depicts distribution of *a* variable bounded at one side. It depicts distribution of time taken by exactly *k* independent events to occur. Gamma distribution is based on two parameter α and θ and is frequently used in queuing theory and reliability analysis. The distribution function is:

$$p(x)dx = \frac{1}{\gamma(a)b^2} x^{a-1} e^{\frac{-a}{b}} dx$$

$$x > 0$$

j) *Chi-squared distribution:* The $x2$ distribution has only one parameter—the number of degrees of freedom. As in the case of *t* distribution, there is a distribution for each degree of freedom and for a very small of degree of freedom the distribution is skewed to the right and as the degree of freedom increases, the curve become more symmetrical. The distribution is represented as:

$$X_i = \sum_i Y_i^2$$

This has a chi-squared distribution with *n* degrees of freedom.

k) *F distribution:* F distribution is defined as the distribution of the ratio of two independent sampling estimates of variance from standard normal distributions. Like *t* and chi-square distributions, the shape of a particular F distribution curve depends on the degree of freedom. If $Y1$ and $Y2$ are chi-squared deviates with $v1$ and $v2$ degrees of freedom then the ratio

$$X = \frac{\left(\dfrac{Y_1}{v_1}\right)}{\left(\dfrac{Y_2}{v_2}\right)}$$

has an F distribution $F(x; v1, v2)$.

l) *T distribution:* T distribution in many ways is like normal distribution, that is, it is symmetric about the mean and it never touches the horizontal axis. Further, the total area under curve in *t* distribution is equal to 1, as in case of normal distribution. However, the *t* distribution curve is flatter than the standard normal distribution, but as the sample size increases, it approaches the standard normal distribution curve. If $Y1$ has a normal distribution and $Y2$ has a chi-squared distribution with v degrees of freedom then the ratio

$$X = \frac{Y_1}{\left(\sqrt{\dfrac{Y_2}{v_2}}\right)}$$

has a *t* distribution $t(x; v)$.

m) *Beta distribution:* Beta distribution is distribution of variables which are bounded at both sides and ranges between 0 and 1. It also depends on two parameters *a* and *b* and is equivalent to uniform distribution in the domain of 0 and 1. The distribution function is:

$$p(x)dx = \frac{\gamma(a+b)}{\gamma(a)\gamma(b)} x^{a-1}(1-x)^{b-1}dx$$

$$0 \le x \le 1$$

n) *Weibull distribution:* Weibull distribution is widely used in survival function analysis. Its distribution depends on parameter β and based on value of β, it can take shape of other distribution. The distribution function is:

$$p(x)dx = \frac{b}{a^b} x^{b-1} \exp(-(x/a)^b)dx$$

$$x \ge 0$$

Appendix C

Z and T distribution

TABLE C1
Z distribution*

x	0.00	0.01	0.02	0.03	0.04	0.05	0.06	0.07	0.08	0.09
-3.0	0.00135	0.00131	0.00126	0.00122	0.00118	0.00114	0.00111	0.00107	0.00104	0.00100
-2.9	0.00187	0.00181	0.00175	0.00169	0.00164	0.00159	0.00154	0.00149	0.00144	0.00139
-2.8	0.00256	0.00248	0.00240	0.00233	0.00226	0.00219	0.00212	0.00205	0.00199	0.00193
-2.7	0.00347	0.00336	0.00326	0.00317	0.00307	0.00298	0.00289	0.00280	0.00272	0.00264
-2.6	0.00466	0.00453	0.00440	0.00427	0.00415	0.00402	0.00391	0.00379	0.00368	0.00357
-2.5	0.00621	0.00604	0.00587	0.00570	0.00554	0.00539	0.00523	0.00508	0.00494	0.00480
-2.4	0.00820	0.00798	0.00776	0.00755	0.00734	0.00714	0.00695	0.00676	0.00657	0.00639
-2.3	0.01072	0.01044	0.01017	0.00990	0.00964	0.00939	0.00914	0.00889	0.00866	0.00842
-2.2	0.01390	0.01355	0.01321	0.01287	0.01255	0.01222	0.01191	0.01160	0.01130	0.01101
-2.1	0.01786	0.01743	0.01700	0.01659	0.01618	0.01578	0.01539	0.01500	0.01463	0.01426
-2.0	0.02275	0.02222	0.02169	0.02118	0.02068	0.02018	0.01970	0.01923	0.01876	0.01831
-1.9	0.02872	0.02807	0.02743	0.02680	0.02619	0.02559	0.02500	0.02442	0.02385	0.02330
-1.8	0.03593	0.03515	0.03438	0.03362	0.03288	0.03216	0.03144	0.03074	0.03005	0.02938
-1.7	0.04457	0.04363	0.04272	0.04182	0.04093	0.04006	0.03920	0.03836	0.03754	0.03673
-1.6	0.05480	0.05370	0.05262	0.05155	0.05050	0.04947	0.04846	0.04746	0.04648	0.04551
-1.5	0.06681	0.06552	0.06426	0.06301	0.06178	0.06057	0.05938	0.05821	0.05705	0.05592
-1.4	0.08076	0.07927	0.07780	0.07636	0.07493	0.07353	0.07215	0.07078	0.06944	0.06811
-1.3	0.09680	0.09510	0.09342	0.09176	0.09012	0.08851	0.08692	0.08534	0.08379	0.08226
-1.2	0.11507	0.11314	0.11123	0.10935	0.10749	0.10565	0.10383	0.10204	0.10027	0.09853
-1.1	0.13567	0.13350	0.13136	0.12924	0.12714	0.12507	0.12302	0.12100	0.11900	0.11702
-1.0	0.15866	0.15625	0.15386	0.15151	0.14917	0.14686	0.14457	0.14231	0.14007	0.13786
-0.9	0.18406	0.18141	0.17879	0.17619	0.17361	0.17106	0.16853	0.16602	0.16354	0.16109
-0.8	0.21186	0.20897	0.20611	0.20327	0.20045	0.19766	0.19489	0.19215	0.18943	0.18673
-0.7	0.24196	0.23885	0.23576	0.23270	0.22965	0.22663	0.22363	0.22065	0.21770	0.21476
-0.6	0.27425	0.27093	0.26763	0.26435	0.26109	0.25785	0.25463	0.25143	0.24825	0.24510
-0.5	0.30854	0.30503	0.30153	0.29806	0.29460	0.29116	0.28774	0.28434	0.28096	0.27760
-0.4	0.34458	0.34090	0.33724	0.33360	0.32997	0.32636	0.32276	0.31918	0.31561	0.31207
-0.3	0.38209	0.37828	0.37448	0.37070	0.36693	0.36317	0.35942	0.35569	0.35197	0.34827

(Table C1 continued)

(*Table C1 continued*)

x	0.00	0.01	0.02	0.03	0.04	0.05	0.06	0.07	0.08	0.09
−0.2	0.42074	0.41683	0.41294	0.40905	0.40517	0.40129	0.39743	0.39358	0.38974	0.38591
−0.1	0.46017	0.45620	0.45224	0.44828	0.44433	0.44038	0.43644	0.43251	0.42858	0.42465
−0.0	0.50000	0.49601	0.49202	0.48803	0.48405	0.48006	0.47608	0.47210	0.46812	0.46414
0.0	0.50000	0.50399	0.50798	0.51197	0.51595	0.51994	0.52392	0.52790	0.53188	0.53586
0.1	0.53983	0.54380	0.54776	0.55172	0.55567	0.55962	0.56356	0.56749	0.57142	0.57535
0.2	0.57926	0.58317	0.58706	0.59095	0.59483	0.59871	0.60257	0.60642	0.61026	0.61409
0.3	0.61791	0.62172	0.62552	0.62930	0.63307	0.63683	0.64058	0.64431	0.64803	0.65173
0.4	0.65542	0.65910	0.66276	0.66640	0.67003	0.67364	0.67724	0.68082	0.68439	0.68793
0.5	0.69146	0.69497	0.69847	0.70194	0.70540	0.70884	0.71226	0.71566	0.71904	0.72240
0.6	0.72575	0.72907	0.73237	0.73565	0.73891	0.74215	0.74537	0.74857	0.75175	0.75490
0.7	0.75804	0.76115	0.76424	0.76730	0.77035	0.77337	0.77637	0.77935	0.78230	0.78524
0.8	0.78814	0.79103	0.79389	0.79673	0.79955	0.80234	0.80511	0.80785	0.81057	0.81327
0.9	0.81594	0.81859	0.82121	0.82381	0.82639	0.82894	0.83147	0.83398	0.83646	0.83891
1.0	0.84134	0.84375	0.84614	0.84849	0.85083	0.85314	0.85543	0.85769	0.85993	0.86214
1.1	0.86433	0.86650	0.86864	0.87076	0.87286	0.87493	0.87698	0.87900	0.88100	0.88298
1.2	0.88493	0.88686	0.88877	0.89065	0.89251	0.89435	0.89617	0.89796	0.89973	0.90147
1.3	0.90320	0.90490	0.90658	0.90824	0.90988	0.91149	0.91308	0.91466	0.91621	0.91774
1.4	0.91924	0.92073	0.92220	0.92364	0.92507	0.92647	0.92785	0.92922	0.93056	0.93189
1.5	0.93319	0.93448	0.93574	0.93699	0.93822	0.93943	0.94062	0.94179	0.94295	0.94408
1.6	0.94520	0.94630	0.94738	0.94845	0.94950	0.95053	0.95154	0.95254	0.95352	0.95449
1.7	0.95543	0.95637	0.95728	0.95818	0.95907	0.95994	0.96080	0.96164	0.96246	0.96327
1.8	0.96407	0.96485	0.96562	0.96638	0.96712	0.96784	0.96856	0.96926	0.96995	0.97062
1.9	0.97128	0.97193	0.97257	0.97320	0.97381	0.97441	0.97500	0.97558	0.97615	0.97670
2.0	0.97725	0.97778	0.97831	0.97882	0.97932	0.97982	0.98030	0.98077	0.98124	0.98169
2.1	0.98214	0.98257	0.98300	0.98341	0.98382	0.98422	0.98461	0.98500	0.98537	0.98574
2.2	0.98610	0.98645	0.98679	0.98713	0.98745	0.98778	0.98809	0.98840	0.98870	0.98899
2.3	0.98928	0.98956	0.98983	0.99010	0.99036	0.99061	0.99086	0.99111	0.99134	0.99158
2.4	0.99180	0.99202	0.99224	0.99245	0.99266	0.99286	0.99305	0.99324	0.99343	0.99361
2.5	0.99379	0.99396	0.99413	0.99430	0.99446	0.99461	0.99477	0.99492	0.99506	0.99520
2.6	0.99534	0.99547	0.99560	0.99573	0.99585	0.99598	0.99609	0.99621	0.99632	0.99643
2.7	0.99653	0.99664	0.99674	0.99683	0.99693	0.99702	0.99711	0.99720	0.99728	0.99736
2.8	0.99744	0.99752	0.99760	0.99767	0.99774	0.99781	0.99788	0.99795	0.99801	0.99807
2.9	0.99813	0.99819	0.99825	0.99831	0.99836	0.99841	0.99846	0.99851	0.99856	0.99861
3.0	0.99865	0.99869	0.99874	0.99878	0.99882	0.99886	0.99889	0.99893	0.99896	0.99900

*Z distribution tables can be generated easily by using Excel spreadsheet and inserting function NORMDIST (*x*, mean, standard deviation, cumulative).

TABLE C2
T distribution*

	T distribution				
	Directional Test (One tail probabilities)				
	0.05	0.025	0.01	0.005	0.0005
	Non-Directional Test (Two tail probabilities)**				
df	–	0.05	0.02	0.01	0.001
1	6.31	12.71	31.82	63.66	636.58
2	2.92	4.30	6.96	9.92	31.60
3	2.35	3.18	4.54	5.84	12.92
4	2.13	2.78	3.75	4.60	8.61
5	2.02	2.57	3.36	4.03	6.87
6	1.94	2.45	3.14	3.71	5.96
7	1.89	2.36	3.00	3.50	5.41
8	1.86	2.31	2.90	3.36	5.04
9	1.83	2.26	2.82	3.25	4.78
10	1.81	2.23	2.76	3.17	4.59
11	1.80	2.20	2.72	3.11	4.44
12	1.78	2.18	2.68	3.05	4.32
13	1.77	2.16	2.65	3.01	4.22
14	1.76	2.14	2.62	2.98	4.14
15	1.75	2.13	2.60	2.95	4.07
16	1.75	2.12	2.58	2.92	4.01
17	1.74	2.11	2.57	2.90	3.97
18	1.73	2.10	2.55	2.88	3.92
19	1.73	2.09	2.54	2.86	3.88
20	1.72	2.09	2.53	2.85	3.85
21	1.72	2.08	2.52	2.83	3.82
22	1.72	2.07	2.51	2.82	3.79
23	1.71	2.07	2.50	2.81	3.77
24	1.71	2.06	2.49	2.80	3.75
25	1.71	2.06	2.49	2.79	3.73
26	1.71	2.06	2.48	2.78	3.71
27	1.70	2.05	2.47	2.77	3.69
28	1.70	2.05	2.47	2.76	3.67
29	1.70	2.05	2.46	2.76	3.66
30	1.70	2.04	2.46	2.75	3.65
31	1.70	2.04	2.45	2.74	3.63
32	1.69	2.04	2.45	2.74	3.62
33	1.69	2.03	2.44	2.73	3.61
34	1.69	2.03	2.44	2.73	3.60
35	1.69	2.03	2.44	2.72	3.59
36	1.69	2.03	2.43	2.72	3.58
37	1.69	2.03	2.43	2.72	3.57
38	1.69	2.02	2.43	2.71	3.57
39	1.68	2.02	2.43	2.71	3.56
40	1.68	2.02	2.42	2.70	3.55

(Table C2 continued)

(*Table C2 continued*)

	T distribution				
	Directional Test (One tail probabilities)				
	0.05	0.025	0.01	0.005	0.0005
	Non-Directional Test (Two tail probabilities)				
df	–	0.05	0.02	0.01	0.001
50	1.68	2.01	2.40	2.68	3.50
60	1.67	2.00	2.39	2.66	3.46
70	1.67	1.99	2.38	2.65	3.43
100	1.66	1.98	2.36	2.63	3.39
200	1.65	1.97	2.35	2.60	3.34
∞	1.65	1.96	2.32	2.57	3.29

*T distribution tables can be generated easily by using Excel spreadsheet and inserting function TINV (probability, degree of freedom).

**For two-tailed tests, the alpha is doubled. For example, consider a test of H_0: $\beta = 0$ vs. H_A: $\beta \neq 0$ where the t-statistics is 3.169 with 10 degrees of freedom. In this case the p-value is $2 \times 0.005 = 0.01$.

GLOSSARY

Abstract	a brief summary statement which describes the essential points of a research article.
Adult literacy rate	the proportion of literate population aged 15 years and above. It is a robust indicator of education efforts in a social environment over a period of time.
Action research	another name for programme evaluation of a highly practical nature.
Ageing	one of the various factors that affects the age composition of a population. It is defined as the ratio of the number of elderly persons to the number of children in a population.
Anonymity	in field research, anonymity requires that the researchers make it impossible to identify individuals from the published research.
Anthropology	social science discipline that studies the physical evolution and variety of human beings, as well as the nature and variety of human cultures.
Applied research	research linking basic research methods to practical situations.
Attrition	reduction in the number of participants/respondents in a study. In case of an experimental design, if one group has more attrition than another group, the process can introduce bias and threaten the internal validity of the research.
Averting behaviour techniques	looks at how investing in a particular technology can result in averting adverse environmental effects.
Benchmark	the standard or target value accepted by professional associations or a group of organizations. It may be composed of one or more items.

Beneficiary assessment	involves systematic consultation with project beneficiaries and other stakeholders to help them identify and design development activities.
Bias	an influence that distorts the results of a research study.
Birth rate	the number of births during a stated period divided by population size.
Body mass index	the most widely used measure for assessment of nutritional status in adults as it reflects the affect of both acute and chronic energy deficiency/excess. It is defined as the weight in kilograms divided by the square of the height in metres.
Bracketing	process used by researchers working within the Husserlian phenomenological tradition to identify their preconceived beliefs and opinions about the phenomenon under investigation, in order to clarify how personal biases and experience might influence what is seen, heard and reported.
Categorical variable	variable with discrete values; for example, a person's gender or a person's marital status.
Causal relationship	a relationship where variation in one variable causes variation in another.
Continuous monitoring	an on-going measure of progress which determines accountability in activities related to inputs.
Convenience sample	a case of sampling in which sampling units are selected out of convenience. For example, in clinical practice researchers are forced to use clients who are available as sample, as they do not have much option.
Correlation	a measure of the association between two variables. It means a stronger correlation if it is close to 1.
Covariation	a measure of how two variables vary relative to one another.
Central tendency	measure of the typicality or centrality of a set of scores. The three main measures of central tendency are mean, median and mode.
Clinical trial	large-scale experiment designed to test the effectiveness of a clinical treatment.
Cluster sampling	probability sampling strategy involving successive sampling of units (or clusters); the sampled units progress from larger ones to smaller ones (for example, health authority/health board, trust, senior managers).
Coding	process of allocating codes to responses collected during fieldwork facilitating analysis of data.
Cohort study	a trend study that studies changes in cohorts, i.e., people belonging to an organization or location that experience the same life events over time.

Concentration index	provides a means of quantifying the degree of income-related inequality in a specific health variable.
Confidence interval	identifies a range of values that includes the true population of a particular characteristic at a specified probability (usually 95 per cent).
Concurrent monitoring	used as an evaluation tool in determining accountability in activities related to inputs.
Content validity	tries to assess whether content of the measurement technique is in consonance with the known literature on the topic.
Contingent valuation method	involves setting up a carefully worded questionnaire that asks people their WTP and/or WTA through structured questions.
Confounding variable	variable which is not controlled and which may affect the results of experimental research.
Constant comparative method	method in which newly-gathered data is continually compared with collected data to refine the development of theoretical categories and relationships.
Content analysis	an approach to analysis of documents and text, which seeks to quantify content into meaningful and predetermined (in line with the objectives of the study) categories in a coherent way.
Continuous variable	variable that can take on an infinite range of values along a specific continuum. Examples include weight and height.
Correlation	one of the most widely used measures of association between two or more variables.
Correlation coefficient	indicates both the type of correlation as well as the strength of relationship. Coefficient value determines the strength while the sign indicates whether variables change in the same direction or in opposite directions.
Cost-benefit analysis	determines accountability in outputs related to inputs and thus suggests the technical feasibility of projects.
Crude birth rate	defined as the number of births during a stated period divided by population size.
Customised research	process that is specific to a client's need/project objectives.
Data analysis	goes beyond summary and organization of data to interpreting patterns within data.
Data collection	stage in the research process when information is gathered through surveys, experiments, fieldwork, or indirect methods to generate data.
Data files	files containing the primary data of first-hand observations, field interviews and video footage, along with notes identifying exactly when and where the information was gathered.

Debriefing	explaining the procedures of a research project to participants.
Deductive reasoning	drawing ideas from other ideas or theories and moving logically from general principles or assumptions to more specific ideas.
Dependent variable	referred to by some researchers as response variable/outcome variable. It is defined as variable which might be modified by some treatment or exposure, or a variable which we are trying to predict through research.
Descriptive statistics	summarize data quantitatively by using tables, graphs and measures, such as those of central tendency and variation.
Descriptive study	enumerates descriptive data about the population being studied and does not try to establish a causal relationship between events.
Direct research methods	techniques of data gathering that involve interaction with the individuals or groups being studied, such as through surveys, experiments and participant observation fieldwork.
Dose-response technique	considers physical and ecological links between pollution ('dose') and impact ('response'), and values the final impact at a market or shadow price.
Dropout rate	defined as the percentage of students dropping out of a class/classes in a given year.
Double-barrelled question	question that asks two or even more questions simultaneously; for example, 'What do you think of proposed changes in the country's economic policy and foreign policy'.
Depth interviews	describes a variety of data collection techniques. Used mainly for qualitative research undertaken with individual respondents rather than groups.
Desk research	analysis and documentation of available information for preparing survey instruments. It also paves the way for finalizing sampling and operation plans for developing lists of indicators for the study.
Data saturation	the point at which data collection can cease. This point of closure is arrived at when the information that is being shared with the researcher becomes repetitive and contains no new ideas.
Descriptive statistics	used to describe, summarize, or explain a given set of data.
Environmental management systems	provides a framework for organizations to manage their environmental obligations.
Epi Info	consists of a series of micro-computer programmes developed for epidemiologic investigations.
Ethnography	research methodology associated with anthropology and sociology that systematically describes the culture of a group of people.
Ethnomethodology	systematic study of the ways in which people use social interaction to make sense of their situation and create their 'reality'

Experimental research — research methodology used to establish cause-and-effect relationships between the independent and dependent variables by means of manipulation of variables, control and randomization.

Experimental group — group of subjects who receive the experimental treatment or intervention under investigation in experimental research.

Extraneous variable — variable that interferes with the relationship between the independent and dependent variables and which, therefore, needs to be controlled for in some way.

Feasibility assessment — determines the technical and financial capability of a programme.

Fecundity — defined as the biological capacity of women to reproduce.

Fecundability — a measure of fecundity. It may be defined as a measure of chance of conception.

Fertility — defined as the actual birth performance of women.

Field notes — notes taken by researchers to record unstructured observations they make 'in the field' and their interpretation of those observations.

Focus group — interview conducted with a small group of people to explore their ideas on a particular topic.

Foetal deaths — defined as a death prior to birth.

Frequency distribution — visual display of numerical values ranging from the lowest to the highest, showing the number of times (frequency) each value occurs.

Game theory — a formal study of decision-making where several players must make choices that potentially affect the interests of the other players.

Gini coefficient — measures inequality in distribution and is calculated as the area between a Lorentz curve and the line of absolute equality, and varies between 0 and 1.

Gini index — calculated as the area between a Lorentz curve and the line of absolute equality, expressed in terms of percentage.

Guttman scaling — developed in the 1940s; a technique of mixing questions up in the sequence they are asked so that respondents do not see that several questions are related.

Gross enrolment ratio — enrolment at a specified level of schooling, irrespective of the age of student enrolled, to the population of children in the age group expected to be at that level of schooling as per prevalent norms on school enrolments.

Gross national product — measures the value of production in a country in the short run; also defined as factor income earned from economic activities occurring in one nation.

Grounded theory — research approach used to develop conceptual categories/theories about social processes inductively from real-world observations (data) from a selected group of people.

Hall tests	a group of respondents are recruited to attend a fixed location, often a large room or hall, where they respond—usually as individuals—to a set of stimuli.
Hawthorne effect	defined as tendency of humans to temporarily improve their performance when they are aware it is being studied, especially in a scenario when they think they have been singled out for some experimental treatment.
Hedonic pricing method	involves an assembly of cross-sectional data on house price estimated by estate agents, together with data on factors likely to influence these prices.
Humanistic social research	represents various perspectives in the social sciences, which emphasize ways in which the natural and social sciences differ in their basic assumptions and approaches to research and methods.
Hypothesis	a statement that predicts the relationship between variables (specifically the relationship between the independent and dependent variables).
Impact evaluation	ascertains the project impact by analyzing whether the project's activities and task have been successful in achieving the desired objective and goal.
Indexes	summative measures, constituting a set of items, which measure a latent variable's characteristics.
Independent variable	a variable that explains any influences/changes in the response variable. Also referred to as explanatory variable.
Index of ageing	defined as the ratio of the number of elderly persons to the number of children in a population.
Inductive reasoning	a logical process of reasoning used to develop more general rules from specific observations.
Infant mortality rate	refers to the number of deaths per 1,000 live births in the first year of a child's life.
Inferential statistics	statistics that allow a researcher to make inferences about whether relationships observed in a sample are likely to occur in the wider population from which that sample was drawn.
Inputs	defined as any human, physical and financial resources that are used to undertake a project or initiative.
Interrater reliability	measure of the consistency between the ratings/values assigned to an attribute that is being rated or observed.
Interview	method of data collection involving an interviewer asking questions of another person (a respondent) either face-to-face or over the telephone.
Interval scale	a scale where categories have equal spacing. For example, temperature, as measured in degrees Fahrenheit or Celcius, constitutes an internal scale. We can say that a temperature of 80 degrees is higher than a temperature of 40 degrees, but we still can't say that 80 degrees in twice as hot as 40 degrees.

Joint Forest Management	a concept of developing partnerships between fringe forest user groups and the forest department on the basis of mutual trust and jointly defined roles and responsibilities with regard to forest protection and development.
Kuznets ratios	refer to the share of income owned by the poorest x per cent of the population, or to the ratio of the income shares of the richest y per cent to the poorest x per cent.
Life expectancy	number of years the person is expected to live given the prevailing age-specific mortality rates of the population to which he/she belongs.
Likert scale	method used to measure attitudes, which involves respondents indicating their degree of agreement or disagreement with a series of statements. Scores are summed to give a composite measure of attitudes.
Linear correlation	a statistical measure of the strength of the relationship between variables (for example, treatment and outcome).
Linear regression	prediction equation that estimates the value of the outcome variable (y) for any given treatment variable (x).
Logical framework approach	provides a set of tools that can be used for planning, designing, implementing and evaluating projects.
Lorentz curve	a measure of inequality. It plots the cumulative percentages of total income received against the cumulative percentages of recipients, starting with the poorest individual or household.
Maternal mortality	represents all deaths of women attributed to complications of pregnancy, childbirth and the puerperium occurring within 42 days after the termination of pregnancy.
Mean	most commonly used and accepted measure of central tendency. It is obtained by adding all observations and dividing the sum by the number of observations and should be used in case of interval or ratio data.
Median	defined as the middle value in an ordered arrangement of observations. It is a measure of central tendency if all items are arranged either in ascending or descending order of magnitude.
Measurement scale	measurement of a phenomenon or property means assigning a number or category to represent it.
Micronutrient malnutrition	apart from protein energy malnutrition, micronutrient deficiencies, namely, iodine, iron and vitamin A deficiency are also quite prevalent in India.
Meta-analysis	integrates the outcome estimates from multiple studies to arrive at an overall or summary judgement on an evaluation question.

Method slurring	term used to describe the tendency of some researchers to combine qualitative research approaches without adequately acknowledging the epistemological origins and assumptions that underpin the methodologies they are blending.
Mode	the most frequently occurring value in a group of observations.
Modelling/Simulation	application of specific assumptions to a set of variable factors and the relationships which exist between them is termed as modelling/simulation.
Monitoring	used to track progress of act on a continuous basis. It does so by measuring inputs and outputs and any changes in output due to change in input.
Multivariate analysis	a range of analysis techniques which can examine quantitative data in greater depth than can usually be obtained from a basic cross-analysis of the data by, for example, age, sex and social grade.
Nash equilibrium	John Nash demonstrated that finite games always have an equilibrium point, wherein all players choose actions which are best for them vis-à-vis their opponents' choices.
Natural experiment	a study that uses an uncontrolled real-life event, such as an accident or a change in law, and that looks at human responses to the event as if it were an experimental variable.
Negative skew	a distribution curve with a long tail on the left side, indicating a concentration of cases toward the high end of the measured characteristic.
Net enrolment ratio	refers to proportion of the population of a particular age group, enrolled at a specific level of schooling, to the total population in that age group.
Nominal scale	the lowest level of measurement that involves assigning characteristics to categories which are mutually exclusive, but which lack any intrinsic order.
Non-participant observation	observation of group behaviour without entering into the activities of the group.
Normal distribution	frequency distributions that can be graphically represented as some type of symmetrical bell curve.
Naturalistic paradigm	assumes that there are multiple interpretations of reality and that the goal of researchers working within this perspective is to understand how individuals construct their own reality within their social context.
Needs assessment	determines the programme need from the perspective of all stakeholders.

Network analysis   a vital technique in project management, used widely for the planning, management and control of projects.

Non-parametric statistics   statistical tests that can be used to analyse nominal or ordinal data. They involve fewer rigorous assumptions about the underlying distribution of variables.

Null hypothesis   a statement that there is no relationship between the independent and dependent variables, and that any relationship observed is due to chance or fluctuations in sampling.

Observation   method of data collection in which data are gathered through visual observations. They can be structured observations or unstructured observations.

Old-age dependency ratio   defined as the number of persons in the age group 60 years and above, per 100 persons in the age group 15–59 years.

Omnibus surveys   surveys covering a number of topics, usually for different clients. The samples tend to be nationally representative and composed of types of people for whom there is a general demand.

One-tailed test   used by a researcher when testing a directional (or one-tailed) hypothesis. This type of test of statistical significance uses only one tail of an underlying distribution of scores/values to determine significance.

Operations research   widely used to assess evaluation using a systems model. The model is a collection of logical and mathematical relationships that represents aspects of the situation under study.

Ordinal scale   can be used to rank order a variable, but the intervals between categories are not equal or fixed (for example, strongly agree, agree, neither agree nor disagree, disagree, strongly disagree).

Organizational development   carried out to create change agents in the organization. It is an important tool to assess whether organization dynamics, values, structure or functioning is in consonance with visions or goals sought by an organization.

Outcomes   consequences/result of an intervention; can arise during and after an intervention.

Outcome evaluations   analyse the impact of programme's service delivery and organizational input on desired outcome.

Parameter   signifies the characteristic of a population.

Parametric statistics   a type of inferential statistic that involves the estimation of at least one parameter in case of normal distribution.

Panel study   asks the same questions to the same people time after time.

Phenomenology   a research methodology which has its roots in philosophy and which focuses on the lived experience of individuals.

Population	a group of individual persons, objects, or items from which samples are taken for measurement.
Positivism	paradigm assuming that human behaviour is determined by external stimuli, and that it is possible to use the principles and methods traditionally employed by the natural scientist to observe and measure social phenomena.
Process evaluation	envisages finding statistically significant relationships between activities and inputs.
Purposive/purposeful sampling	a non-probability sampling strategy in which the researcher selects participants who are considered to be typical of the wider population.
Qualitative data	measures behaviour that is not computable by arithmetic relations and is represented by pictures, words or images.
Quantitative data	numerical records that result from a process of measurement and on which basic mathematical operations can be carried out.
Quasi-experiment	a type of experimental design where random assignment to groups is not employed for either ethical or practical reasons, but certain methods of control are employed and the independent variable is manipulated.
Quota sampling	a non-probability sampling strategy where the researcher identifies the various strata of a population and ensures that all these strata are proportionately represented within the sample to increase its representativeness.
Random numbers	sets of numbers lacking any patterned sequence and are generated by a computer programme or a published list of random numbers.
Random sample	a sample drawn in such a way that each and every member or unit of the population has an equal chance of being selected. It is also known as a probability sample.
Range	difference between the highest and lowest scores in a distribution. It is a measure of variability.
Ratio scale	scores are assigned on a scale with equal intervals and also a true 0 point (for example, measurement in yards, feet and inches or in metres and centimetres).
Raw data	research information that has been collected but not yet organized, summarized, or interpreted.
Reliability	the ability of a measurement instrument to measure the same thing each time it is used.
Replication	repeating a research design in its entirety to see if the same results can be obtained. Most often replication is undertaken with experiments and surveys in the social sciences.

Research methods	techniques of systematic, empirical research that have become acceptable in the social sciences.
Research process	sequence or steps of systematic empirical research.
Response rate	percentage of completed questionnaires (or questions within a questionnaire) obtained in a survey.
Response set	tendency of respondents to unwittingly repeat the type of response from one question to another in a questionnaire.
Randomization	random assignment of subjects to experimental and control groups (that is, the allocation to groups is determined by chance).
Randomized controlled trial	a trial in which participants are randomly assigned either to an intervention group (for example, a drug treatment) or to a control group (for example, a placebo treatment).
Reproductive period	the child-bearing period which starts with the onset of menarche and continues till menopause.
Sampling	process of selecting a sub-group of a population to represent the entire population. There are several different types of sampling.
Sampling bias	distortion that occurs when a sample is not representative of the population from which it was drawn.
Sampling error	fluctuation in the value of a statistic from different samples drawn from the same population.
Sampling frame	list of the entire population eligible to be included within the specific parameters of a research study. A researcher must have a sampling frame in order to generate a random sample.
Semiotics	a form of social description and analysis that is used in research. It puts particular emphasis on an understanding and exploration of the cultural context in which the work is taking place.
Sex ratio	defined as number of females per 1,000 males.
Skewness	summarizes the shape of distribution. It measures the extent to which the sample distribution deviates from normal distribution.
Significance level	indicates the risk of the researcher of making a type I error (that is an error that occurs when a researcher rejects the null hypothesis when it is true and concludes that a statistically significant relationship/difference exists when it does not).
Simple random sampling	probability sampling method that gives each eligible element/unit an equal chance of being selected in the sample. Random procedures are employed to select a sample using a sampling frame.
Snowball sampling	a non-probability sampling strategy whereby referrals from earlier participants are used to gather the required number of participants.
Social assessment	helps make the project responsive to social development concerns.

Social audit	tool to assess whether an organization has fulfilled its social commitments and values.
Structured interview	an interview in which the interviewer asks the respondents the same questions using an interview schedule.
Standard deviation	a descriptive statistic used to measure the degree of variability within a set of scores.
Stakeholders' analysis	process that helps to assess the impact of social change as it obtains the views of all partners associated in the process.
Statistic	estimate of a parameter calculated from a set of data gathered from a sample.
Statistical analysis	analysis is based on the principle of gathering data from a sample of individuals and using those data to make inferences about the wider population from which the sample was drawn.
Statistical inference	a procedure using the laws of probability to infer the attributes of a population based on information gathered from a sample.
Statistical test	procedure that allows a researcher to determine the probability that the results obtained from a sample reflect the true parameters of the population.
Sterility	lack of capacity of a woman or a couple to produce a live birth; also called infecundity.
Surrogate market approach	looks at markets for private goods and services, which are related to the environmental commodities of concern.
Sustainable development	development that meets the needs of the present without compromising the ability of future generations to meet their own needs and extending to all the opportunity to fulfill their aspirations for a better life.
Systematic sampling	probability sampling strategy involving the selection of participants randomly drawn from a population at fixed intervals (for example, every 20th name from a sampling frame).
Survey research	research approach designed to collect systematically descriptions of existing phenomena in order to describe or explain what is going on. Data is obtained through direct questioning of a sample of respondents.
Test-retest reliability	means of assessing the stability of a research instrument by calculating the correlation between scores obtained on repeated administrations.
Total fertility rate	summative measure that signifies the average number of children a woman is expected to have during her reproductive life. The average number of children born to women can be simply calculated by

	averaging the number of live births, for women who have passed their reproductive years.
Travel cost method	one of the earliest methods of environmental valuation, which works on weak complementarities. It has been widely used to measure the value of natural resources as a source of recreational activities.
Triangulation	used in a research context to describe the use of a variety of data sources or methods to examine a specific phenomenon either simultaneously or sequentially in order to produce a more accurate account of the phenomenon under investigation.
Type I error	characterized by false rejection of the null hypothesis and is referred by alpha (α) level.
Type II error	corresponds to the acceptance of a false null hypothesis instead of its rejection. The probability of making a type II error is called beta (β) and the probability of avoiding a type II error is called power ($1 - \beta$).
Unstructured interview	an interview, in which the researcher asks open-ended questions that give the respondent considerable freedom to talk freely on the topic and to influence the direction of the interview.
Validity	refers to the accuracy and truth of the data and findings that are produced.
Variable	an attribute or characteristic of a person or an object that takes on different values (that is, it varies) within the population under investigation (for example, age, weight, pulse rate).
Variation	a measure of the spread of the variable, usually used to describe the deviation from a central value (for example, the mean). Numerically it is the sum of the squared deviations from the mean.
Variance	another measure of variability symbolized by s^2. The standard deviation, represented by s, is defined as the positive square root of the variance.
Watershed protection approach	strategy for effectively protecting and restoring aquatic ecosystems for overall rural development.

Bibliography

Acharya, Sarthi (1991). 'Agricultural Incomes and Rural Poverty: An Analysis at Crop–State Level in India'. Working Paper Series No. 102. The Hague: The Institute of Social Studies.

Afifi, A.A. and S.P. Azen (1979). *Statistical Analysis, A Computer Oriented Approach*. New York: Academic Press.

Afifi, A. and V. Clark (1990). *Computer-aided Multivariate Analysis* (2nd edn). New York, NY: Van Nostrand Reinhold.

—— (1996). *Computer-aided Multivariate Analysis* (3rd edn). London: Chapman & Hall.

Agresti, A. and B. Finlay (1997). *Statistical Methods for the Social Sciences*. Upper Saddle River, NJ: Prentice Hall.

Ahluwalia, Isher J. and I.M.D. Little (1998). *India's Economic Reforms and Development: Essays for Manmohan Singh*. New Delhi: Oxford University Press.

Aldenderfer, Mark S. and Roger K. Blashfield (1984). *Cluster Analysis*. Series: Quantitative Applications in the Social Sciences. Newbury Park, CA: Sage Publications.

Altaf, Mir Anjum, Dale Whittington, Haroon Jamal and V. Kerry Smith (1993). 'Rethinking rural water supply policy in the Punjab, Pakistan'. *Water Resources Research*. 29: 1943–54.

American Psychological Association (1985). *Standards for Educational and Psychological Testing*. Washington D.C.: APA.

Andersen, E.B. (1991). *The Statistical Analysis of Categorical Data* (2nd revised edn). New York: Springer Verlag.

Arrow, K.J. (1951). *Social Choice and Individual Values*. New York: John Wiley.

—— (2000). 'Observations on Social Capital', in P. Dasgupta and I. Serageldin (eds), *Social Capital: A Multifaceted Perspective*. Washington D.C.: The World Bank.

Arrow, Kenneth J., B. Bolin, R. Costanza, P. Dasgupta, C. Folke, C.S. Holling, B.O. Jansson, S. Levin, K.G. Maler, C. Perrings and D. Pimentel (1995). 'Economic Growth, Carrying Capacity, and the Environment'. *Science*. 268: 520–21.

Bacharach, Michael (1987). 'A Theory of Rational Decision in Games'. *Erkenntnis*. 27(1987): 17–55.

Balakrishnan, Radhika and Uma Narayan (1996). 'Combining Justice with Development: Rethinking Rights and Responsibilities in the Context of World Hunger and Poverty', in William Aiken and Hugh LaFollette (eds), *World Hunger and Morality*. New Jersey: Prentice Hall.

Baland, J.M. and J.P. Platteau (1996). *Halting Degradation of Natural Resources: Is There a Role for Rural Communities?* Oxford: Clarendon Press.

Banerjee, B. (1983). 'Social Networks in the Migration Process: Empirical Evidence on Chain Migration in India'. *Journal of Developing Areas*. 17: 185–96.

Bardhan, P. (1996). 'Research on Poverty and Development Twenty Years After Redistribution with Growth'. Proceedings of the Annual World Bank Conference on Development Economics, 1995.

Bartelmus, P. (1999). 'Economic Growth and Patterns of Sustainability'. Wuppertal Paper No. 98. Wuppertal Institute, Germany. http://www.wupperinst.org/Publikationen/WP/WP98.pdf [24.2.03]

Bartelmus, Peter and Jan van Tongeren (1994). *Environmental Accounting: An Operational Perspective*. Working Paper Series No. 1. Department for Economic and Social Information and Policy Analysis, United Nations.

Basu, Kaushik (1991). 'The Elimination of Endemic Poverty in South Asia: Some Policy Options', in Jean Drèze and Amartya Sen (eds), *The Political Economy of Hunger: Volume 3. Endemic Hunger*. Oxford: Clarendon Press.

Basu, R.N. (1985). 'India's Immunization Programme'. *World Health Forum*. 6: 35–38.

Basu, S.K. (1985). 'Inbreeding in India: Its Genetic Consequences and Implications in Health Care'. *Population Genetics and Health Care: Issues and Future Strategies*. NIHFW Technical Report 8. New Delhi: National Institute for Health and Family Welfare.

Bean, J. (1975). 'Distribution and Properties of Variance Estimators for Complex Multistage Probability Samples: An Empirical Distribution'. *Vital and Health Statistics*. 2(65). Washington D.C.: US Government Printing Office.

Behling, Orlando and Kenneth S. Law (2000). *Translating Questionnaires and Other Research Instruments: Problems and Solutions*. Series: Quantitative Applications in the Social Sciences No. 133. Thousand Oaks, CA: Sage Publications.

Bell, J. (1993). *Doing Your Research Project: A Guide for First-time Researchers in Education and Social Science* (2nd edn). Buckingham, Philadelphia: Open University Press.

Berger, R.M. and M.A. Patchner (1988). *Implementing the Research Plan: A Guide for the Helping Professions*. Newbury Park, CA: Sage Publications.

Bernstein, Ira H., with Calvin P. Garbin and Gary K. Teng (1988). *Applied Multivariate Analysis*. New York: Springer Verlag.

Berry, W.D. and M.S. Lewis-Beck (eds) (1986). *New Tools for Social Scientists: Advances and Applications in Research Methods*. Beverly Hills, CA: Sage Publications.

Bhatia R., P. Rogers, J. Briscoe, B. Sinha and R. Cestti (1994). *Water Conservation and Pollution Control in Indian Industries: How to Use Water Tariffs, Pollution Charges, and Fiscal Incentives*. Washington D.C.: Water and Sanitation Currents. UNDP-World Bank Sanitation Programme.

Bickman, L. and Rog, D.J. (eds). (1988). *Handbook of Applied Social Research Methods*. Thousand Oaks, CA: Sage Publications.

Binswanger, Hans P. (1991). 'Brazilian Policies That Encourage Deforestation in the Amazon'. *World Development*. 19(7): 821–29.

Binswanger, Hans P. and Pierre Landell-Mills (1995). *The World Bank's Strategy for Reducing Poverty and Hunger: A Report to the Development Community*. Washington D.C.: The World Bank.

Blalock, H. (1979). *Social Statistics*. New York: McGraw-Hill.

Blalock, H.M., Jr. and A. Blalock (eds) (1968). *Methodology in Social Research*. New York, NY: McGraw-Hill.

Bland J.M. and D.G. Altman (1999). 'Measuring Agreement in Method Comparison Studies'. *Statistical Methods in Medical Research*. 8: 135–60.

Boadway, R.W. and N. Bruce (1984). *Welfare Economics*. Oxford: Basil Blackwell.

Bohrnstedt, G.W. and D. Knoke (1988). *Statistics for Social Data Analysis* (2nd edn). Ithaca, IL: F.E. Peacock Publishers.

Boserup, E. (1965). *The Conditions of Agricultural Growth: The Economics of Agricultural Change under Population Pressure*. London: Allen and Unwin.

Box, G.E.P. and G.M. Jenkins (1976). *Time Series Analysis: Forecasting and Control*. San Francisco, CA: Holden Day.

Boyle, G.J. and P.D. Langley (1989). *Elementary Statistical Methods for Students of Psychology, Education and the Social Sciences*. Elmsford, NY: Pergamon.

Brandenburger, Adam (1992). 'Knowledge and Equilibrium in Games'. *Journal of Economic Perspectives*. 6: 83–101.

Brenner, M., J. Brown, J. and D. Canter (eds) (1985). *The Research Interview, Uses and Approaches*. London: Academic Press.

Brogan, D., E. Flagg, M. Deming and R. Waldman (1994). 'Increasing the Accuracy of the Expanded Programme on Immunization's Cluster Survey Design'. *Annals of Epidemiology*. 4(4): 302–11.

Brown, S.R. and L.E. Melamed (1990). *Experimental Design and Analysis*. Newbury Park, CA: Sage Publications.

Carmines, E.G. and R.A. Zeller (1991). *Reliability and Validity Assessment*. Newbury Park, CA: Sage Publications.

Carron, Gabriel and Chau Ta Ngoc (eds) (1980). *Regional Disparities in Educational Development: Diagnosis and Policies for Reduction*. Paris: IIEP.

Cattell, R.B. (1966). 'The Scree Test for the Number of Factors'. *Multivariate Behavior. Research*. 1: 245–76.

Census of India (1954). Literacy and Education Standard. Paper 5.

Centre for Science and Environment (1997). *The State of India's Environment: A Citizen's Report 4—Dying Wisdom: Rise, Fall and Potential of India's Traditional Water Harvesting Systems*. New Delhi: Centre for Science and Environment.

——— (2002). *State of India's Environment: The Citizens Fifth Report, Part I—National Overview* (reprint). New Delhi: Centre for Science and Environment.

Chaudhry, M. Ghaffar (1996). 'Abolishing Poverty and Hunger: A South Asian Perspective'. *Contemporary South Asia*. 5(3): 253–61.

Chitale M.A. (1992). 'Population and Water Resources of India', in V. Gowariker (ed.), *Science, Population and Development*. Pune: Unmesh Publications.

Cho, Lee-Jay, Robert D. Retherford and Minja Kim Choe (1986). *The Own-Children Method of Fertility Estimation*. Honolulu: East-West Center.

Choudhuri, N. (1976). 'What Ails our Elementary Education'. *Secular Democracy*. 8(31, 32 and 33): 1675–81.

Cipplola, Carlo M. (1969). *Literacy and Development in the West*. London: Penguin.

Clark, R. (1991). *Water: The International Crisis*. London: Earthscan.

Cliff, Norman (1987). *Analyzing Multivariate Data*. San Diego: Harcourt Brace Jovanovich Publishers.

Cohen, J. (1988). *Statistical Power Analysis for the Behavioral Sciences*. Hillsdale, NJ: Lawrence Erlbaum Associates.

Converse, Jean and Stanley Presser (1986). *Survey Questions: Handcrafting the Standardized Questionnaire*. Newbury Park, CA: Sage Publications.

Cook, T.D. and W.R. Shadish (1986). 'Program Evaluation: The Worldly Science'. *Annual Review of Psychology*. 37: 193–232.

Cook, T.D. and D.T. Campbell (1979). *Quasi experimentation: Design and Analysis Issues for Field Settings*. Boston: Houghton Mifflin Co.

Cozby, P.C. (1993). *Methods in Behavioral Research* (5th edn). Mountain View, CA: Mayfield Publishing.

Cronbach, L.J. (1951). 'Coefficient Alpha and the Internal Structure of Tests'. *Psychometrika*. 16: 297–334.

Cronk, Brian C. (1999). *How to Use SPSS: A Step-by-Step Guide to Analysis and Interpretation*. Los Angeles: Pyrczak Publishing.

Cropper, M. and W. Oates (1992). 'Environmental Economics: A Survey'. *Journal of Economic Literature*. 30(2): 675–740.

Crotty, M. (1998). *Foundations of Social Research: Meaning and Perspective in the Research Process*. London: Sage Publications.

D'Agostino, R.B. and M.A. Stevens (1986). *Goodness-of-Fit Techniques*. New York: Marcel Dekker.

Daily, G.C. and Ehrlich, P.R. (1996). 'Socioeconomic Equity, Sustainability, and Earth's Carrying Capacity'. *Ecological Applications*. 6(4): 991–1001.

Daly, H.E. and J.B. Cobb (1994). *For the Common Good*. Boston: Beacon.

DANIDA (1990). *Logical Framework Approach for Project Preparation: Handbook on Logical Framework Approach* (2 volumes). Copenhagen: DANIDA.

Danziger, Sheldon H., Gary D. Sandefur and Daniel H. Weinberg (1994). *Confronting Poverty: Prescriptions for Change*. Cambridge, MA: Harvard University Press.

Darling, A., C. Gomez and M. Niklitschek (1993). 'The Question of a Public Sewerage System in a Caribbean Country: A Case Study' in M. Munasinghe (ed.), *Environmental Economics and Natural Resource Management in Developing Countries*. World Bank for CIDIE.

Dasgupta, P. (1982). *The Control of Resources*. Cambridge, MA: Harvard University Press.

——— (1993a). *An Inquiry into Well-Being and Destitution*. Oxford: Clarendon Press.

——— (1993b). 'Natural Resources in the Age of Substitutability', in A.V. Kneese and J.L. Sweeney (eds), *Handbook of Natural Resource and Energy Economics*. Amsterdam: North Holland.

——— (1996). 'The Economics of the Environment'. *Environment and Development Economics*. 1(4): 387–428.

——— (1999). 'Economic Progress and the Idea of Social Capital', in P. Dasgupta and I. Serageldin (eds), *Social Capital: A Multifaceted Perspective*. Washington D.C.: The World Bank.

——— (2000). 'Economic Progress and the Idea of Social Capital', Mimeo. Resources for the Future. Washington D.C. and London School of Economics, London, UK.

——— (2001). *Human Well-Being and the Natural Environment*. Oxford: Oxford University Press.

Dasgupta, P. and K. Maler (1991). 'The Environment and Emerging Development Issues', *Proceedings of the Annual World Bank Conference on Development Economics*. Supplement to the World Bank Economic Review and World Research Observer.

Dasgupta, P. and K.G. Maler (1995). 'Poverty, Institutions, and the Environmental Resource-Base', in J. Behrman and T.N. Srinivasan (eds), *Handbook of Development Economics*, Vol. III(A). Amsterdam: North Holland.

Davison, M.L. (1983). *Multidimensional Scaling.* New York, John Wiley and Sons.

DeVaus, D.A. (1995). *Surveys in Social Research* (4th edn). St. Leonards, NSW: Allen & Unwin.

Dillon, William R. and Matthew Goldstein (1984). *Multivariate Analysis: Methods and Applications.* New York: John Wiley & Sons.

Dower, Nigel (1991). 'World Poverty' in Peter Singer (ed.), *A Companion to Ethics.* Oxford: Blackwell.

Dube, S.C. (1985). 'Cultural Problems in the Economic Development of India'. *Economic Weekly.* 17: 12 January.

Dunteman, George H. (1984). *Introduction to Multivariate Analysis.* Thousand Oaks, CA: Sage Publications.

Dupuit, Jules (1952). 'On the Measurement of the Utility of Public Works'. R.H. Barback (trans.). *International Economic Papers.* 2: 83–110.

Dutta, Bhaskar (1996). 'India: Traditions for Poverty Research', in Else Øyen, S.M. Miller and Syed Abdus Samad (eds), *Poverty: A Global Review: Handbook on International Poverty Research.* Oslo: Scandinavian University Press.

Easter, W., G. Fedder, G.L. Moighe and A.M. Dunda (1993). *Water Resources Management: A World Bank Policy Paper.* Washington D.C.: International Bank for Reconstruction and Development/ The World Bank.

Edwards K.A. (1993). 'Water, Environment and Development: A Global Agenda'. *Water Resources Forum.* 17(1): 59–64.

Ehrlich, P.R., Ehrlich, A.H. and Daily, G. (1995). *The Stork and the Plow: The Equity Answer to the Human Dilemma.* New York: G.P. Putnam's Sons.

Elliot, J. (1991). *Action Research for Educational Change.* Milton Keynes: Open University Press.

El Sarafy, S. (1970). 'Green Accounting and Economic Policy'. *Ecological Economics.* 21: 217–29.

Epstein, Paul R. (1997). 'Climate, Ecology, and Human Health'. *Consequences.* 3: 60–86.

Eraut, M. (1994). *Developing Professional Knowledge and Competence.* London: Falmer Press.

Esrey, Steven, Jean Gough, Dave Rapaport, Ron Sawyer, Mayling Simpson-Herbert, Jorge Vargas and Uno Winblad (1988a). *Ecological Sanitation.* Stockholm, Sweden: Swedish International Development Authority (SIDA).

Esrey, S.A., J.P. Habicht, M.C. Latham, D.G. Sisler and G. Casella (1988b). 'Drinking Water Source, Diarrhoeal Morbidity, and Child Growth in Villages with both Traditional and Improved Water Supplies in Rural Lesotho, Southern Africa'. *American Journal of Public Health.* 78(11): 1451–55.

Fagan R.F. and T.G. Arner (1995). *Epi Info, Version 6: A Word Processing, Database, and Statistics Program for Public Health on IBM-compatible Microcomputers.* Atlanta: Centre for Disease Control and Prevention.

Falkenmark, M. (1989). 'The Massive Water Scarcity Now Threatening Africa: Why isn't it Being Addressed?' *Ambio.* 18(2): 112–18.

Falkenmark, M., J. Lundquist and C. Widstrand (1989). 'Macro-scale Water Scarcity Requires Micro-scale Approaches: Aspects of Vulnerability in Semi-arid Development'. *Natural Resources Forum.* 13: 258–67.

Falkenmark, M. and C. Widstrand (1992). 'Population and Water Resources: A Delicate Balance', *Population Bulletin*, 47(3): 329–51. Washington D.C.: Population Reference Bureau.

FAO (1993). *The State of Food and Agriculture.* FAO Agriculture Series No. 26. Rome: FAO.

Fitz-Gibbon, C.T. (1987). *How to Analyze Data.* Newbury Park, CA: Sage Publications.

Fitz-Gibbon, C.T. and L.L. Morris (1978). *How to Design a Program Evaluation.* Beverly Hills, CA: Sage Publications.

Flury, Bernhard and Hans Riedwyl (1988). *Multivariate Statistics: A Practical Approach*. London: Chapman and Hall.

Foddy, W. (1993). *Constructing Questions for Interviews and Questionnaires: Theory and Practice in Social Research*. Cambridge and New York: Cambridge University Press.

Fortney, J.A. (1987). 'The Importance of Family Planning in Reducing Maternal Mortality'. *Studies in Family Planning*. 18(2): 109–114.

Fowler, F.J. (1995). *Improving Survey Questions: Design and Evaluation*. Thousand Oaks, CA: Sage Publications.

Frankel, M.R. (1971). *Inference from Survey Samples*. Ann Arbor, MI: Institute for Social Research, University of Michigan.

Freer, Spreckley (2000). *Social Audit Toolkit* (3rd edn). Herefordshire: Social Audit Partnership.

Fudenberg, Drew and Jean Tirole (1991). *Game Theory*. Cambridge, MA: MIT Press.

Gaiha, Raghav (1995). 'Poverty, Development, and Participation in India: A Progress Report'. *Asian Survey*. 35(9): 867–78.

Glaser, B. and A. Strauss (1967). *The Discovery of Grounded Theory: Strategies for Qualitative Research*. New York: Aldine De Gruyther.

George, Darren and Paul Mallery. *SPSS for Windows Step by Step: A Simple Guide and Reference*. 13.0 Update. 6th Edition. Boston: Allyn & Bacon.

Gleick, P. (1993a). 'Water and Conflict: Fresh Water Resources and International Security'. *International Security*. 18(1). Summer.

Gleick P. (ed.) (1993b). *Water in Crisis: Guide to the World's Fresh Water Resources*. Stockholm, Sweden: Stockholm Environment Institute.

Goodland, R. and H. Daly (1996). 'Environmental Sustainability: Universal and Non-negotiable'. *Ecological Applications*. 6(4): 1002–17.

Goodman, L.A. and W.H. Kruskal (1954). 'Measures of Association for Cross Classifications'. *Journal of the American Statistical Association*. 49: 732–64.

——— (1959). 'Measures of Association for Cross Classifications, II: Further Discussion and References'. *Journal of the American Statistical Association*. 54: 123–63.

Gore, M.S., I.P. Desai and Suma Chitnis (eds) (1967). *Papers in the Sociology of Education in India*. New Delhi: NCERT.

Gosal, G.S. (1964). 'Literacy in India—An Interpretive Study'. *Rural Sociology*. 29(3): 261–77.

Gosling, Louisa and Mike Edwards (1995). *Toolkits: A Practical Guide to Assessment, Monitoring, Review and Evaluation*. Development Manual 5. UK: Save the Children.

Gough, Kathleen (1968). 'Implications of Literacy in Traditional China and India', in Jack Goody (ed.), *Literacy in Traditional Societies*. Cambridge: Cambridge University Press.

Government of India (1970). *The Report of the University Education Commission, Vol. 1*. New Delhi: Ministry of Education.

——— (1999). State of Forest Report, 1999. Forest Survey of India. Dehradun: Ministry of Environment and Forests.

——— (2000). *National Population Policy 2000*. New Delhi: Ministry of Health and Family Welfare.

——— (2000). *Storage of Rain Water*. New Delhi: Ministry of Water Resources.

——— (2001). *Forest Survey of India*. New Delhi: Ministry of Environment and Forests.

——— (2001–2002). *Annual Report*. New Delhi: Ministry of Water Resources.

Government of India (2003). *Family Welfare Programme in India, Year Book 2001*. New Delhi: Department of Family Welfare, MOHFW.

Government of India, Central Water Commission (1996). *Water and Related Statistics Information System*. New Delhi: Directorate Performance Overview and Management Improvement Organization.

Groombridge, B. (ed.) (1994). *1994 IUCN Red List of Threatened Animals*. Switzerland: IUCN.

Grossman, Gene M. and Alan Krueger (1995). 'Economic Growth and the Environment'. *Quarterly Journal of Economics*. (CX-2): 353–77.

Guba, E.G. and Y.S. Lincoln (1981). *Effective Evaluation: Improving the Usefulness of Evaluation Results Through Responsive and Naturalistic Approaches*. San Francisco, CA: Jossey-Bass.

Gupta, S.P. (1998). 'Poverty and Statistics'. *The Hindu*. 28 February.

Gwatkin, D., S. Rustein, K. Johnson, R.P. Pande and A. Wagstaff (2000). *Socio-Economic Differences in Health, Nutrition and Population in the Philippines*. Washington D.C.: The World Bank.

Hakim, C. (1987). *Research Design: Strategies and Choices in the Design of Social Research*. Boston: Allen and Unwin.

Hansen M.H., W.N. Hurwitz and W.G. Madow (1953). *Sample Survey Methods and Theory, Volume I: Methods and Applications*. New York: Wiley.

Harberger, A.C. (1971). 'Three Basic Postulates for Applied Welfare Economics'. *Journal of Economic Literature*. 9: 785–97.

Hardin, G. (1968). 'The Tragedy of the Commons'. *Science*. 162: 1243–48.

Harris, Richard J. (1975). *A Primer of Multivariate Statistics*. New York: Academic Press.

Hayami, Yujiro and Kikuchi Masao (1981). *Asian Village Economy at the Crossroads: An Economic Approach to Institutional Change*. University of Tokyo Press: Tokyo.

Herrick, Virgil E. and Ralph W. Tyler (1950). *Toward Improved Curriculum Theory*. Chicago: University of Chicago Press.

Hessler, R.M. (1992). *Social Research Methods*. St. Paul: West Pub. Co.

Hicks, John R. (1940). 'The Valuation of the Social Income'. *Economica* (New Series). 7(26): 105–24.

Hicks, J.R. (1946). *Value and Capital: An Inquiry into Some Fundamental Principles of Economic Theory* (2nd edn). Oxford: Oxford University Press.

Hill, M.O. and H.G. Gauch, Jr. (1980). 'Detrended Correspondence Analysis: An Improved Ordination Technique'. *Vegetatio*. 42: 47–58.

Hu, Howard Moeller and W. Dade (1997). 'The Scope' in Howard Moeller Hu and W. Dade (eds), *Environmental Health*. Cambridge MA: Harvard University Press.

Huitt, William G. (1998). *Internal and External Validity*. http://www.valdosta.peachnet.edu/~whuitt/psy702/intro/valdgn.html

Interagency Committee on Integrated Rural Development for Asia and the Pacific (1992). *Partners in Rural Poverty Alleviation: NGO Cooperation*. New York: The United Nations.

International Institute for Population Sciences (IIPS) (1995). *National Family Health Survey (MCH and Family Planning) India 1992–93*. Bombay: IIPS.

Jackson, Bill (1999). *Designing Projects and Project Evaluations Using the Logical Framework Approach*. Gland: IUCN.

Jacobs, M. (1991). *The Green Economy: Environment, Sustainable Development and the Politics of the Future*. London: Pluto Press.

Jodha, N.S. (1995). 'Common Property Resources and the Environmental Context: Role of Bio-physical Versus Social Stress'. *Economic and Political Weekly*. 30(51): 3278–83.

Jones, R.A. (1996). *Research Methods in the Social and Behavioral Sciences* (2nd edn). Sunderland, MA: Sinauer Associates.

Kaiser, H.F. (1960). 'The Application of Electronic Computers to Factor Analysis'. *Educational and Psychological Measurement*. 20: 141–51.

Kalton, G. and D. Kasprzyk (1986). 'The Treatment of Missing Survey Data'. *Survey Methodology*. 12: 1–16.

Kanitkar, Tara (1979). 'Development of Maternal and Child Health Services in India' in K. Srinivasan, P.C. Saxena and T. Kanitkar (eds), *Demographic and Socio-Economic Aspects of the Child in India*. Bombay: Himalaya Publishing House.

Kanji, G.K. (1993). *100 Statistical Tests*. Thousand Oaks, CA: Sage Publications.

Kee, J.E. (1994). 'Benefit–Cost Analysis in Program Evaluation', in J. Wholey, H.P. Hatry and K.E. Newcomer (eds), *The Handbook of Practical Program Evaluation*. San Francisco: Jossey Bass.

Kendall, M. and A. Stuart (1979). *The Advanced Theory of Statistics, Volume 2* (4th edn). London: Griffin.

Keren, G. and C. Lewis (eds) (1993). *A Handbook for Data Analysis in the Behavioral Sciences: Statistical Issues*. Hillsdale, NJ: L. Erlbaum.

Kish, L. (1965). *Survey Sampling*. New York: Wiley.

Klecka, William R. (1980). *Discriminate Analysis*. Series: Quantitative Application in the Social Sciences. Newbury Park, CA: Sage Publications.

Klees, Rita, Joana Godinho and Mercy Lawson-Doe (1999). *Sanitation, Health and Hygiene in World Bank Rural Water Supply and Sanitation Projects*. Europe and Central Asia Regional Studies Program. Washington D.C.: The World Bank.

Klockers, A.J. and G. Sax (1986). *Multiple Comparisons. Quantitative Applications in the Social Sciences* (Series No. 07–061). Newbury Park, CA: Sage Publications.

Knack, Stephen and Philip Keefer (1997). 'Does Social Capital Have an Economic Payoff: A Cross-Country Investigation'. *Quarterly Journal of Economics*. November. 112: 1251–88.

Koudstal, R., F.R. Rigsberman and H. Sauenije (1992). 'Water and Sustainable Development'. *Natural Resources Forum*. 16(4): 277–90.

Krishan, Gopal and Madhav Shyam (1973). 'Spatial Perspective on Progress of Female Literacy in India: 1901–1971'. *Pacific Viewpoint*. 14: 203–06.

Krishnaji, N. (1997). 'Human Poverty Index'. *Economic and Political Weekly*. 32(35): 2202–05.

Kruskal, W.H. and W.A. Wallis (1952). 'Use of Ranks in One-criterion Variance Analysis'. *Journal of the American Statistical Association*. 47: 583–634.

Kumar, S. (1966). 'Pre-primary Education in India since 1947: An Appraisal'. *Indian Education*. (December 1965 and January 1966). 6: 28–31.

Kuznets, Simon (1955). 'Economic Growth and Income Inequality'. *American Economic Review*. 45(1): 1–28.

Kvale, S. (1996). *Interviews: An Introduction to Qualitative Research Interviewing*. Thousand Oaks, CA: Sage Publications.

LaVange, L.M., S.C. Stearns, J.E. Lafata, G.G. Koch and B.V. Shah (1996). 'Innovative Strategies Using SUDAAN for Analysis of Health Surveys with Complex Samples'. *Statistical Methods in Medical Research*. 5: 311–29.

Lee, S.L., R.N. Forthofer and R.J. Lorimor (1988). *Analyzing Complex Survey Data*. Newbury Park, CA: Sage Publications.

Lee, T.R. (1995). 'Financing Investments in Water Supply and Sanitation'. *Natural Resources Forum*. 19(4): 275–84.

Lee, T.R. (1996). 'Alternatives for Private Participation in the Provision of Water Services'. *Natural Resources Forum*. 20(4): 333–42.

Levine, Mark S. (1977). *Canonical Analysis and Factor Comparison*. Series: Quantitative Applications in the Social Sciences. Newbury Park, CA: Sage Publications.

LewisBeck, Michael S. (1980). *Applied Regression, An Introduction*. Series: Quantitative Applications in the Social Sciences. Newbury Park CA: Sage Publications.

Lind, R.C. (ed.) (1982). *Discounting for Time and Risk in Energy Policy*. Baltimore: Johns Hopkins University Press for Resources for the Future.

Lindbeck, A. (1997). 'Incentives and Social Norms in Household Behaviour'. *American Economic Review*. 87(Papers & Proceedings): 370–77.

Listorti J.A. and F.M. Doumani (2001). *Environmental Health: Bridging the Gaps*. World Bank Discussion Paper No. 422. Washington D.C.: The World Bank.

Little, R. and D. Rubin (1987). *Statistical Analysis with Missing Data*. New York: Wiley.

Loether, H.J. and D.G. Mc Tavish (1998). *Descriptive and Inferential Statistics: An Introduction*. (3rd edn). Boston: Allyn and Bacon.

Loucks, D.P. (1994). 'Sustainability Implications for Water Resources Planning and Management'. *Natural Resources Forum*. 18(4): 263–74.

Lyberg, L., P. Biemer, M. Collins, E. De Leeuw, C. Dippo, N. Schwarz and D. Trewin (eds) (1997). *Survey Measurement and Process Quality*. New York, NY: Wiley.

Mager, R. (1962). *Preparing Objectives for Programmed Instruction*. San Francisco: Fearon.

Mateo R.M. (1992). 'Administration of Water Resources: Institutional Aspects and Management Modalities'. *Natural Resources Forum*. 16(2): 117–25.

May, T. (1993). *Social Research: Issues, Methods and Process*. Buckingham, Philadelphia: Open University Press.

Mohr, L.B. (1995). *Impact Analysis for Program Evaluation* (2nd edn). Thousand Oaks, CA: Sage Publications.

de Moivre, A. (1733). *Approximation ad Summam Terminorum Binomii (a + b) in Seriem Expansii*. Printed for private circulation.

Morris, Matthew (1998). 'Social Capital and Poverty in India'. *IDS Working Paper*. 61. January.

Morrison, Donald F. (1990). *Multivariate Statistical Methods*. New York: McGraw-Hill.

Moser, C.A. and G. Kalton (1972). *Survey Methods in Social Investigation* (2nd edn). New York: Basic Books.

Moulin, Herve (1986). *Game Theory for the Social Sciences* (2nd edn). New York: New York University Press.

Munasinghe, Mohan (1992). *Water Supply and Environmental Management: Developing World Applications*. Boulder, CO: Westview Press.

——— (1999). 'Is Environmental Degradation an Inevitable Consequence of Economic Growth: Tunneling Through the Environmental Kuznets Curve'. *Ecological Economics*. 29(1): 89–109.

Nachmias, C. and D. Nachmias (1992). *Research Methods in the Social Sciences* (4th edn). New York: St. Martin's Press.

Nash, J. (1951). 'Non-cooperative Games'. *Annals of Mathematics*. 54: 299–306.

NCERT (1971). *Education and National Development: Report of the Education Commission, 1964–66*. New Delhi: NCERT.

Newcomer, K.E. (1994). 'Using Statistics Appropriately', in J.S. Wholey, H.P. Hatry and K.E. Newcomer (eds), *The Handbook of Practical Program Evaluation*. San Francisco: Jossey Bass. pp. 534–48.

Newton, Rae R. (1999). *Your Statistical Consultant: Answers to Your Data Analysis Questions*. Thousand Oaks, CA: Sage Publications.

Nishisato, S. (1980). *Analysis of Categorical Data: Dual Scaling and its Applications*. Toronto: University of Toronto Press.

North, J.H. and C.C. Griffin (1993). 'Water Source as a Housing Characteristic: Hedonic Property Valuation and Willingness-to-Pay for Water'. *Water Resources Research*. 29(7): 1923–29.

Norusis, Marija J. (1988). *SPSSX User's Guide* (3rd edn). Chicago: SPSS Inc.

Nuna, S.C. (1987). 'Educational Statistics in India: A Need for Appraisal'. *Progressive Educational Herald*. 1(2): 82–86.

Nuna, S.C. (1987). *Education and Development*. New Delhi: NIEPA.

Nurullah, S. and J.P. Naik (1974). *A Students History of Education in India*. New Delhi: Macmillan.

Olsen, Wendy (1994). 'Distress Sales and Rural Credit: Evidence from an Indian Village Case Study', in Tim Lloyd and Oliver Morrissey (eds), *Poverty, Inequality and Rural Development: Case Studies in Economic Development*. Volume 3. Houndmills: St. Martin's Press.

Ostrom, E. (1996a). *Governing the Commons: The Evolution of Institutions for Collective Action*. Cambridge: Cambridge University Press.

——— (1996b). 'Incentives, Rules of the Game, and Development'. *Proceedings of the Annual World Bank Conference on Development Economics*, 1995 (Supplement to the World Bank Economic Review and the World Bank Research Observer).

Pachauri, Saroj (ed.) (1999). *Implementing a Reproductive Health Agenda in India: The Beginning*. New Delhi: Population Council.

Parikh, Jyoti. (2004), 'Environmentally Sustainable Development in India'. http://scid.stanford.edu/events/India2004/JParikh.pdf

Patton, M.Q. (1990). *Qualitative Evaluation and Research Methods*. Newbury Park, CA: Sage Publications.

Paul, Samuel, Suresh Balkrishnan, K. Gopakumar, Sita Sekhar and Vivekananda (2004). 'State of India's Public Services: Benchmark for the States'. *Economic and Political Weekly*. 39(9). 28 February.

Pearce, John, Peter Raynard and Simon Zadek (1996). *Social Auditing for Small Organizations*. The Workbook. London: New Economic Foundation.

Pfeffermann, D. (1993). 'The Role of Sampling Weights when Modeling Survey Data'. *International Statistical Review*. 61: 317–37.

Pigou, A.C. (1920). *The Economics of Welfare*. London: Macmillan.

——— (1952). *The Economics of Welfare* (4th edn). London: Macmillan.

Portney, P.R. and J.P. Weyant (eds) (1999). *Discounting and Inter-generational Equity*. Washington. D.C.: Resources for the Future.

Radhakrishna, R. (2002). 'Agricultural Growth, Employment and Poverty', *Economic and Political Weekly*. 19 January. 37(3): 243–50.

Randhawa, N.S. and Sundaram K.V. (1990). *Small Farmer Development in Asia and Pacific: Some Lessons for Strategy Formulation and Planning*. FAO Economic and Social Development Paper. Rome: FAO.

Rao, C.H. Hanumantha (1994). *Agricultural Growth, Rural Poverty and Environmental Degradation in India*. New Delhi: Oxford University Press.

Rao, T.S. (1972). 'Free Education for All'. *Social Welfare*. 19(9): pp. 18–20. December.

Raza, Moonis and Y.P. Aggarwal (1983). *Inequities in the Levels of Literacy in India*. Occasional Paper 4. New Delhi: NIEPA.

Reid, S. (1987). *Working with Statistics: An Introduction to Quantitative Methods for Social Scientists*. Totowa, NJ: Rowman & Littlefield.

Reynolds, H.T. (1984). *Analysis of Nominal Data* (2nd edn). Quantitative Applications in the Social Sciences (Series No. 07-007). Newbury Park, CA: Sage Publications.

Rosenberg, M. (1968). *The Logic of Survey Analysis*. New York, NY: Basic Books.

Rossi, P.H. and H.E. Freeman (1993). *Evaluation: A Systematic Approach* (5th edn). Thousand Oaks, CA: Sage Publications.

Roy, Sumit (1997). 'Globalisation, Structural Change and Poverty: Some Conceptual and Policy Issues'. *Economic and Political Weekly*. 32: 2117–35. 16–23 August.

Royston, J.P. (1982). 'Expected Normal Order Statistics (Exact and Approximate) AS 177'. *Applied Statistics*. 31: 161–65.

Schein, E.H. (1987). *The Clinical Perspective in Fieldwork*. Newbury, CA: Sage Publications.

Scriven, M. (1991). *Evaluation Thesaurus* (4th edn). Newbury Park, CA: Sage Publications.

Sen, Amartya (1970). *Collective Choice and Social Welfare*. Edinburgh: Oliver and Boyd.

——— (1977). 'Rational Fools: A Critique of the Behavioural Foundations of Economic Theory', *Philosophy & Public Affairs*, 6(4): 317–44.

——— (1981). *Poverty and Famines: An Essay on Entitlement and Deprivation*. Oxford: Clarendon Press.

SIDA (1996). *Guidelines for the Application of LFA in Project Cycle Management*. Stockholm: SIDA.

SIDBI (2000). 'State of the Indian Micro-Finance Industry'. *Handbook of Micro-Finance*. Vol. 1. SIDBI Micro-Finance Consulting Group. Prepared for a training programme for consultants in micro-finance organized in December 2000.

Siegel, S. (1956). *Nonparametric Statistics for the Behavioral Sciences*. New York, NY: McGraw-Hill.

Siegel, S. and N. Castellan, Jr. (1988). *Nonparametric Statistics for the Behavioral Sciences* (2nd edn). New York: McGraw-Hill.

Sinacore, J.M., R.W. Chang and J. Falconer (1992). 'Seeing the Forest Despite the Trees: The Benefit of Exploratory Data Analysis to Program Evaluation Research'. *Evaluation in the Health Progressions*. 15(2): 131–46.

Singh, K. (1994). *Managing Common Pool Resources: Principles and Case Studies*. New Delhi: Oxford University Press.

Skinner, C.J., D. Holt and T.M.F. Smith (1989). *Analysis of Complex Surveys*. New York, NY: Wiley.

Smith, Alan G. (1986). 'Human Rights and Choice in Poverty'. *Journal of Social Studies*. 32: 44–78.

Smith, Allan H., Elena O. Lingas and Mahfuzar Rahman (2000). 'Contamination of Drinking Water by Arsenic in Bangladesh: A Public Health Emergency'. *Bulletin of the World Health Organization*. 78(9). Geneva: WHO.

Snedecor, G.W. and W.G. Cochran (1982). *Statistical Methods*. Ames, IA: Iowa University Press.

Sokhey, Jotna, Y.N. Mathur and Robin Biellik (1993). 'Country Overview: A Report of the International Evaluation of the Immunization Programme in India'. *Indian Pediatrics*. 30(2): 153–74.

Solanes, M. (1992). 'Groundwater and Pollution of Water Resources'. *Natural Resources Forum*. 16(3): 226–31.

Somekh, B. (1989). 'Action Research and Collaborative School Development' in R. McBride (ed.), *The Inservice Training of Teachers*. Lewes, Falmer Press. pp. 32–42.

Sooch, S.S. and V. Ramalingaswami (1965). 'Preliminary Report of an Experiment in Kangra Valley for Prevention of Himalayan Endemic Goitre with Iodised Salt'. *WHO Bulletin*. 32: 229.

Sopher, David E. (1974). 'A Measure of Disparity'. *Professional Geographer*. 26: 389–92.

Spoull, N.L. (1995). *Handbook of Research Methods: A Guide for Practitioners and Students in the Social Sciences* (2nd edn). Metuchen, NJ: Scarecrow Press.

SPSS, Inc. (1988). *SPSS/PC+ V2.0 Base Manual*. Chicago: SPSS Inc.

Srivastava, M.S. and E.M. Carter (1983). *An Introduction to Applied Multivariate Statistics*. New York: North-Holland Publishing.

Stata Corporation (1996). *Stata Technical Bulletin*. STB-31. College Station, TX. pp. 3–42.

Stern, P.C. and L. Kalof (1996). *Evaluating Social Science Research*. New York: Oxford University Press.

Suryanarayana, M.H. (1996). 'Economic Reforms, Nature and Poverty'. *Economic and Political Weekly*. 31(10): 617–24.

The World Bank (1994). 'Hunger is Political Economy'. Development Brief No. 28. January.

Thompson, Bruce (1984). *Canonical Correlation Analysis*. Series: Quantitative Applications in the Social Sciences. Newbury Park, CA: Sage Publications.

Thompson, M. (1980). *Benefit–Cost Analysis for Program Evaluation*. Beverly Hills, CA: Sage Publications.

Thorndike, R.M., G.K. Cunningham, R.L. Thorndike and E.P. Hagen (1991). *Measurement and Evaluation in Psychology and Education* (5th edn). New York, NY: Macmillan.

Tirtha, Ranjit (1966). 'Area Pattern of Literacy in India'. *Manpower Journal*. Vol. 3 and 4.

Torgerson, W.S. (1952). 'Multidimensional Scaling: I. Theory and Method'. *Psychometrika*. 17: 401–19.

Trochim, W. (2005). Research Methods: The Concise Knowledge Base. Cincinnatti, OH: Atomic Dog Publishers. http://www.socialresearchmethods.net.kb

Tryon, R.C. (1939). *Cluster Analysis*. Ann Arbor, MI: Edwards Brothers.

Tyler, R. (1950). *Basic Principles of Curriculum and Instruction*. Chicago: University of Chicago Press.

UNDP-World Bank (1999). 'Willing to Pay but Unwilling to Charge: Do "Willingness to Pay" Studies Make a Difference'. Field Note, New Delhi: UNDP-World Bank Water and Sanitation Program. South Asia.

UNESCO (1975). *Learning To Be*. Paris: UNESCO Press.

Vaidyanathan, A. (1994). *Second India Studies Revisited: Food, Agriculture and Water*. Madras: Madras Institute of Development Studies.

Vanoli André (1995). 'Reflections on Environmental Accounting Issues'. *Review of Income and Wealth*, 41(2): 113–37.

Velleman, P.F. and D.C. Hoaglin (1981). *Applications, Basics, and Computing of Exploratory Data Analysis*. Boston: Duxbury Press.

Vidyasagar, R. (1993). *Water and Sustainable Development: Indian Scenario*. United Nation Publication.

Vir, S. (1994). 'Control of Iodine Deficiency. The National Program–Current Status'. *NFI Bulletin*. 15: 1–4.

Visaria, Pravin and Vijaylaxmi Chari (1998). 'India's Population Policy and Family Planning: Yesterday, Today, and Tomorrow' in Anrudh K. Jain (ed.) *Do Population Policies Matter? Fertility and Policies in Egypt, India, Kenya, and Mexico*. New York: The Population Council.

Vitousek, P.M, H.A. Mooney, J. Lubchenco and J.M. Melillo (1997). 'Human Domination of Earth's Ecosystems'. *Science*. 277: 494–99.

Vogt, W.P. (1993). *Dictionary of Statistics and Methodology: A Non-technical Guide for the Social Sciences*. Thousand Oaks, CA: Sage Publications.

von Neumann, John (1928). *Zur Theorie der Gesellschaftsspiele* (Theory of Parlor Games), Mathematische Annalen.

Vyas, V.S. and Pradeep Bhargava (1995). 'Public Intervention for Poverty Alleviation: An Overview'. *Economic and Political Weekly*. 30(41 & 42): 2559–72.

Walberg, H.J. and G.D. Haertel (eds) (1990). *International Encyclopedia of Educational Evaluation*. New York: Pergamon Press.

Ward, J.H. (1963). 'Hierarchical Grouping to Optimize an Objective Function'. *Journal of the American Statistical Association*. 58: 236–44.

Webster, M. (1985). *Webster's New Collegiate Dictionary*. Meriam Webster Inc.

WHO (1992). *International Statistical Classification of Diseases and Related Health Problems*. Tenth Revision, Vol. 1. Geneva: WHO.

Wiggins, S. (2000). 'Interpretating Changes from the 1970s to the 1990s in African Agriculture Through Village Studies'. *World Development*. 28(4): 631–62.

World Commission on Environment and Development (1987). *Our Common Future*. Oxford: Oxford University Press.

World Resources Institute. *World Resources* Oxford: Oxford University Press.

INDEX

173–74; independent-samples t, 258; Jonckheere-Terpstra, 172–73; Kolmogorov-Smirnov, 100–01; Kolmogorov-Smirnov, modification of, 101; Kolmogorov-Smirnov one-sample, 167–68; Kolmogorov-Smirnov two-sample, 163–64; Kolmogorov-Smirnov Z, 169; Kruskal-Wallis, 172; Levene, 102; Lilliefors, for normality, 101; Mann-Whitney U, 163, 168; McNemar, 171; Median, 172; non-parametric, 164, 166, 168, 172; of internal reliability, 78; one-sample, 164, 166, 168; one-sample t, 164; paired t, 165–66, 174, 238; paired-samples t, 259; parametric, 162, 164; power, of a, 159; Scree, 205; Shapiro-Wilks' W, 100; sign, 163, 169–70; T, 237; three or more sample, 164, 166; three sample, 165; two-sample, 164–66, 168; unpaired t, 165; Wald-Wolfowitz runs, 163, 169; Wilcoxon rank sum, 167; Wilcoxon signed rank, 170–71; Wilcoxon's matched pairs, 163; Wilcoxon-Mann-Whitney, 172
text import wizard, 247
Theil measures, 340
Thurstone scales, 74
time series, 66; design, 66
Total Fertility Rate (TFR), 277
Total Internal Renewable Water Resources (IRWR), 320
total sanitation campaign, 335
total utility, 41
transition, demographic, model, 271–72
trend study, 65
true cohort method, 313
Tshuprow's t, 127

uncertainty coefficients, 129
Universal Elementary Education (UEE), 308
Universal Immunization Programme (UIP), 288
use value, 366
utility, concept of, 41; diminishing marginal, 41; maximization, 41
Uttar Pradesh Basic Education Programme, 310

vaccination, measles, 288
validity, 77; construct, 79; content, 79; discriminate, 79; methods of measuring, 79
valuation, contingent, method, 329; contingent, technique, 367; direct, techniques, 367; economic, 366; indirect, techniques, 367; techniques, 366
value, base, 38; existence, 366
variable, association between, 146; dependent, 122; dependent, encoding, 193; dropping a, 234; extraction of factors among, 205; statistics for ordinal/ranked, 131; status, 223

variance, and standard deviation, 144; methods of, estimation, 114
variation, coefficient of, 144, 340
vasectomy, 292; conventional, 292
vertical and horizontal associations, 36
vision statement, 51
Vitamin A deficiency, 295, 297

Ward's method, 211
water, access to potable, 325; availability, 324; availability of safe drinking, 326; availability of safe drinking, supply, 325; contamination, 356; contamination problems, 325; domestic, use, 324; drinking, 324; drinking, availability in urban areas, 325; efficient utilization of, resources, 321; growing competition for, 223; internal renewable, resources, 320; management of, resource, 328; natural renewable, resource, 320; optimum utilization of, resources, 322; piped, supply, 333; public waste, disposal, 330; quality of, 321; quality problems, 326; rural, supply, 325; scarcity of, 326; sharing of, resources, 328; source of, supply in the urban areas, 324; total availability of, resources, 320; unpolluted, 375; urban, supply, 325; use and control of resources, 321; utilization of river, 328; withdrawals and desalination, 320
watershed, management, 223; protection approach, 223
weight for age (W/A), 300
weight for height (W/H), 299
weighted average link method, 211
weighting in case of under-representation of strata, 112
weighting to account for the probability of selection, 112
welfare, collective, state of a society, 40; economics, 40–43; individual, functions of a society, 40; new, economics approach, 40; of society, 42; social, 40; social, maximization, 42; theory, 40
Wilcoxon test, calculation of, statistics, 171
Wilk's Lambda, 184, 190
Winsorized mean, 140
World Commission on Environment and Development (WCED), 349

Yates correction, 127
Yule's Q, 130–31

z distribution, 96
Z score, 301
zero-sum game, 44

ABOUT THE AUTHOR

Kultar Singh is founding member and Director, Sambodhi Research and Communications. He has worked extensively on research projects covering a wide gamut of development issues, including poverty, livelihood, health and nutrition, and HIV/AIDS. He has garnered extensive quantitative research experience during his association with organisations such as ACNielsen ORGMARG, CARE, BASICS and PFI.

Mr Singh has also written extensively on social and developmental issues. His interests include development research and project planning management, and advanced data analysis using quantitative and qualitative statistical software such as SPSS, STATA, EPI Info, ATLAS Ti and N6.